Introduction to Computers, C and Data Structures

Dr. K. Kalyani Radha

M.Tech., Ph.D.,

ASSISTANT PROFESSOR,

DEPARTMENT OF MECHANICAL ENGINEERING,

JNTUA COLLEGE OF ENGINEERING,

ANANTAPUR.

FIRST EDITION : 2011

Himalaya Publishing House

MUMBAI • NEW DELHI • NAGPUR • BENGALURU • HYDERABAD • CHENNAI • PUNE • LUCKNOW • AHMEDABAD • ERNAKULAM • BHUBANESWAR • INDORE • KOLKATA • GUWAHATI

First Edition : 2011

Published by	:	Mrs. Meena Pandey for **Himalaya Publishing House Pvt. Ltd.**, "Ramdoot", Dr. Bhalerao Marg, Girgaon, **Mumbai - 400 004.** Phone: 022-23860170/23863863, Fax: 022-23877178 **E-mail: himpub@vsnl.com; Website: www.himpub.com**
Branch Offices	:	
New Delhi	:	"Pooja Apartments", 4-B, Murari Lal Street, Ansari Road, Darya Ganj, New Delhi - 110 002. Phone: 011-23270392, 23278631; Fax: 011-23256286
Nagpur	:	Kundanlal Chandak Industrial Estate, Ghat Road, Nagpur - 440 018. Phone: 0712-2738731, 3296733; Telefax: 0712-2721215
Bengaluru	:	No. 16/1 (Old 12/1), 1st Floor, Next to Hotel Highlands, Madhava Nagar, Race Course Road, Bengaluru - 560 001. Phone: 080-32919385; Telefax: 080-22286611
Hyderabad	:	No. 3-4-184, Lingampally, Besides Raghavendra Swamy Matham, Kachiguda, Hyderabad - 500 027. Phone: 040-27560041, 27550139; Mobile: 09848130433
Chennai	:	No. 85/50, Bazullah Road, T. Nagar, Chennai - 600 017. Phone: 044-28144004/28144005
Pune	:	First Floor, "Laksha" Apartment, No. 527, Mehunpura, Shaniwarpeth (Near Prabhat Theatre), Pune - 411 030. Phone: 020-24496323/24496333
Lucknow	:	Jai Baba Bhavan, Church Road, Near Manas Complex and Dr. Awasthi Clinic, Aliganj, Lucknow - 226 024. Phone: 0522-2339329, 4068914; Mobile: 09305302158, 09415349385, 09389593752
Ahmedabad	:	114, "SHAIL", 1st Floor, Opp. Madhu Sudan House, C.G. Road, Navrang Pura, Ahmedabad - 380 009. Phone: 079-26560126; Mobile: 09327324149, 09314679413
Ernakulam	:	39/104 A, Lakshmi Apartment, Karikkamuri Cross Rd., Ernakulam, Cochin - 622011, Kerala. Phone: 0484-2378012, 2378016; Mobile: 09344199799
Bhubaneswar	:	5 Station Square, Bhubaneswar - 751 001(Odisha). Mobile: 09861046007
Indore	:	Kesardeep Avenue Extension, 73, Narayan Bagh, Flat No. 302, IIIrd Floor, Near Humpty Dumpty School, Indore - 452 007 (M.P.). Mobile: 09301386468
Kolkata	:	108/4, Beliaghata Main Road, Near ID Hospital, Opp. SBI Bank, Kolkata - 700 010, Phone: 033-32449649, Mobile: 09910440956
Guwahati	:	House No. 15, Behind Pragjyotish College, Near Sharma Printing Press, P.O. Bharalumukh, Guwahati - 781009 (Assam). Mobile: 09883055590, 09883055536
DTP by	:	HPH, Editorial Office, Bhandup (Swapnali)
Printed at	:	**7 Hills Printers**, Hyderabad.

Dedicated

to my parents

Preface

In recent years, there has been a major trend towards the usage of C among serious programmers. Among the many reasons for C's popularity, programs written in C compile into smaller programs that execute efficiently.

This book introduces introduction to computers assuming that the reader will not have any prior knowledge of computers. The book begins with basics of computers, algorithms and flowcharts. This course material provides instructions in computer programming with C and Data Structures. It includes complete and understandable explanations of the commonly used features of the topics chosen by creating a friendly approach which makes the students feel interested in learning the new concepts. In addition, the material presents a contemporary approach to programming, stressing the importance of clarity, legibility, modularity and efficiency in program design with graphical representations. Thus, the reader is exposed to the principles of good programming practice as well as the specific rules of using C and Data Structures. Examples of programs are presented throughout the text, beginning with the first chapter. The use of an interactive programming style is emphasized throughout the text. This volume can be used by the beginners in the programming as well as professionals. It is particularly well suited for an introductory programming course and I am confident that the book covers all the concepts of C and Data Structures and serves as an ideal companion for all the students.

The book is divided into two parts: Part I – Introduction to Computers and C Language; Part II – Data Structures. Part I covers the fundamentals of Computers, Introduction to C language, Fundamentals concepts in C like loops, variables, arrays, strings, functions, pointers, structures and unions, file management and dynamic memory allocation, with numerous example programs. Part II covers the concepts of abstract data type, memory allocation, linear and non-linear data structures, searching and sorting techniques with algorithms and example programs.

I express my gratitude to the Almighty, without whose blessing the task would have not been completed within time.

I express my gratitude to my Guru's Dr. K. Rajagopal, Professor, Department of Mechanical Engineering, JNTUCE, Hyderabad and Dr. E. Lakshmi Nagesh, Principal, Netaji Institute of Technology, Nalgonda District for all the encouragement they have given to me at all times in the completion of this book.

I thank my friend S. Naga Sarada for her support and constant encouragement.

With a deep sense of affection I am grateful to my parents K. Prabhakar Rao and Vimala Devi, my brother Kishore Kumar for the love, moral support and cooperation they have provided for me to finish this book.

Finally, I express my special thanks to Mr. Krishna Poojari and Mr. Shankar Yadav, Himalaya Publishing House Pvt. Ltd., Hyderabad, for bringing out the book in the present elegant form.

Author

Contents

Part - I

Introduction to Computers and C Programming

Part - II

Data Structures

Detailed Contents

Part - I
Introduction to Computers and C Programming

PART-I

Introduction to Computers and C Programming

CHAPTER 1

Introduction to Computers

WHAT IS A COMPUTER?

A computer is an electronic machine that manipulates data according to a list of instructions.

It accepts input (data), processes it and gives output (information).

COMPUTER ORGANIZATION AT A GLANCE

A basic computer consists of three components: CPU (Central Processing Unit), I/O (Input/Output), and Memory as illustrated in Figure.

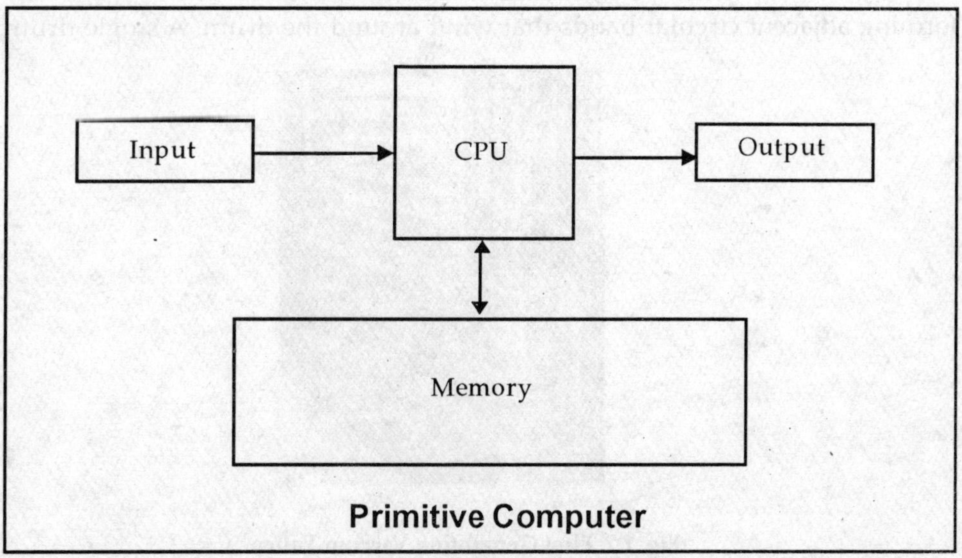

Fig. 1.1: The Central Processing Unit

The CPU receives the data through the input device and processes it according to the given set of instructions. The processed data is returned to Memory or is presented to the user through the output device. CPU consists of Arithmetic and Logic Unit (ALU), Control Unit (CU) and Registers.

GENERATIONS OF COMPUTERS

The history of computer development is often referred to in reference to the different generations of computing devices. A generation refers to the state of improvement in the product development process. This term is also used in the different advancements of new computer technology. With each new generation, the circuitry has gotten smaller and more advanced than the previous generation before it. As a result of the miniaturization, speed, power, the computer memory has proportionally increased. New discoveries are constantly being developed that affect the way we live, work and play.

Each generation of computers is characterized by major technological development that fundamentally changed the way computers operate, resulting in increasingly smaller, cheaper, more powerful and more efficient and reliable devices. Read about each generation and the developments that led to the current devices that we use today.

First Generation (1940-1956): Vacuum Tubes

The first computers used vacuum tubes for circuitry and magnetic drums for memory, and were often enormous, taking up entire rooms. A magnetic drum, is a metal cylinder coated with magnetic iron-oxide material on which data and programs can be stored. The tracks on a magnetic drum are assigned to channels located around the circumference of the drum, forming adjacent circular bands that wind around the drum. A single drum can have

Fig. 1.2: First Generation Vaccum Tubes

upto 200 tracks. As the drum rotates at a speed of up to 3,000 rpm, the device's read/write heads deposit magnetized spots on the drum during the write operation and sense these spots during a read operation. This action is similar to that of a magnetic tape or disk drive.

They were very expensive to operate and in addition to using a great deal of electricity, generated a lot of heat, which was often the cause of malfunctions. First generation computers relied on machine language to perform operations, and they could only solve one problem at a time. Machine languages are the only languages understood by computers, they are almost impossible for humans to use because they consist entirely of numbers. Computer Programmers, therefore, use either **high-level programming languages** or **an assembly programming language**. An assembly language contains the same instructions as a machine language, but the instructions and variables have names instead of being just numbers.

Programs written in **high-level programming languages** retranslated into assembly language or machine language by a compiler. Assembly language program retranslated into machine language by a program is called an assembler (assembly language compiler).

Every CPU has its own unique machine language. Programs must be rewritten or recompiled, therefore, to run on different types of computers. Input was based on punch card and paper tapes, and output was displayed on printouts.

The UNIVAC and ENIAC computers are examples of first-generation computing devices. The UNIVAC was the first commercial computer delivered to a business client, the US Census Bureau in 1951.

Second Generation (1956-1963): Transistors

Transistors replaced vacuum tubes and used in the second generation computers. Transistor is a device composed of semiconductor material that amplifies a signal or opens or closes a circuit. Invented in 1947 at Bell Labs, transistors have become the key ingredient of all digital circuits, including computers. Prior to the invention of transistors, digital circuits were composed of vacuum tubes, which had many disadvantages. They were much larger, required more energy, dissipated more heat, and were more prone to failures. It's safe to say that without the invention of transistors, computing as we know it today would not be possible.

The transistor was invented in 1947 but did not see widespread use in computers until the late 50s. The transistor was far superior to the vacuum tube, allowing computers to become smaller, faster, cheaper, more energy-efficient and more reliable than their first generation predecessors. Though the transistor still generated a great deal of heat that subjected the computer to damage, it was a vast improvement over the vacuum tube. Second generation computers still relied on punched cards for input and printouts for output.

Fig. 1.3: Second Generation Transistors

Second generation computers moved from cryptic binary machine language to symbolic, or assembly languages, which allowed programmers to specify instructions in words. High level programming languages were also being developed at this time, such as early versions of COBOL and FORTRAN. These were also the first computers that stored their instructions in their memory, which moved from a magnetic drum to magnetic core technology.

The first computers of this generation were developed for the atomic energy industry.

Third Generation (1964-1971): Integrated Circuits

The development of the integrated circuit was the hallmark of the third generation of computers. Transistors were miniaturized and placed on silicon chips, called semiconductors, which drastically increased the speed and efficiency of computers.

Silicon is the basic material used to make computer chips, transistors, silicon diodes and other electronic circuits and switching devices because its atomic structure makes the element an ideal semiconductor. Silicon is commonly doped, or mixed with other elements, such as boron, phosphorous and arsenic to alter its conductive properties.

A chip is a small piece of semiconducting material (usually silicon) on which an integrated circuit is embedded. A typical chip is less than ¼-square inches and can contain millions of electronic components (transistors). Computers consist of many chips placed on electronic boards called printed circuit boards. There are different types of chips. For example, CPU chips (also called microprocessors) contain an entire processing unit, whereas memory chips contain blank memory.

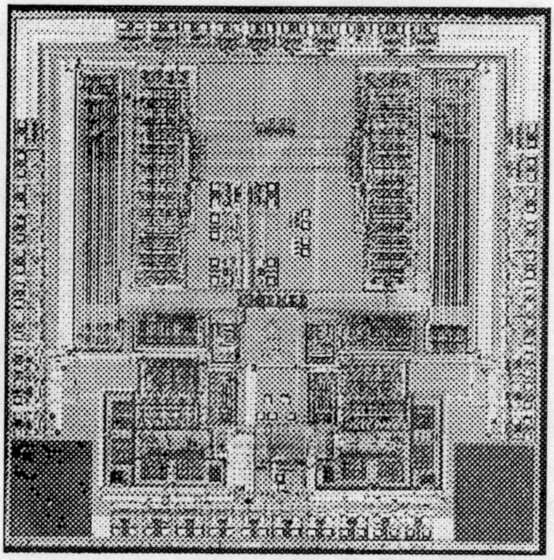

Fig. 1.4: Third Generation Integrated Circuits

Computer chips, both for CPU and memory are composed of semiconductor materials. Semiconductors make it possible to miniaturize electronic components such as transistors. Not only does miniaturization mean that the components take up less space, it also means that they are faster and require less energy.

Instead of punched cards and printouts, users interacted with third generation computers through keyboards and monitors and interfaced with an operating system, which allowed the device to run many different applications at one time with a central program that monitored the memory.

Fourth Generation (1971-Present): Microprocessors

The microprocessor brought the fourth generation of computers, as thousands of integrated circuits we rebuilt onto a single silicon chip. A silicon chip that contains a CPU. In the world of personal computers, the terms microprocessor and CPU are used interchangeable. Microprocessors also control the logic of almost all digital devices from clock radios to fuel-injection systems for automobiles.

Three basic characteristics differentiate microprocessors:

- **Instruction Set:** The set of instructions that the microprocessor can execute.
- **Bandwidth:** The number of bits processed in a single instruction.
- **Clock Speed:** Given in megahertz (MHz), the clock speed determines how many instructions per second the processor can execute.

In both cases, the higher the value, the more powerful the CPU. For example, a 32-bit microprocessor that runs at 50MHz is more powerful than a 16-bit microprocessor that runs at 25MHz.

Fig. 1.5 : Fourth Generation Computer

The CPU is the brain of the computer. Sometimes referred to simply as the processor or central processor, the CPU is where most calculations take place. On large machines, CPUs require one or more printed circuit boards. On personal computers and small workstations, the CPU is housed in a single chip called a microprocessor.

Two typical components of a CPU are:

- The arithmetic logic unit (ALU), which performs arithmetic and logical operations.
- The control unit, which extracts instructions from memory, decodes and executes them, calling on the ALU when necessary.

As these small computers became more powerful, they could be linked together to form networks, which eventually led to the development of the Internet. Fourth generation computers also saw the development of (Graphic User Interfaces) GUIs, the mouse and handheld devices.

Fifth Generation (Present and Beyond): Artificial Intelligence

Fifth generation computing devices, based on artificial intelligence, are still in development, though there are some applications such as voice recognition being used today.

Fig. 1.6: Fifth Generation Computing Devices

Artificial Intelligence is the branch of computer science concerned with making computers behave like humans. Artificial intelligence includes:

- **Games Playing**: programming computers to play games such as chess and checkers.
- **Expert Systems**: programming computers to make decisions in real-life situations (for example, some expert systems help doctors diagnose diseases based on symptoms).
- **Natural Language**: programming computers to understand natural human languages.
- **Neural Networks**: systems that simulate intelligence by attempting to reproduce the types of physical connections that occur in animal brains.
- **Robotics**: programming computers to see, hear and react to other sensory stimuli.

Voice Recognition

The field of computer science that deals with designing computer systems that can recognize spoken words. Note that voice recognition implies only that the computer can take dictation, not that it understands what is being said. Comprehending human languages falls under a different field of computer science called natural language processing. A number of voice recognition systems are available in the market. The most powerful can recognize thousands of words. However, they generally require an extended training session during which the computer system becomes accustomed to a particular voice and accent. Such systems are said to be speaker dependent.

The use of parallel processing and superconductors is helping to make artificial intelligence a reality. Parallel processing is the simultaneous use of more than one CPU to execute a program. Ideally, parallel processing makes a program run faster because there are more engines (CPUs) running it. In practice, it is often difficult to divide a program in such a way that separate CPUs can execute different portions without interfering with each other.

The goal of fifth-generation computing is to develop devices that respond to natural language input and are capable of learning and self-organization. Here, natural language means a human language. For example, English, French and Chinese are natural languages.

COMPUTER HISTORY

Here are some computers that came and went in the history of computing.

ENIAC

Fig. 1.7: An Image of the ENIAC in Use

A behemoth of a machine weighing 27 tonnes, ENIAC stands for Electronic Numerical Integrator and Computer. Acronym for Electronic Numerical Integrator and Computer, the world's first operational electronic digital computer, developed by Army Ordinance to compute World War II ballistic firing tables. The ENIAC, weighing 30 tonnes, using 200 Kilowatts of electric power and consisting of 18,000 vacuum tubes, 1,500 relays, and hundreds of thousands of resistors, capacitors and inductors, was completed in 1945. In addition to ballistics, the ENIAC's field of application included weather prediction, atomic-energy calculations, cosmic-ray studies, thermal ignition, random-number studies, wind-tunnel design and other scientific uses. The ENIAC soon became obsolete as the need arose for faster computing speeds. The ENIAC saw service until October 2, 1955.

Altair 8800

A microcomputer design from 1975, the Altair is the computer that is believed to have started the personal computer revolution. It also formed the basis of Microsoft's first product: a programming language called Altair Basic. The computer was sold as a kit requiring assembly by the user, although pre-assembled kits could be bought for a higher price. The Altair defined sales forecasts by selling thousands instead of hundreds to computer hobbyists, accelerating a growing hacker culture.

IBM PC

The grand daddy of all current personal computers, the IBM PC was introduced in 1981. It was capable of running 3 different operating systems at launch, although the most popular of which was PC DOS. The IBM PC introduced the concept of the BIOS (Basic Input Output System), which was propriety at the time, although now reverse engineered and considered the *de facto* standard in firmware interfacing. Because of its success, many manufacturers were encouraged to create clones with the same feature set as the PC, which we use today as our computers.

Commodore 64

Fig. 1.8: Commodore 64C System with 1541-II Floppy Drive and 1084S RGB Monitor

An 8-bit computer introduced in January 1982, the Commodore rose to become the best selling personal computer of all time. Utilizing the Commodore BASIC programming language licensed from Microsoft, the Commodore was able to host over 10,000 commercial programs. Aside from office productivity tools such as word processors and spreadsheets, the Commodore was also host to a number of games and even game development environments.

Due to its advanced graphics and audio systems along with the inclusion of a cartridge slot, the Commodore was seen more as a gaming device than a productivity tool. Over 20,000 games were released for the Commodore, upto the video game crash of 1983. The sheer popularity of the Commodore 64 also saw the rise in prominence of software piracy.

Macintosh

First introduced by Apple in 1984, the Macintosh was the first computer to use a mouse and graphical user interface rather than a command-line interface. Until the dominance of the IBM PC, the Macintosh saw use primarily as a desktop publishing tool. However, due to the immense cost of porting command-line interface programs to the GUI, software development was initially slow.

TYPES OF COMPUTERS

Mainframe

Fig. 1.9: Mainframe Computer

Mainframes are computers where all the processing is done centrally and the user terminals are called "dumb terminals" since they only input and output (and do not process). Mainframes are computers used mainly by large organizations for critical applications, typically bulk data processing such as census. Examples: banks, airlines, insurance companies and colleges.

Workstation

Workstations are high-end, expensive computers that are made for more complex procedures and are intended for one user at a time. Some of the complex procedures consist of science, mathematics and engineering calculations and are useful for computer design and manufacturing. Real workstations are not usually sold in retail. Perhaps the first computer that might qualify as a "workstation" was the IBM 1620.

Fig. 1.10: Sun SPARC Station

The Personal Computer or PC

PC is an abbreviation for a Personal Computer, it is also known as a Microcomputer. Its physical characteristics and low cost are appealing and useful for its users. The capabilities of a personal computer have changed greatly since the introduction of electronic computers.

Fig. 1.11: A Personal Computer (PC)

By the early 1970s, people in academic or research institutions had the opportunity for single-person use of a computer system in interactive mode for extended durations, although these systems would still have been too expensive to be owned by a single individual. The introduction of the microprocessor, a single chip with all the circuitry that formerly occupied large cabinets lead to the proliferation of personal computers after about 1975. Early personal computers generally called microcomputers, sold often in kit form and in limited volumes. By the late 1970s, mass-market pre-assembled computers allowed a wider range of people to use computers, focusing more on software applications and less on development of the processor hardware. Throughout the 1970s and 1980s, home computers were developed for household use, offering some personal productivity, programming and games, while somewhat larger and more expensive systems were aimed for office and small business use.

Today, a personal computer is an all rounded device that can be used as a productivity tool, a media server and a gaming machine. The modular construction of the personal computer allows components to be easily swapped out when broken or upgraded.

Microcontroller

Fig. 1.12: A Microcontroller

Microcontrollers are minicomputers that enable the user to store data, do simple commands and tasks with little or no user interaction with the processor. These single circuit devices have minimal memory and program length but can be integrated with other processors for more complex functionality. Many such systems are known as Embedded Systems. Microcontrollers are important; they are used everyday in devices such as appliances and automobiles.

Server

Similar to mainframes in that they serve many uses with the main difference that the users (called clients) do their own processing usually. The server processes are devoted to sharing files and managing log on rights. A server is a central computer that contains collections of data and programs. Also called a network server, this system allows all connected users to share and store electronic data and applications. Two important types of servers are file servers and application servers.

Fig. 1.13: Server

Supercomputer

Fig. 1.14: Supercomputer

Supercomputers were introduced in the 1960s as the world's most advanced computer. These computers were used for complex calculations such as forecasting weather and quantum physics. Today, supercomputers are one of a kind; they are fast and very advanced. The term supercomputer is always evolving as tomorrow's normal computers or today's supercomputer. As of November 2008, the fastest supercomputer is the IBM Roadrunner. It has a theoretical processing peak of 1.71 petaflops and has currently peaked at 1.456 petaflops.

CLASSIFICATION OF COMPUTERS

Computers are broadly divided into three types. They are:

Analog Computers: An analog computer uses an analog signal for its operation. They work on the principle of measuring of signal and they are very accurate but costly.

Digital Computers: They work with digital signal using 0s and 1s. The basic principle is counting of digits. These computers can perform a variety of operations and are less expensive compared to analog computers. Mainly used for scientific purposes.

Hybrid Computers: A hybrid computer is a combination of both digital and analog computers.

HARDWARE

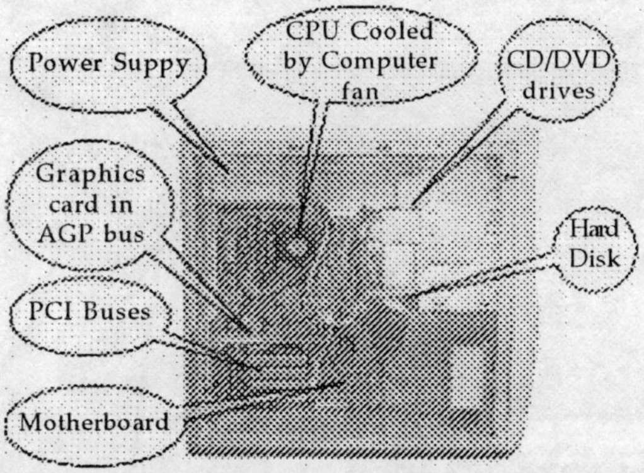

Fig. 1.15: Physical Hardware Elements of a Computer

Hardware refers to the physical elements of a computer. Also referred to as the machinery or the equipment of the computer. Examples of hardware in a computer are the keyboard, monitor, mouse and the processing unit. However, most of a computer's hardware cannot be seen; in other words, it is not an external element of the computer, but rather an internal one, surrounded by the computer's casing. A computer's hardware is comprised of many different parts, but perhaps the most important of these is the motherboard. The motherboard is made up of even more parts that power and control the computer.

In contrast to software, hardware is a physical entity, while software is a non-physical entity. Hardware and software are interconnected, without software; the hardware of a computer would have no function. However, without the creation of hardware to perform tasks directed by software via the central processing unit (box), software would be useless.

Different Parts of the Computer Hardware

Motherboard: A motherboard is a piece of hardware in a computer which is the central circuit board. It is called a "mother" board in the sense that it joins all internal components and peripherals in a computer together so that the computer can function.

Ports: Ports are used by a motherboard to interface with electronics both inside and outside of the computer.

Serial: A really old piece of technology, serial ports was once used as a connection port for old mice. Serial ports can be found in motherboards predating the year 2000.

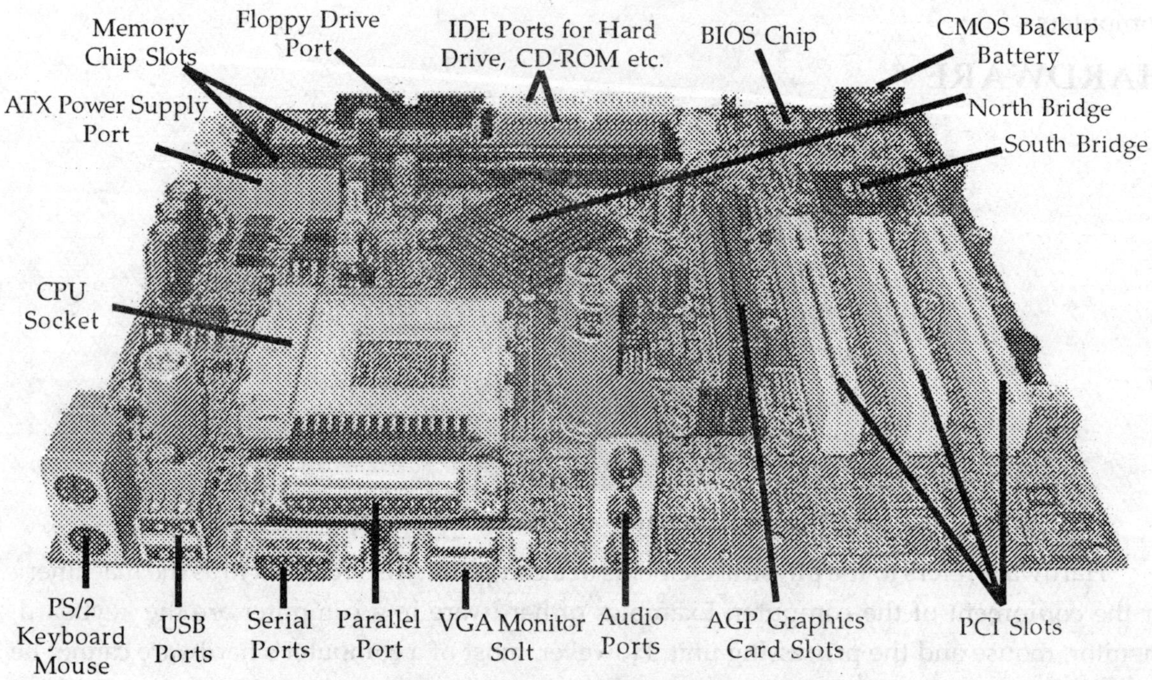

Fig. 1.16: Motherboard Containing all the Internal Parts

PS/2: PS/2 ports have been around for a very long time; however they are still included in motherboards being manufactured today since they are the *de facto* standard in connecting peripherals such as your keyboard and mouse to the computer. PS/2 based mice and keyboards are slowly being superseded by USB technology.

Parallel: Parallel ports are used to connect other peripherals such as joysticks, and printers. Similar to the serial port, this technology is slowly being phased out in favour of USB. Parallel ports can still be found in many motherboards today.

SCSI: Pronounced "scuzzy", this was used primarily as a connection interface for tape drives and hard disk drives. SCSI has been superseded in favour of newer and cheaper technologies such as USB and Firewire.

USBL: Universal Serial Bus (USB) is a connectivity specification, currently at version 2, and known as "hi-speed USB". It is one of the most successful interconnect in computing history. It operates at 480 Mbps and can be found in over 2 billion PC, CE, and mobile devices. USB has strong consumer brand recognition and a reputation for ease-of-use.

Firewire: Technically known as the IEEE 1394 interface, but dubbed by Apple as Firewire, this connection medium hoped to surpass USB in terms of speed and popularity. While it did outperform USB v2 in speed tests, uptake was very limited due to the existing widespread use of USB.

Slots: Slots are an opening in a computer where a circuit board can be inserted to add new capabilities. All personal computers contain expansion slots for adding more memory, graphics capabilities, and support for special devices.

Graphics card: Graphic cards- are also called video card's or a video adapter. They convert signals into video signals so that the images can be displayed on the monitor. Graphics cards are designed to offload rendering from the CPU. They are powered by the motherboard and require a PCIX or PCIX 2.0 slot to install. Some cards require more power and thus will need a 6-8 pin connector that runs directly to the power supply. Typical sizes include 128-1024MB of memory.

Sound card: A sound card, also referred to as an audio card facilitates the input and output of audio signals to and from a computer under the control of computer programs. Sound cards for computers were uncommon until 1988, which left the single internal PC speaker as the only way early PC software could produce sound and music. Uses of a sound card include the audio components for multimedia applications such as games, video/audio editing software and music composition. Most computers today have sound capabilities built into the motherboard, while others require additional expansion cards.

NIC (Network Interface Cards): A network card, network adapter, LAN Adapter or NIC (network interface card) is a piece of computer hardware designed to allow computers to communicate over a computer network. Used for remote communication via cable. Data is transmitted over a cable network. The NIC connects computers and other devices such as printers and many modern motherboards have NICs built in by default.

PC card: A PC card is a peripheral interface device that is located on the side of a typical laptop computer. Originally used as a memory expansion tool; the PC card has many uses such as the use to house network cards, modems, and hard disks. An example of a PC card is a wireless expansion card for laptops, allowing older laptops to connect to wireless networks.

SOFTWARE

Software, commonly known as programs, consists of all the electronic instructions that tell the hardware how to perform a task. These instructions come from a software developer in the form that will be accepted by the operating system that they are based on. For example, a program that is designed for the Windows operating system will only work for that operating system. Compatibility of software will vary as the design of the software and the operating system differ. Software that is designed for Windows XP may experience compatibility issue when running under Windows 2000 or NT or other versions.

Software can also be described as a collection of routines, rules and symbolic languages that direct the functioning of the hardware.

Software is capable of performing specific tasks as opposed to hardware which only perform mechanical tasks that they are mechanically designed for. Practical computer systems divide software systems into three major classes:

(1) **System software:** Helps run computer hardware and computer system. Computer software includes operating system, device drivers, diagnostic tools and more.

(2) **Programming software:** Software that assists a programmer in writing computer programs.

(3) **Application software:** Allows users to accomplish one or more tasks.

The term "software" is sometimes used in a broader context to describe any electronic media content which embodies expressions of ideas such as film, tapes, records, etc. Software is the electronic instruction that tells the computer to do a task.

OS: The operating system (software platform) is a master program required for a computer to run. On a standard personal computer, an operating system arranges simple tasks like handling signals from input and output devices, managing memory usage and controlling peripherals. DOS, Windows, Mac OS and Linux are some examples of personal computer operating systems. Operating systems are also needed to run the application software which most people use computers for, most application programs depend on specific Operating systems (like Windows and Microsoft Office.)

Boot: In computing, booting (or booting up) is a process that loads the operating system on to RAM (random access memory) where it can be used. ROM (read only memory) is what instructs the operating system to load into RAM.

A "cold boot" is the process of turning the computer on from the "off" position. This usually takes longer to load the system than a warm boot.

A "warm boot" is the process of restarting the computer from the "on" position. This takes less time as the operating system is still running, and only needs to be copied onto the RAM.

A "boot disk" is a copy of the operating system, usually kept on a CD or floppy disk. When a hard drive's operating system is not working, rebooting the computer with the boot disk inside allows the system to be accessed.

A "flash booter" is the first application that runs after a reboot. It lives in the Flash Memory and its job is to decide if an application needs more time, or if it is ready to run by "jumping" the execution on the application. It also allows programming and erasing new applications on the Electronic Control Unit. An operating system has two jobs: to coordinate the computer's resources and to service applications.

UTILITIES

Also know as service programs. Utilities perform a variety of functions like disk defragmenting or data compression.

Driver: A computer driver is a program that controls a device. There are device drivers for printers, displays, CD-ROM readers, diskette drives, and so on. For other device, you may need to install a new driver when you connect the device to your computer. In DOS systems, drivers are files with a.SYS extension. In Windows environments, drivers often have a.DRV extension.

A driver acts like a *translator* between the device and programs that use the device. Each device has its own set of specialized commands that only its driver knows. In contrast, most programs access devices by using generic commands. The driver, therefore, accepts generic commands from a program and then translates them into specialized commands for the device.

Backup: Making copies of data in case the original data is lost or destroyed. The two reasons for backing up your files is: (a) disaster recovery – to restore the files to an operational state following a disaster, and (b) to restore small numbers of files after they have been corrupted or accidentally deleted.

FIRMWARE

Fig. 1.17: Firmware

Firmware is both hardware and software. It is a computer chip that performs only one function.

Examples are a video card and sound card. Can be explained as programming instructions that are stored in a read only memory and can only be used by connecting them with software. Used so that processing happens quicker as in video and sound cards.

BLOCK DIAGRAM OF A COMPUTER

Central Processing Unit (CPU)

The main unit inside the computer is the CPU. This unit is responsible for all events inside the computer. It controls all internal and external devices, performs arithmetic and logic operations. The operations a microprocessor performs are called the instruction set of this processor. The instruction set is "hardwired" in the CPU and determines the machine language for the CPU. The more complicated the instruction set is, the slower the CPU works. Processors differ from one another by the instruction set. If the same program can run on two different computer brands, they are said to be compatible.

Control Unit (CU)

The control unit directs and controls the activities of the internal and external devices. It interprets the instructions fetched into the computer, determines what data, if any, are needed, where it is stored, where to store the results of the operation and sends the control signals to the devices involved in the execution of the instructions.

PROCESSING

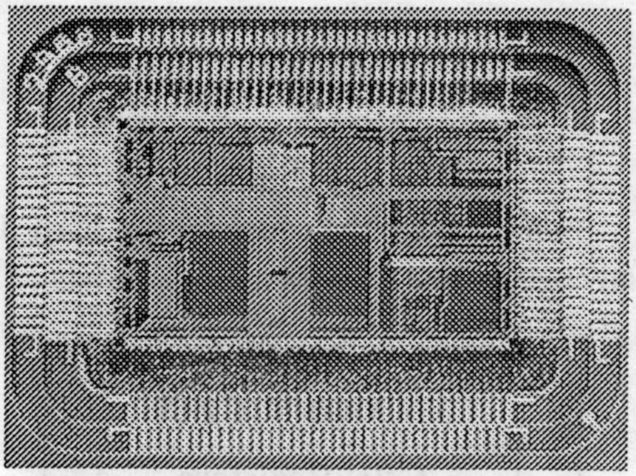

Fig. 1.18: Processor in a Computer

Processor is the brain of a computer. It's also called the "CPU" and it is a microchip.

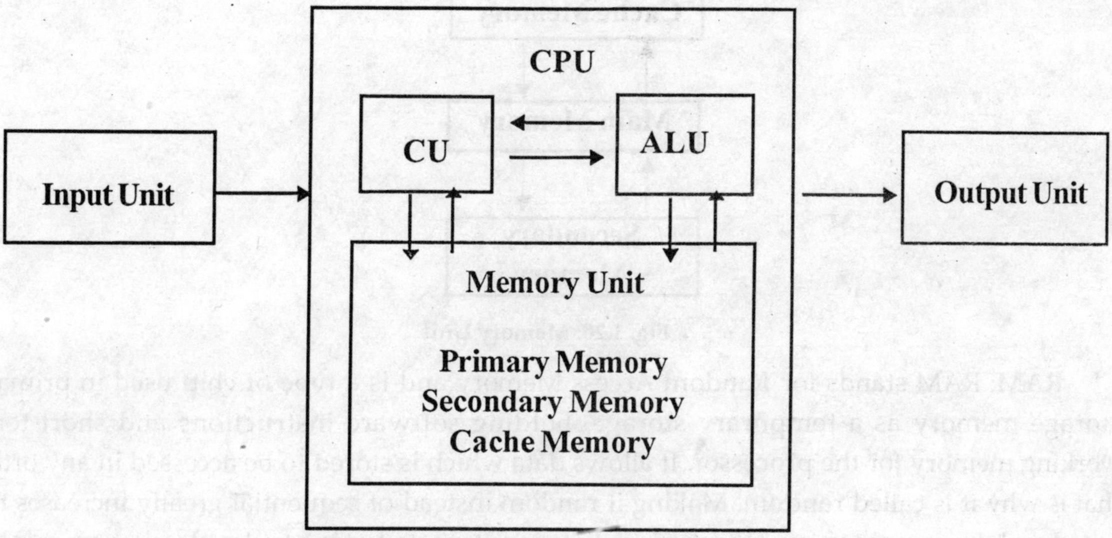

Fig. 1.19· Block Diagram of a Computer

Arithmetic and Logic Unit (ALU)

The arithmetic and logic unit (ALU) is the part where actual computations take place. It consists of circuits which perform arithmetic operations (e.g., addition, subtraction, multiplication, division) over data received from memory and capable to compare numbers.

While performing these operations, the ALU takes data from the temporary storage area inside the CPU named registers. Registers are a group of cells used for memory addressing, data manipulation and processing. Some of the registers are general purpose and some are reserved for certain functions. It is a high-speed memory which holds only data for immediate processing and results of this processing. If these results are not needed for the next instruction, they are sent back to the main memory, and registers are occupied by the new data used in the next instruction.

MEMORY UNIT

Primary Memory

Primary storage or memory, means the space on the hard drive that is briefly used for working space. This usually occurs in a chip. Memory consists of four types of memory chips RAM, ROM, CMOS and flash.

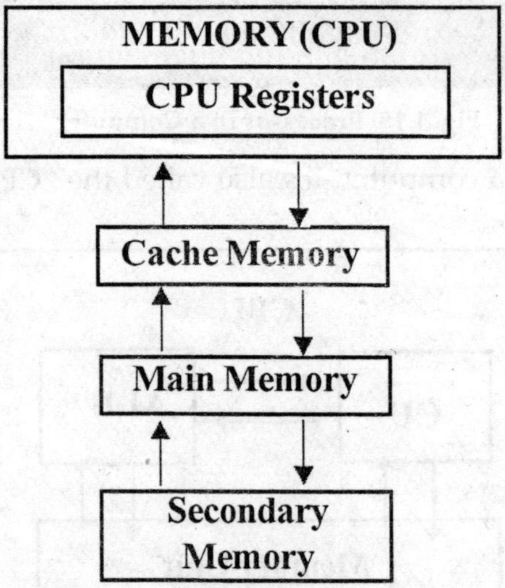

Fig. 1.20: Memory Unit

RAM: RAM stands for Random Access Memory and is a type of chip used in primary storage memory as a temporary storage, holding software instructions and short-term working memory for the processor. It allows data which is stored to be accessed in any order that is why it is called random. Making it random instead of sequential greatly increases the speed and the computer can operate since time is not wasted going to the place where needed data is stored (as in tape backups).

- **Volatile:** Volatile is a descriptive word for RAM which is short-term memory; when the computer loses power, the temporary storage will be lost. In order to prevent data from being lost, it must be saved to a hard disk.

- **Fast:** RAM (in most cases) work faster than a hard drive, and some, faster than flash memory (which isn't volatile). This greater speed is why it's still used in computers today. Computers will run faster and more efficiently with more amounts of RAM. The suggested amount of RAM for current operating systems such as Windows Vista/xp and OSX 10.5 to run smoothly with the weight of shared graphics memory and programs is 1024 megabytes.

Currently, RAM comes in three types: DDR1, DDR2 and DDR3. DDR1 and DDR2 are currently used. DDR3 operates at a higher frequency and has three data transfer channels thus increasing bandwidth. Newly developed SSD hard disks currently are capable of meeting and exceeding the transfer rate of DDR1 and DDR2. A 32-bit operating system is only capable of utilizing 4GB RAM. However 64-bit is capable of supporting much more memory.

ROM: ROM refers to a read only memory chip that cannot be written on or erased by the computer user without special equipment. While using ROM, contents are not lost when power to the computer is no longer available. Since it does not need power and cannot be rewritten, the only things put on are starting (booting) instructions.

CMOS: CMOS stands for Complementary Metal Oxide Semiconductor. This is a technology used in chips and analog circuits. Don't lose contents when turned off even if the content was not saved. Also keeps the time and date current even when the computer is turned off.

Secondary Memory

Computer storage is often referred to as secondary memory where the data is more permanently stored.

Floppy Disks: A "floppy disk" (or diskette) is a form of magnetic data storage; thin, flexible, soft, flat piece of mylar plastic, packaged in a 3.5 inch plastic case. The reason it is called a floppy is because obsolete (8 and 5.25 inch formats) types would "flop" as you waved them. Floppy disks were invented by IBM and were a popular form of data storage from the 1970s to the 1990s. The key to their widespread use was their inexpensive cost and ease of portability. Information could be transferred to a floppy disk, stored, disk removed, then inserted into another system to then be accessed.

Zip Disks: A zip drive is a secondary storage device that uses zip disks. Zip disks are cartridges similar to floppy disks but capable of storing 70-500 times more memory. Zip disks are disks with a special high quality magnetic coating that have a capacity of 100, 250 or 750MB. Zip drives are almost obsolete.

Hard Drives: A hard-disk drive is non-volatile device used for storage that is located inside the computer case. Like the floppy drive, it holds its data on rotating platters with a magnetic upper exterior which are changed or read by electromagnetic tipped arms that move over the disk as it spins.

Tape Drives: A tape drive is a storage device that uses a streaming magnetic tape to store data. Instead of allowing random access to data, tape drives only allow sequential access to data. It must wind between reels to find any particular piece of data at any given time. Tape drives are used for archival storage of data stored on hard drives.

Cache Memory

Cache memory is a fast semiconductor memory that is used to increase the speed of processing of data and instructions. It is placed in between the CPU and the main memory. It is much faster than main memory.

The concept of cache memory is introduced in computers to increase the speed of the processing by reducing the access time and fetch time. Cache memory stores the instructions and data which are to be immediately executed. It is used to reduce the access time for address, instructions or data which are normally stored in the main memory. Thus, the cache memory increases the speed of the system. Generally, cache memory sizes are 64k, 128k, etc. which are small in size.

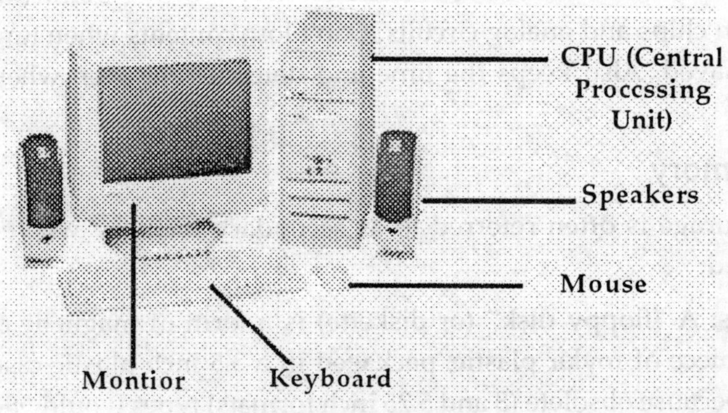

Fig. 1.21: Different Parts of a PC

INPUT UNIT

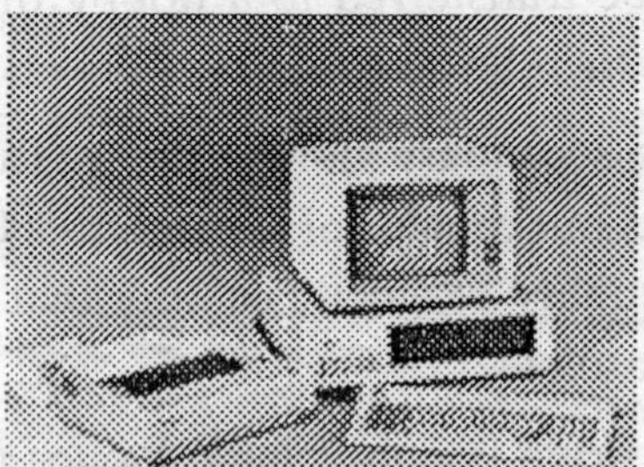

Fig. 1.22: Input Device Keyboard

Whatever goes into the computer; Input can take a variety of forms, from commands you enter from the keyboard to data from another computer or device. A device that feeds data into a computer, such as a keyboard or mouse, is called an input device.

Input Devices

Keyboard: The keyboard is the most popular input device for a computer. It translates numbers, letters, symbols and control keys into signals that can be interpreted by the PC. Most English keyboards today are based on the qwerty design. Some specialist keyboards have extra function keys that perform special actions when pressed.

Mouse/Pointing Device: Another type of input device that uses a pointing or insertion device instead of characters from a keyboard. With the rise in graphical user interfaces, mice became the most commonly used method in controlling a computer. A mouse is used to manipulate objects and text, etc. on the computer screen. This device can be plugged into the back of a computer, the back of a keyboard or can even be cordless.

Touch Pad/Pointing Stick: Touch pads are most commonly built into a laptop computer. A touch pad is a rectangular plastic piece which can control the pointer on a computer simply by dragging your finger across its surface. A pointing stick resembles a pencil eraser and is commonly located in between keys on a laptop keyboard. To control the pointer on the computer with a pointing stick, you use your finger to bend the stick in the direction you would like the pointer to move.

Stylus: A Stylus (which is Latin for stake or pointed object) is a small pen-like device used to enter data by reacting to a touch-sensitive screen or film. Styli allow a user to input handwriting specific pieces of information like signatures. Many artists also utilize styli with the use of a tablet. One important feature of a stylus is its tip which ideally is made of a firm but non-scratching form of plastic. The body of a stylus can be made from anything ranging from synthetic plastic to bronze or chrome in some situations.

Light Pen: Light pen is a device which looks like a pen connected to the computer. The user can bring the pen to which ever they want to locate. A computer input device with a light-sensitive wand works with CRT monitors. Used like/for a touch screen with higher accuracy than fingers.

Digitizer: A digitizer is a "pointing" technology implemented on computer tablets. It consists of the "tablet", an electronically integrated surface representative (to the computer) of an XY-axis grid. Using the electronic stylus (pen), the tablet will detect the stylus' movements and convert it into digital signals for the computer to use. Commonly used in the engineering and architecture.

Scanner: A scanner is a device that uses light to read an image or text and turn it into a digital message. This media can then be used to store, change and send the image or text. There are various types of scanners. The three most common are Drum, flatbed and hand. Drum scanners use photomultiplier tubes (PMT). Flatbed scanners use a glass pane and a bright light. Hand scanners are dragged across the image manually.

OUTPUT UNIT

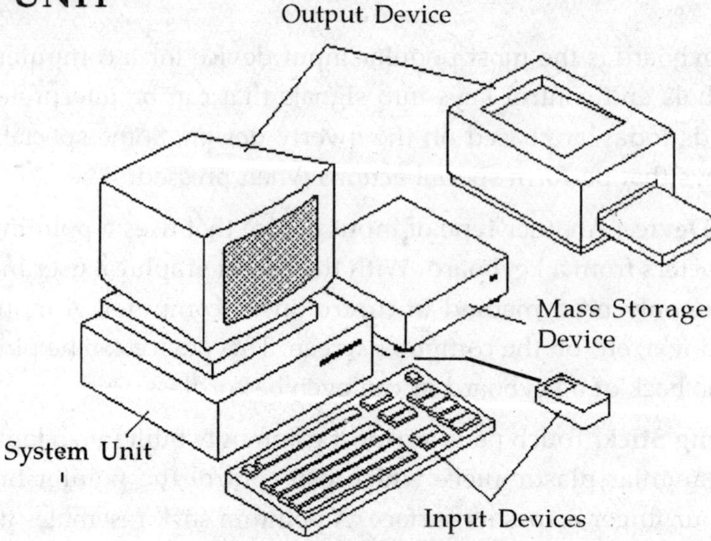

Fig. 1.23: Output Devices of a Computer

Anything that comes out of a computer. Output can be display screens, loudspeakers, and printers.

Output Devices

Auditory: A computer can produce sound in the form of beeps from the piezo speaker on its motherboard, or it can use a sound card to produce true tone sounds that sound like the real thing.

Speakers: This is the primary method of sound output in most computers today. Sound is translated from bits to electrical signals in a sound card, which then channels the signals to the speakers.

MIDI (Musical Instrument Digital Interface): Allows electronic musical instruments and computers to communicate, control and synchronize each other was invented. Unlike mp3 or WAV files, MIDI does not transmit an audio signal or media, instead, it simply transmits digital data "event messages" such as the pitch and intensity of musical notes to play, control signals for parameters such as volume, vibrato and panning, cues and clock signals to set the tempo. Therefore, the "music" you get from MIDI files are simple instrumental sounds.

MIC: Also known as "microphone": a device used to change sound into electric signals. Microphones are used in telephones, tape recorders, hearing aids and many other devices.

Printer: A printer is a device that prints text or images on paper. It makes a physical copy of it with ink on paper.

STORAGE DEVICES

Computer data storage is referred to as storage or memory, which can save digital data. Examples are RAM, hard disks or removable memory sticks.

Fig. 1.24: RAM in a Computer

Names for Different Sizes of Data

When choosing a new computer, we come across terms such as "300GB hard drive" and "500MB download", and to the uninitiated, this can be somewhat disconcerting. Data in a computer is represented in a series of bits. Since the birth of computers, bits have been the language that controls the processes that take place inside that mysterious black box called the computer. In this, we look at every language that the computer uses to do its work.

Binary: Binary numeral system is using two symbols, usually "0" and "1". A binary number can be represented by bits. Binary refers to the system of information transfer through the processor. The binary code occurs in digits of 0 and 1. The processor understands these codes as off and on respectively. In the computer, 0 is represented by the electrical current off and 1 by current being on.

Bit: A bit is simply a 1 or a 0, i.e., a true or a false. It is the most basic unit of data in a computer. It's like the dots and dashes in Morse code for a computer. It's also called machine language.

Byte: In computer science, a byte is a unit of measurement of information storage, that equals '8 bits', can be used to represent letters and numbers. For example, the number 01000001 is 8 bits long, and represents the letter A in ASCII.

KB: A kB is a unit of data that equals 1024 bytes. This is because 8 bytes cannot contribute into 1000.

MB: Megabyte is 1024kB; the kilobyte squared, 10242 bytes.

GB: A gigabyte is a unit of data storage worth a billion bytes meaning either exactly 1 billion bytes (10243) or approximately 1.07 billion bytes. Gigabytes are presented as 1 billion bytes and not 10243.

TB: A terabyte is 10244 and is defined as about one trillion bytes, or 1024 gigabytes. Data centres such as those operated by Google handle thousands if not millions of terabytes of data each day.

PB: A petabyte is a unit of information or computer storage equal to one quadrillion bytes (10245). Microsoft stores on 900 servers a total of approximately 14 petabytes.

MEASUREMENTS OF DATA SPEED

Today, there are generally two ways of describing data transfer speeds: in *bits* per second, or in *bytes* per second.

Bps: Known as bits per second, bps was the main way of describing data transfer speeds several decades ago. Bps was also known as the baud rate, therefore, a 600 baud modem is one which could transfer data at around 600bps.

Kbps: Kilobits per second or 1000 bits per second.

Mbps: 1,000,000 bits per second (usually used in describing internet download/upload speeds).

Gbps: 1,000,000 kilobits per second or 1,000,000,000 bits per second. This term is most commonly heard in local area networks, where the close proximity of machines allows for lightening fast data transfer rates.

TYPES OF CODES

EBCDIC: Extended Binary Coded Decimal Interchange Code: A binary code used with large computers, such as mainframes. This code uses 8 bits (0's or 1's) for each character and was developed by IBM in 1963 and 1964.

ASCII: Pronounced: "ask-ee". A type of binary code that uses 1 byte (8 bits) for each character. A total of 256 characters. ASCII is the most common code used in microcomputers. ASCII stands for American Standard Code for Information Interchange. It is a "numerical representation of a character". It is used to transfer documents between computers with .txt (for text) extension.

Unicode: Unicode is a type of binary coding which uses an exclusive number for every character. It uses up to 4 bytes (currently 21 bits) for each of these characters, *instead* of the 1 byte per character of EBCDIC. Unicode can handle 2,097,152 (221) character combinations (instead of the 256 characters of ASCII) which means *most* of the world's written languages can be represented by a single character set.

In text processing, Unicode takes the role of providing a unique code point — a number, not a glyph — for each character. In other words, Unicode represents a character in an abstract way and leaves the visual rendering (size, shape, font or style) to other software, such as a web browser or word processor.

VIRUS

A virus is a program that can destroy and corrupt data on a computer. It can come through a floppy disk, CD or USB, but now usually comes through email.

Viruses are programs that can copy themselves and create problems in one computer without the user ever knowing or authorizing it. Virus can only be spread by when they are taken to an uninfected computer.

INTERFACES

Interfaces are the functioning of two things, e.g., the way software and hardware interacts or how either would interact with a person, i.e., the user.

CUI (User Interface): You type commands into the computer. It's not easy to remember all the commands, and it looks less exciting than a GUI, but it works faster because you're not making the computer waste time showing pretty icons and background images.

GUI (User Interface): It allows people to interact with a computer and computer-controlled devices using graphical icons, visual indicators or special graphical elements called "widgets". These icons are used in conjunction with text, labels or text navigation.

PROGRAMMING LANGUAGES

Programming languages are divided into two: Low-level language and High-level language.

Low-level Languages

Both machine language and assembly language are called low-level languages which are machine-oriented and machine-dependent.

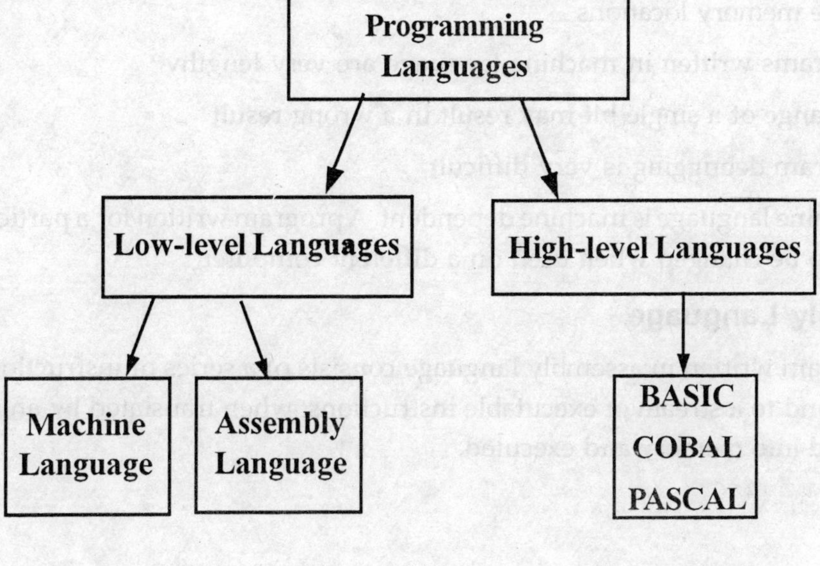

1. Machine Language

The fundamental method of representing information to computer is the electric pulse, which is also known as binary representation. Sometimes referred to as machine code or object code, machine language is a collection of binary digits or bits (0's and 1's) that the computer reads and interprets. Machine language is the only language a computer is capable of understanding.

The computer uses only the machine language when executing a program. The reason is that the computer can understand the machine language and process very fast. There is a specific binary code for each instruction. The instruction in machine language is a sequence of 0's and 1's.

The machine language instruction consists of an operation code and an operand or an address of operands.

The operation code defines the function that the computer must perform. For example, the addition of two numbers. The operand represents the variables involved in the operation. But the machine language is efficient only for the computers and is inefficient for the programmers.

Each microprocessor has its own instruction set and corresponding machine codes.

Advantages

- Computer understands the machine language.
- Time taken to execute the program is less.

Disadvantages

- Programmer has to remember the binary equivalent operational code and addresses of the memory locations
- Programs written in machine language are very lengthy
- A change of a single bit may result in a wrong result
- Program debugging is very difficult
- Machine language is machine dependent. A program written for a particular computer has to be changed when used on a different computer.

2. Assembly Language

A program written in assembly language consists of a series of instructions mnemonics that correspond to a stream of executable instructions, when translated by an assembler that can be loaded into memory and executed.

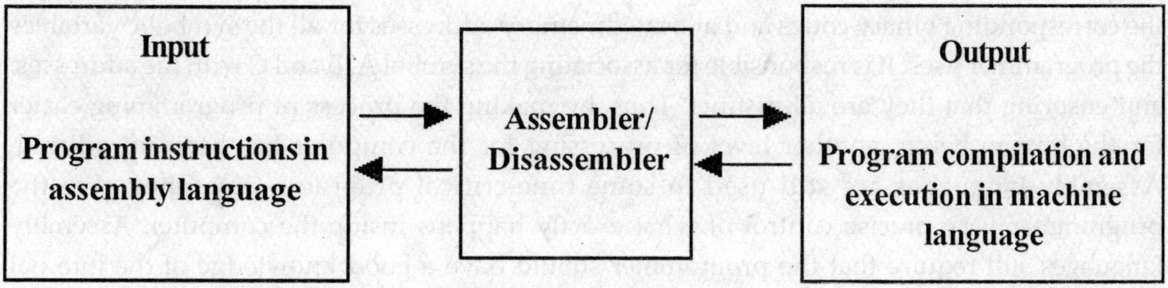

The mnemonic "mov" is an operation code or opcode, and was chosen by the instruction set designer to abbreviate "move." A comma-separated list of arguments or parameters follows the opcode; this is a typical assembly language statement. Transforming assembly into machine language is accomplished by an assembler, and the reverse by a disassembler. Unlike in high-level languages, there is usually a one-to-one correspondence between simple assembly statements and machine language instructions. However, in some cases, an assembler may provide pseudo instructions which expand into several machine language instructions to provide commonly needed functionality.

The bookkeeping involved in machine language programming is very tedious. If a programmer is modifying a program and decides to insert an extra data item, the addresses of other data items may be changed. The programmer will have to carefully examine the whole program deciding which bit patterns represent the addresses which have changed, and modify them.

Human beings are notoriously bad at simple repetitive tasks; computers thrive on them. Assembly languages are a more human friendly form of machine language. Machine language commands are replaced by mnemonic commands on a one-to-one basis. The assembler program takes care of converting from the mnemonic to the corresponding machine language code. The programmer can also use symbolic addresses for data items. The assembler will assign machine addresses and ensure that distinct data items do not overlap in storage, a depressingly common occurrence in machine language programs. For example, the short section of program might be written in assembly language as:

Operation Code	Address
LOAD	A
ADD	B
STORE	C

Obviously, this leaves less scope for error but since the computer does not directly understand assembly language this has to be translated into machine language by a program called an assembler. The assembler replaces the mnemonic operation codes such as ADD with the corresponding binary codes and allocates memory addresses for all the symbolic variables the programmer uses. It is responsible for associating the symbol A, B and C with the addresses, and ensuring that they are all distinct. Thus, by making the process of programming easier for the human being, another level of processing for the computer has been introduced. Assembly languages are still used in some time-critical programs since they give the programmer very precise control of what exactly happens inside the computer. Assembly languages still require that the programmer should have a good knowledge of the internal structure of the computer. For example, different ADD instructions will be needed for different types of data item. Assembly languages are still machine-specific and hence the program will have to be rewritten if it is to be implemented on another type of computer.

A sample program to add two numbersm

RD A	Read a number into memory location A
RD B	Read a second number into memory location B
CLA A	Clear the ALU and add the number in A to it
ADD B	Add the number in B to the ALU
ST SUM	Store the result from the ALU into location SUM
PRT SUM	Send the number in SUM to the printer
HALT	Stop processing.

Advantages

- No need of remembering all binary OP codes and addresses of the memory locations.
- Program debugging is comparatively easier.
- Less time is required in writing the program.
- Less chances of making errors.
- Language is simpler than machine language.

Disadvantages

- Execution of program takes more time as it has to be converted into machine language.
- Assembly language is machine-oriented, i.e., it is designed for specific computer. Program has to be rewritten for a different machine

High-level Languages

Very early in the development of computers, attempts were made to make programming easier by reducing the amount of knowledge of the internal workings of the computer that was needed to write programs. If programs could be presented in a language that was more familiar to the person solving the problem, then fewer mistakes would be made. High-level programming languages allow the specification of a problem solution in terms closer to those used by human beings. These languages were designed to make programming far easier, less error-prone and to remove the programmer from having to know the details of the internal structure of a particular computer. These high-level languages were much closer to human language. One of the first of these languages was Fortran II which was introduced in about 1958. In Fortran II, our program above would be written as:

C = A + B

which is obviously much more readable, quicker to write and less error-prone. As with assembly languages the computer does not understand these high-level languages directly and hence they have to be processed by passing them through a program called a compiler which translates them into internal machine language before they can be executed.

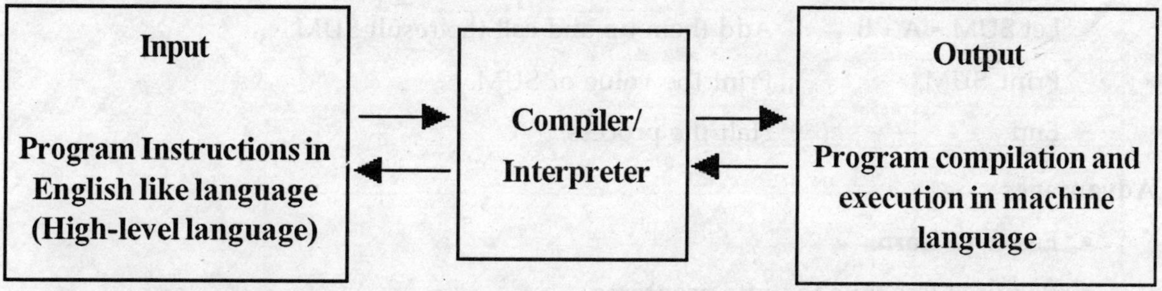

Another advantage accrues from the use of high-level languages if the languages are standardized by some international body. Then each manufacturer produces a compiler to compile programs that conform to the standard into their own internal machine language. Then it should be easy to take a program which conforms to the standard and implement it on many different computers merely by recompiling it on the appropriate computer. This great advantage of portability of programs has been achieved for several high-level languages and it is now possible to move programs from one computer to another without too much difficulty. Unfortunately, many compiler writers add new features of their own which means that if a programmer uses these features then their program becomes non-portable. It is well worth becoming familiar with the standard and writing programs which obey it, so that your programs are more likely to be portable. As with assembly language, human time is saved at the expense of the compilation time required to translate the program to internal machine language. The compilation time used in the computer is trivial compared with the human time saved, typically seconds as compared with weeks.

Many high-level languages have appeared since Fortran II (and many have also disappeared!), among the most widely used have been:

COBOL	Business applications
FORTRAN	Engineering and Scientific Applications
PASCAL	General use and as a teaching tool
C & C++	General Purpose – currently most popular
PROLOG	Artificial Intelligence
JAVA	General Purpose – gaining popularity rapidly

All these languages are available on a large variety of computers.

A Program to Add two numbers in a High-level Language (True BASIC)

A sample program:

Input A, B	Read two numbers A and B.
Let SUM = A + B	Add them up and call the result SUM.
Print SUM	Print the value of SUM.
End	Halt the process.

Advantages

- Easier to learn.
- Required less time to write programs.
- Easier to maintain.
- Not machine-dependent.

Disadvantages

- Less efficient as they take more execution time.
- Giving an instruction in high-level language does not tell how the computer works.
- Compiler has to be loaded in main memory which is limited in size.

TRANSLATORS

Translator is a software that accepts one language as input and convert it into another language. The input for any translator is to be converted to another language. The input for any translatór is called as source language or source code and output of any translator is called as object language or object code. There are two types.

Compilers vs Interpreters

Compiler - spends some time evaluating the entire program and then translates all the programming statements of a program into a machine level program, which is then executed at once.

Interpreter - translates interactively each programming statement into an immediately usable machine language instruction. Although an interpreter slows down the execution speed of a program somewhat, it does not require extra steps to compile and link like a compiler.

Any high-level language can either be interpreted or compiled.

ALGORITHM

- An algorithm is the step-by-step solution to a certain problem.
- A procedure for solving a problem in terms of the actions to be executed and the order in which those actions are to be executed.

The steps are normally "sequence", "selection", "iteration" and a case-type statement.

Example: On a separate sheet of paper, list all the known possible steps in preparing/ performing the following activities; be as descriptive and specific as you can be:

- Cooking/Frying an egg, sunny-side up
- The activities you do and the vehicles you ride on your way to school
- Walking your dog at the park

These activities above might seem easy, but as you perform the tasks, you will encounter a series of trial-and-error sub-activities. For beginners, this is normal and you may tend to miss a few steps. The solution to the case of egg frying should look like this:

(1) Get the frying pan.

(2) Get the oil.

  (a) Do you have oil?

    (1) If yes, put it in the pan.

    (2) If no, do you want to buy oil?

    (3) If yes, then go out and buy.

    (4) If no, you can terminate.

(3) Turn on the stove.

(4) Etc...

For the case of frying an egg sunny side-up, have you forgotten to state that you will heat up the pan? Or may be put in some oil? Should you put some oil in first before heating the pan, or should you heat the pan and then put some oil in? These are the possible conditions that you may encounter in preparing the algorithms for this task.

PSEUDOCODE

Pseudocode (pronounced SOO-doh-kohd) is a detailed yet readable description of what a computer program or algorithm must do, expressed in a formally-styled natural language rather than in a programming language. Pseudocode is sometimes used as a detailed step in the process of developing a program. It allows designers or lead programmers to express the design in great detail and provides programmers a detailed template for the next step of writing code in a specific programming language.

Example:

Write a program that obtains two integer numbers from the user. It will print out the sum of those numbers.

Prompt the user to enter the first integer

Prompt the user to enter a second integer

Compute the sum of the two user inputs

Display an output prompt that explains the answer as the sum

Display the result

SYNTAX

Syntax is the grammar, structure, or order of the elements in a language statement. Syntax applies to computer languages as well as to natural languages. Usually, we think of syntax as "word order." However, syntax is also achieved in some languages such as Latin by inflectional case endings. In computer languages, syntax can be extremely rigid as in the case of most assembler languages or less rigid in languages that make use of "keyword" parameters that can be stated in any order.

FLOW CHARTS

Flow chart is a graphical representation of algorithm. It is used to represent algorithm steps into graphical format. It also gives us an idea to organize the sequence of steps or events necessary to solve a problem with the computer. In other words, flow charts are symbolic diagrams of operations and the sequence, data flow, control flow and processing logic in information processing. These charts are used to understand any working sequence of the program.

Advantages of Flow Chart

(1) It provides an easy way of communication because any other person besides the programmer can understand the way they are represented.

(2) It represents the data flow.

(3) It provides a clear overview of the entire program and problem and solution.

(4) It checks the accuracy in logic flow.

(5) It documents the steps followed in an algorithm.

(6) It provides the facility for coding.

(7) It provides the way of modification of running program.

(8) They show all major elements and their relationship.

Terminator: This symbol represents the beginning and end point in a program. We use start and stop option in it.

Input/Output Symbol: This symbol is used to take any input or output in the algorithm.

Process Symbol: A rectangle indicates the processing, calculation and arithmetic operations.

Decision Symbol: It is used when we want to take any decision in the program.

Connector Symbol: This symbol is used to connect the various portions of a flow chart. This is normally used when the flow chart is split between two pages.

Data Flow Symbol: This symbol is used to display the flow of the program. It shows the path of logic flow in a program.

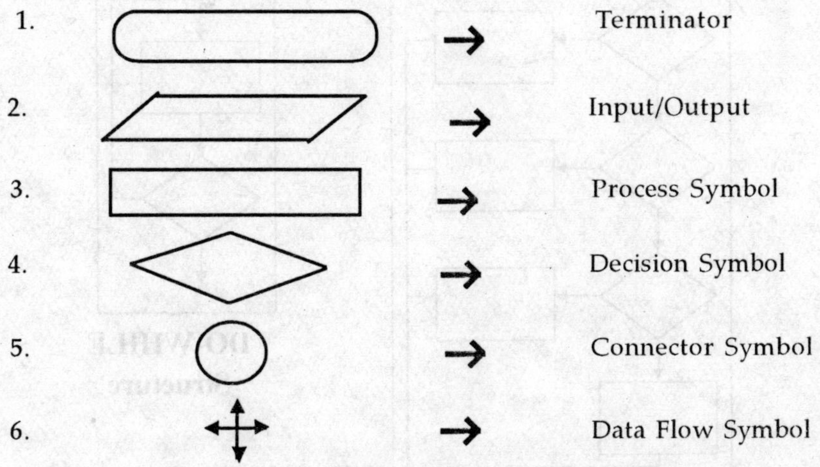

Data Flow Symbol: This symbol is used to display the flow of the program. It shows the path of logic flow in a program.

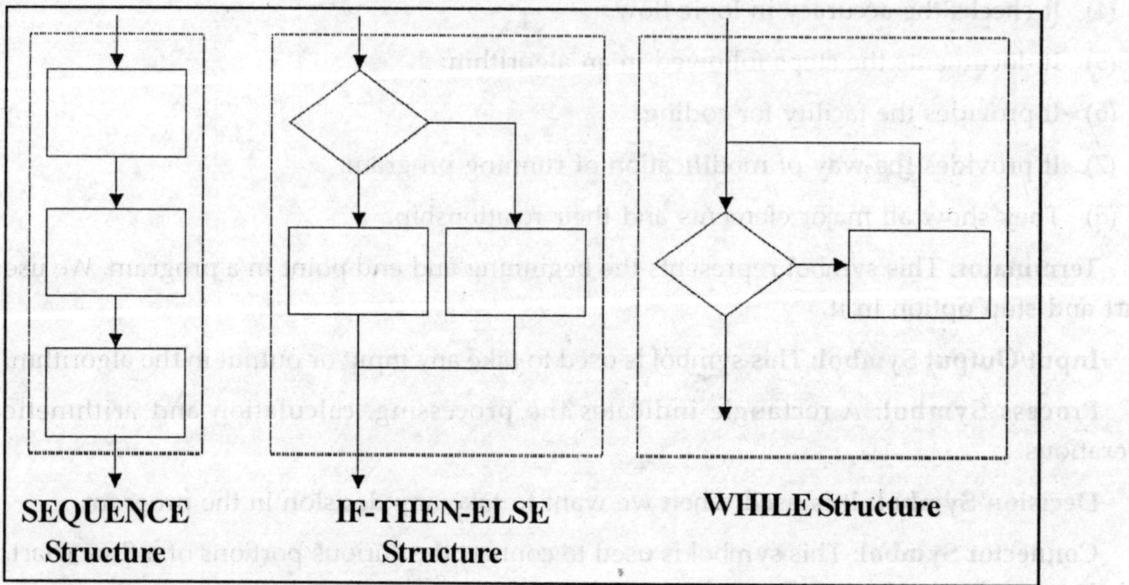

Basic Flow Chart Structures:

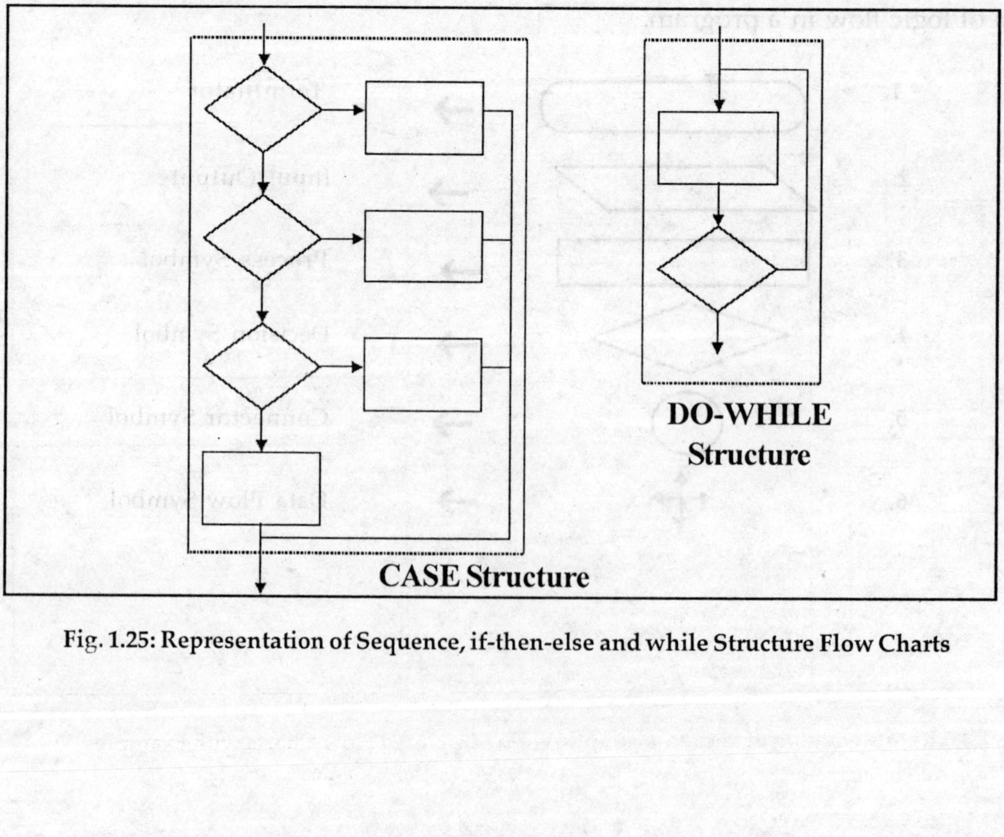

Fig. 1.25: Representation of Sequence, if-then-else and while Structure Flow Charts

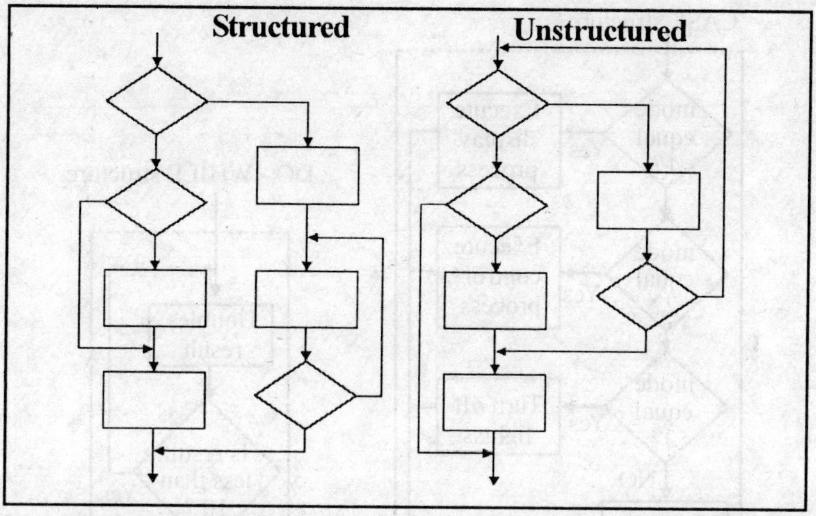

Fig. 1.26: Representation of Case Structure and do-while.. Structure Flow Charts

Examples of Using Flow Charts

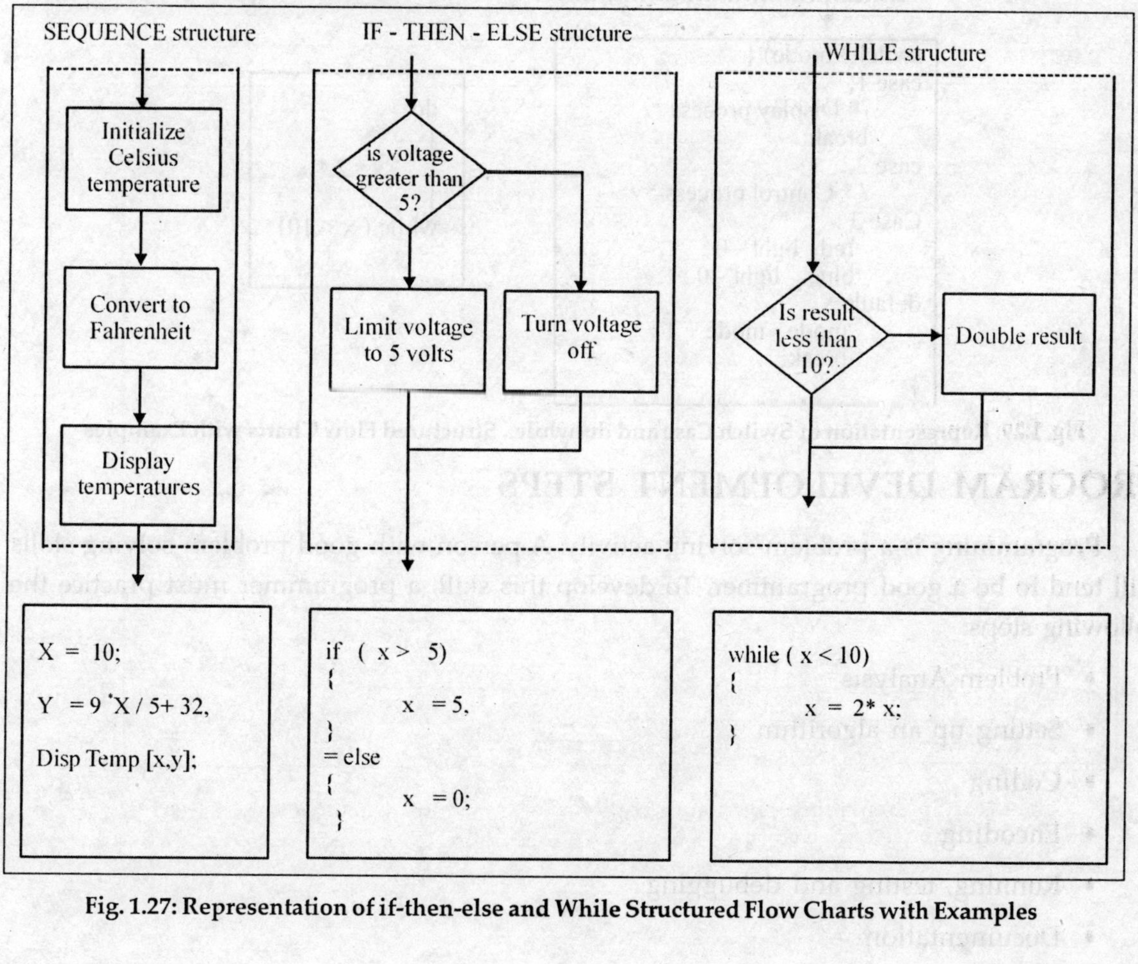

Fig. 1.27: Representation of if-then-else and While Structured Flow Charts with Examples

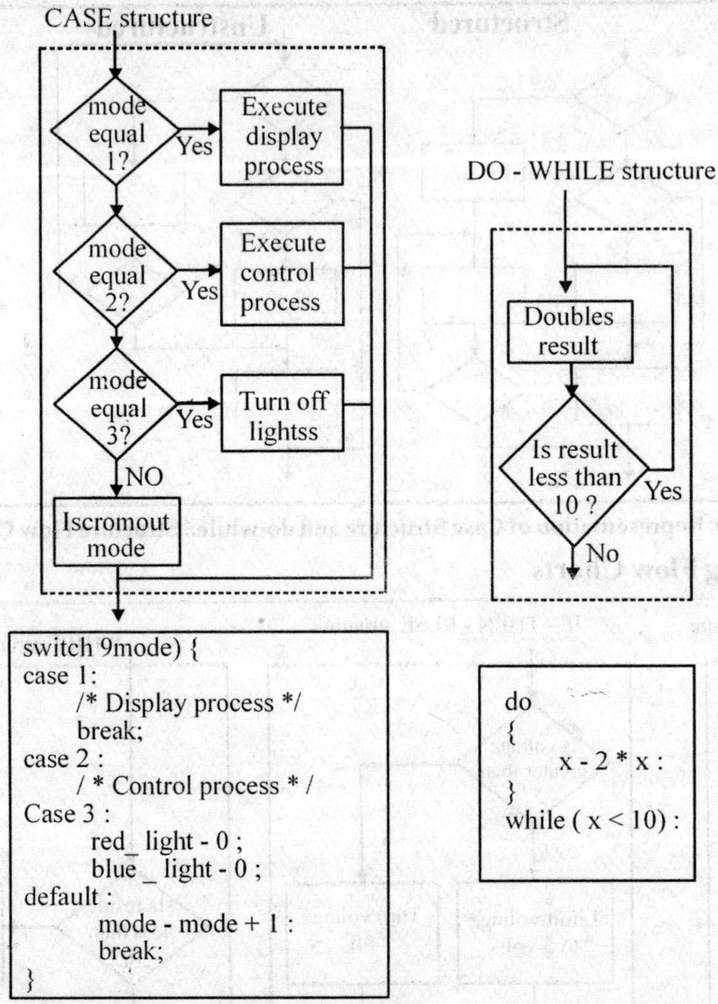

Fig. 1.29: Representation of Switch Case and do-while.. Structured Flow Charts with Examples

PROGRAM DEVELOPMENT STEPS

Programming is a problem-solving activity. A person with good problem-solving skills will tend to be a good programmer. To develop this skill, a programmer must practice the following steps:

- Problem Analysis
- Setting up an algorithm
- Coding
- Encoding
- Running, testing and debugging
- Documentation

Review Questions

1. What is a computer? Enumerate various types of computers.
2. Find out how many computer languages are classified into various generations (first generation to fifth generation languages)? To which generation C belong to?
3. What are the hardware and software and what do they include?
4. What is a compiler? Give three examples of compilers.
5. What are the object code and executable code?
6. What are the various components of a computer with an example for each?
7. Explain the importance of verification and validation for problem solving with computers.
8. What has to be done before a program can be executed in a computer? How is the program executed by the CPU?
9. What benefit derives from the 'stored program concept'?
10. What are the tasks carried out by the Central Processing Unit.
11. What are the major differences between main memory and external memory?
12. What is stored in main memory? What is stored in external memory?
13. How is information represented inside computer systems?
14. Why do we write programs in high-level languages?
15. What is ALU? Distinguish between cache memory and associate memory.
16. What is a register? How are registers used in CPU?
17. What is meant by mainframe computer? Where can mainframes be found? For what are they generally used?
18. What is a minicomputer? How do minicomputers differ from mainframes?
19. What is a personal computer? How do personal computers differ from others?
20. What is computer memory? What kinds of information are stored in a computer's memory?
21. What is a bit? What is a byte? What is the difference between a byte and a bit?
22. What terms are used to describe the size of a computer's memory? What are some typical memory sizes?
23. Name some typical auxiliary storage devices. How does this type of device differ from the computer's main memory?
24. What is machine language? How does machine language differ from high-level languages?
25. Name some commonly used high-level languages. What are the advantages of using high-level languages?
26. What are the steps involved in going from the specification of a problem to producing an executable program which will solve the problem?

27. What are the algorithm and the flow chart?

28. Write the various steps involved in executing a C program and illustrate it with the help of flow chart.

29. What is a flow chart? Explain the different symbols used in flow chart.

30. What are the basic characteristics of an algorithm? Explain with an example.

31. What is meant by compilation? What is meant by interpretation? How do these two processes differ?

32. Write an algorithm to find the roots of a quadratic equation for all the cases.

ઉઉઉ

CHAPTER 2

Introduction to C Language

BACKGROUND

In the early days of computers, the only programming languages available to programmers were two low level languages: machine and assembly language. Programming in these languages was tedious and time consuming because the programmers had to manage the hardware itself (memory, stack, interrupts, etc.). When computers became increasingly available, many high-level languages such as FORTRAN, PASCAL and BASIC were developed in order to make the underlying hardware invisible to the programmer and to make the syntax easier; therefore making computers easier and faster to program.

In 1972, the Unix operating system was being developed with the concept of a system programming language having attributes of both "low" and "high" level languages, which have the advantage of allowing the programmers to take control of the underlying hardware if desired.

Brian W. Kernigahn and Dennis M. Ritchie developed C at Bell Laboratories (AT&T Bell Labs). Their underlying goal was to develop a language which is simple and flexible enough to be used in a variety of different processors (two early versions were name A and B) with a Unix operating system.

In 1983, the American National Standards Institute (ANSI) formed a committee to produce a C programming language standard. This "ANSI C" was completed in 1988. Although it was originally intended to run under UNIX, there has been a great interest in running it under the MS-DOS operating system on the IBM PC and compatibilities. It is an excellent language for this environment because of the simplicity of expression, the compactness of the code and the wide range of applicability.

IMPORTANCE OF C

"C" language is a language that combines all the elegance and power of assembly language with all the readability and maintainability. It is often called as a middle level computer language, as it has the features of both high-level language (BASIC, PASCAL, etc.) and low-level (assembly) language.

C is a general purpose programming language with features: economy of expression, modern flow control and data structure, and a rich set of operators.

Important Features of C

- It is robust language whose rich setup of built-in functions and operators can be used to write any complex program.
- It has the ability to extend itself. A C program is basically a collection of functions that are supported by the C library. We can continuously add our own functions to the library with the availability of the large number of functions.
- It is highly portable, i.e., software written for one computer can be run on another computer, with little or no modification.
- Program written in C are efficient due to several variety of data types and powerful operations.
- There are 32 keywords, several standard functions available which can be used for developing a program.
- C language is well suited for structured programming, this requires user to think of a problem in terms of function or modulus or block. A collection of these modulus make a program debugging and testing easier.
- Pointer implementation extensive use of pointers for memory, array, structures and functions.
- It allows dynamic allocation of memory while writing a program and can request the operating system to allocate/release the memory.
- The program written in C complier combines the capabilities of an assembly language with the features of high-level language and well suited for writing both system software and business package.

Drawbacks

- There is no runtime checking.
- As the program extends, it is very difficult to fix the bugs.

- Structured programming serves well upto a point, but beyond that an entirely new paradigm, i.e., object-oriented programming (OOP) is required.

SOFTWARE DEVELOPMENT METHOD

Software development is the set of activities and processes that will eventually result in a software product. This may include inventing, improving, selecting among alternative solutions, and then describing computer programs that meet user requirements within the constraints of the environment. Adopting a good software development methodology will eventually lead to a software product that meets most, if not all of the agreed requirements, within the given constraints that which includes cost and schedule.

The following are the sequence of operations used for software development:

- Specify the problem requirements
- Analyze the problem
- Design the algorithm to solve the problem
- Implement the algorithm
- Test and verify the completed program
- Maintain and update the program

C INTEGRATED DEVELOPMENT ENVIRONMENT

When writing a C program, environment modern versions of the language are usually accompanied with an Integrated Development Environment (IDE). These applications allows you to write the program, organize your source code, debug your programs, compile them, build them into a final executable to be distributed, and execute the programs, as well as a number of associated tasks, such as loop-up online help on various aspects of the language and IDE. Turbo C compiler (DOS) based (very small and fast) and Borland C Builder compilers are used to run the C program.

BASIC STRUCTURE OF A 'C' PROGRAM

Same as that of a structure of a human being, containing head, body, hands and legs. C program also has a structure.

C program consists of a set of one or more functions which performs a specific task when a group of statements are executed. It is divided into six different sections. They are:

1. Documentation Section
2. Link Section
3. Definition Section
4. Global Declaration Section

→ Optional Section

5. main Function Section

    {
        Declaration statements;
        Executable statements;
    }

→ Must be used

6. Sub-program function section

    Function1(){
        Declaration statements;
    Executable statements;
        }
    Function2(){
        Declaration statements;
        Executable statements;
        }
        .
        .
        .
        .
    Functionn (){
        Declaration statements;
        Executable statements;
        }

→ User-defined Functions

A SIMPLE C PROGRAM

```
/* My first program in C language*/
#include <stdio.h>
main() {printf("This is my first C program"); // prints onto the screen
}
```

Example:

```
// Program to find the area of glass and length of wood
#include <stdio.h>
void main (void) {
float height, width, area, wood_length;
scanf ("%f", &height);
scanf ("%f", &width);
area = 2 * height * width;
wood_length = 2 * ( height + width) * 3.25;
printf ("The area of glass is : %f metres.\n",area);
printf ("The length of wood is : %f feet.\n", wood_length);
}
```

//	Singe line comments, tells the compiler not to compile this line only.
/*..........*/	Multiple line comments, tells the compiler not to compile these lines.
#include	This is a pre-processor directive. It is not part of our program, it is an instruction to the compiler to make it do something. It tells the C compiler to the contents of a file, in this case the system file .h. The compiler knows it is a system file, and therefore must be looked for in a special place, by the fact that the name is enclosed in < > characters.
<stdio.h>	This is the name of the standard library definition file for all STanDard Input Output. Your program will almost certainly want to send stuff to the screen and read things from the keyboard. .h is the name of the file in which the functions that we want to use are defined. A function is simply a chunk of program that we want to use a lot, so we stuck it in a parcel and gave it a name.
.h	The < > characters around the name tell C to look in the system area for the file stdio.h. If I had given the name ".h" instead it would tell the compiler to look in the current directory. This means that I can set up libraries of my own routines and use them in my programs, a very useful feature.

void	Literally, this means nothing. In this case, it is referring to the function whose name follows.
main	The function is actually the one which is run when your program is used. A C program is made up of a large number of functions. Each of these is given a name by the programmer and they refer to each other as the program runs. C regards the name " " as a special case and will run this function first. If you forget to have a main function, or mistype the name, the compiler will give you an error.
(void)	This is a pair of brackets enclosing. This actually tells the compiler that the function has no parameters. A parameter to a function gives the function something to work on.
{	This is a *brace.* As the name implies, braces come in packs of two, i.e., for every open brace there must be a matching close. Braces allow me to lump pieces of program together. Such a lump of program is often called a *block*. A block can contain the declaration of variable used within it, followed by a sequence of program statements which are executed in order. In this case, the braces enclose the working parts of the function. When the compiler sees the matching close brace at the end, it knows that it has reached the end of the function and can look for another (if any). The effects of an un-paired brace are invariably fatal....
float	Our program needs to remember certain values as it runs. Notably, it will read in values for the width and height of the windows and then calculate and print values for the glass area and wood length. C calls the place where values are put variables. At the beginning of any block, you can tell C that you want to reserve some space to hold some data values. Each item you can hold a particular kind of value. Essentially, C can handle three types of data, floating point numbers, integer numbers and characters (i.e., letters, digits and punctuation).
height, width, area,wood_length	You declare some variables of a particular type by giving the type of the data, followed by a list of the names you want the variables to have. A list of items in C is separated by the character. In this case it is a list of variable names. Once the compiler has seen the word it is expecting to see the name of at least one variable that is to be created. The compiler works its way down the list, creating boxes which can hold floating point values and giving them the appropriate names. From this point on we can refer to the above names, and the compiler will know that we are using that particular variable.
	The semicolon marks the end of the list of variable names, and also the end of that declaration statement. All statements in C programs are separated by the ; character, this helps to keep the compiler on the right track. The ; character is actually very important. It tells the compiler where a given statement ends. If the compiler does not find one of these where it expects to see one it will produce an error. This is called as "Statement Terminator".

scanf	This line is a call to the function. The compiler knows that this is a function call by the fact that it is followed by a parameter list. What the compiler does at this point is parcel up the parameters you have given and then call scanf, passing the parameter information on. This function is expecting a particular sequence and type of parameters. The compiler knows what looks like and the kind of information uses is expecting because it has already seen the file .h, which is where this function is defined. The compiler can now check that the way we have used agrees with the definition.
"%f"	This is the set of parameters to the call of. scanf is short for scan formatted. The function is controlled by the format string, which is the first parameter to the function. The second and successive parameters are addresses into which puts the values it has been told to fetch.
&height	In C, a function cannot change the value of a parameter which is supplied to it. This is quite a departure from other languages, which let you do this. It does make life more complicated, when you want your function to be able to change the value of something. The way that you get theeffect is by cheating. Instead of passing the variable height we have instead supplied &height. The & is very important. When the compiler sees the & it regards this as an instruction to create a pointer to the given variable, and then pass this pointer to. This means that when runs it is given a pointer to where the result is to be placed, which is OK.
);	The) character marks the end of the list of parameters to and the; then end of this statement.
scanf ("%f", & width);	The function of this line is identical to the one above, except that the result is placed into the variable called.
area = 2 * height * width;	This is an assignment. The assignments are the bread and butter of programming. A good proportion of your programs will be instructions to assign new values to variables, as the various results are calculated. C uses the = character to make assignments happen. The first part of this statement is the name of a previously defined variable. When this program runs, the expression is worked out and then the result is placed in the specified variable. In this case, the expression works out the total amount of glass needed. This result is then placed in the variable.
wood_length = 2 * (height + width) * 3.25;	This is an expression much like above, this time it is important that you notice the use of parenthesis to modify the order in which values are calculated in the expression. Normally, C will work out expressions in the way you would expect, i.e., all multiplication and division will be 3.2 done first, followed by addition and subtraction.
printf("The area of glass needed is : %f metres. \n", area);	The function is the opposite of. It takes text and values from within the program and sends it out onto the screen. Just like it is common to all versions of C and just like it is described in the system file .h. The first parameter to is the format string, which contains text, value descriptions

	and formatting instructions.This is another format string. The text in this message will appear as it is given, although` the delimiters will not be printed. Like the % tells that a value description follows, the meaning that a floating point value is to be printed. You can get quite clever with place markers, using them to specify exactly how many spaces to fill with the value and, with real numbers, how many places after the decimal point to print, for example: Format command %d I want you to print the value of a signed, decimal integer %c I want you to print the character which responds to this value (more on characters a little later)%f I want you to print the value of a signed, decimal, floating point number. I want to see the result with a floating decimal point. %5d I want you to print the decimal integer in five character positions, right justified. %6.2f I want you to print the decimal floating point number in six character positions, right justified and to an accuracy of two decimal places.The rest of the text is quite straight forward, until we get to the \ character, which marks a formatting instruction. These instructions allow you to tell to do things like take a new line, move the cursor to the start of the line and etc. The \ is followed by a single character which identifies the required function. In the case of our program we want to take a new line at that point, and that is what n does. Note that unlike many languages, print statements do not automatically take a new line. This means that the programmer has to do more, but does make for greater flexibility.
}	This closing brace marks the end of the program. The compiler will now expect to see the end of the file or the start of another function. If it does not, it means that you have got an unmatched brace somewhere in the program, which will almost certainly mean your program will not work properly.

EXECUTION OF C PROGRAM

Steps to be followed in writing and running a C program.

(1) Creating the source program: The test of a program is called the source code. The source code is a set of sequenced statements which are to be executed by the complier. This source code is saved as ".c" extension file in Turbo C BIN.

(2) Linking and compilation of the program: The text program "*.c" is linked to the system library and compiled using "control+F9" keys. If there are no errors, the command produces an executable file.

(3) Program execution: During execution, the program may request for some data to be executed using "Alt+F5" keys and the output is displaced on the DOS prompt. Sometimes, the program does not produce desired results. Then it is necessary to correct the source code. And after modifying, the entire process will be repeated again.

LOADING TURBO C

(1) Without Hard disk

A:\> TC

F:\LIT1> TC

(2) With hard disk

C:\> CD TC

C:\TC> CD BIN

C:\TC\BIN> TC

Menu Options in Menu Bar

File

Edit

Compile

Run

Project

Options

Debug

Break/Watch

To Open Menu options → Press Alt and follow by highlighted character

Alt + F → For Opening File menu

File Menu Options

Load

Pick

New

Save

Write to

Directory

Change dir

OS Shell

Quit

Alt + F + L or F3	→	For Opening an exist file
Alt + F + P or Alt + F3	→	For Opening an recent files
Alt + F + N	→	For Opening a Blank Screen
Alt + F + S or Alt + F2	→	For Saving a File
Alt + F + W	→	To Create a Duplicate file
Alt + F + D	→	To Open a file from any Drive or Director
Alt + F + C	→	To Change Current Source Path
Alt + F + O	→	To quit from C temporarily
Alt + F + Q or Alt + X	→	To exit from C permanently
Alt + C→ C (or) Alt + F9		To Compile a C program
Alt + R→ R (or) Ctrl + F9		To Run a C Program
Alt + F5	→	To Display User Screen
Alt + P + R	→	To Remove Messages

Review Questions

1. Where was C originally developed and by whom?
2. To what extent do individual versions of C differ from one another? Has the language been standardized?
3. What are the major components of a C program?
4. How can comments be included within C program? Where can comments be placed?
5. What is meant by a computer program? What, in general, happens when a computer program is executed?
6. What are the general characteristics of C language?
7. Are C programs required to be typed in lowercase? Can uppercase be used for anything in a C program? Explain.
8. What is the purpose of main() function?
9. What items of punctuation is used at the end of most C statements? Do all statements end this way?
10. What are the steps involved in writing and executing a C program?

CHAPTER 3

Variables, Constants and Expressions

C TOKENS

In a C source program, the basic element recognized by the compiler is the "token." A token is source-program text that the compiler does not break down into component elements.

The smallest units in a C program such as individual words and punctuation marks are called "C tokens". For example, the words main, brace, parenthesis are all tokens of 'C' program. The C tokens are classified as:

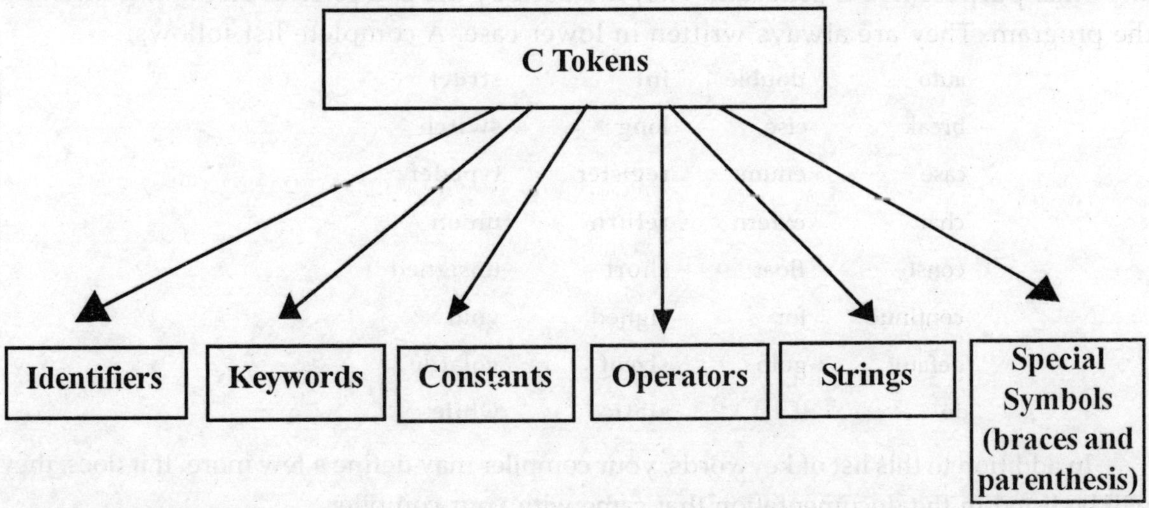

IDENTIFIERS

Identifiers are distinct names given to program elements such as constants, variables, etc. An identifier is used for any variable, function, data definition, etc. In the C programming language, an identifier is a combination of alphanumeric characters, the first being a letter of the alphabet or an underline, and the remaining being any letter of the alphabet, any numeric digit, or the underline.

Two rules must be kept in mind when naming identifiers.

1. The case of alphabetic characters is significant. Using for a variable name is not the same as using and neither of them is the same as using for a variable name. All three refer to different variables.
2. According to the ANSI-C standard, at least 31 significant characters can be used and will be considered significant by a conforming "ANSI C" compiler. If more than 31 are used, all characters beyond the 31st may be ignored by any given compiler.

A *valid identifier* is a sequence of one or more letters, digits or underscore characters (_). Neither spaces nor punctuation marks or symbols can be part of an identifier. Only letters, digits and single underscore characters are valid. In addition, variable identifiers always have to begin with a letter. They can also begin with an underline character (_), but in some cases these may be reserved for compiler specific keywords or external identifiers, as well as identifiers containing two successive underscore characters anywhere. In no case, they can begin with a digit.

KEYWORDS

There are 32 keywords in C. These have predefined uses and cannot be used for any other purpose in a C program. They are used by the compiler as an aid to compiling the program. They are always written in lower case. A complete list follows;

auto	double	int	struct
break	else	long	switch
case	enum	register	typedef
char	extern	return	union
const	float	short	unsigned
continue	for	signed	void
default	goto	sizeof	volatile
do	if	static	while

In addition to this list of keywords, your compiler may define a few more. If it does, they will be listed in the documentation that came with your compiler.

DATA TYPES IN C LANGUAGE

A programming language is proposed to help programmer to process certain kinds of data and to provide useful output. The task of data processing is accomplished by executing series of commands called program. A program usually contains different types of data types (integer, float, character, etc.) and need to store the values being used in the program. C language is rich of data types. A C programmer has to employ proper data type as per his requirement.

C has different data types for different types of data and can be broadly classified as:

(1) Primary data types

(2) Secondary data types

Syntax: datatype <variablename>;

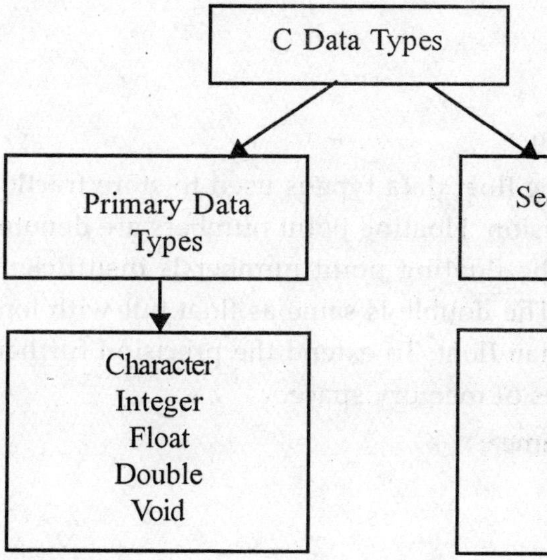

1. Primary Data Types

Primary data types consist following data types.

(a) Character Type: Character type variable can hold a single character. As there are signed and unsigned int (either short or long), in the same way there are signed and unsigned chars; both occupy 1 byte each, but having different ranges. Unsigned characters have values between 0 and 255, signed characters have values from –128 to 127.

Syntax: char <variablename>;

Example: char ch = 'a';

Example: char a, b, g, S, j;

(b) Integer Type: Integers are whole numbers with a range of values, which are machine-dependent. Generally, an integer occupies 2 bytes memory space and its value range limited to -32768 to +32767 (i.e., -215 to +215-1). A signed integer use one bit for storing sign and rest 15 bits for number.

To control the range of numbers and storage space, C has three classes of integer storage namely short int, int and long int. All three data types have signed and unsigned forms. A short int requires half the amount of storage than normal integer. Unlike signed integer, unsigned integers are always positive and use all the bits for the magnitude of the number. Therefore, the range of an unsigned integer will be from 0 to 65535. The long integers are used to declare a longer range of values and it occupies 4 bytes of storage space.

Syntax: int <variable name>;

Example:

int num1;

short int num2;

long int num3;

Example: int 5, 6, 100, 2500.

(c) Floating Point Type: The float data type is used to store fractional numbers (real numbers) with 6 digits of precision. Floating point numbers are denoted by the keyword float. When the accuracy of the floating point number is insufficient, we can use the double to define the number. The double is same as float but with longer precision and takes double space (8 bytes) than float. To extend the precision further, we can use long double which occupies 10 bytes of memory space.

Syntax: float <variable name>;

Example:

float num1;

double num2;

long double num3;

Example: float 9.125, 3.1254.

(d) Void Type: The void type has no values, therefore we cannot declare it as variable as we did in case of integer and float.

The void data type is usually used with function to specify its type. Like in our first C program, we declared "main()" as void type because it does not return any value. The concept of returning values will be discussed in detail in the C functions.

2. Secondary Data Types

Secondary data types will be discussed in detail in further chapters.

User-defined Type Declaration

C language supports a feature where user can define an identifier that characterizes an existing data type. This user-defined data type identifier can later be used to declare variables. In short, its purpose is to redefine the name of an existing data type.

Syntax: typedef <type> <identifier>;

Example: typedef int number;

FUNDAMENTAL DATA TYPES

When programming, we store the variables in our computer's memory, but the computer has to know what kind of data we want to store in them, since it is not going to occupy the same amount of memory to store a simple number than to store a single letter or a large number, and they are not going to be interpreted in the same way.

The memory in our computers is organized in bytes. A byte is the minimum amount of memory that we can manage. A byte can store a relatively small amount of data: one single character or a small integer (generally an integer between 0 and 255). In addition, the computer can manipulate more complex data types that come from grouping several bytes, such as long numbers or non-integer numbers.

Next, you have a summary of the basic fundamental data types in C and the range of values that can be represented with each one:

Name	Description	Size*	Range*
char	Character or small integer	1 byte	signed:-128 to 127 unsigned: 0 to 255
short int (short)	Short Integer	1 byte	signed:-128 to 127 unsigned: 0 to 255
int	Integer	2 bytes	signed: -32768 to 32767 unsigned: 0 to 65535
long int (long)	Long integer	4 bytes	signed: -2147483648 to 2147483647 unsigned: 0 to 4294967295
bool	Boolean value. It can take one of two values: true or false.	1 byte	true or false
float	Floating point number.	4 bytes	+/- 3.4e +/- 38 (~7 digits)
double	Double precision floating point number.	8 bytes	+/- 1.7e +/- 308 (~15 digits)
long double	Long double precision floating point number.	10 bytes	+/- 1.7e +/- 308 (~15 digits)
wchar_t	Wide character.	2 *or* 4 bytes	1 wide character

*The values of the columns *Size* and *Range* depend on the system the program is compiled for. The values shown above are those found on most 32-bit systems. But for other systems, the general specification is that int has the natural size suggested by the system architecture (one *"word"*) and the four integer types — char, short, int and long — each one be at least as large as the one preceding it, with char being always one byte in size. The same applies to the floating point types float, double and long double, where each one must provide at least as much precision as the preceding one.

VARIABLES

A variable is one which can hold a single data at a time.

A variable is a name given to the space in the memory for holding data such as integers, characters, floating point numbers, strings, etc. Using a variable name is more convenient than using the memory locations. There are certain rules for naming variables for which you need to refer to the rules for identifiers.

Declaration of Variables

To declare a variable means to create a memory space for the variable depending on the data type used and associate the memory location with the variable name. In C, all the variables should be declared before it can be used. Also you cannot redeclare a variable once it has been already declared.

The general pattern for declaring a variable is as follows:

, , ;

Example:

int age;

int age, count, i,j;

float amount, rateofinterest, totalbalance;

char ch;

Declaration Versus Definition

Definition is the place where variable is created (allocated storage).

Declaration is a place where nature (type) of variable is stated, but no storage is allocated.

Constant Variables

A constant variable is also called a named constant. A named constant is really a variable whose content is read only and cannot be changed while the program is running. Here is a declaration of a named constant.

const float pi = 3.14;

It looks just like a regular variable declaration except that the word const appears before the data type name.

const is a qualifier that tells the compiler to make the variable read only. Its value will remain constant throughout the programs execution.

An initialization value must be given when declaring a variable with the const qualifier, or an error will result when the program is compiled. A compiler error will also result if there is any statement in the program that attempt to change the contents of a named constant.

TYPES OF QUALIFIERS

- const
- volatile

The const qualifier is used to tell C that the variable value cannot change after initialization.

const float pi = 3.14159;

pi cannot be changed at a later time within the program.

Another way to define constants is with the #define preprocessor which has the advantage that it does not use any storage.

CONSTANTS

The term constant means that it does not change during the execution of program. Constants may be classified as:

1. Integer Constant
2. Floating Point Constant

1. Integer Constant

Integer constants are whole numbers without any fractional parts. There are three types of Integer constants:

(i) Decimal constant (base 10)

(ii) Octal Constant (base 8)

(iii) Hexa decimal constant (base 16)

Allowed digit in decimal constant 0,1,2,3,4,5,6,7,8,9. The digits of one octal constant can be 0,1,2,3,4,5,6,7 and that in hexadecimal constants are 0,1,2,3,4,5,6,7,8,9,A,B,C,D,E,F.

Rules for Decimal Constant

A decimal integer constant must have at least one digit and must be written without a decimal point. The first digit in the constant should not be 0. It may have either sign + or –. If either sign does not proceed to the constant, it is assumed to be positive.

Following are valid decimal integer constants:

(i) 12345

(ii) 3468

(iii) – 9746

The following are invalid decimal integer constants:

(i) 11. (decimal point not allowed)

(ii) 45,256 (comma not allowed)

(iii) $ 125 (currency symbol not allowed)

(iv) 025 (first digit should not be 0 for a decimal integer)

(v) *f* 248 (first symbol not a digit)

Rules for Octal Constant

An octal constant must have at least one digit and start with the digit 0. It must be written without a decimal point. It may have either sign + or –. A constant which has no sign is taken as positive.

The following are valid octal constants:

(i) 0245

(ii) – 0467

(iii) + 04013

The following are invalid octal constants:

(i) 25 (Does not begin with 0)

(ii) 0387 (8 is not an octal digit)

(iii) 04.32 (Decimal point not allowed)

Rules for Hexadecimal Constant

A hexadecimal constant must have at least one hexadecimal digit and start with Ox or OX. It may have either sign.

The following are valid hexadecimal constants:

(i) OX 14 AF

(ii) OX 34680

(iii) –OX 2673E

The following are invalid hexadecimal constants:

(i) Ox14AF

(ii) OX34680

(iii) –Ox2673E

2. Floating Point Constants

A floating point constant may be written in one or two forms could be fractional form or the exponent form, the rules for writing a floating point constant in these two forms is given as follows.

Rules for Fractional Form

A floating point constant in a fractional form must have at least one digit to the right of the decimal point. It may have either the + or the – sign preceding it. If a sign does not precede it, then it is assumed to be positive.

Following are valid floating point constants:

(i) 1.0

(ii) –0.5678

(iii) 5800000.0

(iv) –0.0000156

Following are invalid:

(i) 1 (Decimal point missing)

(ii) 1. (No digit following decimal point)

(iii) –1/2 (Symbol/illegal)

(iv) .5 (No digit to the left of the decimal)

(v) 58, 678.94 (Comma not allowed)

Rules for Exponential Form

A floating point constant in the exponent form consists of a mantissa and an exponent. The mantissa must have at least one digit. It may have a sign. The mantissa is followed by the letter E or e and the exponent. The exponent must be an integer without a decimal point and must have at least one digit. A sign for the exponent is optional.

The following are valid floating point constants in exponent form:

(i) (a) 152 E08 (b) 152.0 E8 (c) 152 e+8 (d) 152 E+08 (e) 15.2 e9 (f) 1520 E7

(ii) –0.148E-5

(iii) 152.859 E25

(iv) 0.01540 e05

The following are invalid:

(i) 152.AE8 (Mantissa must have a digit following).

(ii) 152*e9 (* not allowed).

(iii) +145.8E (No digit specified for exponent).

(iv) –152.9E5.5 (Exponent cannot be a fraction).

(v) 0.158 E+954 (Exponent too large).

(vi) 125, 458.25 –5 (Comma not allowed in mantissa).

(vii) 02E8 (A digit must precede in mantissa).

DATA TYPE MODIFIERS

We have so far learned about the fundamental data types, why they are used, their default sizes and values. Now let us understand the need for data type modifiers and the way they can be used.

Let us consider an example of a program, which will accept an age from the user to do some processing. Because the age is represented in numbers, so we will have to use the integer data type int. We all know that even under exceptional case, an age of a person cannot exceed more than 150. Now, that we are using an integer data type it occupies 2 bytes of memory, which would not be required to represent the value 150. Instead the value 150 could easily be saved in an integer of 1 byte in size, but the default size of an integer is 2 bytes. So we have a problem here. Well, not that we can't solve. To override the default nature of a data type, C has provided us with data type modifiers as follows:

Signed: By default, all data types are declared as signed. Signed means that the data type is capable of storing negative values.

Unsigned: To modify a data type's behavior so that it can only store positive values, we require to use the data type unsigned.

For example, if we were to declare a variable age, we know that an age cannot be represented by negative values and hence, we can modify the default behavior of the int data type as follows:

Example: unsigned int age;

This declaration allows the age variable to store only positive values. An immediate effect is that the range changes from (-32768 to 32767) to (0 to 65536).

Long: Many times in our programs we would want to store values beyond the storage capacity of the basic data types. In such cases, we use the data type modifier long. This doubles the storage capacity of the data type being used.

Example: long int annualsalary

This declaration will make the storage capacity of variable annualsalary to 4 bytes.

The exception to this is long double, which modifies the size of the double data type to 10 bytes. Please note that in some compilers this has no effect.

Short: If long data type modifier doubles the size, short on the other hand reduces the size of the data type to half. Please refer to the example of age variable to explain the concept of data type modifiers. The same will be achieved by providing the declaration of age as follows:

Example: short int age;

This declaration above will provide the variable age with only 1 byte and its data range will be from -128 to 127.

FORMAT SPECIFIERS

Tells the printf() function the format of the output to be printed out.

No.	Format Specifier	Output Type	Output Example
1	%d	Signed decimal integer	76
2	%i	Signed decimal integer	76
3	%o	Unsigned octal integer	134
4	%u	Unsigned decimal integer	76
5	%x	Unsigned hexadecimal (small letter)	9c
6	%x	Unsigned hexadecimal (capital letter)	9C
7	%f	Intger including decimal poing	76.0000
8	%e	Signed floating point (using e notation)	7.6000e+01
9	%E	Signed floating point (using E notation)	7.6000E+01
10	%g	The shorter between %f and %e	76
11	%G	The shorter between %f and %E	76
12	%x	Character	'7'
13	%s	String	'76'

ESCAPE SEQUENCES

Character	Operation
\n	New line
\t	Horizontal tab
\v	Vertical tab
\a	To beep the speaker
\′	Single quote
\″	Double quote
\?	Question mark
\\	Back slash
\0	NULL

ARITHMETIC OPERATIONS

There are five arithmetic operators in C. They are:

Operator	Purpose
+	Addition
–	Subtraction
*	Multiplication
/	Division
%	Remainder after integer division

The operator % is known as the modulus operator.

Example: Suppose that a and b are integer variables whose values are 10 and 3 respectively, several arithmetic expressions involving these variables are shown below together with their resulting values.

Expression	Value
a + b	13
a – b	7
a * b	30
a / b	3
a % b	1

Now, suppose that v1 and v2 are floating point variables whose values are 12.5 and 2.0 respectively. Several arithmetic expressions involving these variables are shown below, together with their resulting values.

Expression	Value
v1 + v2	14.5
v1 – v2	10.5
v1 * v2	25.0
v1 / v2	6.25

Now, suppose c1 and c2 are character type variables that represent the characters P and T, respectively. Several arithmetic expression that make use of these variables are shown below together with their resulting values (based upon the ASCII character set).

Expression	Value
C1	80
C1 + C2	164
C1 + C2 +5	169
C1 + C2 +'5'	217

P is encoded as (decimal) 80, T is encoded as 84 and 5 is encoded as 53 in the ASCII character set, as shown above.

Suppose that a and b are integer variables whose values are 11 and –3, respectively. Several arithmetic expressions involving these variables are shown below, together with their resulting values.

Expression	Value
a+b	8
a–b	14
a*b	-33
a/b	-3

TYPECAST

The value of an expression can be converted to a different data type. If desired to do so, the expression must be preceded by the name of the desired data type enclosed in parentheses.

Syntax: (data type) expression

This type of construction is known as a cast. It is also called a type cast. Suppose that i is an integer variable whose value is 7, and f is floating point variable whose value is 8.5. The expression (i + f) % 4 is invalid because the first operand (i + f) is floating point rather than integer. However, the expression ((int) (i + f)) % 4 forces the first operand to be an integer and is therefore valid, resulting in the integer remainder 3.

UNARY OPERATORS

C includes a class of operators that act upon a single operand to produce a new value such operators are known as unary operators. Unary operators usually precede their single operands, though some unary operators are written after their operands.

(i) Unary Minus: Unary minus is an unary operator where a minus sign precedes a numerical constant, a variable or an expression. In C, all numeric constants are positive. Thus, a negative number is actually an expression consisting of the unary minus operator followed by a positive number.

Example: –743, –0 × 7FFF, –0.2, –5E – 8, – root 1, – (x + y) – 3 * (x + y)

(ii) Increment Operator and Decrement Operator: The increment operator (+ +) causes its operand to be increased by one whereas the decrement operator (– –) causes its operand to be decreased by one. The operand used with each of these operators must be a single variable.

e.g., Suppose i is an integer variable that has been assigned a value of 5. The expression ++i, causes the value of i to be increased by one, whereas the decrement operator (- - i) causes the value to be decreased by 1 so, now the new variable of i will be 4.

i ++ means i = i + 1

– – i means i = i – 1

The increment and decrement operators can each be utilized in two different ways, depending on whether the operator is written before or after the operand. If the operator precedes the operand (e.g., ++ i), then the operand will be altered in value before it is utilized for its intended purpose within the program. If however, the operator follows the operand (e.g., i ++), then the value of the operand will be altered after it is utilized.

Example: printf ("i = %d\n", i);

printf ("i = % d\n", ++i);

printf ("i = %d\n", i);

There printf statements will generate following three lines of output.

i = 1

i = 2

i = 2

Now let us take the second case

printf ("i = %d\n", i);

printf ("i = %d\n", i++);

printf ("i = %d\n", i)

The statement will generate the following three lines of output

i = 1

i = 1

i = 2

LOGICAL OPERATORS

There are two logical operators also available in C. They are (Logical Not!):

Operator	Meaning
&&	and
||	or

The result of a logical **and** operation will be true only if both operands are true whereas the result of a logical **or** operation will be true if either operand is true or if both operands are true.

In other words, the result of a logical **or** operation will be false only if both operands are false. Suppose i is an integer variable whose value is 7, f is a floating point variable whose value is 5.5 and C is a character variable that represents the character 'w', several complex logical expressions that make use of these variables are shown below:

Expression	Interpretation	Value
(i > = 6)&&(c = = 'w')	true	1
(i >= 6)&&(c = = 119)	true	1
(f < 11) && (i > 100)	false	0
(i= 'p') || ((i + f) < (10)	true	1

RELATIONAL OPERATORS

These are four relational operators in C. They are:

Operator	Meaning
<	Less than
<=	Less than or equal to
>	Greater than
>=	Greater than or equal to

EQUALITY OPERATORS

There are two equality operators in C which are as follows:

Operator	Meaning
= =	Equal to
! =	Not equal to

Expression	Interpretation	Value
i < j	true	1
(i + j) > = k	true	1
(j + k) > (i + 5)	false	0
k ! = 3	false	0
j = 2	true	1

The six operators mentioned above are used to form logical expressions representing conditions that are either true or false.

The resulting expression will be of type integer, since true is represented by the integer value 1 and false is represented by the value 0.

Example: Let us suppose i, j and k are integer variables whose values are 1, 2 and 3 respectively. Several logical expressions involving these variables are shown below.

Expression	Interpretation	Value	Meaning
(i > = 6) & (c == 'w')	true	1	Both operands are true, hence expression is true.
(i > = 6) | | (c = = 119)	true	1	Both operands are true, hence expression is true.
(f < 11) & is& (i > 100)	false	0	Second operand is false, hence expression false.
(c1 == 'p') |((i + f) < = 10)	true	1	First operand is true, hence expression is | true.

ASSIGNMENT OPERATORS

The commonly used assignment operator is " =". Assignment expressions that make use of this operator are written in the form.

identifier = expression

Here, identifier represents a variable and expression represents a constant, a variable or a more complex expression.

Example: Here are some typical assignment expressions that make use of the = operator.

a = 3

x = y

sum = a + b

area = length * width

BITWISE OPERATION AND OPERATOR INTRODUCTION

A bitwise operation operates on one or more bit patterns or binary numerals at the level of their individual bits. C Programming provides us six operators for manipulation of data at bit level. These operators operates on integer, character but not on float, double. Using Bitwise Operators, we can manipulate individual bits.

Following are six bitwise operators:

Operator	Name of Operator
~	One's Compliment
>>	Right Shift
<<	Left Shift
&	Bitwise AND
|	Bitwise OR
^	Bitwise XOR

Rules of Bitwise Operators:

Input Bits		AND	OR	XOR
0	0	0	0	0
0	1	0	1	1
1	0	0	1	1
1	1	1	1	0

BITWISE OPERATORS — SHIFT, LOGICAL, ROTATION AND MASKS

Bit Shifts

The bit shifts are sometimes considered as bitwise operations, since they operate on the binary representation of an integer instead of its numerical value; however, the bit shifts do not operate on pairs of corresponding bits, and therefore cannot properly be called bitwise operations. In this operation, the digits are moved, or shifted, to the left or right. Registers in a computer processor have a fixed number of available bits for storing numerals, so some bits will be "shifted out" of the register at one end, while the same number of bits are "shifted in" from the other end; the differences between bit shift operators lie in how they compute the values of those shifted in bits.

Arithmetic Shift

In an arithmetic shift, the bits that are shifted out of either end are discarded. In a left arithmetic shift, zeros are shifted in on the right; in a right arithmetic shift, the sign bit is shifted in on the left, thus preserving the sign of the operand. For example, consider an 8-bit register:

00010111 LEFT SHIFT

= 00101110

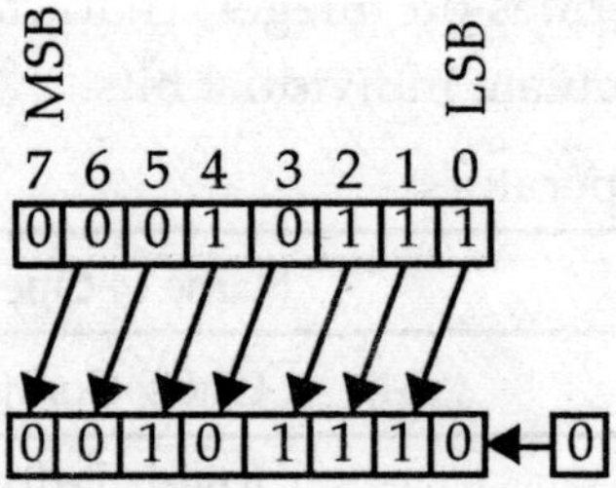

Fig. 3.1: Left Shift

00010111 RIGHT SHIFT

= 00001011

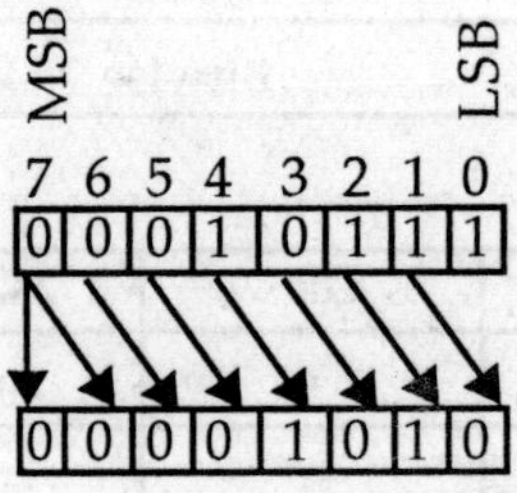

Fig. 3.2: Right Shift

A left arithmetic shift by n is equivalent to multiplying by 2n (provided the value does not overflow), while a right arithmetic shift by n of a two's complement value is equivalent to dividing by 2n and rounding toward negative infinity. If the binary number is treated as ones' complement, then the same right shift operation results in division by 2n and rounding toward zero.

Logical Shift

In a logical shift, the bits that are shifted out are discarded, and zeros are shifted in (on either end). Therefore, the logical and arithmetic left shifts are exactly the same operation. However, the logical right shift inserts bits with value 0 instead of copying in the sign bit.

Hence the logical shift is suitable for unsigned binary numbers, while the arithmetic shift is suitable for signed two's complement binary numbers.

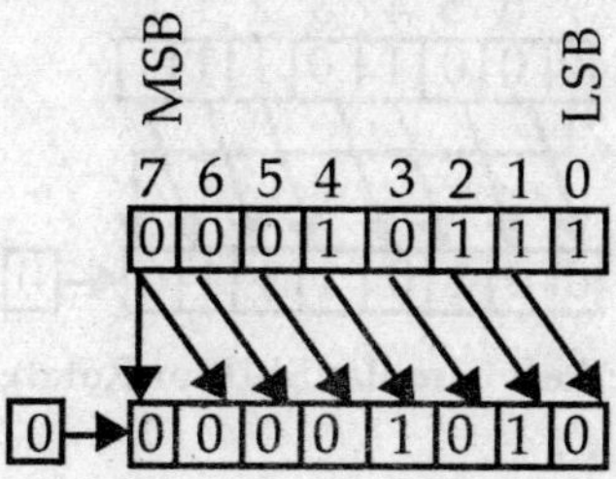

Fig. 3.3: Logical Shift Right

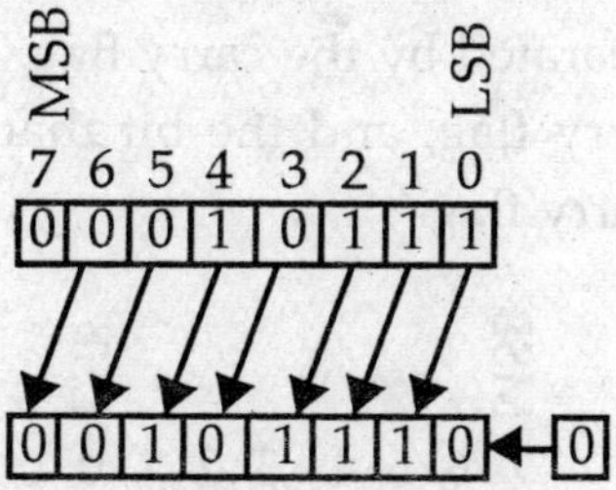

Fig. 3.4 : Logical Shift Left

Rotation

Rotate No Carry

Another form of shift is the circular shift or bit rotation. In this operation, the bits are "rotated" as if the left and right ends of the register were joined. The value that is shifted in on the right during a left shift is whatever value was shifted out on the left, and *vice versa.* This operation is useful if it is necessary to retain all the existing bits, and is frequently used in digital cryptography.

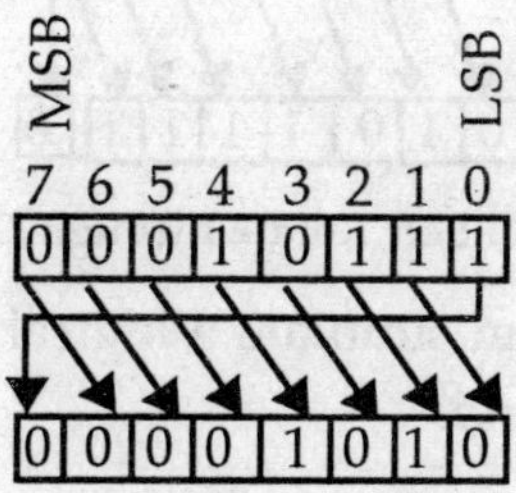

Fig. 3.5: Right Circular Shift or Rotate

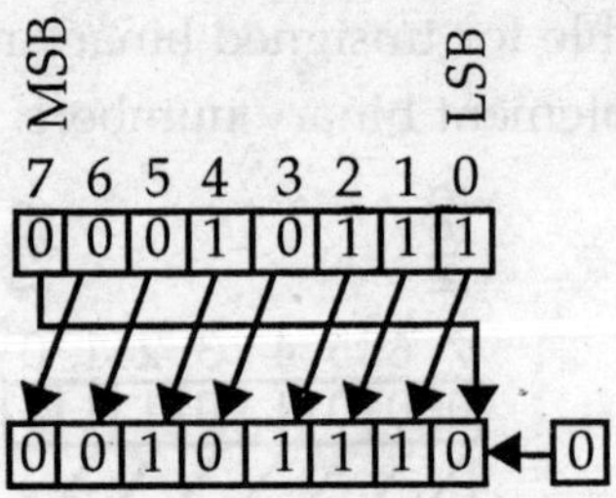

Fig. 3.6: Left Circular Shift or Rotate

Rotate through Carry

Rotate through carry is similar to the rotate no carry operation, but the two ends of the register are considered to be separated by the carry flag. The bit that is shifted in (on either end) is the old value of the carry flag, and the bit that is shifted out (on the other end) becomes the new value of the carry flag.

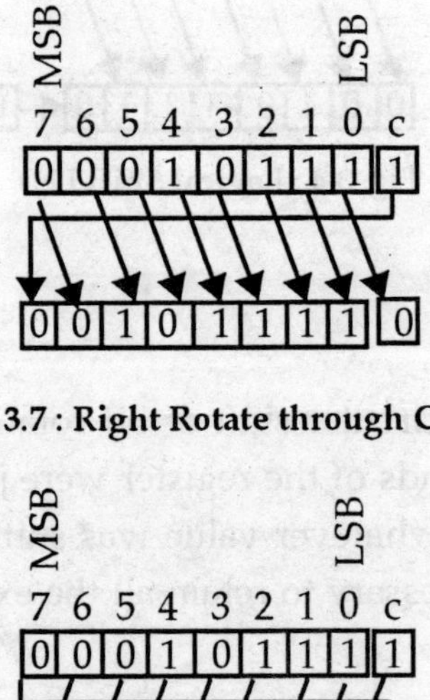

Fig. 3.7 : Right Rotate through Carry

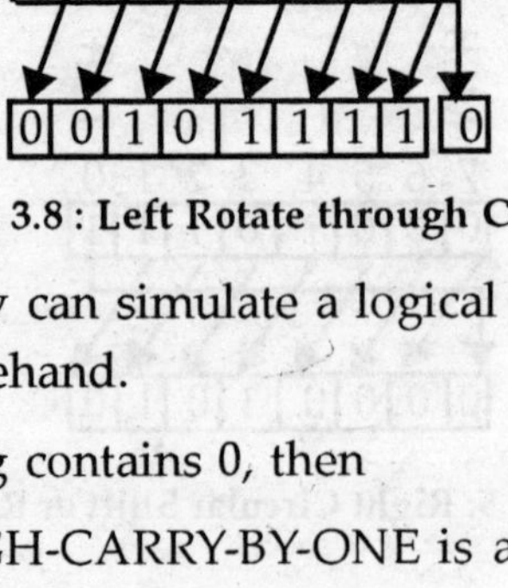

Fig. 3.8 : Left Rotate through Carry

A single rotate through carry can simulate a logical or arithmetic shift of one position by setting up the carry flag beforehand.

For example, if the carry flag contains 0, then

x RIGHT-ROTATE-THROUGH-CARRY-BY-ONE is a logical right shift,

and if the carry flag contains a copy of the sign bit, then

x RIGHT-ROTATE-THROUGH-CARRY-BY-ONE is an arithmetic right shift.

For this reason, some microcontrollers such as PICs just have rotate and rotate through carry, and don't bother with arithmetic or logical shift instructions.

Rotate through carry is especially useful when performing shifts on numbers larger than the processor's native word size, because if a large number is stored in two registers, the bit that is shifted off the end of the first register must come in at the other end of the second. With rotate-through-carry, that bit is "saved" in the carry flag during the first shift, ready to shift in during the second shift without any extra preparation.

Applications

Bitwise operations are necessary for much low-level programming, such as writing device drivers, low-level graphics, communications protocol packet assembly and decoding.

Masks

Masking means blocking. Masking is the process of changing bits in a byte.

It is the process by which, only required data is retained and the rest is blocked (i.e., masked).

Masking can be done by using bitwise operators, among them the AND (&) is most commonly used.

For example, consider a process of masking in which we want Last 4LSB bits, so mask it with: (0000 0000 0000 1111)

Num 1: 1000 0001 1110 1011

&: 0000 0000 0000 1111

The result would be

Num 1: 0000 0000 0000 1011 //the first 12 bits are masked

The portion to be retained is written as 1 and the portion to be masked is written as 0.

THE CONDITIONAL OPERATOR

Conditional operator is (? :). An expression that makes use of the conditional operator is called a conditional expression.

For example, expression 1? expression 2 : expression 3

When evaluating a conditional expression, expression 1 is evaluated first. If the expression 1 is true, then expression 2 is evaluated and this becomes the value of conditional expression. However, if expression 1 is false, then expression 3 is evaluated and this becomes the value of the conditional expression.

For example: In the conditional expression shown below, suppose f and g are floating point variables. The conditional expression is,

(f < g)? f : g

It takes the value f if f is less than g, otherwise the conditional expression takes the value of g. In other words, conditional expression returns the value of the smaller of the two variables.

PRECEDENCE OF OPERATORS AND ASSOCIATIVITY

C operators in order of *precedence* (highest to lowest). Their *associativity* indicates in what order operators of equal precedence in an expression are applied.

Operator	Description/Operator Type	Associativity
() [] . -> ++ —	Parentheses (function call) (see Note 1) Brackets (array subscript) Member selection via object name Member selection via pointer Postfix increment/decrement (see Note 2)	left-to-right
++ /— + /- ! /~ (*type*) * & sizeof	Prefix increment/decrement Unary plus/minus Logical negation/bitwise complement Cast (change *type*) Dereference Address Determine size in bytes	right-to-left
* / %	Multiplication/division/modulus	left-to-right
+ -	Addition/subtraction	left-to-right
<< >>	Bitwise shift left, Bitwise shift right	left-to-right
< ,<= > , >=	Relational less than/less than or equal to Relational greater than/greater than or equal to	left-to-right
== , !=	Relational is equal to/is not equal to	left-to-right
&	Bitwise AND	left-to-right
^	Bitwise exclusive OR	left-to-right
|	Bitwise OR	left-to-right
&&	Logical AND	left-to-right
||	Logical OR	left-to-right
?:	Ternary (conditional) operator	right-to-left
= += ,-= *= ,/= %= ,&= ^= , |= <<=, >>	Assignment Addition/subtraction assignment Multiplication/division assignment Modulus/bitwise AND assignment Bitwise exclusive/ OR assignment Bitwise shift left/right assignment	right-to-left
,	Comma (separate expressions)	left-to-right

Note 1: Parentheses are also used to group sub-expressions to force a different precedence; such parenthetical expressions can be nested and are evaluated from inner to outer.

Note 2: Post-fix increment/decrement have high precedence, but the actual increment or decrement of the operand is delayed (to be accomplished sometime before the statement completes execution). So in the statement = x * z++; the current value of ? is used to evaluate the expression (*i.e.,* ++ evaluates to) and only incremented after all else is done.

EVALUATION OF EXPRESSIONS

An arithmetic expression is a combination of variables, constants and operators arranged as per the syntax of the language. Expressions are evaluated using an assignment statement:

variable = expression;

The expression is evaluated first and then the result replaces the previous value of the variable on the left-hand side.

Example:

x = a + b * c;

y = a + b / c – d;

Algebraic expression	C expression
a × b – c	a * b - c
$3x^2 - 2y + 5z - 6$	3 * x * x – 2 * y + 5 * z - 6
(m – n) (p + q) r/t	(m – n) * (p + q) * r/t
A/B + C	A/B + C

Rules

- First parenthesized sub-expressions from left to right are evaluated.
- If parenthesis is nested, the evaluation begins with the innermost sub-expression.
- When parenthesis is used, the expressions within parenthesis assume highest priority.
- The precedence rule is applied for evaluating sub-expressions.
- The associativity rule is applied for evaluating when two or more operations of the same precedence level appear in a sub-expression.

Example

X = 4 * 2/3 + 10/5 + 8 – 1 + 9/6

Step-wise evaluation of the above expression:

Expression	Operation
X = 8/3 + 10/5 + 8 – 1 + 9/6	*
= 2 + 10/5 + 8 – 1 + 9/6	/
= 2 + 2 + 8 – 1 + 9/6	/
= 2 + 2 + 8 – 1 + 1	/
= 4 + 8 – 1 + 1	+
= 12 – 1 + 1	+
= 11 + 1	-
= 12	+

DATA INPUT AND OUTPUT — C CONSOLE I/O

Console I/O, in general, means communications with the computer's keyboard and display. However, in most modern operating systems, the keyboard and display are simply the default input and output devices, and user can easily redirect input from, say a file or other program and redirect output to, say, a serial I/O port:

type infile > myprog > com

The program itself, "myprog", doesn't know the difference. The program uses console I/O to simply read its "standard input (stdin)" — which might be the keyboard, a file dump, or the output of some other program — and print to its "standard output (stdout)" — which might be the display or printer or another program or a file. The program itself neither knows nor cares.

PREPROCESSOR COMMANDS

The C Preprocessor is not part of the compiler, but is a separate step in the compilation process. In simplistic terms, a C Preprocessor is just a text substitution tool.

The unconditional directives are:

#include - Inserts a particular header from another file

#define - Defines a preprocessor macro

#undef - Undefines a preprocessor macro

The conditional directives are:

#ifdef - If this macro is defined

#ifndef - If this macro is not defined

#if - Test if a compile time condition is true

#else - The alternative for #if

#elif - #else an #if in one statement

#endif - End preprocessor conditional

Other directives include:

- Stringization, replaces a macro parameter with a string constant

- Token merge, creates a single token from two adjacent ones

STANDARD HEADER FILES

Prototypes of the library functions are given in several standard header files. For example, stdio.h contains prototypes for printf, scanf, putchar and getchar. Other standard header files are:

assert.h	assertions
ctype.h	character class tests
float.h	system limits for floating point types
limits.h	system limits for integral types
math.h	mathematical functions
setjmp.h	non-local jumps
signal.h	signals and error handling
stdarg.h	variable length parameter lists
stdlib.h	utility functions; number conversions, memory allocation, exit and system
string.h	string functions
time.h	date and time functions

To include these standard header files in your code, use the preprocessor directive #include and place along brackets around the name of the file

Example: #include<math.h>

Console I/O Requires the Declaration

#include <stdio.h>

In 'C' language, input and output of data is done by a collection of library functions like getchar, putchar, scanf, printf, gets and puts. These functions permit the transfer of information between the computer and the standard input/output devices. The library function getchar and putchar as the name suggests, allow single characters to be transferred into and out of the computer, scanf and printf permit the transfer of single characters, numerical values and strings, gets and puts facilitate the input and output of strings. An input/output function can be accessed from anywhere within a program simply by writing the function name, followed by a list of parameters enclosed in parentheses. Some input/output functions do not require parameters, but the empty parentheses must appear. 'C' includes a collection of header files that provide necessary information in support of the various library functions. The header file stdio.h contains the information about input/output library functions.

Useful functions include:

printf()	Print a formatted string to stdout.
scanf()	Read formatted data from stdin.
putchar()	Print a single character to stdout.
getchar()	Read a single character from stdin.
puts()	Print a string to stdout.
gets()	Read a line from stdin.

PC-based compilers also have an alternative library of console I/O functions. These functions require the declaration:

#include <conio.h>

The three most useful PC console I/O functions are:

getch() Get a character from the keyboard (no need to press Enter).

getche() Get a character from the keyboard and echo it.

kbhit() Check to see if a key has been pressed.

* The "printf()" function, as explained previously, prints a string that may include formatted data:

printf ("This is a test!\n"); – which can include the contents of variables:

printf ("Value1: %d Value2: %f\n", intval, floatval);

READING A CHARACTER

getchar Function

The getchar function reads a single character from standard input. It takes no parameters and its returned value is the input character. In general, a reference to the getchar function is written as

charactervariable = getchar();

For example char c;

```
c = getchar();
```

The second line causes a single character to be entered from the standard input device and then assigned to c. If an end-of-file condition is encountered when reading a character with the getchar function, the value of the symbolic constant EOF(end of file) will automatically be returned. This function can also be used to read multicharacter strings, by reading one character at a time within a multipass loop.

WRITING A CHARACTER

putchar Function

The standard C function that prints or displays a single character by sending it to standard output is called putchar. This function takes one argument, which is the character to be sent. It also returns this character as its result. If an error occurs, an error value is returned. Therefore, if the returned value of putchar is used, it should be declared as a function returning an int.

For example:

```
putchar ('N');
putchar ('a');
putchar ('t');
putchar ('i');
putchar ('o');
putchar ('n');
putchar ('a');
putchar ('l');
```

When putchar is used, however, each character must be output separately. The parameter to the function calls in the given statements are character constants, represented between apostrophes as usual. Of course, the arguments could be character variables instead.

FORMATTED INPUT

scanf Function

Input data can be entered into the computer from a standard input device by means of C library function scanf. This function can be used to enter any combination of numerical values, characters single character and strings. The function returns the number of data items that have been entered successfully.

In general terms, the scanf function is written as:

scanf (string, parameter 1, parameter 2..., parameter n);

Where string = string containing certain required formatting information, and parameter 1, parameter 2 = parameters that represent the individual input data item.

The control string or string comprises individual groups of characters, with one character group for each input data item. Each character group must start with per cent sign (%). In the string, multiple character groups can be contiguous, or separated by white space characters. The conversion character that is used with % sign are many in number and all have different meaning corresponding to type of data item that is to be input from keyboard. Some of the conversion characters are listed below:

Conversion character - Meaning

c type of data item is single character

d type of data item is decimal integer

e type of data item is floating point value

f type of data item is floating point value

h type of data item is short integer

i type of data item is decimal, hexadecimal or octal integer

o type of data item is octal integer

s type of data item is string

u type of data item is unsigned decimal integer

[. . .] type of data item is string which may include white space characters.

The parameters are written as variables or arrays, whose types match the corresponding characters groups in the control string. Each variable name must be preceded by an ampersand (&).

For example: Suppose there are three variables.

char name[10], int roll_no, float marks;

then the scanf statement for these three variables will be:

scanf("%s %d %f," name, &roll_no, &marks);

This statement contains three character groups. %s represents that first parameter is string, i.e., name. The second character group %d, represents that the parameter is decimal integer value, and third character group %f represents that the parameter is floating point value. It is to be noted here that roll_no and marks that are only variables not arrays and are preceded by ampersand sign unlike name which is a character array. The order of data items depends upon the requirement of user, but the order of character group should match with the order of data items.

If two or more data items are entered, they must be separated by white space characters. Data items may continue onto two or more lines, since the newline character is considered to be a white space character. It is already stated that s-type conversion character applies to a string terminated by a white space character. Therefore, a string that includes white space characters cannot be entered in this manner. To do so, the s-type conversion character within the control string is replaced by a sequence of characters enclosed in square brackets designated as [...]. White space characters may be included within the brackets, thus accommodating strings that contain such characters. When the program is executed, successive characters will continue to be read from the standard input device as long as each input character matches one of the characters enclosed within the brackets. The order of the characters within the square brackets need not correspond to the order of the characters being entered. Input characters may be repeated. The string will terminate, however once an input character is encountered that does not match any of the characters within the brackets. A null character \0 will then automatically be added to the end of the string.

Another way to do this is to precede the characters within the square brackets by a circumflex (^). This causes the subsequent characters within the brackets to be interpreted in the opposite manner. Thus, when the program is executed, successive characters will continue to be read from the standard input device as long as each input character does not match one of the characters enclosed within the brackets. If the characters within the brackets are simply the circumflex followed by a new line characters, then the string entered from the standard input device can contain any ASCII characters except the newline character.

For example:

```
char school [40];
scanf ("%[^\n]", school);
```

Through this statement, any string of undetermined length (but not more than 40 characters) will be entered from the standard input device and assigned to school.

If the string entered through keyboard is "National Open School", then it is assigned to array 'school'. If you want to limit or to restrict the width of the data item, you can define it with the help of an unsigned integer indicating the field width, which is placed within the control string, between the % and the conversion character. The data item may be composed of fewer characters than the specified field width. But you cannot exceed the number of characters in the actual data item than specified field width. Any character that extends beyond the specified field width will not be read, incorrectly interpreted as the components of next data item. Such leftover characters may be:

For example:

int x,y,z;

scanf("%3d % 3d %3d", & x, &y, &z);

If the data input from the keyboard is 1,2,3, then the result is:

x = 1, y = 2 , z = 3

But suppose if the data input is 123, 456, 789, then it will result in:

x = 123, y = 456, z = 789

If the input is 1234 5678 9, then

x = 123, y = 4, z = 567

The remaining two digits (8 and 9) would be ignored, unless they were read by a subsequent scanf statement.

If the control string contains multiple character groups without interspersed white space characters, then whitespace characters within the input data will be interpreted as a data item. To skip this and read the next nonwhitespace character, the conversion group %s should be used.

FORMATTED OUTPUT

printf Function

The printf function is used to print out a message, either on screen or paper. The letter "f" in printf could stand for either "formatted" or "function" and it is equivalent to the WRITE statement in Pascal, only more powerful. It is similar to the input function scanf except that its purpose is to display data rather than to enter data into the computer. So, printf function moves data from the computer's memory to the standard output device, whereas the scanf function enters data from the standard input device and stores it in the computer's memory.

The general form is:

printf (string, parameter 1, parameter 2,……, parameter n)

where string refers to a string that contains formatting information, and parameter 1, parameter 2… parameter n are arguments that represents the individual output data items. The parameters can be written as constants, single variable or array names or more complex expressions.

Unlike scanf function, the parameters in a printf function do not represent memory addresses and therefore they are not preceded by ampersand (&) sign. The control string or string is composed of individual groups of characters, with one character group for each output data item. Each character group must start with a per cent sign like in scanf function followed by a conversion character indicating the type of the corresponding data item. Multiple character groups can be contiguous, or they can be separated by other characters, including whitespace characters. Some of the conversion characters are given below:

c type of data item is displayed as a single character

d type of data item is displayed as a signed decimal integer

e type of data item is displayed as a floating point value with an exponent

f type of data item is displayed as a floating point value without an exponent

o type of data item is displayed as an octal integer without a leading zero

s type of data item is displayed as a string

u type of data item is displayed as an unsigned decimal integer

x type of data item is displayed as a hexadecimal integer, without the leading fx

Let us consider an example of printf.

Suppose there are three variables,

char name[10], int roll_no, float marks;

then the printf statement to display all these three variables is:

printf("%s %d %f", name, roll_no, marks);

Within the printf function, the control string or string is "%s %d %f". It contains three characters groups. The first character group %s indicates that the first parameter represents a string. The second character group %d indicates that the second parameter represents a decimal integer value and the third character group %f indicates that the third parameter represents a floating point value.

It is to be noted here that the parameters are not preceded by ampersands as in scanf. The printf function interprets s-type conversion differently than the scanf function. In the printf function, s-type conversion is used to output a string terminated by the null character (\0). White space characters may be included within the string.

For example:

```
char school[40];

scanf("%[^\n]" ,school);

printf("%s",school);
```

If the string entered through keyboard is "National Open School", then it will print it as it is on the screen through printf statement. A concept of minimum field width in a printf statement, can be specified by preceding the conversion character by an unsigned integer. If the number of characters in the corresponding data item is less than the specified field width, then the leading blanks will be added in front of data item to fill the specified field. But if the number of characters in the corresponding data item is greater than the specified field width, then the extra space will be allocated to display the whole data item as contrary to scanf function in which there is a concept of maximum field width as stated earlier. It is also possible to specify the maximum number of decimal places for a floating point value or the maximum number of characters for a string. This is known as precision. This is an unsigned integer that is always preceded by a decimal point. If a minimum field width is specified in addition to the precision, then the precision specification follows the field width specification.

For example:

float a = 456.789;

printf ("%7f % 7.3f %7.1 f", a,a,a);

The result is 456.789000 456.789 456.7

Minimum field width and precision specification can be applied to character data as well as numerical data. When applied to a string, the minimum field width is interpreted in the same manner as with a numerical quantity. The field width specification will not prevent the entire string from being displayed. The precision specification will determine the maximum number of characters that can be displayed. If the precision specification is less than the total number of characters in the string, the excess rightmost characters will not be displayed. This will occur even if the minimum field width is larger than the entire string, resulting in the addition of leading blanks to the truncated string.

For example:

char school[9];

printf("%7s %12s % 12.3s %.3s, school, school, school, school);

Suppose the string is 'National', then the output is:

Nationa .... National........... Nat Nat

The first string is shown as input even this consists of 8 characters and the field width specification is 7 characters. So, it overrides the minimum field width specification. The second string is padded with 4 leading blanks to make 12 as field width specification. Third string is padded with 12 leading blanks and only 3 characters are shown because of 3 character precision specification and the last string also displays only 3 characters but there are no leading blank spaces because of no minimum field width specification. So, second string in this case is right justified in the output. In addition to the field width, the precision and the conversion character, each character group within the control string can include a flag, which affects the appearance of the output. The flag must be placed immediately after the percent sign.

READING AND WRITING STRINGS

gets and puts Function

'C' contains a number of other library functions that permit some form of data transfer into or out of the computer. gets and puts functions facilitate the transfer of strings between the computer and the standard input/output devices. Each of these functions accepts a single argument or parameter. The parameter must be a data item that represents a string. The string may include whitespace characters. In the case of gets, the string will be entered from the keyboard and will terminate with a new line character.

The gets and puts functions are alternative use for scanf and printf for reading and displaying strings.

For example:

```
char school[40];
gets(school);
puts(school);
```

These lines use the gets and puts to transfer the line of text into and out of the computer. When this program is executed, it will give the same result as that with scanf and printf function for input and output of given variable or array.

Review Questions

1. What is a C token? Explain tokens in C language.
2. What is the difference between declaring a variable and defining a variable?
3. What is an assignment statement? What is the relationship between an assignment statement and an expression statement?
4. What are keywords in C? What restrictions apply to their use?
5. Name and describe the four basic data types in C with an example.
6. Explain the preprocessor directives in C language.
7. Which bitwise operator is suitable for checking whether a particular bit is ON or OFF?
8. Which bitwise operator is suitable for turning OFF a particular bit in a number?
9. What characters comprise the C character set?
10. Distinguish between the binay and unary minus.
11. What role is played by parenthesis in evaluating expressions?

12. Summarize the rules for naming identifiers. Can digits be included in an identifier name? Can any special character be included?
13. When writing integer constants, how are decimal constants, octal constants and hexadecimal constants distinguished from one another.
14. What are unsigned integer constants? What are long integer constants? How can they be written and identified?
15. Describe two different ways that floating point constants be written. What special rules apply in each case?
16. What is a character constant? How do character constants differ from numeric type constants?
17. What is ASCII character set? How common is its use?
18. What is an escape sequence? What is its purpose?
19. What is a string constant? How do string constants differ from character constants? Do string constants represent numerical values?
20. What is a variable? Explain with an example.
21. What is the purpose of a type declaration? What are the components of a type declaration?
22. What is an expression? What kind of information is represented by an expression?
23. What is an operator? Describe different types of operators that are included within the C language.
24. What is an operand? What is the relationship between operators and operands?
25. Describe the arithmetic operators in C.
26. What is meant by operator precedence? What are the relative precedences of the arithmetic operators?
27. Write a short note on rotation of operators.
28. What is masking? Why we use masking in C?
29. What is meant by associativity? What is the associativity of the arithmetic operators?
30. When should parenthesis be included within an expression?
31. Describe about the relational operators included in C.
32. Describe the equality operators in C. How do they differ from the relational operator?
33. Describe the use of the conditional operator to form conditional expressions. How a conditional expression is evaluated?
34. Describe the logical not operator. What is its purpose? Within which group this is included? How many operands does it require?
35. Explain all of the increment, decrement and bitwise operators in C with examples.
36. State the rules that are applied while evaluating expressions in arithmetic type conversion.

CHAPTER 4

Control Statements

A program consists of a number of statements which are usually executed in sequence. Programs can be much more powerful if we can control the order in which statements are run.

Statements fall into three general types;

- Assignment, where values, usually the results of calculations, are stored in variables.
- input/Output, data is read in or printed out.
- Control, the program makes a decision about what to do next.

(1) Types of Selection statements:

- The if else Statement
- The switch Statement

(2) Types of Repetition statements:

- Loops
- The for Loop
- The while Loop
- The do-while Loop

(3) Types of other statements related to looping:

- The break Statement
- The continue Statement
- The goto Statement

if STATEMENT

The general format of an **if statement** in C is:

```
if (test){
statement;
}
```

The statement (or compound statement) can be followed by an **else** clause.

```
if (test){
statement;
}
else
{
statement;
}
```

Note that the semicolon is needed before the else. Below is an example of an **if** statement.

```
if (number > 0)
printf("Number positive\n");
else
{
printf("Number negative\n");
printf("or zero\n");
}
```

Nested if else is shown in the following example:

```
if (number > 100)
printf("Large\n");
else if (number > 0)
printf ("Not large but positive\n");
else if (number = = 0)
printf("or zero\n");
else
```

```
printf("Negative \n");
```

Care is needed to match the **else** clause with the correct **if**.

THE if else STATEMENT

This is used to decide whether to do something at a special point, or to decide between two courses of action.

The statement (or compound statement) can be followed by an **else** clause.

```
if (test){
statement;
}
else
{
statement;
}
if (test){
statement;
}
```

The following test decides whether a student has passed an exam with a pass mark of 45.

```
if (result >= 45)
printf("Pass\n");
else
printf("Fail\n");
```

It is possible to use the if part without the else.

```
if (temperature < 0)
printf("Frozen\n");
```

Each version consists of a test (this is the bracketed statement following the if). If the test is true, then the next statement is obeyed. If it is false, then the statement following the else is obeyed if present. After this, the rest of the program continues as normal.

If we wish to have more than one statement following the if or the else, they should be grouped together between curly brackets. Such a grouping is called a compound statement or a block.

```
if (result >= 45)
{     printf("Passed\n");
printf("Congratulations\n");
}
else
{     printf("Failed\n");
printf("Good luck in the results\n");
}
```

Sometimes we wish to make a multi-way decision based on several conditions. The most general way of doing this is by using the else if variant on the if statement. This works by cascading several comparisons. As soon as one of these gives a true result, the following statement or block is executed, and no further comparisons are performed.

NESTED if else

If we write an entire if else construct within the body of the if statement or the body of an else statement, this is called 'nesting' of ifs.

Example:

```
if(condition){
if(condition)
statement;
else
{
statement;
}
}
else
statement;
if (result >= 75)
printf("Passed: Grade A\n");
else if (result >= 60)
printf("Passed: Grade B\n");
```

```
else if (result >= 45)
printf("Passed: Grade C\n");
else
printf("Failed\n");
```

In this example, all comparisons test a single variable called result. In other cases, each test may involve a different variable or some combination of tests. The same pattern can be used with more or fewer else if's, and the final one else may be left out. It is up to the programmer to devise the correct structure for each programming problem.

THE switch STATEMENT

This is another form of the multiway decision. It is well structured, but can only be used in certain cases where;

- Only one variable is tested, all branches must depend on the value of that variable. The variable must be an integral type (int, long, short or char).
- Each possible value of the variable can control a single branch. A final, catch all, default branch may optionally be used to trap all unspecified cases.

The general format is:

```
switch (expression){
case value1: statements1;
case value2: statements2;
/* more cases */
default: defaultstatements;
}
```

Semantically, this is different to the Pascal case. If the expression is equal to value1, then statement1 is executed, followed by statement2, then all other statements including default statements. If the expression is equal to value2, then statement2 is executed, followed by all other statements including default statements. To get the same effect as Pascal, it is necessary to put a break after every set of statements, to prevent execution of all subsequent statements in the switch. The following fragment of code illustrates the use of break.

```
/*assume char op; */
scanf("%c", &op);
switch(op){
case '+' : printf("%d", x + y); break;
```

```
case '-' : printf("%d", x - y); break;
case '*' : printf("%d", x * y); break;
case '/' : printf("%d", x / y); break;
default: break;
}
```

This is a function which converts an integer into a vague description. It is useful where we are only concerned in measuring a quantity when it is quite small.

```
estimate(number)
int number;
/*Estimate a number as none, one, two, several, many */
{switch(number){
case 0 :
printf("None\n");
break;
case 1 :
printf("One\n");
break;
case 2 :
printf("Two\n");
break;
case 3 :
case 4 :
case 5 :
printf("Several\n");
break;
default :
printf("Many\n");
break;
}
}
```

Each interesting case is listed with a corresponding action. The break statement prevents any further statements from being executed by leaving the switch. Since case 3 and case 4 have no following break, they continue on allowing the same action for several values of numbers.

Both if and switch constructs allow the programmer to make a selection from a number of possible actions.

The other main type of control statement is the loop. Loops allow a statement, or block of statements, to be repeated. Computers are very good at repeating simple tasks many times, the loop is C's way of achieving this.

LOOPS

C gives you a choice of three types of loop, while, do while and for.

- The while loop keeps repeating an action until an associated test returns false. This is useful where the programmer does not know in advance how many times the loop will be traversed.
- The do-while loops are similar, but the test occurs after the loop body is executed. This ensures that the loop body is run at least once.
- The for loop is frequently used, usually where the loop will be traversed a fixed number of times. It is very flexible, and novice programmers should take care not to abuse the power it offers.

THE for LOOP

The for loop works well where the number of iterations of the loop is known before the loop is entered. The head of the loop consists of three parts separated by semicolons.

- The first is run before the loop is entered. This is usually the initialization of the loop variable.
- The second is a test, the loop is exited when this returns false.
- The third is a statement to be run every time the loop body is completed. This is usually an increment of the loop counter.

for Statement

The C for statement offers much more than the equivalent counted loop in Pascal.

The general format is:

for (*initial; condition; increment/decrement*){

Statement;

```
}
```

Where initial is a statement that initializes values prior to the execution of the loop.

The expression condition must hold true for an iteration of the loop to start. The increment/decrement statement is executed for each iteration, after the iteration has completed.

```
for (n=1; n<=10; n++){
printf("%3d", n);
}
```

This will print out the numbers 1 to 10. The curly brackets are not necessary as there is only a single statement.

It is not always necessary to have all parts of the **for** statement, parts can be left empty. The following code has the same functionality as the above.

```
n=0;
for (; ++n<=10; ){
printf("%3d", n);
}
```

In this case, the initialization is outside the loop. The incrementing of **n** occurs as part of the final test. As the operator is first, the incrementing happens before the comparison. If the test were replaced by:

```
n++<=10;
```

The loop would be executed 11 times.

```
for (hi = 100, lo = 0; hi >= lo; hi--, lo++)
```

The for loop is extremely flexible and allows many types of program behavior to be specified simply and quickly.

Example: To write the simple interest problem using the for loop

```
/*Calculation of simple interest for 3 sets of p,n and r*/
int p,n, count;
float r, si;
for(count = 1; count <=3; count = count +1){
printf("Enter values of p,n and r");
scanf("%d %d %f", & p, & n, & r);
si = p * n * r / 100;
```

```
printf("Simple interest = Rs %f \n", si);
}
}
```

THE while LOOP

The while loop repeats a statement until the test at the top proves false.

As an example, here is a function to return the length of a string. Remember that the string is represented as an array of characters terminated by a null character '\0'.

The syntax of a while statement is:

while *(expression)*{

statement;

}

The expression is usually a relational expression. The statement is either a compound statement enclosed in curly brackets or single statement.

For example:

```
n = 1;
while (n <= 10){
printf("%3d", n);
n++;
}
```

This will print out the numbers 1 to 10.

The positioning of the curly brackets and the indentation are according to the programmer's preference.

```
/* Calculation of simple interest for 3 sets of p, n and r */
main( )
{int p,n, count;
float r, si;
count = 1;
while(count < = 3){
printf("\n Enter values of p, n and r");
scanf("%d %d %f", & p, & n, & r);
```

```
si = p*n*r/100;
printf("simple interest = Rs. %f", si);
count = count +1;
}
```

THE do...while LOOP

This is very similar to the while loop except that the test occurs at the end of the loop body. This guarantees that the loop is executed at least once before continuing. Such a set-up is frequently used where data is to be read. The test then verifies the data, and loops back to read again if it is unacceptable.

do...while Statement

The syntax of a **do...while** statement is:

```
do{
statement;
}while (expression);
```

where the compound statement is always executed at least once.

```
do
{
printf("Enter a number that is not 7");
scanf("%d",&n);
} while (n==7);
```

This will loop until the user types something other than a 7.

If the final expression is replaced by:

```
(n=7)
```

Regardless what the user types **n** will be set to 7. The expression returns true each time it executes and so the program will loop infinitely.

```
do
{
printf("Enter 1 for yes, 0 for no :");
scanf("%d", &input_value);
} while (input_value != 1 && input_value != 0);
```

There is a minor difference between the working of while and do-while loops. The difference is the place where the condition is tested. The while tests the condition before executing any of the statements within the while loop. As against this, the do-while tests the condition after having executed the statements within the loop.

Example:

```
main( ){
while(5<1)
printf("Hello\n");
}
```

In the above example, the printf will not get executed at all since the condition fails at the first time itself. Now let's write the same program using a do-while loop.

```
main( ){
do
{
 printf ("Hello\n");
} while (5<1);
}
```

In the above program, the printf( ) would be executed once, since first the body of the loop is executed and then the condition is tested.

THE break STATEMENT

We have already met break in the discussion of the switch statement. It is used to exit from a loop or a switch, control passing to the first statement beyond the loop or a switch.

With loops, break can be used to force an early exit from the loop, or to implement a loop with a test to exit in the middle of the loop body. A break within a loop should always be protected within an if statement which provides the test to control the exit condition.

Example: /*The following program is to determine whether a number is prime or not*/

```
main( ){
int num, i;
printf("Enter a number");
scanf("%d", &num);
  i = 2;
```

```
while (i < = num -1) {
if (num%i= = 0){
printf("Not a prime number");
break;
}
i + +;
}
if(i = = num)
printf("Prime number");
}
```

THE continue STATEMENT

This is similar to break but is encountered less frequently. It only works within loops where its effect is to force an immediate jump to the loop control statement.

- In a while loop, jump to the test statement.
- In a do-while loop, jump to the test statement.
- In a for loop, jump to the test, and perform the iteration.

Example:

```
main( ){
    int i,j;
    for(i = 1; i< = 2; i++){
     for(j=1; j<=2; j++){
if (i= =j)
continue;
printf("\n%d%d\n", i,j);
}
}
}
```

The output of the above program would be....

12

21

When the value of i equal to that of j, the continue statement takes the control to the for loop (inner) bypassing rest of the statements pending execution in the for loop(inner).

THE go to STATEMENT

C has a goto statement which permits unstructured jumps to be made.

The syntax of a goto statement is:

goto *label*;

Where ***label*** is a local label, terminated by a colon.

For example:

```
again;
/* code*/;
goto again;
```

Example:

```
void function(void)
{
while ( ... )
for( ... )
if (disaster) goto error;
error:
return;
}
```

Exit STATEMENT

This statement causes close all files and buffers, and terminate the program.

Syntax:- exit(n);

Value of n is assign by the function, to indicate termination status.

exit(0) → used for terminate from Simple Program

exit(1) → used for terminate from user-defined function in Main Program

exit(2) → used for terminate from Complex Program

C PROGRAM EXAMPLES

/*Program to Print Even Numbers in the Given Range*/

```
#include <stdio.h>
#include <conio.h>
void main(){
int r,i;
clrscr();
printf("enter the range:");
scanf("%d",&r);
i=1;
while(i<=r) {
if(i%2==0)
printf("%d\t",i);
i++;
}
getch();
}
```

/*Program to Find Factorial of a Given Number Using While Loop*/

```
#include <stdio.h>
#include <conio.h>
void main(){
int n,f,i;
clrscr();
printf("enter n value");
scanf("%d",&n);
i=n;
f=1;
while(i>0){
f = f * i;
```

```
i = i-1;
}
printf("factorial of%d a given number%d",n,f);
getch();
return(0);
}
```

/*Program to Find Factorial of a Given Number Using for Loop*/

```
#include <stdio.h>
#include <conio.h>
void main(){
int a,b=1;
clrscr();
printf("enter any value");
scanf("%d",&a);
for(;a>0;){
b=b*a;
a--;
}
printf("factorial of a given number %d",b);
getch();
}
```

/*Program to Find Fibonacci Series Using for Loop*/

```
#include <stdio.h>
#include <conio.h>
void main(){
int a,b,c=0;
clrscr();
for(a=-1,b=1,c=1;a+b<=100;){
c=a+b;
```

```
printf("\t %d",c);
a=b;
b=c;
}
getch();
}
```

/*Program to Find Fibonacci Series Using While*/

```
#include <stdio.h>
#include <conio.h>
void main(){
int a=-1,b=1,c,n,i=1;
clrscr();
printf("enter n value");
scanf("%d",&n);
while(i<=n){
c=a+b;
printf("\t %d",c);
a=b;
b=c;
i++;
}
getch();
}
```

/*Program — Palindrome of a Number*/

```
#include <stdio.h>
#include <conio.h>
void main(){
int n,t,s,rem;
clrscr();
```

```
printf("enter a number:");
scanf("%d",&n);
t=n;
s=0;
while(n>0){
rem=n%10;
s=(s*10)+rem;
n=n/10;
}
if(t==s)
printf("%d is a palindrome",t);
else
printf("%d is not a palindrome",t);
getch();
}
```

/*Program to Check Whether a No is a Palindrome or Not*/

```
#include <stdio.h>
#include <conio.h>
void main(){
int n, num, digit, sum =0,rev=0;
printf("enter the number");
scanf("%d",&num);
n=num;
do{
digit=num%10;
sum=sum + digit;
rev=(rev*10)+digit;
num=num/10;
}
```

```
while(num!=0);
printf("sum of the digits of the number=%d\n",sum);
printf("the reverse of the number=%d\n",rev);
if(n==rev)
printf("the given number is a palindrome");
else
printf("the number is not a palindrome");
getch();
}
```

```
/*Program to Print
1
2 2
3 3 3 */
#include <stdio.h>
#include <conio.h>
main(){
int i,j,a=1,b=0,c=0;
clrscr();
for(i=1,b=0;i<=5;i++,b++){
printf("\n");
for(j=1;j<=i;j++){
c=a+b;
printf("%d ",c);
}
}
getch();
}
```

/*Program to find the Length of a Given Number*/

```
#include <stdio.h>
#include <conio.h>
void main(){
int num, rem, count =0;
clrscr();
printf("\n enter the number\n");
scanf("%d",&num);
while(num>0){
num=num/10;
count++;
}
printf("the number of digits in a given number is %d",count);
getch();
}
```

/*Program to Find Whether a Number is Prime or Not*/

```
#include <stdio.h>
#include <conio.h>
void main(){
int n, i=2;
clrscr();
printf("\n enter a number\n");
scanf("%d",&n);
while(i<n){
if(n%i==0)
break;
i++;
}
if(i= =n){
```

```
printf("%d is a prime",n);
}
else
printf("%d is not a prime",n);
getch();
}
```

/*Program – Sum of Digits of a Given Number*/

```
#include <stdio.h>
#include <conio.h>
main(){
int r,s;
long n;
clrscr();
printf("enter any number:");
scanf("%1d",&n);
s=0;
while(n>0){
r=n%10;
s=s+r;
n=n/10;
}
printf("the sum of digits is %d",s);
getch();
}
```

/*Program to Find Out the Leap Year*/

```
#include <stdio.h>
#include <conio.h>
main(){
int year;
```

```
clrscr();
printf("enter the year:");
scanf("%d",&year);
if((year%4==0)&&(year%100!=0)||(year%400==0))
printf("it is a leap year");
else
printf("it is not a leap year");
getch();
}
```

/*Program to Find Whether a Number is Armstrong Number or Not*/

```
#include <stdio.h>
#include <conio.h>
void main(){
int n,s, r, t;
clrscr();
printf("Enter any number");
scanf("%d", &n);
t=n;
s = 0;
while(n>0){
r=n%10;
s=s+(r*r*r);
n=n/10;
}
if (t==s)
printf("%d is an Armstrong number",t);
else
printf("%d is not an Armstrong number",t);
getch();
}
```

/*Program to Find the Distance Travelled*/

```
#include <stdio.h>
#include <conio.h>
void main(){
float s,u,a,t,p,q,t1,s1,r,o,z;
clrscr();
printf("enter u r choice");
{
printf("Enter the values  of u,a");
scanf("%f %f",&u,&a);
printf("\n  enter t value");
scanf("%f",&t);
p=u*t;
q=0.5*(a*t*t);
s = (p + q);
scanf("%f",&s);
printf("enter t1");
scanf("%f",&t1);
r=u*t1;
o=0.5*(a*t1*t1);
s1=(r + o);
scanf("%f",&s1);
}
printf("the distance travel in time interval t,t1 %f-%f  =%f",s1,s,s1-s);
getch();
}
```

/*Program to Find the Roots of a Quadratic Equation*/

```
#include <stdio.h>
#include <conio.h>
```

```
#include <math.h>
main(){
int a,b,c;
float r,x,y;
clrscr();
printf("\t Enter the values of a,b,c:");
scanf("%d %d %d",&a,&b,&c);
if((b*b)>=(4*a*c)){
x=((-b)+r)/(2*a);
y=((-b)-r)/(2*a);
printf("The roots are: %f %f",x,y);
}
else
{
printf("Roots are imaginary");
}
getch();
}
```

/*Program to Print Numbers from 1 to 100*/

```
#include <stdio.h>
#include <conio.h>
void main(){
int i=1;
clrscr();
while(i<=100){
printf("%d\t",i);
i++;
}
getch();
}
```

/*Program to Print Numbers from 100 to 1*/

```
#include <stdio.h>
#include <conio.h>
void main(){
int i=100;
clrscr();
while(i>=1){
printf("%d\t",i);
i--;
}
getch();
}
```

/*Program to Print ASCII Values*/

```
#include <stdio.h>
#include <conio.h>
void main(){
int i;
clrscr();
for(i=0;i<25;i++)
printf("%d = %c",i,i);
getch();
}
```

/*Program to Print Even Numbers*/

```
#include <stdio.h>
#include <conio.h>
void main(){
int r,i;
clrscr();
printf("enter the range:");
scanf("%d",&r);
```

```
i=1;
while(i<=r){
if(i%2= =0)
printf("%d\t",i);
i++;
}
```

/*Program to Find Factorial of a Given Number Using for Loop*/

```
#include <stdio.h>
#include <conio.h>
void main(){
int a,b=1;
clrscr();
printf("enter any value");
scanf("%d",&a);
for(;a>0;){
b=b*a;
a--;
}
printf("factorial of a given number %d",b);
getch();
}
```

/*Program to Find Fibonacci Series*/

```
#include <stdio.h>
#include <conio.h>
void main() {
int a,b,c,n;
clrscr();
printf("enter n value");
scanf("%d", &n);
```

```
for(a=0,b=1,c=1;c<n;c=a+b,a=b,b=c)
printf("\t %d",c);
getch();
}
```

/*Program to Find Fibonacci Series Using for Loop*/

```
#include <stdio.h>
#include <conio.h>
void main(){
int a,b,c=0;
clrscr();
for(a=-1,b=1,c=1;a+b<=100;){
c=a+b;
printf("\t %d",c);
a=b;
b=c;
}
getch();
}
```

/*Program to Find Fibonacci Series Using While*/

```
#include <stdio.h>
#include <conio.h>
void main(){
int a=-1,b=1,c,n,i=1;
clrscr();
printf("enter n value");
scanf("%d",&n);
while(i<=n){
c=a+b;
printf("\t %d",c);
```

```
a=b;
b=c;
i++;
}
getch();
}
```

/*Program to Find a Perfect Number*/

```
#include <stdio.h>
#include <conio.h>
void main(){
int n, i,s;
clrscr();
printf("enter any no:");
scanf("%d", &n);
i=1;
s=0;
while(i<n){
if(n%i==0)
s=s+i;
i++;
}
if(s==n)
printf("%d is a perfect number",n);
else
printf("%d is not a perfect number",n);
getch();
}
```

/*Program to Find the Grade from the Given Percentage Using Switch*/

```
#include <stdio.h>
#include <conio.h>
```

```
void main(){
int p,q;
clrscr();
printf("enter the percentage of the student:");
scanf("%d",&p);
if(p>=75)
q=1;
if((p<75)&&(p>=65))
q=2;
if((p<65)&&(p>=55))
q=3;
if((p<55)&&(p>=45))
q=4;
if((p<=45))
q=5;
switch(q){
case 1: printf("the grade for %d  per cent is A",p);break;
case 2: printf("the grade for %d per cent is B",p);;break;
case 3: printf("the grade for  %d per cent is C",p);;break;
case 4: printf("the grade for  %d per cent is D",p);;break;
default : printf("the option you have entered is wrong");
}
getch();
}
```

/*Program to Print Greatest of Three Numbers*/

```
#include <stdio.h>
#include <conio.h>
void main(){
```

```
int a,b,c;
clrscr();
printf("enter any three numbers");
scanf("%d %d %d",&a,&b,&c);
if((a>b)&&(a>c))
printf("a is the greatest number %d",a);
if((b>a)&&(b>c))
printf("b is the greatest number %d",b);
if((c>a)&&(c>b))
printf("c is the greatest number %d",c);
getch();
}
```

Review Questions

1. What is meant by looping? Describe different forms of looping with an example.
2. Write short notes on iterative statements in C.
3. What is the purpose of while statement? When is the logical expression evaluated? What is the minimum number of times that a while loop is executed?
4. How is the execution of a while loop terminated?
5. What is the purpose of a do..while statement? How does it differ from while statement?
6. What is the minimum number of times a do..while loop can be executed? Compare with a while loop and explain the reasons for the differences.
7. What is the purpose of a for statement? How does it differ from while and do..while statements?
8. How many times a for loop is executed show using an example?
9. What rules apply to nested loops? Can one type of loop be embedded within another?
10. What is the purpose of if-else statement? In what way is this statement different from the while, do..while and for statements?
11. Compare the use of the if-else statement with the use of the? operator. In particular, in what way can the? operator be used in place of an if-else statement.
12. What is the purpose of the switch statement? When a switch statement used?

13. What is the difference between 'break' and 'continue' statements?
14. Explain about goto statement with a simple example?
15. What is conditional execution?
16. What is the purpose of comma operator? Within which control statement does the comma operator usually appear?
17. Why the use of goto statement generally discouraged? Under what conditions might be goto statement helpful? What types of usage should be avoided and why?
18. Suppose a break statement is included within the innermost of several nested control statements. What happens when the break statement is included?

CHAPTER

5

Functions

INTRODUCTION

Functions are the building blocks of a C program. Functions are sections of code that perform a single, well-defined service. All executable code in C is within a function. Functions take any number of parameters and return a maximum of 1 value. A parameter is a value passed to a function that is used to alter its operation or indicate the extent of its operations.

FUNCTION DECLARATION

A function consists of three parts:

(i) Return type – any standard or user-defined data type

(ii) Function name – any name except reserved key words

(iii) Signature – list of the arguments to be passed to the function

STRUCTURE OF A FUNCTION

```
<return type> FunctionName (Argument1, Argument2, Argument3......)
{
Statement1;
Statement2;
Statement3;
}
```

A function in C looks like this:

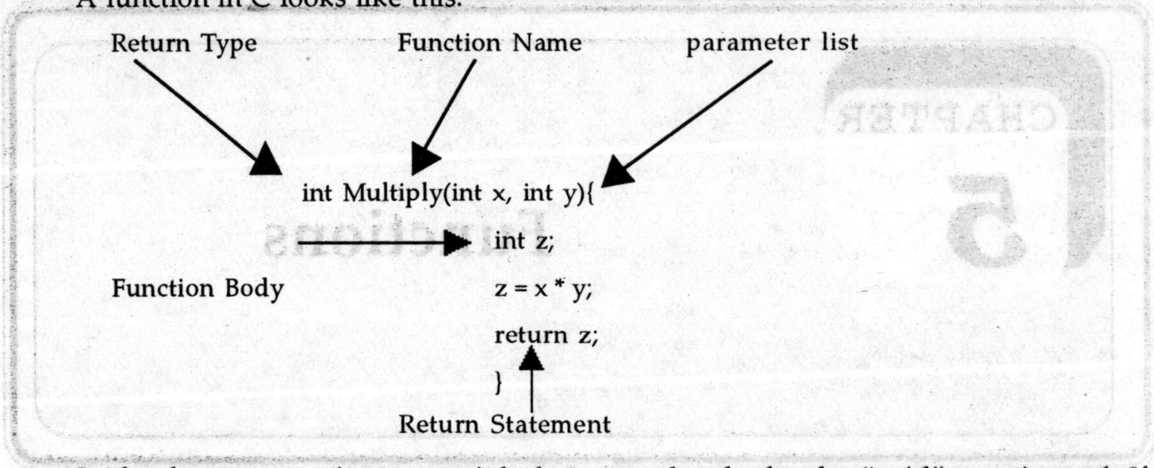

In the data type section, you might have wondered why the "void" type is used. If a function does not return a value or there are no parameters, the type void is used.

Example:

```
void PrintHello(void){
printf("Hello World"); /* printf prints a string to the screen*/
return;
}
```

Another question you might ask is which function is executed first in a program. In C, the function named "main" is executed first. Like variables, all functions except the "main" function must be declared before it is defined.

RETURN STATEMENT

The body of the function looks like the code:

Syntax: return;

This is the means by which the function returns the value to whatever called it. If our function has a type other than void, it must return a value of the appropriate type. You return a value by placing it in the program, after the return keyword.

FUNCTION DEFINITION

Syntax:

```
[return type] function name (argument list)
arguments declaration;
{
```

local variable declarations;

statements;

[return expression]

}

(or)

[return type] function name (argument list with declaration)

{

local variable declarations;

statements;

[return expression]

}

Example:

```
int add(a, b) or int add(int a, int b)
int a,b;
{
int y;
y=a+b;
return y;
}
```

When the value of y which is the addition of the values of a and b, the last two statements i.e., y=a+b; and return(y); can be combined as return (a+b);

Example:

```
int mul(int a, int b);//function declaration
main()
{
int a,b;
scanf("%d %d",&a,&b);
int result=mul(a,b);//function call
printf("%d",result);
}
```

```
//function definition
int mul(int x, int y)
{
return (x*y);
}
```

TERMINOLOGIES

Calling Function

The function which calls another function is termed as calling function.

Example: From above example, main() is calling function.

Called Function

The function which gets called is termed as called function.

Example: From above example, mul() is called function.

Actual Arguments

The arguments that are passed to a function during calling are called as actual arguments.

Example: a,b are called as actual arguments in the line int result=mul(a,b);//function call

Formal Arguments

The arguments which are mentioned in the function definition are called as formal arguments.

Example: x and y are formal arguments as they are present in the function definition.

Library Functions

Functions present in the standard libraries are known as library functions.

Example: printf(), scanf() etc.

User-defined Functions

Functions written by us are called as user-defined functions.

Example:

```
int add(int a, int b)
{
  ——;
}
```

FUNCTION CALL

A function can be called from any other function using its name and passing the arguments, if any.

FUNCTION PROTOTYPES

The prototype of a function provides the basic information about a function which tells the compiler that the function is used correctly or not. It contains the same information as the function header contains. The prototype of the function in the above example would be like int sum (int x, int y);

The only difference between the header and the prototype is the semicolon; there must a semicolon at the end of the prototype.

Void Type

Sometimes a function may not return any value, in such a case its data type becomes void.

For example:

void display( )

Why We Use Functions?

The most important reason to use functions is to aid in the conceptual organization of a program.

Another reason to use functions is to reduce the complexity of the program. Any sequence of instructions that appears in program more than once is a set of statements for being made into a function. The function's code is stored in only one place in memory, even though the function is executed many times in the course of the program.

Two Reasons

Writing functions avoids rewriting the same code over and over. Suppose that there is a section of code in a program that calculates area of a triangle. If, later in the program we want to calculate the area of a different triangle we won't like to write the same instructions all over again. Instead we would prefer to jump to a "section of code" that calculates area and then jump back to the place from where you left off. This section of code is nothing but a function.

Using functions, it becomes easier to write programs and keep track of what they are doing. If the operation of a program can be divided into separate activities, and each activity is placed in a different function, then each could be written and checked more or less independently. Separating the code into modular functions also makes the program easier to design and understand.

DECLARING A FUNCTION

Any function by default returns an int value. If we desire that a function should return a value other than an int, then it is necessary to explicitly mention so in the calling functions as well as in the called function.

For example:

```
main( ){
float a,b,
printf ("\n Enter any number");
scanf ("\% f", &a );
b = square (a);
printf ("\n square of % f is % f", a,b);
}
square (float x){
float y;
y = x * x;
return (y);
}
```

The output of this program is:

Enter any number 2.5

square of 2.5 is 6.000000

Here, 6 is not a square of 2.5.

This happened because any C function, by default, always returns an integer value.

The following program segment illustrates how to make square( ) capable of returning a float value.

```
main( ){
float square( );
float a, b;
printf ("\n Enter any number");
scanf ("%f" &a);
b = square(a);
```

```
printf ("\n square of % f is % f," a, b);
}
float square(float x){
float y;
y= x *x;
return(y);
}
```

Output:

Enter any number 2.5

Square of 2.5 is 6.2500000

There are basically two types of functions:

1. Library functions. Example: printf(), scanf(), etc.
2. User-defined function. Example: the function as message mentioned above.

The following point must be noted about functions:

(i) C program is a collection of one or more functions.

(ii) A function gets called when the function name is followed by a semicolon:

For example:

```
main( ){
message( );
}
```

Function is defined when function name is followed by a pair of braces in which one or more statements may be present.

For example:

```
message( ){
statement 1;
statement 2;
statement 3;
}
```

Any function can be called from any other function even main( ) can be called from other functions.

For example:

```
main( ){
message( );
}
message( ){
printf ("\n Hello");
main( );
}
```

A function can be called any number of times.

For example:

```
main(){
message( );
message( );
}
message( ){
printf ("\n Hello");
}
```

The order in which the functions are defined in a program and the order in which they get called need not necessarily be same.

For example:

```
main( ){
message 1( );
message 2( );
}
message 2( ){
printf ("\n I am learning C");
}
message 1( ){
printf ( "\n Hello");
}
```

A function can call itself such a process is called "**recursion**".

A function can be called from other function, but a function cannot be defined in another function. The following program code would be wrong, since "India" is being defined inside another function main( ).

```
main( ){
printf ("\n I am in main function");
India( ){
printf {"\n I am in India");
}
}
```

Any C program contains at least one function.

If a program contains only one function, it must be main( ).

In a C program, if there are more than one functions present then one of these functions must be main( ) because program execution always begins with main( ).

There is no limit on the number of functions that might be present in a C program.

Each function in a program is called in the sequence specified by the functions calls in main( ).

After each function has done its thing, control returns to the main( ), when main( ) runs out of function calls, the program ends.

Advantages of Using Functions

There are many advantages in using functions in a program, they are:

It makes possible top-down modular programming. In this style of programming, the high-level logic of the overall problem is solved first while the details of each lower-level functions is addressed later. The length of the source program can be reduced by using functions at appropriate places.

A function may be used later by many other programs, this means that a C programmer can use functions written by others, instead of starting over from scratch.

A function can be used to keep away from rewriting the same block of codes which we are going to use two or more locations in a program. This is especially useful if the code involved is long or complicated.

PARAMETERS

Arguments are also known as parameters (in fact the term parameter is commonly used). They are used to communicate data between the calling function and the called function.

The parameters are of two types. They are:

(1) Actual parameters

(2) Formal parameters (Dummy parameters)

The variables that are used while calling a function are known as actual parameters. The variables that are used in function definition are known as formal parameters. The names of actual parameters and the formal parameters can be same or can be different. Even though the names are same, the "C" compiler treats them as different variables.

For example:

Let us consider the following statement:

max = maximum(a,b,c);

Here, we are passing values of a, b, c to function maximum.

a, b, c are known as actual parameters.

maximium (x,y,z)

In the function definition, we are using x, y, z, these variables are known as formal parameters.

The values of the actual parameters are copied into formal parameters. The value of a is copied into x; value of b is copied into y; value of c is copied into z.

TYPES OF FUNCTIONS

A function may belong to any one of the following categories:

- Functions with no arguments and no return values
- Functions with arguments and no return values
- Functions with arguments and return values
- Functions with no arguments and return values
- Functions that return multiple values

Functions with No Arguments and No Return Value

A C function without any arguments means you cannot pass data (values like int, char, etc.) to the called function. Similarly, function with no return type does not pass back data to the calling function. It is one of the simplest types of function in C. This type of function which does not return any value cannot be used in an expression. It can be used only as independent statement.

For example:

```
#include <stdio.h>
#include <conio.h>
void printline(){
int i;
printf("\n");
for(i=0;i<30;i++){
printf("-");
}
printf("\n");
}
void main(){
clrscr();
printf("Welcome to function in C");
printline();
printf("Function easy to learn");
printline();
getch();
}
```

Output

Welcome to function in C

Function easy to learn.

Explanation

The above C program example illustrates that how to declare a function with no argument and no return type.

Line 3-10: This C code block is a user-defined function (UDF) whose task is to print a horizontal line. This is a simple function and a basic programmer can understand this. As you can see in line no. 6, the declaration of a "for loop" which loops 30 times and prints "-" symbol continuously.

Line 11-18: These lines are "main()" function code block. Line no. 13 and 15 simply prints two different messages. And line no. 14 and 16 calls our user-defined function "printline()".

Functions with Arguments and No Return Value

In our previous example, what we have noticed is that "main()" function has no control over the UDF "printfline()", it cannot control its output. Whenever "main()" calls "printline()", it simply prints line every time. So the result remains the same.

A C function with arguments can perform much better than previous function type. This type of function can accept data from calling function. In other words, you send data to the called function from calling function but you cannot send result data back to the calling function. Rather, it displays the result on the terminal. But we can control the output of function by providing various values as arguments.

For example:

```
#include <stdio.h>
#include <conio.h>
void add(int x, int y){
int result;
result = x+y;
printf("Sum of %d and %d is %d.\n\n",x,y,result);
}
void main(){
clrscr();
add(30,15);
add(63,49);
add(952,321);
getch();
}
```

Output

Sum of 30 and 15 is 45

Sum of 63 and 49 is 112

Sum of 952 and 321 is 1273

Explanation

This program simply sends two integer arguments to the UDF "add()" which, further, calculates its sum and stores in another variable and then prints that value.

Line 3-7: This C code block is "add()" which accepts two integer type arguments. This UDF also has a integer variable "result" which stores the sum of values passed by calling function (in this example "main()"). And line no. 6 simply prints the result along with argument variable values.

Line 8-14: This code block is a "main()" function but only line no. 10, 11, 12 is important for us now. In these three lines, we have called same function "add()" three times but with different values and each function call gives different output. So, we can control function's output by providing different integer parameters which was not possible in function type 1. This is the difference between "function with no argument" and "function with argument".

Functions with Arguments and Return Value

This type of function can send arguments (data) from the calling function to the called function and wait for the result to be returned back from the called function back to the calling function. And this type of function is mostly used in programming world because it can do two-way communications; it can accept data as arguments as well as can send back data as return value. The data returned by the function can be used later in our program for further calculations.

```
#include <stdio.h>
#include <conio.h>
int add(int x, int y){
int result;
result = x+y;
return(result);
}
void main(){
int z;
clrscr();
z = add(952,321);
printf("Result %d.\n\n",add(30,55));
printf("Result %d.\n\n",z);
```

```
getch();
}
```

Output

Result 85

Result 1273

Explanation

This program sends two integer values (x and y) to the UDF "add()", "add()" function adds these two values and sends back the result to the calling function (in this program to "main()" function). Later result is printed on the terminal.

Line No. 3-7: Look line no. 3 carefully, it starts with int. This int is the return type of the function, means it can only return integer type data to the calling function. If you want any function to return character values, then you must change this to char type. On line no. 6 you can see return statement, return is a keyword and in bracket we can give values which we want to return. You can assign any integer value to experiment with this return which ultimately will change its output.

Line No. 8-15: In this code block, only line no. 11, 12 and 13 is important. We have declared an integer "z" which we used in line no. 11. The integer variable is used in UDF "add()" returns an integer value on calling. To store that value, we have declared an integer value. We have passed 952, 321 to the "add()" function, which finally return 1273 as result. This value will be stored in "z" integer variable. Now we can use "z" to print its value or to other function.

You will also notice some strange statement in line no. 12. Actually, line no. 12 and 13 does the same job, in line no. 13 we have used an extra variable whereas on line no. 12 we directly printed the value without using any extra variable. This is simply to show you how we can use function in different ways.

Functions with No Arguments but Returns Value

We may need a function which does not take any argument but only returns values to the calling function then this type of function is useful. The best example of this type of function is "getchar()" library function which is declared in the header file "stdio.h". We can declare a similar library function of own.

For example:

```
#include <stdio.h>
#include <conio.h>
```

```
int send(){
int no1;
printf("Enter a no:");
scanf("%d",&no1);
return(no1);
}
void main(){
int z;
clrscr();
z = send();
printf("\nYou entered: %d", z);
getch();
}
```

Output

Enter a no: 6

You entered : 6

Explanation

In this program, we have a UDF which takes one integer as input from keyboard and sends back to the calling function.

RECURSION

In C, functions can call themselves. A function is recursive if a statement in the body of the function calls itself. Sometimes called circular definition, recursion is the process of defining something in terms of itself.

Examples of recursion abound. A recursive way to define an integer number is as the digits: 0, 1, 2, 3, 4, 5, 6, 7, 8, and 9 plus or minus an integer number.

The main advantage of recursive function is clear, short and simple programs.

Example:

```
int fact(int x)
{
int f=1;
```

```
if(x>1)
f=x*fact(x-1);
return(f);
}
```

TOWERS OF HANOI

The Tower of Hanoi or Towers of Hanoi is a mathematical game or puzzle. It consists of three rods, and a number of disks of different sizes which can slide onto any rod. The puzzle starts with the disks in a neat stack in ascending order of size on one rod, the smallest at the top, thus making a conical shape.

The objective of the puzzle is to move the entire stack to another rod, obeying the following rules:

- Only one disk may be moved at a time.
- Each move consists of taking the upper disk from one of the rods and sliding it onto another rod, on top of the other disks that may already be present on that rod.
- No disk may be placed on top of a smaller disk.
- The puzzle can be played with any number of disks. The number of moves required to solve a Tower of Hanoi puzzle is 2n-1, where n is the number of disks.

For example, consider three pegs A, B and C. And initial positions of all n disks are on peg A. The solution is to move these disks on to peg B may be in two ways.

For an even number of disks:

- make the legal move between pegs A and B
- make the legal move between pegs A and C
- make the legal move between pegs B and C
- repeat until complete

For an odd number of disks:

- make the legal move between pegs A and C
- make the legal move between pegs A and B
- make the legal move between pegs B and C
- repeat until complete

In each case, a total of 2n-1 moves are made.

Recursive Solution

A key to solving this puzzle is to recognize that it can be solved by breaking the problem down into a collection of smaller problems and further breaking those problems down into even smaller problems until a solution is reached. The following procedure demonstrates this approach.

- Label the pegs A, B, C—these labels may move at different steps
- Let n be the total number of discs (here n = 6).
- Number the discs from 1 (smallest, topmost) to n (largest, bottommost)

To move n discs from peg A to peg C:

(1) move n"1 discs from A to B. This leaves disc #n alone on peg A

(2) move disc #n from A to C

(3) move n 1 discs from B to C so they sit on disc #n

The above is a recursive algorithm: to carry out steps 1 and 3, apply the same algorithm again for n 1. The entire procedure is a finite number of steps, since at some point the algorithm will be required for n = 1. This step, moving a single disc from peg A to peg B, is trivial.

The following is a procedure for moving a tower of n disks from a peg A onto a peg C, with B being the remaining third peg:

Step 1: If h > 1then, first use this procedure to move the h-1 smaller disks from peg A to peg B.

Step 2: Now the largest disk, i.e., disk h-1 can be moved from peg A to peg C.

Step 3: If h > 1 then, again use this procedure to move the h-1 smaller disks from peg B to peg C.

Algorithm

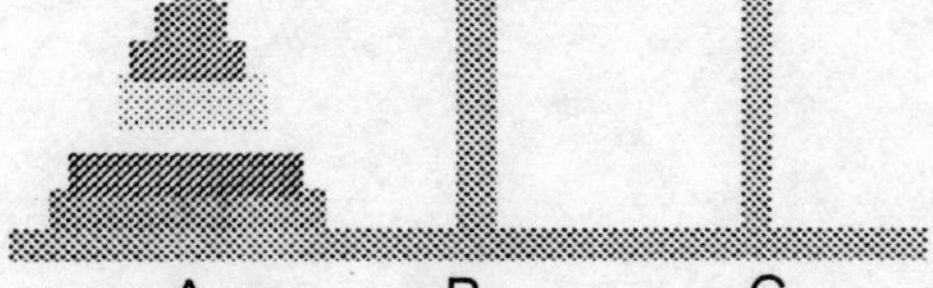

Step 1

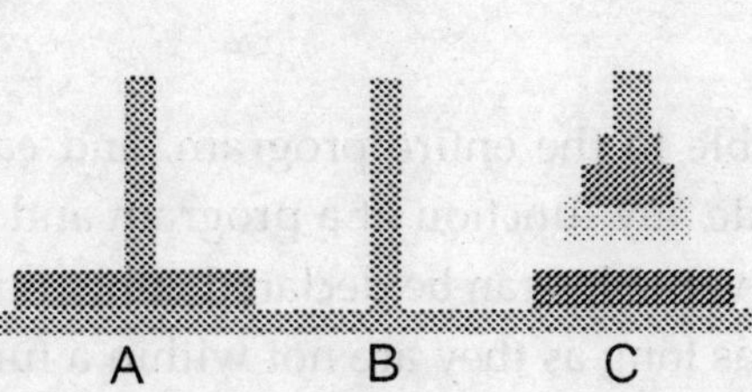

Step 2

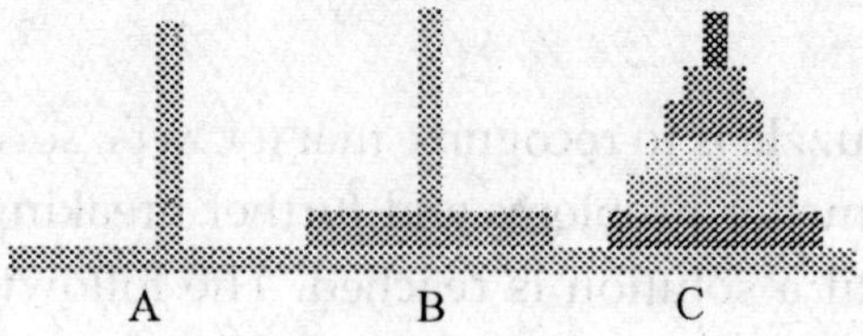

Step 3

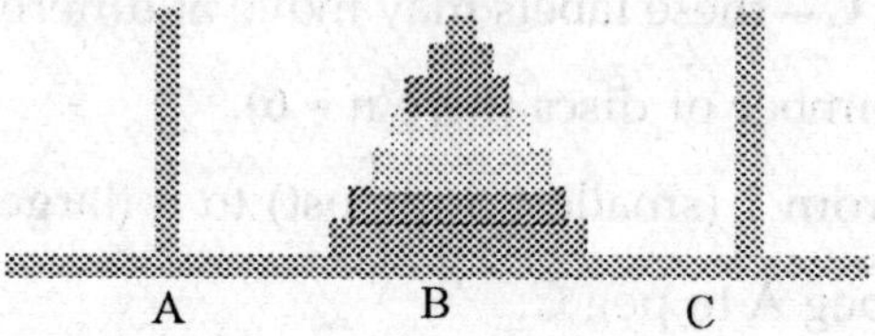

Step 4

Procedure:

```
MoveStack(n,A,C,B:Integer);
begin
if n=1
then MoveOne(A,C); {If there's only one to move, move it}
else
begin
{Move n-1 disks from peg A to peg B using C as the spare}
MoveStack(n-1,A,B,C);
MoveOne(A,C); {Move 1 disk to Peg C}
{Then move n-1 disks from B  to  C using A as the spare}
MoveStack(n-1,B,C,A);
end;
end;
```

VARIABLE STORAGE CLASSES

Global Variables

Global variables are visible to the entire program, and can be used anywhere in the code. They are declared outside any function of a program and hold their value throughout the program execution. These variables can be declared either outside the main( ) or declared any where before its first use as long as they are not within a function. However, it is best to declare global variables at the top of the program.

Example:

```
int ctr;                /* ctr is a global */
void book(void);
void main(void){
ctr = 10;
book( );
}
void book(void){
ctr=2;
——
——
}
```

Static Variables

Static variables are similar to automatic variables except that they retain the latest value when the block/function in which they are declared is reinvoked. The scope of such variables is limited to the block or the function in which they are declared.

Syntax:

```
static type variable_list;
```

Examples:

```
static int  a,b,c;
static float r,s;
```

There are two types of static variables:

1. Local static variable
2. Global static variable

The scope of the local static variable is local to that function in which they appear while the scope of the global static variable is throughout the program.

Following program is to understand the use of local static variable.

```
main( ){
int no,i;
printf("Enter the number whose table is required:");
```

```
scanf("%d",&no);
for(i=1;i<=10;i++)
func(no);
}
func(no)
int no;
{
static int step=0;
step = step + no;
printf("%d",step);
}
```

Output

5 10 15 20 25 30 35 40 45 50

Following program is to understand the use of global static variable:

```
static int no;
main( ){
no=5;
printf("In main() no = %d\n",no);
func1();
func2();
printf("After function call no = %d\n",no);
}
func1(){
int x=5;
no=no+x;
printf("\n func1() no = %d\n",no);
}
func2(){
int x=5;
no=no+x;
printf("\n func2() no = %d\n",no);
}
```

Output

in main() no = 5

in func1() no = 10

in func2() no = 15

After function call no = 15

TYPES OF STORAGE CLASSES

Mainly four storage classes are there:

- auto
- static
- register
- extern

auto	The default class. Automatic variables are local to their block. Their storage space is reclaimed on exit from the block.
register	If possible, the variable will be stored in a processor register. May give faster access to the variable. If register storage is not possible, then the variable will be of automatic class. Use of the register class is not recommended, as the compiler should be able to make better judgment about which variables to hold in registers, in fact injudicious use of register variables may slow down the program.
static	On exit from block, static variables are not reclaimed. They keep their value. On re-entry to the block, the variable will have its old value.
extern	Allows access to external variables. An external variable is either a global variable or a variable defined in another source file. External variables are defined outside of any function. (Note: Variables passed to a function and modified by way of a pointer are not external variables).
static external	External variables can be accessed by any function in any source file which make up the final program. Static external variables can only be accessed by functions in the same file as the variable declaration.

1. Auto

Automatic variables are declared inside a particular function and they are created when the function is called and destroyed when the function exits. Automatic variables are local or private to a function in which they are defined. By default, all the variables declared without any storage specification is automatic.

Scope: Within the block in which the variables are declared

Lifetime: Upto the closing brace of that code block

Storage: Allocated in stack

Example:

```
{
int Count;
auto int Month;
}
```

The example above defines two variables with the same storage class. Auto can only be used within functions, i.e., local variables.

/*Program to Illustrate the Working of Auto Variables*/

```
#include <stdio.h>
void main(){
int m=1000;
function2();
printf("%d\n",m);
}
function1(){
int m=10;
printf("%d\n",m);
}
function2(){
int m=100;
function1();
printf("%d\n",m);
}
```

A local variable declared in main lives throughout the whole program although it is accessible only in the main. A program with two subprograms function1 and function2 with m as automatic variable and is initialized to 10, 100, 1000 in function1, function2 and main respectively. When executes, main calls function2 which in turn calls function1. When main is active m = 1000. But when function2 is called, the main m is temporarily put on the shelf and the new local m = 100 becomes active. Similarly, when function1 is called both previous values of m are put on shelf and latest value (m = 10) become active, as soon as it is done main (m = 1000) takes over. The output clearly shows that value assigned to m in one function does not affect its value in the other function. The local value of m is destroyed when it leaves a function.

2. Static

Static is the default storage class for global variables.

Scope: Within the block in which the variables are declared.

Lifetime: Throughout the program.

Storage: Allocated in static storage

Note:

Static variable will be initialized automatically to NULL values. If a variable is declared with only the static storage class, its type is taken to be static int, i.e., static a = 10 is equivalent to static int a = 10.

Example:

```
static int Count;
static int Road;
main(){
printf("%d\n", Count);
printf("%d\n", Road);
}
```

The two variables above (Count and Road) both have a static storage class.

A static variable is initialized only once, when the program is compiled. It is never initialized again.

Example:

A program to illustrate the working of static variables

```
#include <stdio.h>
```

```
main(){
int j;
for(j=1;j<3;j++)
stat();
}
stat()
{
static int x=0;
x = x+1;
printf("x=%d\n",x);
}
```

During the first call to stat in the example shown above, x is incremented to 1. Since x is static, this value persists and therefore the next call adds another 1 to x giving it a value of 2. The value of x becomes 3 when third call is made. If we had declared x as an auto, then output would here been x = 1 all the three times.

'Static' can also be used to describe the visibility of objects.

For example:

```
static int x = 37;
static void f(){}
```

says that x and f() are not visible outside the source file where they're defined, and

```
void f(){
static int x = 47;
}
```

says that x is not visible outside of f().

There is an important use for static storage class in returning values. Let us consider an example.

```
char *Func(void);
main(){
char *Text1;
Text1 = Func();
```

```
}
char *Func(void){
char Text2[10]="martin";
return(Text2);
}
```

'Func' returns a pointer to the memory location where 'Text2' starts but Text2 has a storage class of auto and will disappear when we exit the function and could be overwritten by something else.

To overcome that problem, we have to declare Text2 variable as:

```
static char Text2[10]="martin";
```

As the lifetime of static is throughout the lifetime of the program, Text2 variable will exist even after the end of the function.

A variable can exist without being visible. If the variable is static, its lifetime is throughout the program where visibility is within that function/file. (This is proved from above example, Text2 variable's visibility ends after Func() returned, but lifetime still exists).

Static functions in C, not only a variable but also a function can be 'static'. A static function will become local to the file it is defined and will not be visible in any other source file.

Example:

```
static void f(){}
```

3. Register

Register variables are a special case of automatic variables. Automatic variables are allocated storage in the memory of the computer; however, for most computers, accessing data in memory is considerably slower than processing in the CPU. These computers often have small amounts of storage within the CPU itself where data can be stored and accessed quickly. These storage cells are called registers.

Normally, the compiler determines what data is to be stored in the registers of the CPU at what times. However, the C language provides the storage class register so that the programmer can "suggest" to the compiler that particular automatic variables should be allocated to CPU registers, if possible. Thus, register variables provide a certain control over efficiency of program execution. Variables which are used repeatedly or whose access times are critical may be declared to be of storage class register.

Allocating memory for variable in register is only suggestion to the compiler, not a compulsion.

Scope: Within the block in which the variables are declared

Lifetime: Upto the closing brace of that code block

Storage: Stored in register

Example:

register int Miles;

By using register storage class, we cannot improve program efficiency.

For example, if too many register variables are declared, or there are not enough registers available to store all of them, values in some registers would have to be moved to temporary storage in memory in order to clear those registers for other variables. Thus, much time may be wasted in moving data back and forth between registers and memory locations. In addition, the use of registers for variable storage may interfere with other uses of registers by the compiler, such as storage of temporary values in expression evaluation. In the end, use of register variables could actually result in slower execution. Register variables should only be used if you have a detailed knowledge of the architecture and compiler for the computer you are using. It is best to check the appropriate manuals if you should need to use register variables.

One disadvantage of register variables is we cannot apply unary '&' operator on the register variables as they don't have the memory locations.

4. Extern

In C, programmers are allowed to build libraries of functions. This means that function(s) required to run a program can be saved in separate file(s) which can be compiled separately and linked up with the file containing the main() function prior to running the program. In this case, however, if the function(s) use the same variable then their declaration would be done as follows:

```
int val;
main( ){
--
--
printf("Enter value:");
scanf("%d",&val);
calc( );
}
```

```
calc (){
extern int val;
——
——
}
```

Here that though val is available globally in program A, it has been declared again within the function calc() in program B, however the qualifier extern has been added to its declaration. The extern declaration in program B indicates to the compiler that the variable used in this program file has been declared in another program file. The extern declaration does not cause memory to be reserved for the variable. This is because memory is reserved when the variable is declared as global and the same variable cannot have two different memory locations.

If a function is defined in the same program file as the global variable and it uses the variable, then it can also contain an extern declaration for that variable, though it is not necessary.

Every C variable has a storage class and a scope. The storage class determines the part of memory where storage is allocated for an object and how long the storage allocation continues to exist. It also determines the scope which specifies the part of the program over which a variable name is visible, i.e., the variable is accessible by name.

The extern defines a global variable that is visible to ALL object modules. When you use 'extern' the variable cannot be initialized at all, what it does is point the variable name at a storage location that has been previously defined.

Scope: Within the file in which the variables are declared

Lifetime: Throughout the duration of the program

Storage: Allocated in the heap

Review Questions

1. Is main() a user-defined function. How does it differ from other user-defined functions?
2. Distinguish between the following: (i) actual and formal arguments and (ii) global and local variables.
3. What does a static variable mean?
4. Where are the auto variables stored?
5. What are the differences between formal arguments and actual arguments?
6. What is a function? Is the use of functions required when writing a C program?
7. State several advantages to the use of functions.
8. What is meant by a function call? From what parts of a program can a function be called?

9. What are arguments? What is their purpose?
10. What is the purpose of a return statement?
11. Explain about the Towers of Hanoi as a mathematical game or puzzle.
12. What are the three principal components of a function definition?
13. How is the first line of a function definition written? What is the use of each item, or group of items?
14. Describe about storage allocation and scope of global, extern, static, local and register variables?
15. What are register variables? What are the advantages of using register variables?
16. What are storage memory, default value, scope and life of Static and External storage class?
17. Can using the register storage class always improve program efficiency?
18. Why is it sometimes desirable to pass a pointer to a function as an argument?
19. What are formal arguments? What are actual arguments? What is the relationship between formal and actual arguments?
20. How are formal arguments declared in a function?
21. What relationship must exist between the data type that appears in the first line of the function definition and the expression that is included in the return statement?
22. Can a function be called from more than one place within a program?
23. Explain the difference between a function declaration and a function definition.
24. What is the purpose of keyword void in a function declaration and function definition?
25. What advantage is there in using function prototypes in a program?
26. What is recursion? What is its advantage?
27. What is recursion? Write a program using recursion (factorial)?
28. What is scope and storage allocation of global and extern variables? Explain with an example.
29. What is scope and storage allocation of static, local and register variables? Explain with an example.

ଓଓଓ

CHAPTER 6

Arrays and Strings

An array in C is a group of same type of variables referenced under a common name using an index. String in C, on other hand, is another name for character array terminated with a null character and has some special properties. Both arrays and strings are stored in continuous memory location. An array is one which can hold more than one data or variable at a time but of same data type. Also array can be single or multidimensional widening the field of situation which they can be applied to.

TYPES OF ARRAYS

(1) Single Dimensional Array

(2) Two-dimensional Array

(3) Multidimensional Array

(4) Passing Array as Parameter

(5) Initializing Array

(6) Variable Length Array

(7) Strings

SINGLE DIMENSIONAL ARRAY

Also known as 1-D array because of its logical representation of one dimension data.

The general form of declaration of 1-D Array is –

Datatype arrayname [size];

Here, 'datatype' is the type of the variables collected under the common name. The 'arrayname' is the common name used to reference the collected variables. The 'size' is the size of the array or the number of variables collected in the array. One important thing is that in this declaration the size should be constant hence making array of this type static with fixed size. This may seem to be a very big restriction on arrays but dynamic variable length arrays can be created in C using dynamic memory allocation.

Each element in the array is stored in contiguous memory location. Total size of array is product of size of the each variable and number of each variable.

Diagram below shows the logical memory representation of 1-D Array (A — Array Name, X — Array Starting Memory Location, V - Size of each element in Bits).

A[0]	A[1]	A[2]	N elements	A[N+1]	A[N+2]	A[N+3]
X	X+V	X+2V	X+3V	X+NV	X+(N+1)V	X+(N+2)V

Elements in array are accessed through an index with valid value 0 to n-1 if n is the size of the array.

One other point to be always kept in mind is that the array boundary can be over-runned since C provides no boundary checking and it is a sole responsibility of the programmer. This is a very dangerous situation because your code is modifying memory outside of what is allocated to it. You may write into some critical data, Operating System Memory, Stack etc., which may lead to severe program and Operating System crashes.

Following C program shows how to use a one-dimensional array in C.

```
// Program showing potential use of 1-D Array
#include <stdio.h>
int main(){
int value [1000],i; // Declaring an Array
for (i = 0; i<1000; i++){
 value [i] = i; // Loading the Array
}
for (i = 0; i<1000; i++){
printf ("\n%d",value [i]); // Displaying the Array
}
return 0;
}
```

TWO DIMENSIONAL ARRAY

Next in complexity to one-dimensional array are two-dimensional arrays, also known as 2-D array.

The general form of declaration of 2-D Array is:

Data type arrayname [size1] [size2];

Here, 'size1' is the number of 1-D Arrays and 'size2' is the size of each of that 1-D Array.

2-D arrays can be mentally represented as a matrix with 'size1' number of rows and 'size2' number of columns. This can be shown in the table below:

N elements

A[0][0]	A[0][1]	A[0][2]		A[0][N+1]	A[0][N+2]	A[0][N+3]
A[1][0]	A[1][1]	A[1][2]		A[1][N+1]	A[1][N+2]	A[1][N+3]
A[2][0]	A[2][1]	A[2][2]		A[2][N+1]	A[2][N+2]	A[2][N+3]
M elements						
A[M+1][0]	A[M+1][1]	A[M+1][2]		A[M+1][N+1]	A[M+1][N+2]	A[M+1][N+3]
A[M+2][0]	A[M+2][1]	A[M+2][2]		A[M+2][N+1]	A[M+2][N+2]	A[M+2][N+3]

Total size of the 2-D array = size1 * size2 * size of each variable.

In 2-D array also, the index begins with 0 for both parameters. Row value can have possible values 0 to size1 - 1 and columns can have possible values from 0 to size2 - 1.

C program below shows the declaration and input/output operations on a 2-D array.

```
// Program showing potential use of 2-D Array
#include <stdio.h>
int main(){
int value [100] [100],i,j; // Declaring an Array
for (j = 0; j<100; j++){
for (i = 0; i<100; i++){
value [j] [i] = j*100+i; // Loading the Array
}
}
for (j = 0; j<100; j++){
for (i = 0; i<100; i++){
printf ("\n%d",value [j] [i]); // Displaying the Array
```

```
}
}
return 0;
}
```

MULTIDIMENSIONAL ARRAY

C Programming language allows more than 2-D array where most of other languages of its class does not show that C is designed to allow scope for infinite applications.

The general form of declaration of Multidimensional array is:

Data type arrayname [size1] [size2] .... [sizeX];

The array of type above is called X-D array.

Size of this X-D array = size1 * size2 * size3 * ... * sizeX * size of each variable.

Though allowed array of greater dimension than 3-D is not used because size of the array increases exponentially as dimension increases. Also time to access array indexes increases decreasing the programs efficiency.

Following diagram shows logical memory representation of a 3-D array as array of 2-D arrays –

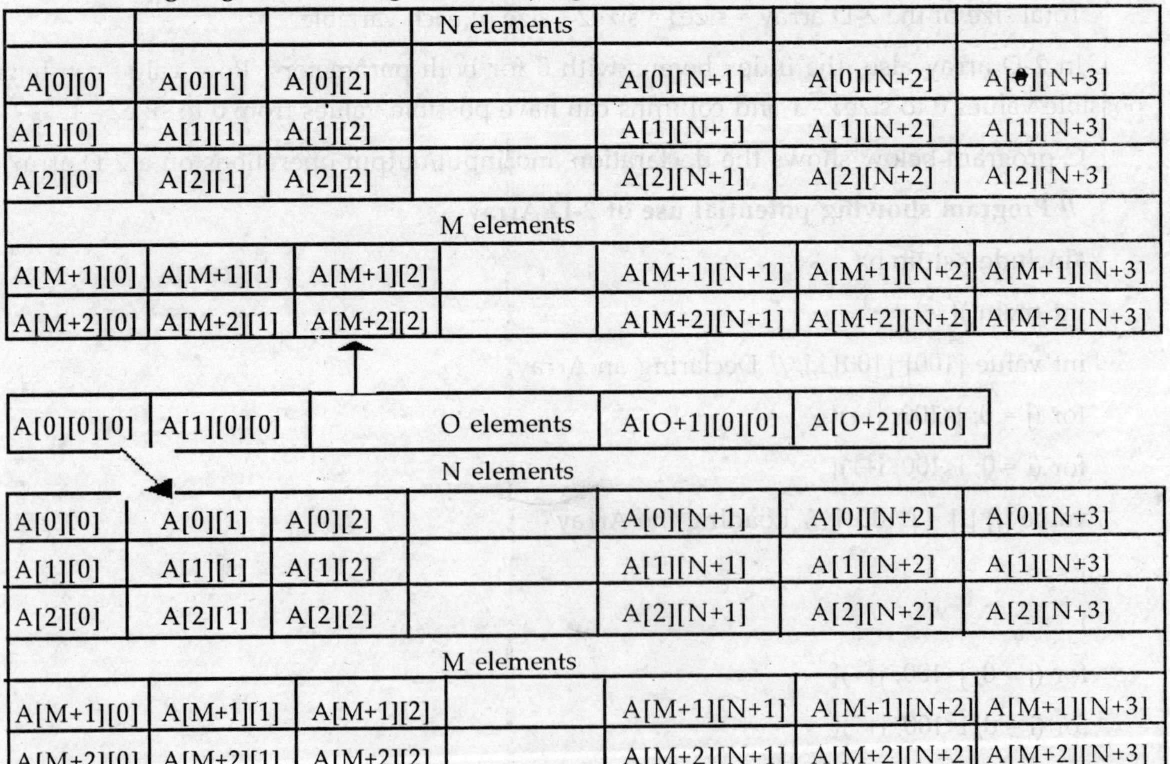

C program below shows the declaration and input/output operations on a 3-D array.

```
// Program showing potential use of 3-D Array
#include <stdio.h>
int main(){
int value [10] [10] [10] ,i,j,k; // Declaring an Array
for (k = 0; k<10; k++){
for (j = 0; j<10; j++){
for (i = 0; i<10; i++){
value [k] [j] [i] = k*10+j*10+i; // Loading the Array
}
}
}
for (k = 0; k<10; k++){
for (int j = 0; j<100; j++){
for (int i = 0; i<100; i++){
printf ("\n%d",value [k] [j] [i]); // Displaying the Array
}
}
}
return 0;
}
```

PASSING ARRAY AS PARAMETER

In C, entire array cannot be passed as parameter to function entirely. Instead only the base address of the pointer is passed as an argument. This leads to restriction that arrays can be passed only by call by reference method unlike any other variables which can be passed both by call by reference and call by value. This restriction can be easily overcome by declaring passed argument as constant pointer making the function unable to modify the parameter passed simulating call by value to certain extent.

General form passing array as parameter is:

return_type function_name (name [size1] [size2] .... [sizeX]);

Also the left most size (size1) is optional because compiler can calculate its value from the size of array but rest of the sizes is necessary so another general form is:

return_type function_name (name [ ] [size2] .... [sizeX]);

C program below shows the passing of a 1-D, 2-D and 3-D array as parameter to functions.

```
// Program showing passing of 1-D, 2-D and 3-D Array as parameter
#include <stdio.h>
void input1D (int data [1000]);
void input2D (int data [100][100]);
void input3D (int data [10][10][10]);
void display1D (int data []);
void display2D (int data [][100]);
void display3D (int data [][10][10]);
int main(){
int array1D [1000];
int array2D [100] [100];
int array3D [10] [10] [10];
// Passing Array by First Form
void input1D (int array1D []);
void input2D (int array2D [][100]);
void input3D (int array3D [][10][10]);
// Passing Array by second Form
void display1D (int display1D []);
void display2D (int display2D [][100]);
void display3D (int display3D [][10][10]);
return 0;
}
void input1D (int data [1000]){
int value [1000],i; // Declaring an Array
for (i = 0; i<1000; i++){
value [i] = i; // Loading the Array
```

```
}
}
void input2D (int data [100][100]){
 int value [100] [100],i,j; // Declaring an Array
for (j = 0; j<100; j++){
for (i = 0; i<100; i++){
value [j] [i] = j*10+i; // Loading the Array
}
}
}
void input3D (int data [10][10][10]){
int value [10] [10] [10] ,i,j,k; // Declaring an Array
for (k = 0; k<10; k++){
for (j = 0; j<10; j++){
for (i = 0; i<10; i++){
value [k] [j] [i] = k*10+j*10+i; // Loading the Array
}
}
}
}
void display1D (int data []){
int value [1000],i;
for (i = 0; i<1000; i++){
value [i] = i; // Loading the Array
}
}
void display2D (int data [][100]){
int value [100] [100],i,j
for (j = 0; j<100; j++){
```

```
for (i = 0; i<100; i++){
printf ("\n%d",value [j] [i]); // Displaying the Array
}
}
}
void display3D (int data [][10][10]){
int value [10] [10] [10] ,i,j,k;
for (k = 0; k<10; k++){
for (int j = 0; j<100; j++){
for (int i = 0; i<100; i++){
printf ("\n%d",value [k] [j] [i]); // Displaying the Array
}
}
}
}
```

INITIALIZING ARRAY

Values in array can be initialized at the time of their declaration. This is important because they may contain garbage value, if not initialized properly and their usage may be dangerous. Some compilers make sure that initialized values be 0 or NULL.

The general form of array initialization is:

Type name [size1] [size2] .... [sizeX] = {values};

Values is a comma separated list of constants or variables, which in case of multi-dimensional array is in subaggregated form.

If array is half or partially initialized, the rest of the values are automatically changed to zero or NULL.

C program below shows the initialization of a 1-D and 2-D array.

```
// Program showing initialization of 1-D and 2-D Array
#include <stdio.h>
int main(){
int array1D [10], array2D [2] [5], i,j; // Declaring an Array
```

```
array1D = {0,1,2,3,4,5,6,7,8,9}; // Initialization of 1D Array
array2D = {
// Initialization of 2D Array
{1,1},
{2,2},
{3,3},
{4,4},
{5,5},
};
for (i = 0; i<10; i++){
printf ("\n%d",array1D [i]); // Displaying the Array
}
for (j=0; j<2; j++){
for (i = 0; i<5; i++){
printf ("\n%d",array2D [j] [i]); // Displaying the Array
}
}
return 0;
}
```

One thing that can be noted is that during initialization that left most index is optional (that means all index in 1-D Array). This is because the compiler automatically set its value to the minimum value of the size required to store all the initializations safely. This feature provides an innate advantage of overcoming the human error of wrong index value calculation. Now we re-write the above program to show the feature of unsized array initialization in C.

The general form of unsized array initialization is:

```
type name (name [] [size2] .... [sizeX]) = {values};
```

```
// Program showing unisized array initialization of 1-D and 2-D Array
#include <stdio.h>
int main(){
int i,j;
```

```
int array1D [] = {0,1,2,3,4,5,6,7,8,9}; // Unsized Array Initialization of 1D Array
int array2D [][2] = { // Unsized Array Initialization of 2D Array
{1,1},
{2,2},
{3,3},
{4,4},
{5,5},
};
for (i = 0; i<10; i++){
printf ("\n%d",array1D [i]);
}
for (j=0; j<2; j++){
for (i = 0; i<5; i++){
printf ("\n%d",array2D [j] [i]);
}
}
return 0;
}
```

VARIABLE LENGTH ARRAY

As discussed above, the size of the array has to be constant otherwise program wont compile. This imposes a severe instruction on the array because its size is limited at compile time. As a result, the array formed is static who's size cannot be neither decreased nor increased. This is often against what is required because in many programs size of the array required is known only at run time. For overcoming this restriction, we use variable length array whose length can be varied at run time. There are two methods.

In first method, we use dynamic memory allocation which will be discussed latter in detail. We take a quick look here how it can solve the problem. We will use malloc function to get us memory for the array dynamically and the amount of memory fetched is also calculated at run time based on parameter passed to the function. We also use a little use of pointers which is discussed in details in next chapter.

/*Program below shows the potential use of dynamic memory allocation to create variable length array*/

```
#include <stdio.h>
#include <alloc.h>
int * createarray (int length)
// This function creates array dynamically on basis of parameter passed and return its base.
{
int *array;
array = (int *) malloc(length * size of (int));
return array;
}
int main(){
int* array1;
int* array2;
array1 = createarray (1000); //Creates array of size 1000.
array2 = createarray (10000); //Creates array of size 10000.
return 0;
}
```

This program construct is itself called variable length array and is used to create variable length arrays. One important restriction is that they can create only local dynamic arrays, i.e., global scope dynamic array is not allowed. They work because they allow a variable to be used as declaring array size whose value is evaluated at run time.

/* Program below shows the correct use to construct variable length array and to create dynamic arrays*/

```
#include <stdio.h>
void createarray (int length)
// This function creates array dynamically on basis of parameter passed
{
  int array [length];
  for (i = 0; i<length; i++){
```

```
array [i] = i; // Loading the Array
    }
for (i = 0; i<length; i++){
printf ("\n%d",array [i]); // Displaying the Array
}
}
int main (){
createarray (1000); //Creates array of size 1000.
return 0;
}
```

STRINGS

A string is a sequence of characters or an array of characters. Any sequence or set of characters defined within double quotation symbols is a constant string. In C, it is required to do some meaningful operations on strings. They are:

- Reading string
- Displaying strings
- Combining or concatenating strings
- Copying one string to another.
- Comparing string and checking whether they are equal
- Extraction of a portion of a string

Strings are stored in memory as ASCII codes of characters that make up the string appended with '\0' (ASCII value of null). Normally, each character is stored in one byte; successive characters are stored in successive bytes.

INITIALIZING STRINGS

Following the discussion on character arrays, the initialization of a string must be of the following form which is simpler to one-dimensional array.

```
char month1[ ]={'j','a','n','u','a','r','y'};
```

Then the string month is initialized to January. This is perfectly valid but C offers a special way to initialize strings.

The above string can be initialized as:

```
char month1[]="january";
```

The characters of the string are enclosed within a part of double quotes. The compiler takes care of string enclosed within a pair of double quotes. The compiler takes care of storing the ASCII codes of characters of the string in the memory and also stores the null terminator in the end.

/* Program to read and print a string variable*/

```
#include <stdio.h>
main(){
char month[15];
printf ("Enter the string");
gets (month);
printf ("The string entered is %s", month);
}
```

In this example, string is stored in the character variable month, the string is displayed in the statement.

```
printf("The string entered is %s", month");
```

It is one-dimensional array. Each character occupies a byte. A null character (\0) that has the ASCII value 0 terminates the string. The figure shows the storage of string "january" in the memory recall that, while '\0' specifies a single character whose ASCII value is zero.

j

a

n

u

a

r

y

\0

Character string terminated by a null character '\0'.

ARRAY OF STRINGS

A string variable is any valid C variable name and is always declared as an array. The general form of declaration of a string variable is:

char string_name[size];

The size determines the number of characters in the string name.

Example:

char month[10];

char address[100];

The size of the array should be one byte more than the actual space occupied by the string since the complier appends a null character at the end of the string.

Reading Strings from the Terminal

The function scanf with %s format specification is needed to read the character string from the terminal.

Example:

char address[15];

scanf("%s",address);

The scanf statement has a drawback, it just terminates the statement as soon as it finds a blank space, suppose if we type the string, new york, then only the string new will be read and since there is a blank space after word "new" it will terminate the string.

Note that we can use the scanf without the ampersand symbol before the variable name.

In many applications, it is required to process text by reading an entire line of text from the terminal.

The function getchar can be used repeatedly to read a sequence of successive single characters and store it in the array.

We cannot manipulate strings since C does not provide any operators for string. For instance, we cannot assign one string to another directly.

For example:

string="xyz";

string1=string2;

The above statements are not valid.

To copy the chars in one string to another string, we may do so on a character to character basis.

Writing Strings to Screen

The printf statement along with format specifier %s to print strings on to the screen. The format %s can be used to display an array of characters that is terminated by the null character.

For example:

printf("%s",name);

can be used to display the entire contents of the array name.

STRING/DATA CONVERSION

Arithmetic Operations on Characters

We can also manipulate the characters as we manipulate numbers in C language. Whenever the system encounters the character data, it is automatically converted into an integer value by the system. We can represent a character as an interface by using the following method.

X='a';

printf("%d\n",x);

The executed program displays 97 on the screen. Arithmetic operations can also be performed on characters for example x='z'-1; is a valid statement. The ASCII value of 'z' is 122, the statement therefore will assign 121 to variable x.

It is also possible to use character constants in relational expressions

For example:

ch>'a' && ch < = 'z' will check whether the character stored in variable ch is a lower case letter. A character digit can also be converted into its equivalent integer value suppose the expression a=character-'1';

where a is defined as an integer variable and character contains value 8

then a= ASCII value of 8 ASCII value '1'=56-49=7.

We can also get the support of the C library function to convert a string of digits into their equivalent integer values.

The general format of the function in x=atoi(string)

Here, x is an integer variable and string is a character array containing string of digits.

STRING MANIPULATION FUNCTIONS

String Operations (string.h)

C language recognizes that string is a different class of array by letting us input and output the array as a unit and is terminated by null character. C library supports a large number of string handling functions that can be used to array out many of the string manipulations such as:

- Length (number of characters in the string)
- Concatenation (adding two are more strings)
- Comparing two strings.
- Substring (extract substring from a given string)
- Copy (copies one string over another)

To do all the operations described here, it is essential to include string.h library header file in the program.

The nine most commonly used functions in the string library are:

strlen - get string length

strcat - concatenate two strings

strcmp - compare two strings

strcpy - copy a string

strcmpi - compares two strings but not case sensitive

strlwr - converts all characters in a string from uppercase to lowercase

strrev - reverses the characters in a string

strupr - converts all characters in a string from lower case to uppercase.

strncmp - compares the first N characters of each string/ compare parts of two strings

Other operations are:

strchr - string scanning operation

strncat - concatenate one string with part of another

strncpy - copy part of a string

strrchr - string scanning operation

strlen() Function

This function counts and returns the number of characters in a string. The length does not include a null character.

Syntax n=strlen(string);

Where n is integer variable. This receives the value of length of the string.

Example:

length=strlen("Hollywood");

The function will assign number of characters 9 in the string to an integer variable length.

```
\/*Program to find the length of the string using strlen() function*/
#include <stdio.h>
include <string.h>
void main(){
char name[100];
int length;
printf("Enter the string");
gets(name);
length=strlen(name);
printf("\nNumber of characters in the string is=%d", length);
}
```

strcat() Function

When you combine two strings, you add the characters of one string to the end of other string. This process is called concatenation. The strcat() function joins two strings together. It takes the following form:

strcat(string1,string2)

The string1 and string2 are character arrays. When the function strcat is executed, string2 is appended to string1. The string at string2 remains unchanged.

Example:

```
strcpy(string1,"Mera");
strcpy(string2,"bharath");
Printf("%s",strcat(string1,string2);
```

From the above program segment, the value of string1 becomes Merabharath. The string at str2 remains unchanged as bharath.

strcmp() Function

In C, you cannot directly compare the value of two strings in a condition like if(string1==string2).

Most libraries, however, contain the strcmp() function, which returns a zero if 2 strings are equal, or a non-zero number if the strings are not the same. The syntax of strcmp() is given below:

strcmp(string1,string2)

The string1 and string2 may be string variables or string constants. Some computers return a negative value if the string1 is alphabetically less than the second and a positive number if the string is greater than the second.

Example:

strcmp("Newyork","Newyork") will return zero because 2 strings are equal.

strcmp("their","there") will return a -9 which is the numeric difference between ASCII 'i' and ASCII 'r'.

strcmp("The", "the") will return -32 which is the numeric difference between ASCII "T" & ASCII "t".

strcmpi() Function

This function is same as strcmp() which compares two strings but not case sensitive.

Example:

strcmpi("THE","the"); will return 0.

strcpy() Function

C does not allow you to assign the characters to a string directly as in the statement name="Robert";

Instead use the strcpy() function found in most compilers.

The syntax of the function is illustrated below:

strcpy(string1,string2);

strcpy function assigns the contents of string2 to string1. string2 may be a character array variable or a string constant.

strcpy(Name,"Robert");

In the above example Robert is assigned to the string called Name.

strlwer () Function

This function converts all characters in a string from uppercase to lowercase.

Syntax:

strlwr(string);

For example:

strlwr("EXFORSYS") converts to exforsys.

strrev() Function

This function reverses the characters in a string.

Syntax:

strrev(string);

For example:

strrev("program") reverses the characters in a string into "margorp".

strupr() Function

This function converts all characters in a string from lower case to uppercase.

Syntax:

strupr(string);

For example:

strupr("exforsys") will convert the string to EXFORSYS.

Example

```
/*Program to / Use String Functions*/
#include <stdio.h>
#include <string.h>
void main(){
char s1[20],s2[20],s3[20];
int x,l1,l2,l3;
printf("Enter the strings");
scanf("%s%s",s1,s2);
x=strcmp(s1,s2);
if(x!=0) {
printf("\nStrings are not equal\n");
strcat(s1,s2);
}
else
printf("\nStrings are equal");
strcpy(s3,s1);
```

```
l1=strlen(s1);
l2 =strlen(s2);
l3=strlen(s3);
printf("\ns1=%s\t length=%d characters\n",s1,l1);
printf("\ns2=%s\t length=%d characters\n",s2,l2);
printf("\ns3=%s\t length=%d characters\n",s3,l3);
}
```

strncmp() Function

This function compares the first N characters of each string. If the first string is greater than the second, it returns a number greater than zero. If the second string is greater, it returns a number less than zero. If the strings are equal, it returns 0. Its prototype is:

int strncmp(const char *first, const char *second, size_t N);

C Program Examples

```
/*Program to Print
1
2 3
4 5 6
7 8 9 10*/
#include <stdio.h>
int main(){
int i, j, ctr = 1;
for (i = 1; i < 5; i++){
for (j = 1; j <= i; j++){
printf("%2d ", ctr++);
}
printf("\n");
}
return 0;
}
```

/*Program to Print an Array in Ascending or Descending Order*/

```
#include <stdio.h>
#include <conio.h>
void main(){
int i,j,a[50],n,t,opt,s;
printf("enter the size of the array");
scanf("%d",&n);
printf("enter the elements of the array");
for(i=0;i<n;i++)
scanf("%d",&a[i]);
printf("1.ascending order\n 2.descending order\n");
printf("enter your option");
scanf("%d",&opt);
switch(opt){
case 1: for(i=0;i<n-1;i++){
 for(j=i+1;j<n;j++){
if(a[i]>a[j]){
s=a[i];
a[i]=a[j];
a[j]=s;
}
}
}
printf("\n the sorted nos are");
for(i=0;i<n;i++)
printf("%d",a[i]);
break;
case 2: for(i=0;i<n-1;i++){
for(j=i+1;j<n;j++){
```

```
if(a[i]<a[j]){
s=a[i];
a[i]=a[j];
a[j]=s;
}
}
}
printf("\n the sorted nos in descending order are");
for(i=0;i<n;i++)
printf("%d",a[i]);
break
}
getch();
}
```

/*Program to Find the Sum of Any Two Matrices*/

```
#include <stdio.h>
#include <conio.h>
void main(){
int m,n,p,q,i,j;
 int a[10][10],b[10][10],c[10][10];
clrscr();
printf("A, B are two matrices of order m*n, p*q");
printf("\nenter the values of m,n,p,q:");
scanf("%d%d%d%d",&m,&n,&p,&q);
if(m==p && n==q){
printf("enter the elements of matrix A:");
for(i=0;i<m;i++){
for(j=0;j<n;j++)
scanf("%d",&a[i][j]);
```

```
}
printf("enter the elements of matrix B:");
for(i=0;i<p;i++){
for(j=0;j<q;j++)
scanf("%d",&b[i][j]);
}
printf("the resultant matrix after addition is:");
for(i=0;i<p;i++){
for(j=0;j<q;j++){
c[i][j]=a[i][j]+b[i][j];
printf("%d\t",c[i][j]);
}
printf("\n");
}
}
else
printf("the order of the matrices should be same");
getch();
}
```

/*Program to Find the Determinant of a 2 × 2 matrix*/

```
#include <stdio.h>
#include <conio.h>
void main(){
int i,j,det,a[2][2];
clrscr();
printf("enter the elements of matrix A:");
for(i=0;i<2;i++){
for(j=0;j<2;j++)
scanf("%d",&a[i][j]);
```

```
}
det=a[0][0]*a[1][1]-a[0][1]*a[1][0];
printf("determinant =%d\t",det);
getch();
}
```

/*Program to Accept an Array in Matrix Form and Display*/

```
#include <stdio.h>
#include <conio.h>
void main(){
int i,j,p,q,a[10][10];
printf("enter the order of matrix");
scanf("%d %d",&p,&q);
for(i=0;i<p;i++){
for(j=0;j<q;j++){
 printf("enter%drow%dcolumn elements",i+1,j+1);
 scanf("%d",&a[i][j]);
}
}
for(i=0;i<p;i++){
for(j=0;j<q;j++){
printf("  %d\t",a[i][j]);
}
printf("\n");
}
}
```

/*Program to Find the Determinant and Inverse of a 2 × 2matrix*/

```
#include <stdio.h>
#include <conio.h>
void main(){
```

```
int i,j,det,a[2][2],b[2][2];
clrscr();
printf("enter the elements of matrix A:");
for(i=0;i<2;i++){
for(j=0;j<2;j++)
scanf("%d",&a[i][j]);
}
det=a[0][0]*a[1][1]-a[0][1]*a[1][0];
printf("determinant =%d\t",det);
b[0][0]=a[1][1]/det;
b[0][1]=-a[0][1]/det;
b[1][0]=-a[1][0]/det;
b[1][1]=a[0][0]/det;
printf("\nthe inverse of matrix is:\n");
for(i=0;i<2;i++){
for(j=0;j<2;j++){
printf("%d\t",b[i][j]);
}
printf("\n");
}
getch();
}
```

/*Program to Find the Transpose of a Matrix*/

```
#include <stdio.h>
#include <conio.h>
void main(){
int i,j,m,n,a[10][10],b[10][10];
clrscr();
printf("order of matrix A");
```

```
printf("enter the values of m & n:");
scanf("%d%d",&m,&n);
printf("enter the elements of matrix A:");
for(i=0;i<m;i++){
for(j=0;j<n;j++)
scanf("%d",&a[i][j]);
}
printf("\nthe transpose of matrix is:\t");
for(i=0;i<m;i++){
for(j=0;j<n;j++){
b[i][j]=a[j][i];
printf("%d\t",b[i][j]);
}
printf("\n");
}
getch();
}
```

/*Program to Find the Product of Two Matrices*/

```
#include <stdio.h>
#include <conio.h>
void main(){
int m,n,p,q,s,i,j,k;
int a[10][10],b[10][10],c[10][10];
clrscr();
printf("enter the order and elements of matrix A:");
scanf("%d%d",&n,&m);
for(i=0;i<n;i++){
for(j=0;j<m;j++)
scanf("%d",&a[i][j]);
```

```
}
printf("enter the order and elements of matrix B:");
scanf("%d%d",&p,&q);
for(j=0;j<p;j++){
for(k=0;k<q;k++)
scanf("%d",&b[j][k]);
}
if(m==p){
printf("the resultant product matrix is:\n");
for(i=0;i<n;i++){
for(k=0;k<q;k++){
s=0;
for(j=0;j<p;j++){
s=s+(a[i][j]*b[j][k]);
}
c[i][k]=s;
printf("%d\t",c[i][k]);
}
printf("\n");
}
}
else
printf("the matrices cannot be multiplied");
getch();
}
```

/*Program — Array Sorting*/

```
#include <stdio.h>
#include <conio.h>
void main(){
```

```
int i,j,p,q,t,s,a[10][10],b[30];
printf("enter the order of the matrix");
scanf("%d %d",&p,&q);
printf("enter %d values of p and %d q",p,q);
t=0;
for(i=0;i<p;i++){
for(j=0;j<q;j++){
scanf("%d",&a[i][j]);
b[t]=a[i][j];
t++;
}
}
for(i=0;i<t;i++){
for(j=i+1;j<t;j++){
if(b[i]<b[j]){
s=b[i];
b[i]=b[j];
b[j]=s;
}
}
}
printf("\n the elements of matrix A are");
for(i=0;i<p;i++){
printf("\n");
for(j=0;j<q;j++)
printf("%d\t",a[i]);
}
t=0;
for(i=0;i<p;i++){
```

```
for(j=0;j<q;j++){
a[i][j]=b[t];
t++;
}
}
printf("after sorting");
for(i=0;i<p;i++){
printf("\n");
for(j=0;j<q;j++)
printf("%d\t",a[i][j]);
}
getch();
}
```

/*Program to Print Sequence of Characters*/

```
#include <stdio.h>
#include <conio.h>
void main(){
char s[20],s2[20];
clrscr();
int i,j;
printf("enter a string\n");
scanf("%s",s);
printf("\n\n");
for(i=0;i<=10;i++){
j=i+1;
printf("%-2.*s\n",j,s);
}
printf("— — — — — — — — — — — — — \n");
for(i=10;i>=0;i—){
```

```
j=i+1;
printf("%-12.*s\n",j,s);
}
printf("————————————\n");
}
```

/*Program to Concatenate Two Strings*/

```
#include <stdio.h>
#include <string.h>
#include <conio.h>
void main(){
char s1[20],s2[20];
clrscr();
printf("enter any two strings\n");
gets(s1);
gets(s2);
puts(strcat(s1,s2));
getch();
}
```

/*Program — Copying Two Strings*/

```
#include <stdio.h>
#include <conio.h>
#include <string.h>
void main(){
char s1[20],s2[20];
clrscr();
int i;
printf("enter any  string\n");
gets(s1);
gets(s2);
```

```
strcpy(s1,s2);
//printf("after copying the string s2 to s1: %s",s1);
i=strlen(s1);
printf("\nthe length of the string %s is %d",s1,i);
getch();
}
```

/*Program — Comparing Two Strings*/

```
#include <stdio.h>
#include <conio.h>
#include <string.h>
void main(){
char s1[20],s2[20];
clrscr();
int i,j;
printf("enter any two strings\n");
gets(s1);
gets(s2);
i=strcmp(s1,gets(s1));
j=strcmp(s1,s2);
printf("\n%s,%s",s1[20],s2[20]);
printf("%d%d",i,j);
getch();
}
```

/*Program to Copy One String into Another*/

```
#include <stdio.h>
#include <conio.h>
void main(){
char s1[20],s2[20];
clrscr();
```

```
int i;
printf("enter a string in string s2\n");
scanf("%s",s2);
for(i=0;s2[i]!='\0';i++)
s1[i]=s2[i];
s1[i]='\0';
printf("\n");
printf("after copying in s1 :%s\n",s1);
printf("no. of strings=%d\n",i);
}
```

/*Program to Reverse a String without Using String Function*/

```
#include <stdio.h>
#include <conio.h>
void main(){
int i;
char s[20];
clrscr();
printf("enter any string\n");
scanf("%s",&s);
for(i=0;s[i]!='\0';i++){
for(i=i-1;i>=0;i++)
printf("%c",s[i]);
}
getch();
}
```

/*Program — Using String Handling Functions*/

```
#include <stdio.h>
#include <conio.h>
#include <string.h>
```

```
void main(){
char s1[20],s2[20],s3[20];
clrscr();
int x,i,j,k;
printf("enter any two string constants\n");
scanf("%s%s",s1,s2);
x=strcmp(s1,s2);//comparing the strings s1 and s2
if(x!=0){
printf("\n strings are not equal");
}
else
printf("\n strings are equal\n");
strcpy(s3,s1);// copying s1 to s3
printf("\nafter copying string s1 to s3%s",s3);
i=strlen(s1);//to find the length of each string
j=strlen(s2);
k=strlen(s3);
printf("\ns1=%s\t length=%d characters\n",s1,i);
printf("\ns3=%s\t length=%d characters\n",s2,j);
printf("\ns3=%s\t length=%d characters\n",s3,k);
getch();
}
```

/*Program to Count Characters, Special Characters and Words Using Strings*/

```
#include <stdio.h>
#include <conio.h>
#include <string.h>
#include <stdlib.h>
void main(){
char s[20];
```

```
clrscr();
int nch=0,nw=0,nsch=0,i=0;
printf("enter any string\n");
gets(s);
while(s[i]!='\0'){
if((s[i]>='a')&& (s[i]<='z'))
nch++;
else if(s[i]=='\0'){
nw++;
nch++;
}
else
nsch++;i++;
}
printf("no. of characters in agiven string are %d\n",nch);
printf("no. of special characters in a given string are %d\n",nsch);
printf("no. of words in a given string are %d\n",nw);
getch();
}
```

/*Program — Reverse of a String*/

```
#include <stdio.h>
#include <conio.h>
#include <string.h>
void main(){
char s[20];
clrscr();
printf("enter any string\n");
gets(s);
puts(strrev(s));
```

```
getch();
}
```

/*Program to Compare Two Strings Without Using String Functions*/

```
#include <stdio.h>
#include <string.h>
#include <conio.h>
#define null '\0'
void main(){
char s1[20],s2[20];
clrscr();
printf("enter any two strings\n");
gets(s1);
gets(s2);
strcmp(s1,s2);
getch();
}
strcmp(char *s,char *t){
while(*t!=null){
if(*t!=*s)
break;
t++;
s++;
}
*s=null;
if(*t==*s)
printf("the two strings are same");
else
printf("th e two strings are different");
return(*t);
}
```

/*Program to Sort Strings*/

```
#include <stdio.h>
#include <conio.h>
#include <string.h>
void main(){
int i,j,d;
char a[10][10],temp[10];
clrscr();
printf("enter the no. of strings:\n");
scanf("%d",&d);
printf("\n entered strings are: %d\n",d);
printf("enter the strings");
for(i=0;i<=d;i++)
gets(a[i]);
printf("the entered strings are:\n");
for(i=0;i<=d;i++)
printf("\n%s",a[i]);
for(i=0;i<=d;i++){
for(j=i+1;j<=d;j++){
if((strcmp(a[i],a[j])>0)){
strcpy(temp,a[i]);
strcpy(a[i],a[j]);
strcpy(a[j],temp);
}
}
}
printf("\n");
printf("\n sorted strings are:");
for(i=0;i<=d;i++)
printf("\n%s",a[i]);
getch();
}
```

Review Questions

1. Define an array. What are the types of array operations?
2. In what way does an array differ from an ordinary variable?
3. What conditions must be satisfied by all of the elements of any given array?
4. Suggest a practical way to visualize one-dimensional and two-dimensional arrays.
5. How are arrays processed in C? Can entire arrays be processed with single instructions, without repetition?
6. What is a matrix? Explain its uses with an example
7. What are arrays? Explain two-dimensional array.
8. How are multidimensional arrays defined? Compare with the manner in which one-dimensional arrays are defined.
9. What is a string? Explain all string handling functions.
10. Explain how strings can be stored using multidimensional arrays?
11. What are the string in-built functions available? Write in detail about each one of them with an example.
12. The names of employees of an organization are stored in three arrays, namely, first name, second name and last name. Write a program to concatenate the three parts into one string to be called name.
13. Write a program to replace a particular word by another word in a given string.
14. How can a list of strings be stored within a two-dimensional array? How can the individual strings be processed? What library functions are available to simplify string processing?

CHAPTER 7

Pointers

INTRODUCTION

Pointer is a variable which stores the memory address of a computer which may contain other variable or even another pointer.

If a variable contains address of another variable, then it is said that first variable points to second. Pointer can also be represented as a reference to another variable but there is very subtle difference in the two statements which is mostly dependent upon situation and environment. Pointers enable us to effectively represent complex data structures, to change values as arguments to functions, to work with memory which has been dynamically allocated and to more concisely and efficiently deal with arrays.

Pointer is generally of size of integer on the machine but it may be of different type which indicates the type of variable the pointer is pointing to decide pointer's properties and behavior. Pointer of one type cannot be implicitly converted from one type to another but can be explicitly converted using type casting. In such a conversion, a pointer always assumes that it is pointing to an object of its type but reality may differ and if used incorrectly may lead to disasters including permanent machine damage.

DECLARING A POINTER VARIABLE

Declaring a pointer variable is quite similar to declaring a normal variable all you have to do is to insert a star '*' operator before it.

General form of pointer declaration is:

data type * name;

where data type represent the type to which pointer thinks it is pointing to.

Multiple pointers of similar type can be declared in one statement but make sure you use * before every one otherwise they will become a variable of that type.

THE * & OPERATORS

It is important to note that all operations performed on pointers are done through two operators '*' (star) and '&' (ampercent). '&' is a unary operator that returns a memory address of a variable. '*' is complement of '&' and return value stored at a memory location stored in a pointer. '*' can be interpreted as statement "at address" while '&' can be interpreted as statement "address of".

"&" gives the address of something in memory, i.e., it generates a *pointer* to the object

- gives what is pointed at by a pointer (called *dereferencing*).

For example, assuming the following declaration:

int i = 17;

Then the expression "&i" generates a *pointer* to the variable i. We can then find out what this pointer is pointing at by applying the * operator to the newly generated pointer; thus *&i should have the value 17.

POINTER ASSIGNMENT

This is a type of expression used to assign value of one pointer to another using assignment operator '='. In this, value of righthand side points to memory address of variable stored in lefthand side pointer. As a result, both pointers point to same memory location after this expression.

Pointer of similar type can be used in expression easily as shown below but for different type pointers you need to type cast them as shown in the below program.

```
#include <stdio.h>
int main(){
char ch = a;
char* p1, *p2;
p1 = &ch;
p2 = p1; // Pointer assignment taking place
printf (" *p1 = %c and *p2 = %c", *p1,*p2); // Prints 'a' twice
return 0;
}
```

POINTER CONVERSION

Pointer conversion is a very powerful yet very dangerous feature. Before the concept of pointer conversion, you must understand the concept of a void pointer. Void pointer technically is a pointer which is pointing to the unknown. Void pointer has special property that it can be typecasted into any other pointer without any typecasting though every other conversion needs a typecasting. Also in dynamic memory allocation function such as malloc( ) and alloc ( ) returns void pointer which can be easily converted to other types which we come across in dynamic memory allocation chapter later on.

There is a pointer called null pointer which seems like void pointer but is entirely different. Null pointer is a pointer which points to nothing. In fact, it points to the base address of the CPU register and since register is not addressable in usage of a null pointer, it will lead to crash or at minimum a segmentation fault.

Be careful while typecasting one pointer to another because even after typecasting your pointer can point to anything but it will still think it is pointing to something of it declared type and have properties of the original type.

Type conversion is a powerful feature but yet it may be difficult to remove bugs and crashes and should be used with uttermost vigilance. It may also lead to unexpected and unreliable results but program would compile successfully.

Example below shows a type casting of one pointer into another:

```
#include <stdio.h>
int main(){
int i = 10;
char* p1
int *p2;
p2 = &i;
p1 = (char *) p2; // Typecasting and Pointer Conversion
printf (" *p1 = %c And *p2 = %d", *p1,*p2);
// Output maybe unexpected depending critically on computer and compiler.
return 0;
}
```

THE NULL POINTER AND POINTER TO VOID

The constant 0 when used in a pointer context (e.g., assigned to a variable of any pointer type or compared with a pointer value) is replaced by a null pointer of the appropriate type. Such a pointer is used to indicate that a pointer does not point anywhere or is invalid. The preprocessor constant NULL (defined in the header file stdio.h) can be used instead of the constant 0.

Library functions that return pointers return NULL if an error occurs. The value of a pointer should always be checked to ensure that it is not NULL before attempting to dereference it. Attempting to dereference a NULL pointer will give a run time error on some systems.

Pointer to void (void *) is ANSI C's generic pointer type. Functions, such as malloc(), which return a generic pointer, return void *. Values of type void * can be assigned to any other pointer type without a cast, but this is potentially dangerous, as the object pointer references may not be of the same type as the pointer to which it is being assigned.

For example:

```
char *a;

void *b;

b="Hello";

a=b;

printf("%s",a);
```

POINTER ARITHMETIC

Pointer arithmetic is quite different from normal arithmetic, unless and until you are working on char type pointers, reason being they are 1 byte long under all environments.

Not all arithmetic operations are defined in pointers. You can increment them, decrement them, add and subtract integer values from them. You even can subtract two pointers. But you cannot add two pointers, multiply, divide, modulus them. You cannot add or subtract values other than integer.

Now, pointer arithmetic may look a little weird but it has a deep sense attach to it.

Now, consider a pointer X, its current value that address it is pointing to is 1000 (just assuming). We make another assumption about the size of the data types. Size of data type is machine dependent, for example, int can be 16, 32, or 64 bit long depending upon your machine.

Now if this X pointer is char type (assumed 1 byte or 8 bit long) then X++ will have value 1001 and X– – will have value 999. Now if this X pointer is integer type (assumed 2 byte or 32 bit long) than X++ will have value 1002 and X– – will have value 998. Again if this X pointer is float type (assumed 4 byte or 32 bit long) than X++ will have value 1004 and X – – will have value 9996. Also if this X pointer is double type (assumed 8 byte or 64 bit long) than X++ will have value 1008 and X – – will have value 992.

Reason is when you increment a pointer of certain base type it increases its value in such a way that it points to next element of its base type. If you decrement a pointer, its value decrease in such a way that it points to previous value of its base type. So increment as well as decrement in fixed quanta of size of the base type.

You can add or subtract any integer value, in such a case value of pointer get increase and decrease by the product of the value to be added or subtract and size of the base type.

Pointer of user-defined types such as structures and union also increase by the quanta of their bit values which can be determined using size of operator.

Pointer arithmetic in C may look a bit strange but it is extensively used in programming and provides unmatched efficiency in performance of task such as accessing an array.

POINTER COMPARISON

Two pointers can be compared no matter where they point. Comparison can be done using <, >, =, <= and >= operators. Though it is not forcibly implied but comparison of two pointers become sensible only when they are related such as when they are pointing to elements of same arrays. Comparison of two unrelated pointers is unpredictable and the code should not rely upon it. All the comparison is generally done on the basis of memory organization in the host machine.

Following C example shows a potential use of pointer comparison in C.

```
#include <stdio.h>
int main(){
int data[100];
int* p1;
int *p2;
for (int i = 0; i <100;i++){
data[i] = i;
}
p1 = &data [1];
```

```
p2 = &data [2];
if (p1 > p2){
printf ("\n\n p1 is greater than p2");
}
else
{
printf ("\n\n p2 is greater than p1");
}
}
```

ARRAYS AND POINTERS

Array and Pointers in C are very closely related. In fact, they are so similar to each other in nature that they can be used interchangeably in each other positions most of the time.

Important link joining them is that array name without the brackets is the pointer name and other end a pointer can be indexed as if it's an array. Consider following C program for better understanding in which cycle through the elements of array using a pointer as an array name and through pointer arithmetic.

```
#include <stdio.h>
int main(){
int data[100];
int* p1;
for (int i = 0, i <100;i++){
data[i] = i;
}
p1 = data; //Assigning base address of an array to pointer
for (int i = 0; i <100;i++) //Accessing Array using Index
{
printf ("\n%d",p1[i]);
}
for (int i = 0; i <100;i++) //Accessing Array using Pointer Arithmetic
{
```

```
printf ("\n%d",*(p1 +i));
}
return 0;
}
```

Pointers like any other data type can be arrayed. This array is called array of pointers and is quite useful programming method. Array of pointers are declared as shown below.

data type *variable_name [array_size];

For example: To declare an array of 5 integer pointers we will use declaration:

int *array [5];

The C program below will show you a simple use of array of pointers in C programming.

```
#include <stdio.h>
int main(){
int data[5];
int *array[5];
for (int i = 0; i <5;i++){
data[i] = i;
}
//Assigning address of elements of array data to array of pointers.
for (int i = 0; i <5;i++){
array[i] = &data[i];
}
for (int i = 0; i <5;i++) //Accessing Array value using index
{
printf ("\n%d",data[i]);
}
for (int i = 0; i <5;i++) //Accessing Array value using array of pointers
{
printf ("\n%d",*array[i]);
}
return 0;
}
```

MULTIPLE INDIRECTION

Well, in C, it is permitted for a pointer to point to another pointer. As a result, many layers of pointer can be formed and this is called multiple indirections. As such there is no limitation on the level of indirection but including great depth of indirection, it is difficult to follow and may lead to errors. Normally, more than two level depth indirection are required.

A pointer to a pointer has declaration similar to that of a normal pointer but have more asterix sign before them indicating the depth of the pointer.

```
int ** pointer;
```

The above statement creates a pointer which points to pointer to a variable with int value.

Consider an example:

```
#include <stdio.h>
int main(){
int i = 10;
int **p1
int *p2;
p2 = &i;
p1 = &p2; // Multiple indirection
printf (" **p1 = %d And *p2 = %d", **p1,*p2); //Statement will show 10 twice.
return 0;
}
```

POINTER INITIALIZATION

When it comes to pointer initialization, C programming standard goes null. Standard does not force any initialization to a non-static local pointer but it does state that global pointers and static pointers get automatically initialized to null. So, initialized non-static local pointer contains an unknown value. If you try to use this pointer without giving it proper value, you may crash your program and even operating system in extreme cases and permanent damage to computer in terms of software and hardware can occur. So pointers are very nasty if used incorrectly.

Most important term in pointer initialization would be "null". It is a standard practice of top quality C programmers that any pointer which is not pointing to valid memory location should be initialized to null showing that it is pointing to nothing and should not be used. In fact, a null pointer is pointing to something, it is pointing to the base address of your CPU register. Now since register of CPU cannot be addressed the use of such pointer leads to abnormal termination of the program with a probable segmentation fault at runtime but no serious damage will be done to the machine. A MACRO name NULL is also defined in many standard headers such as <stdio.h>.

You can initialize a pointer to null using 2 methods as shown below:

variable_type *pointer_name = 0;

or

variable_type *pointer_name = NULL;

Even though null pointer should not be used directly, it does have some indirect uses such as; they can be used in a comparison with other pointer. They mark an end of something such as their extensive use in data structures.

Also char pointers which are capable of saving strings or char array can be initialized in more spectacular way as shown below:

char *pointer_name = "string value here";

In such a statement, you may wonder since p is not an array and no memory is allocated to it so where the string is actually stored. Answer to this question can be found in the technique used by C compilers to handle string constants. To handle such constants, the compiler creates a string table in which dynamic memory is allocated to pointer from heap and string is stored in this string table.

POINTER TO A FUNCTION

One of the rarest used yet powerful features of C programming language is the pointer to a function. As most of the people don't know that every function defined in C programming language have a base address attached to it. This base address acts as an entering point into that function. As you can now guess, this address can be stored in a specially designed pointer known as function pointer. Address of the function can be obtained by using pointer name without parenthesis.

Once stored, this pointer can be of tremendous use such that, it can be used to call that function but most important feast it let you attain is that it allows you to pass function as arguments to other functions as if it was a variable.

The trickiest thing about pointer to a function is declaration of the pointer that holds the base address of the function, rest is piece of cake. The general form of declaration of a pointer to a function is:

return_type (* pointer_name) (variable1_type variable1_name, variable2_type, variable2_name,....);

The declaration above tells compiler that pointer of name pointer_name will store an address of function which return a value of return_type type. Also it will take variables of name variable1_name, variable2_name of type variable1_type, variable2_type respectively and so on.

The simple C example below will further clear the concept of pointer to a function.

```
#include <stdio.h>
int add(int a, int b, int c){
return a+b+c;
}
int main(){
int (*function_pointer) (int,int,int);
//Declaration of function pointer for storage of base address of function add.
function_pointer = add;
printf ("%d", function_pointer (1,2,3)); //Print 6 as output
return 0;
}
```

POINTER DRAWBACKS

Pointers have tremendous power but the power can swing both sides, good and evil. Pointer if used incorrectly leads to very difficult unearth bugs which will most probably make you go wild. Pointers itself are not any trouble but the value they are storing can be. If it contains an incorrect value, it can lead to disasters of massive magnitude when used.

When you use this incorrect pointer to read a memory location, you may be reading an incorrect garbage value which if unluckily accepted by your program as assumed correct value nothing can help you. Consider a scenario in banking in which any customers real account value is switched with this garbage value, he can become a millionaire or beggar in a second, or think that in a rocket launching software you use this incorrect value as launching angle and crashing the billion dollar masterpiece. These scenarios are just my imagination running wild but you cannot ignore the fact that they are possible.

Now when you use this incorrect pointer to write a memory location, you may be writing an unknown memory location. If you have a large memory in the system, maybe you are using a unassigned memory but if that memory by any luck is a memory used by OS or Hardware and you are modifying it you maybe corrupting the Operating System software or damaging the hardware and their drivers. Also it is a possibility that you maybe using a memory location already in use by your software storing some essential data and you are unknowingly modifying it. You maybe are writing over your own code and data.

Such bugs and errors created by the pointers may not show up immediately but come up later and it is at that time difficult to predict that it was the pointer to blame.

UNUTILIZED POINTERS

Carefully look at the C program below:

```
#include <stdio.h>
int main(){
int a, *p;
a = 1;
*p = a;
return 0;
}
```

Now, notice that pointer p above is pointing to some unknown location. Maybe if you are lucky, then the compiler or OS points it to some safe location but it is just an assumption. It can be pointing to any damn memory location in the system. Now, the code above write value 1 into the unknown memory location pointed to by p. There is a large possibility with large program in small environment that p is pointing something vital which is now destroyed. To avoid this error, pointer initialization must be used so that pointer is pointing to nothing and compiler issue an error (runtime or compile time) when you use that pointer incorrectly and some damage control can happen.

Correct and safe program would be:

```
#include <stdio.h>
int main(){
int a, *p = NULL;
a = 1;
*p = a; //This would generate a run time error always and a compile time error in smart
compilers.
return 0;
}
```

Incorrect Pointer Usage

Carefully look at the example below:

```
#include <stdio.h>
#include <alloc.h>
int main(){
int a, *p = NULL;
p = (int *) malloc (sizeof (int));
a = 1;
p = a;
printf ("%d",*p); //This will print garbage value
return 0;
}
```

Seeing above code, I guess you can easily point the error. Line p = a; is incorrect and should be p = &a;. The point is this may be a syntax error by the programmer or a logical error by a beginner. Compiler should give warning but no compiler would produce error, in fact, even a warning is only an assumption and may not occur. The reason being compiler except this because every point in memory is represented in hexadecimal number in which this decimal number is implicitly converted. It is a rare but useful thing in special circumstances to use hardcode memory values especially in case of hardware programming and system programming where values of memory address such as port address always remain constant for the machine for which the program is being used. But this concept allows accidental error like above which may prove dangerous. So stay cautious of such error while programming.

Correct and safe program would be:

```
#include <stdio.h>
#include <alloc.h>
zint main(){
int a, *p = NULL;
p = (int *) malloc(sizeof (int));
a = 1;
p = &a;
printf ("%d",*p);
```

```
return 0;
}
```

Incorrect Pointer Comparison

Carefully look at the example below:

```
#include <stdio.h>
#include <alloc.h>
int main(){
int *p = NULL, *q = NULL;
p = (int *) malloc(sizeof (int));
q = (int *) malloc(sizeof (int));
if ( p < q )
prinf ("\np is less than q"); //This will print garbage value
else
printf ("\np is greater than q");
return 0;
}
```

The comparison of pointer as done above is absolutely incorrect, reason being that both p and q pointers in the above code are entirely unrelated and the output of the above code cannot be predicted. Comparison done above is entirely dependent upon compiler, operating system and to great extent luck. When pointer comparison is performed, the comparison is done between the integer values of the memory locations they are pointing to. Now this memory location assigned to them is not fixed and is entirely random. So, p can be either less or greater than q each with 50% probability in mathematics terms. So, the comparison cannot be relied upon in the bottom line. But this comparison if used correctly can be useful in logically related memory allocation such as in arrays. Also in very rare conditions you may even want to use this unrelated pointer comparisons.

Failure to do pointer re-initialization

Carefully look at the C program below:

```
#include <stdio.h>
#include <alloc.h>
int main(){
```

```
int i;
int *p = (int *) malloc(sizeof (int) * 10);
int *q;
q = p;
for (i = 0; i < 10; i++){
*p = i;
p++;
}
 for (i = 0; i < 10; i++){
 printf ("%d", *p); //Prints Garbage Value
 *p++;
}
return 0;
}
```

The mistake above is very common and creates a bug very tough to found. The point is when in the above code p is allocated memory and is used to load int values using pointer arithmetic and then when same pointer is used to display the loaded values, output will be garbage value. The reason for this that p is not re-initialized to memory address it was given during dynamic memory allocation. So, p keeps running ahead of its last left position that is from the end of its allocated memory and runs into unknown memory locations next in serial and only god knows what it will read and destroy when used for writing memory location. This problem can be easily avoided by rc initializing p to its original value

Correct and safe program would be:

```
#include <stdio.h>
#include <alloc.h>
int main(){
 int i;
 int *p = (int *) malloc(sizeof (int) * 10 );
 int *q;
 q = p;
 for (i = 0; i < 10; i++){
```

```
*p = i;
p++;
}
p = q;
for (i = 0; i < 10; i++){
printf ("%d ", *p); //Prints Value 1 to 10;
*p++;
}
return 0;
}
```

POINTERS AND FUNCTIONS

Call by Value

In the preceding examples, we have seen that whenever we called a function we have always passed the values of variables to the called function. Such function calls are called 'calls by value' by this what it meant is that on calling a function we are passing the values of variables to it.

The example of call by value are shown below:

```
sum = calsum(a, b, c);
f = factr(a);
```

In this method, the value of each of the actual arguments in the calling function is copied into corresponding formal arguments of the called function. With this method, the changes made to the formal arguments in the called function have no effect on the values of actual argument in the calling function. The following program illustrates this.

```
main( ){
int a = 10, b=20;
swapy (a,b);
printf ("\na = % d b = % d", a,b);
}
swapy (int x, int y){
int t;
```

```
t = x;
x = y;
y = t;
printf ("\n x = % d y = % d" , x, y);
}
```

The output of the above program would be;

x = 20, y = 10

a = 10, b = 20

Call by Reference

In the second method, the addresses of actual arguments in the calling function are copied into formal arguments of the called function. This means that using these addresses we would have an access to the actual arguments and hence we would be able to manipulate them. The following program illustrates this.

```
main( ){
int a = 10, b =20,
swapr (&a, &b);
printf ("\n a = %d b= %d", a, b);
}
swapr (int *x, int * y){
int t;
t = *x
*x = *y;
*y = t;
}
```

The output of the above program is:

a = 20, b =10

Functions that Return Multiple Values

So far, we have learned and seen that in a function, return statement was able to return only single value. That is because, a return statement can return only one value. But if we want to send back more than one value then.

The arguments used are send values to the called function, in the same way we can also use arguments to send back information to the calling function. The arguments that are used to send back the data are called Output Parameters.

It is a bit difficult because this type of function uses pointers.

Let's see an example:

```
#include <stdio.h>
#include <conio.h>
void calc(int x, int y, int *add, int *sub){
*add = x+y;
*sub = x-y;
}
void main(){
int a=20, b=11, p,q;
clrscr();
calc(a,b,&p,&q);
printf("Sum =  %d, Sub = %d",p,q);
getch();
}
```

Output:

Sum = 31, Sub = 9

Explanation:

Logic of this program is that we call UDF "calc()" and sends argument then it adds and subtract that two values and store those values in their respective pointers. The "*" is known as indirection operator whereas "&" known as address operator. We can get memory address of any variable by simply placing "&" before variable name. In the same way, we get value stored at specific memory location by using "*" just before memory address.

Line no. 3-6: This UDF function is different from all above UDF because it implements pointer. Line no. 3 looks something strange, let's have a clear idea of it. "calc( )" function has four arguments, first two arguments need no explanation. Last two arguments are integer pointer which works as output parameters (arguments). Pointer can only store address of the value rather than value but when we add * to pointer variable then we can store value at that address.

Line no. 7-13: When we call "calc()" function in the line no. 10, then following assignments occurs. Value of variable "a" is assigned to "x", value of variable "b" is assigned to "y", address of "p" and "q" to "add" and "sub" respectively. In line no. 4 and 5, we are adding and subtracting values and storing the result at their respective memory locations. This is how the program works.

Pointers for Interfunction Communication

On many occasions, we may want to write a program to which a user-defined function can be passed. For example, one can write a general program to solve an ordinary differential equation. We would then like to have it in such a way that a user can write a function, which evaluate all the derivatives of the particular problem, and pass it to the ODE solver. We will now see how this can be achieved by using a pointer.

Function name can be used as a pointer to point to functions like the name of the array is a pointer to its base address. We can also define a pointer, point it to a function and then use that pointer to invoke the function. The pointer to a function should be of the same "type" as the function.

If we have to pass a function pointer to another function, we have to define them as "external". That is they are "global" to the program and is defined outside any function boundaries. Consider the following example.

/*Program — Pointer to a function and passing the pointer to a function*/

```
#include <math.h>

#include <stdio.h>

float cube(float);

main(){

float b;

void (*func_ptr)();

void myfunction();

b=2.0;

func_ptr=myfunction;

(*func_ptr)(b,&cube);

}

void myfunction (x,powerthree)

float x;
```

```
float (*powerthree)(float);
{
float z;
x=2*x;
z=(*powerthree)(x);
printf("%f\n", z);
}
float cube(x)
float x;
{
float z;
z=x*x*x;
return z;
}
```

Here, cube is an external function and is defined outside of the function boundaries. This function calculates the 3rd power of any floating point variable passed to it and returns it as a floating point. Thus, this function is of the type "float". In the main function, we have defined a pointer func_ptr. Since we want to use it to a function which is of the type "void" we need to define this pointer also as "void".

The function myfunction has a floating point and a function pointer as its arguments. Instead of invoking this function directly, we use func_ptr for it. Note that we are passing the address of the external function, cube, as an argument here. "myfunction" receives it as a floating point 'x' and function 'powerthree'. When 'powerthree' is called inside this function, it is actually invoking the function cube, which is supplied as external.

Pointers: Pointing to the Same Address

Here is a cool aspect of C: any number of pointers can point to the same address. For example, you could declare p, q, and r as integer pointers and set all of them to point to i, as shown here:

```
int i;
int *p, *q, *r;
p = &i;
q = &i;
r = p;
```

Note that in this code, r points to the same thing that p points to, which is i. You can assign pointers to one another, and the address is copied from the right-hand side to the left-hand side during the assignment. After executing the above code, this is how things would look:

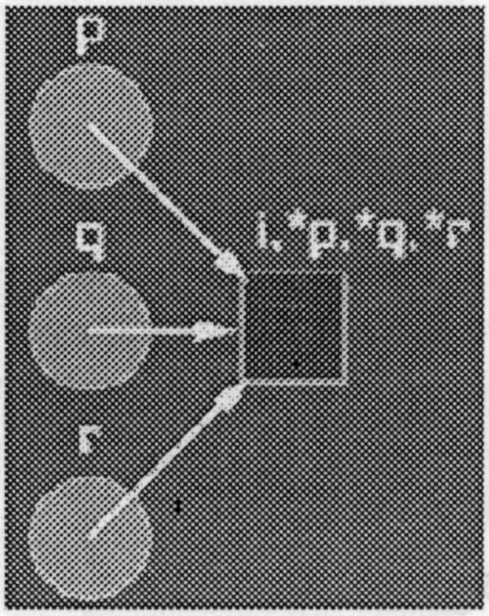

Fig. 7.1: Pointer Pointing to the Same Address

The variable i now has four names: i, *p, *q and *r. There is no limit on the number of pointers that can hold (and therefore point to) the same address.

Pointers to Pointers

It is possible and often useful to create pointers to pointers. This technique is sometimes called a handle, and is useful in certain situations where the operating system wants to be able to move blocks of memory on the heap around at its discretion.

The following example demonstrates a pointer to a pointer:

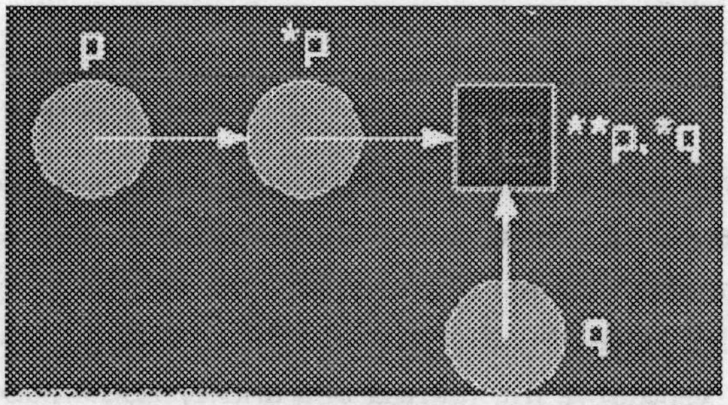

Fig. 7.2: A Pointer to a Pointer

```
int *q;
p = (int **)malloc(sizeof(int *));
*p = (int *)malloc(sizeof(int));
**p = 12;
q = *p;
printf("%d\n", *q);
free(q);
free(p);
```

Windows and OS use this structure to allow memory compaction on the heap. The program manages the pointer p, while the operating system manages the pointer *p. Because the OS manages *p, the block pointed to by *p (**p) can be moved, and *p can be changed to reflect the move without affecting the program using p. Pointers to pointers are also frequently used in C to handle pointer parameters in functions.

Command Line Arguments

C provides a fairly simple mechanism for retrieving command line parameters entered by the user. It passes an argv parameter to the main function in the program. The argv structures appear in a fair number of the more advanced library calls in C programming.

For example:

```
#include <stdio.h>
int main(int argc, char *argv[]){
int x;
printf("%d\n",argc);
for (x=0; x<argc; x++)
printf("%s\n",argv[x]);
return 0;
}
```

In this code, the main program accepts two parameters, argv and argc. The argv parameter is an array of pointers to string that contains the parameters entered when the program is invoked at the UNIX command line. The argc integer contains a count of the number of parameters. This particular piece of code types out the command line parameters. To try this, compile the code to an executable file named aaa and type aaa xxx yyy zzz. The code will print the command line parameters xxx, yyy and zzz, one per line.

The char *argv[] line is an array of pointers to string. In other words, each element of the array is a pointer, and each pointer points to a string (technically, to the first character of the string). Thus, argv[0] points to a string that contains the first parameter on the command line (the program's name), argv[1] points to the next parameter, and so on. The argc variable tells you how many of the pointers in the array are valid. You will find that the preceding code does nothing more than print each of the valid strings pointed to by argv.

Dangling Pointer

Dangling pointers in computer programming are pointers that do not point to a valid object of the appropriate type. Dangling pointers arise when an object is deleted or deallocated, without modifying the value of the pointer, so that the pointer still points to the memory location of the deallocated memory. As the system may reallocate the previously freed memory to another process, if the original program then dereferences the (now) dangling pointer, unpredictable behaviour may result, as the memory may now contain completely different data. This is especially the case if the program writes data to memory pointed by a dangling pointer, as silent corruption of unrelated data may result, leading to subtle bugs that can be extremely difficult to find, or cause segmentation faults (*NIX) or general protection faults (Windows).

In other words, dangling pointer points to a memory location which is being removed.

For example:

```
int* a = new int;
int *b = a;
delete b;
```

Now, 'a' will be a dangling pointer.

Dangling pointer leads to the memory leak problems.

Memory Leak

A memory leak in computer science is a particular type of unintentional memory consumption by a computer program where the program fails to release memory when no longer needed.

For example:

```
void f(void)
{
void* s;
s = malloc(50); /* get memory */
return;
}//control comes out w/o freeing the memory....
```

Memory leaks occur when memory allocated to a pointer is not deleted and the pointer goes out of scope. This allocated memory never gets deallocated and remains in the heap until the system is restarted.

For example:

```
void foo(){
int* ptr = new int;
*ptr = 10;
...
...
}
```

Since ptr is allocated memory using 'new', but no 'delete' is called, hence memory allocated to ptr will leak.

```
#include <stdio.h>
#include <stdlib.h>
#include <string.h>
#define BLOCKSIZE 20;
int main(){
char *ptr;
ptr (char *)malloc(BLOCKSIZE);
if(ptr! NULL)
strcpy(ptr "JNTU");
printf("content s" ptr);
printf("naddress u" ptr);
free(ptr);
printf("nAfter free");s
printf("ncontent s" ptr);
printf("naddress u" ptr);
}
```

Output:

content JNTU

address 134520840 //(just an example)

After free

content

address 134520840 //same as the previous address

From the above example, after free() also 'i' keeps the address but content is deallocated. So now, it is not pointing to any valid memory location. Hence, 'ptr' is now dangling pointer which is probably having an address but not pointing to any valid memory location. So it is good practice to assign NULL after freeing the allocated memory as below.

ptr NULL;

In this way, dangling problem can be solved.

C Program Examples

/*Program – Implementation of Pointers*/

```
#include <stdio.h>
#include <conio.h>
main(){
char c,*t;
int a,*f;
float b,*s;
clrscr();
f=&a;
s=&b;
t=&c;
printf("enter char, int and float:");
scanf("%c%d%f",&c,&a,&b);
printf("char at c: %c",*t);
printf("address of c:  %d",t);
printf("value of a: %d",*f);
printf("address of a:  %d",f);
```

```
printf("value of b: %f",*s);
printf("address of b:  %d",s);
getch();
}
```

/*Program to find the biggest and lowest values using pointers*/

```
#include <stdio.h>
#include <conio.h>
void main(){
int a[20],d,i;
int *ptr,*big,*low;
clrscr();
printf("enter the size of the integer array\n");
scanf("%d",&d);
printf("\n enter %d values",d);
for(i=0;i<d;i++)
scanf("%d",&a[i]);
ptr=a;
*big=0;
for(i=0;i<d;i++){
if(*big<*ptr)
*big=*ptr;
if(*low>*ptr)
*low=*ptr;
ptr++;
}
printf("\n elements of array :\n");
for(i=0;i<d;i++)
printf("%d\t",a[i]);
printf("\n the biggest value of array: %d",*big);
```

```
printf("\n the lowest value of array: %d",*low);
getch();
}
```

/*Program to read an array of integers using pointers*/

```
#include <stdio.h>
#include <conio.h>
void main(){
int a[20],d,i;
int *ptr;
clrscr();
printf("enter the size of the integer array\n");
scanf("%d",&d);
printf("\n enter %d values",d);
for(i=0;i<d;i++)
scanf("%d",&a[i]);
ptr=a;
printf("\n elements of array :\n");
for(i=0;i<d;i++){
printf("%d\t",*ptr);
ptr++;
}
getch();
}
```

/*Program to find factorial of a given number using pointers and functions*/

```
#include <stdio.h>
#include <conio.h>
int factorial(int n, int *fact){
int i, *fact;
fact=1;
```

```
for(i=1;i<n;i++){
*fact=*fact*i;}
return(1);
}
void main(){
int n,fact=1;
clrscr();
printf("enter n value");
scanf("%d",&n);
factorial(n,&fact);
printf("factorial of a given number%d",fact);
getch();
}
```

/*Program using pointers to find lowest and biggest number*/

```
#include <stdio.h>
#include <conio.h>
main(){
int a[20], i, d;
int *ptr,*big,*low;
clrscr();
printf("enter dimension");
scanf("%d",&d);
printf("enter %d values:",d);
for(i=0;i<d;i++)
scanf("%d",&a[i]);
ptr=a;
*big=0;
for(i=0;i<d;i++){
if(*big<*ptr)
```

```
*big=*ptr;
if(*low>*ptr)
*low=*ptr;
ptr++;
}
printf("elements of array a:\n");
for(i=0;i<d;i++)
printf("%d\t",a[i]);
printf("the biggest value of array:%d\n",*big);
printf("the lowest value of array:%d",*low);
getch();
}
```

Review Questions

1. How to use pointers as arguments in a function? Explain through an example.
2. Explain the process of accessing a variable through its pointer. Give an example.
3. What is a pointer? How a pointer is initialized?
4. Explain the difference between the 'call by reference' and 'call by value'.
5. What is Pass by Value? Write a C program showing this concept.
6. What is Pass by Reference? Write a C program showing this concept.
7. What are the advantages of using pointers in a program?
8. Define Array of pointers.
9. What kind of information does a pointer variable represent?
10. What is the relationship between the address of a variable and the corresponding pointer variable?
11. What is the purpose of the indirection operator? To what type of operand must the indirection operator be applied?
12. What is the purpose of a dangling pointer?
13. What are the reasons of memory leaks? How can it be rectified?
14. What is the purpose of a pointer to pointer? Expalin with an example.

ଔଔଔ

CHAPTER 8

Structures and Unions

STRUCTURE

A structure is a convenient tool for handling a group of logically related data items. We can also say that the structure is one which can hold more than one data at a time and of different data types. Structure helps to organize complex data in a more meaningful way. It is powerful concept that we may use in designing a program.

Syntax: The general format of a structure:

```
struct tag_name
{
data type member1;
data type member2;
data type member3;
- - -
- - -
data type member m;
}
obj1, obj2;
```

struct is the keyword

tag_name is the structure name

member1, member2 and member3 ..... member m are the structure members such as variables and arrays

obj1 and obj2 are the structure objects. These are used in order to access the structure members.

STRUCTURE DEFINITION

A structure definition creates a format that may be used to declare structure variables consider the following example.

```
struct book_bank
{
char title [20];
char author [15];
int pages;
float price;
};
```

Here, keyword **struct** hold the details of four fields these fields are title, author, pages, and price, these fields are called **structure elements**. Each element may belong to different types of data. Here, **book_bank** is the name of the structure and is called the structure tag.

It simply describes as shown below.

struct book-bank

title array of 20 characters

author array of 15 characters

pages integer

price float

ACCESSING STRUCTURES

The members of a struct can be accessed by their name preceded by a dot '.' and the name of the member.

For example:

```
struct point
{
int x;
int y;
}mypoint;
```

The struct with tag name "point" then consists of two integer members x and y.

The members of a struct can be accessed by their name preceded by a dot '.'

mypoint.x= 4;

mypoint.y= 3;

and for pointers to structures with '->':

struct tag-name* ptr;

ptr->member;

Pointer to struct variables are also possible:

struct point A = { 3, 4 };

struct point *ptrA= &A;

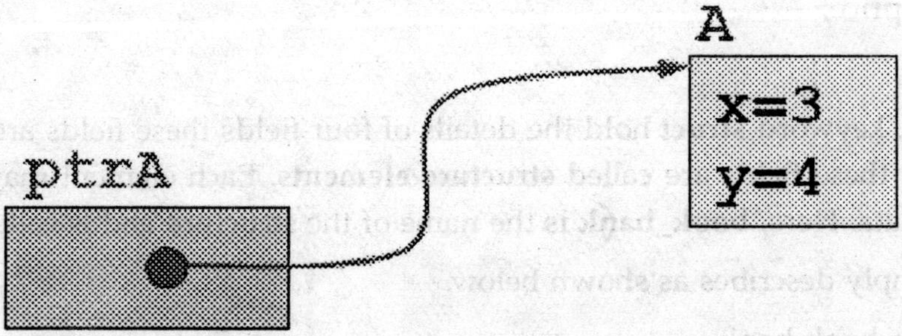

However, there is an important difference. Members in struct variables are accessed using a dot '.' between variable name and the name of the struct member. But using a pointer to a structs the arrow '->'has to be used for the accessing the member.

A.x = 5;

A.y = 6;

ptrA->x = 2;

ptrA->y = 5;

Since pointer **ptrA** points to **A** the members of variable are manipulated.

printf("(%d, %d)\n", A.x, A.y);=>(2, 5)

ARRAY OF STRUCTURES

Each element of the array itself is a structure. See the example shown below. Here we want to store data of 5 persons for this purpose; we would be required to use 5 different structure variables, from sample1 to sample 5. To have 5 separate variable will be inconvenient.

```
# include <stdio.h>
main( ){
struct person{
```

```
char name [25];
char age;
};
struct person sample[5];
int index;
char into[8];
for( index = 0; index <5; index ++){
printf("Enter name;");
gets(sample [index]. name);
printf("%age;");
gets(info);
sample [index]. age = atoi (info);
}
for (index = 0; index <5; index++){
printf("name = %s\n", sample [index]. name);
printf("Age = %d \n", sample [index]. age);
}
getch( );
}
```

The structure type person is having two elements: Name is an array of 25 characters and character type variable **age.**

Using the Statement

struct person sample[5];

We are declaring a 5 element array of structures. Here, each element of sample is a separate structure of type person.

We then define 2 variable indexes and an array of 8 characters' **info.** Here, the first loop executes 5 times, with the value of index varying from 0 to 4. The first printf statement displays. Enter name gets( ) function waits for the input string. For the first time, the name you enter will go to sample[0]. name. The second printf display **age** the number you type is will be 5 stored as character type, because the member age is declared as character type. The function **atoi( )** converts this into an integer. atoi stands for **alpha to integer**. This will be stored in sample[0].age. The second **for** loop is responsible for printing the information stored in the array of structures.

STRUCTURES WITHIN STRUCTURES OR NESTED STRUCTURES

Structure within a structure means nesting of structures. Let us consider the following structure defined to store information about the salary of employees.

```
struct salary{
char name[20];
char department[10];
int basic_pay;
int dearness_allowance;
int city_allowance;
}employee;
```

This structure defines name, department, basic pay and three kinds of allowance. We can group all the items related to allowance together and declare them under a substructure as shown below:

```
struct salary
{
char name [20];
char department[10];
struct
{
int dearness;
int hous_rent;
int city;
}allowance;
}employee;
```

The salary structure contains a member named **allowance** which itself is a structure with three members. The members contained in the inner, structure namely dearness, hous_rent, and city can be referred to as:

employee allowance. dearness

employee. allowance. hous_rent

employee. allowance. city

An innermost member in a nested structure can be accessed by chaining all the concerned structure variables (from outermost to innermost) with the member using dot operator. The following being invalid.

employee. allowance (actual member is missing)

employee. hous_rent (inner structure variable is missing)

POINTERS AND STRUCTURES

A pointer to a structure can be declared like this:

gridtype *ptrb;

and this can be associated with an existing variable like this:

ptrb = &b;

To obtain the **x** member of ***ptrb,** we do either:

(*ptrb).x

or use the specially provided operator **->**

ptrb->x

***ptrb.x** does not work because the precedence of dot is higher than *, and this is the reason for the existence of the **->** operator.

If we have:

```
typedef struct{
int x;
int y;
} gridtype;
gridtype a, *aptr =&a;
```

then the following are equivalent:

a.x

aptr->x

(*aptr).x

The priorities indicate that:

++ aptr->x

increments the **x** member. If it was required to increment **aptr,** brackets should be used.

A FUNCTION RETURNING A STRUCTURE

Function to Return Structure

```
gridtype makeplace (int xx, int yy){
gridtype temp;
temp.x = xx;
temp.y = yy;
return temp;
}
```

The scoping of C means it is acceptable to use **x** and **y** in place of **xx** and **yy**:

```
gridtype makeplace (int x, int y){
gridtype temp;
temp.x = x;
temp.y = y;
return temp;
}
```

This will be more readable to some programmers.

To return a pointer to a **gridtype** will require memory to be allocated, as in the following:

```
gridtype *makeplace (int xx, int yy){
gridtype *temp;
temp = malloc(sizeof(gridtype));
if (temp == NULL)
exit (1); /* error */
temp -> x = xx;
temp -> y = yy;
return temp;
}
```

The programmer will need to free the space allocated to this **gridtype** when it is no longer needed.

PASSING A STRUCTURE AS A WHOLE TO A FUNCTION

Structures are passed to functions by way of their pointers. Thus, the changes made to the structure members inside the function will be reflected even outside the function.

```
# include <stdio.h>
typedef struct
{
char *name;
int acc_no;
char acc_types;
float balance;
} account;
main( ){
void change(account *pt);
static account person = {"chetan", 4323, 'R', 12.45};
printf("%s %d %c %2.f \n", person.name, person.acc_type, person.acc_type, person.
balance);
change(&person);
printf("%s %d %c %2.f \n", person.name, person.acc_type,person.acc-type, person.
balance);
getch( );
}
void change(account *pt){
pt - > name =" Rohit R";
pt - > acc_no = 1111;
pt - > acc_type = 'c';
pt - > balance = 44.12;
}
```

Output

```
Chetan    4323   R   12.45
Rohit R   1111   c   44.12
```

UNIONS

Unions, like structure contain members, whose individual data types may vary. This is a major distinction between them in terms of storage. In structures, each member has its own storage location, whereas all the members of a union use the same location. Like structures, a union can be declared using the keyword **union** as follows:

The general formats of a union thus, can be shown as:

```
union tag{
member 1;
member 2;
- - -
- - -
member m;
};
```

The general format for defining individual union variables:

Storage-class union tag variable 1, variable 2,........., variable n;

Storage-class and **tag** are optional variable 1, variable 2 etc. are **union** variable of type **tag.**

Declaring **union** and defining variables can be done at the same time as shown below:

```
Stroage-calss union tag{
member 1;
member 2;
- - -
- - -
- - -
member m;
} variable 1, variable 2;
```

For example:

```
union item{
int m;
float x;
```

char c;

} code;

This declares a variable **code** of type **union** item. The union contains item members, each with a different date type. However, we can use only one of them at a time. This is due to the fact that only one location is allocated for a union variable, irrespective of its size.

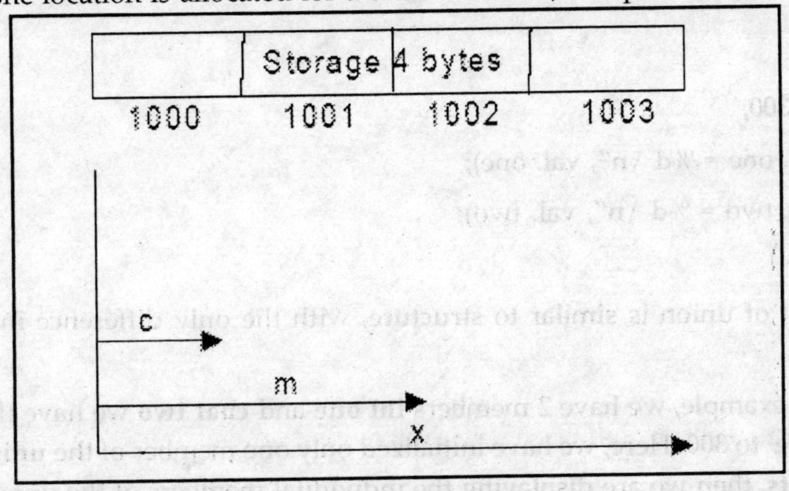

Fig. Compiler allocation in terms of union

The compiler allocates a piece of storage that is large enough to hold the largest variable type in the union. In the declaration above, the member x requires 4 bytes which is the largest among the members. The above figure shows how all the three variables share the same address, this assumes that a **float** variable requires 4 bytes of storage.

To access a union member, we can use the same syntax that we as for structure members, that is,

code. m

code. x

code. c are all valid

When accessing member variables, we should make sure that we are accessing the member whose value is currently in storage.

For example:

```
code. m = 565;

code. x = 783.65;

printf("%d", code. m); would produce erroneous output.

# include <stdio.h>
```

```
main( ){
union
{
int one;
char two;
} val;
val. one = 300;
printf("val. one = %d \n", val. one);
printf("val. two = %d \n", val. two);
}
```

The format of union is similar to structure, with the only difference in the keyword used.

The above example, we have 2 members **int one** and **char two** we have then initialized the member '**one**' to 300. Here, we have initialized only one member of the **union**. Using two **printf** statements, then we are displaying the individual members of the union **val** as:

val. one = 300
val. two = 44

As we have not initialized the char variable **two,** the second **printf** statement will give a random value of 44.

BIT FIELDS

A is declared by suffixing the field name with a colon followed by the number of bits used by the bit field. A bit field can be declared in any integer type (the ANSI standard allows only types int and unsigned int for bit fileds. The other possible types are extensions allowed by different compilers such as COSMIC compiler, and by most compilers targetting microcontrollers). The reference type used is considered to be the *allocation unit,* meaning that an integer of that type is open and filled until there is no more space available. Any bit field overlapping an allocation unit boundary is allocated in a new integer.

For example:

```
struct{
char a:4;
char b:3;
char c:2;
}
```

This structure defines 3 bit fields based on a *char* allocation unit. A first char is open and bit fields **a** and **b** are allocated inside. There is not enough space available to allocate bit field **c**. A new char is then opened and bitfield **c** is allocated inside. This structure is thus occupying 2 bytes in memory.

A bit field without name may be used to skip the corresponding amount of bits in the allocation unit. A zero bit field width is forcing the opening of a new allocation unit.

ENUMERATIONS

An enumeration consists of a set of named integer constants. An enumeration type declaration gives the name of the (optional) enumeration tag and defines the set of named integer identifiers (called the "enumeration set", "enumerator constants", "enumerators", or "members"). A variable with enumeration type stores one of the values of the enumeration set defined by that type.

Variables of enum type can be used in indexing expressions and as operands of all arithmetic and relational operators. Enumerations provide an alternative to the #define preprocessor directive with the advantages that the values can be generated for you and obey normal scoping rules.

In ANSI C, the expressions that define the value of an enumerator constant always have int type; thus, the storage associated with an enumeration variable is the storage required for a single int value. An enumeration constant or a value of enumerated type can be used anywhere the C language permits an integer expression.

Syntax:

enum-specifier:

enum identifier opt { enumerator-list }

enum identifier

The optional identifier names the enumeration type defined by enumerator-list. This identifier is often called the "tag" of the enumeration specified by the list. A type specifier of the form

enum identifier { enumerator-list }

declares identifier to be the tag of the enumeration specified by the enumerator-list nonterminal. The enumerator-list defines the "enumerator content." The enumerator-list is described in detail below.

If the declaration of a tag is visible, subsequent declarations that use the tag but omit enumerator-list which specify the previously declared enumerated type. The tag must refer to a defined enumeration type, and that enumeration type must be in current scope. Since the enumeration type is defined elsewhere, the enumerator-list does not appear in this declaration. Declarations of types derived from enumerations and typedef declarations for enumeration types can use the enumeration tag before the enumeration type is defined.

Syntax:

enumerator-list:

enumerator

enumerator-list, enumerator

enumerator:

enumeration-constant

enumeration-constant = constant-expression

enumeration-constant:

identifier

Each enumeration-constant in an enumeration-list names a value of the enumeration set. By default, the first enumeration-constant is associated with the value 0. The next enumeration-constant in the list is associated with the value of (constant-expression + 1), unless you explicitly associate it with another value. The name of an enumeration-constant is equivalent to its value.

You can use enumeration-constant = constant-expression to override the default sequence of values. Thus, if enumeration-constant = constant-expression appears in the enumerator-list, the enumeration-constant is associated with the value given by constant-expression. The constant-expression must have int type and can be negative.

The following rules apply to the members of an enumeration set:

An enumeration set can contain duplicate constant values. For example, you could associate the value 0 with two different identifiers, perhaps named null and zero, in the same set.

The identifiers in the enumeration list must be distinct from other identifiers in the same scope with the same visibility, including ordinary variable names and identifiers in other enumeration-lists.

Enumeration tags obey the normal scoping rules. They must be distinct from other enumeration, structure, and union tags with the same visibility.

Example:

```
enum DAY          /* Defines an enumeration type  */
{
saturday,     /* Names day and declares a      */
```

```
sunday = 0,    /* variable named workday with   */
monday,        /* that type                     */
tuesday,
wednesday,     /* wednesday is associated with 3 */
thursday,
friday
} workday;
```

The value 0 is associated with saturday by default. The identifier sunday is explicitly set to 0. The remaining identifiers are given the values 1 through 5 by default.

In this example, a value from the set DAY is assigned to the variable today.

```
enum DAY today = wednesday;
```

Note that the name of the enumeration constant is used to assign the value. Since the DAY enumeration type was previously declared, only the enumeration tag DAY is necessary.

To explicitly assign an integer value to a variable of an enumerated data type, use a typecast:

```
workday = (enum DAY) (day_value - 1);
```

This cast is recommended in C but is not required.

```
enum BOOLEAN  /* Declares an enumeration data type called BOOLEAN */
{
false,    /* false = 0, true = 1 */
true
};
enum BOOLEAN end_flag, match_flag; /* Two variables of type BOOLEAN */
```

This declaration can also be specified as:

```
enum BOOLEAN { false, true } end_flag, match_flag;\
```

or as

```
enum BOOLEAN { false, true } end_flag;
enum BOOLEAN match_flag;
enum BOOLEAN { false, true } end_flag;
enum BOOLEAN match_flag;
```

An example that uses these variables might look like this:

```
if (match_flag == false)
{
.
. /* statement */
.
}
end_flag = true;
```

Unnamed enumerator data types can also be declared. The name of the data type is omitted, but variables can be declared. The variable response is a variable of the type defined:

```
enum { yes, no } response;
```

SELF-REFERENTIAL STRUCTURES

It is possible to have a member of a structure as a pointer to itself. In a structure, if one or members are pointers pointing to the same structure, and then this type of structure is known as self-referential structure.

Syntax: The general format of a structure:

```
typedef struct structure_name
{
member 1;
member 2;
- - -
- - -
- - -
member m;
struct struct_name *p;
} NODE;
```

Example:

```
typedef struct selfreference
{
int data;
struct selfreference *np;
```

```
} NODE;
```

np is a member which is a pointer to struct selfreference.

Recursive declaration of a structure is not allowed in C language. It is illegal to use the structure itself as its member. Instead a pointer may be used to point any structure.

There is another indirect way to create a self-referential structure.

For example:

```
struct one
{
    .......
    .......
    struct two *t; // t points to structure two
};
struct two
{
    .........
    .........
    struct one *o; // o points to structure one
}
```

The structure *one* has a member 't' pointing to the structure *two*, which has member 'o' pointing to the structure *one*. An indirect recursive declaration of a pointer to a structure results in a self-referential structure.

C PROGRAM EXAMPLES

/*Program — pointers using structures*/

```
#include <stdio.h>
#include <conio.h>
#include <string.h>
void main(){
struct book{
char name[20],author[20];
}b,*ptr;
```

```
clrscr();
printf("enter name:\n");
gets(b.name);
printf("enter author:\n");
gets(b.author);
ptr=&b;
printf("\n book name: %s",ptr->name);
printf("\n book author: %s",ptr->author);
getch();
}
```

/*Program to print employee name and salary using structures and pointers*/

```
#include <stdio.h>
#include <conio.h>
#include <math.h>
#define size 5
struct emp
{
int no;
float sal;
char name[20];
}e;
void main(){
struct emp e[3];
float a;
int i;
clrscr();
for(i=0;i<3;i++){
printf("enter emp code : \n");
scanf("%d",&e[i].no);
printf("enter emp name : \n");
```

```
//flushall();
scanf("%s",&e[i].name);
printf("enter temp float value : ");
scanf("%f",&a);
printf("enter emp sal : \n");
scanf("%f",&e[i].sal);
}
printf(" emp code   emp name     emp sal : \n");
for(i=0;i<3;i++)
printf("\n%d%s%f",e[i].no,e[i].name,e[i].sal);
getch();
}
```

/*Program — concept of structure within structure*/

```
#include <stdio.h>
#include <conio.h>
struct empdet
{
char name[20];
struct dateofjoin
{
int dd,mm,yyyy;
}doj;
int salary;
};
main(){
struct empdet emp;
clrscr();
printf("enter emp name:");
scanf("%s",emp.name);
```

```
printf("enter emp date of join in the format dd mm yyyy:");
scanf("%d %d %d",&emp.doj.dd,&emp.doj.mm,&emp.doj.yyyy);
printf("enter emp salary:");
scanf("%d",&emp.salary);
printf(" emp delatils are\n:");
printf("employee name%s\n",emp.name);
printf("\ndate of join: date%d\t month%d\t year%d\n", emp.doj.dd, emp.doj.mm,
emp.doj.yyyy);
printf("employee salary%d\n",emp.salary);
}
```

/*Program — student-wise total for three students using array of structure*/

```
#include <stdio.h>
#include <conio.h>
#include <stdlib.h>
struct student{
int no,marks[3],total;
char name[20];
};
main(){
struct student stu[3];
int i=0,j=0;
clrscr();
for(i=0;i<3;i++){
printf("enter student details : \n");
printf("enter student id : \n");
scanf("%d",&stu[i].no);
printf("enter student name: ");
gets(stu[i].name);
stu[i].total=0;
for(j=0;j<3;j++) {
```

```
printf("enter marks%d:",j+1);
scanf("%d",&stu[i].marks[j]);
stu[i].total=stu[i].total+stu[i].marks[j];
}
printf("\n\n");
}
printf("the studentwise total marks are\n");
for(i=0;i<3;i++){
printf("student %d details\n",i+1);
printf("student id: %d\n:",stu[i].no);
printf("student name%s",stu[i].name);
for(j=0;j<3;j++)
printf("marks %d %d\n:",j+1,stu[i].marks[j]);
printf("total marks %d:",stu[i].total);
printf("\n\n");
}
}
```

Review Questions

1. What is a structure? Explain the components of a structure.
2. What is a member? What is the relationship between a member and a structure?
3. Describe the syntax for defining the composition of a structure. Can individual members be initialized within a structure type declaration?
4. How is the structure member accessed? And how can it be processed?
5. When are arrays of structures used? Declare a variable as array of structure and initialize it.
6. Differentiate a variable, array and a structure using an example.
7. How does a structure differ from a union?
8. How structure elements are accessed using pointer? Which operator is used? Give an example.
9. Write a program to use structure within union. Display the contents of structure elements.
10. What is structure within structure? Give an example for it.
11. Write a C program to illustrate the concept of structure within structure.

12. What are the advantages of using unions?
13. Define bit field in structures.
14. Define enumerations.
15. Discuss the usage of pointer-based expression using structures.
16. How can an individual structure member be accessed in terms of its corresponding pointer variable?
17. What is a self-referential structure? For what kinds of applications are they useful?

CHAPTER 9

File Management

BASIC CONCEPTS

- Real-life situations involve large volume of data and in such cases, the console oriented I/O operations pose two major problems.
- It becomes cumbersome and time-consuming to handle large volumes of data through terminals.
- The entire data is lost when either the program is terminated or computer is turned off. Therefore, it is necessary to have more flexible approach where data can be stored on the disks and read whenever necessary, without destroying the data. This method employs the concept of files to store data.

C supports a number of functions that have the ability to perform basic file operations, which include:

(1) Naming a file

(2) Opening a file

(3) Reading from a file

(4) Writing data into a file

(5) Closing a file

FILE OPERATION FUNCTIONS

Function Name	Operation
fopen()	Creates a new file for use/Opens a new existing file for use
fclose()	Closes a file which has been opened for use
getc()	Reads a character from a file

Function Name	Operation
putc()	Writes a character to a file
fprintf()	Writes a set of data values to a file
fscanf()	Reads a set of data values from a file
getw()	Reads a integer from a file
putw()	Writes an integer to the file
fseek()	Sets the position to a desired point in the file
ftell()	Gives the current position in the file
rewind()	Sets the position to the beginning of the file

STREAMS

Streams are a portable way of reading and writing data. They provide a flexible and efficient means of I/O.

A stream is a file or a physical device (e.g., printer or monitor) which is manipulated with a pointer to the stream. There exists an internal C data structure, FILE, which represents all streams and is defined in stdio.h. We simply need to refer to the FILE structure in C programs when performing I/O with streams.

We just need to declare a variable or pointer of this type in our programs.

For example, we must open a stream before doing any I/O, then access it and then close it.

Stream I/O is BUFFERED: i.e., to say a fixed "chunk" is read from or written to a file via some temporary storage area (the buffer). This is illustrated in Fig. 9.1. Always the file pointer actually points to this buffer.

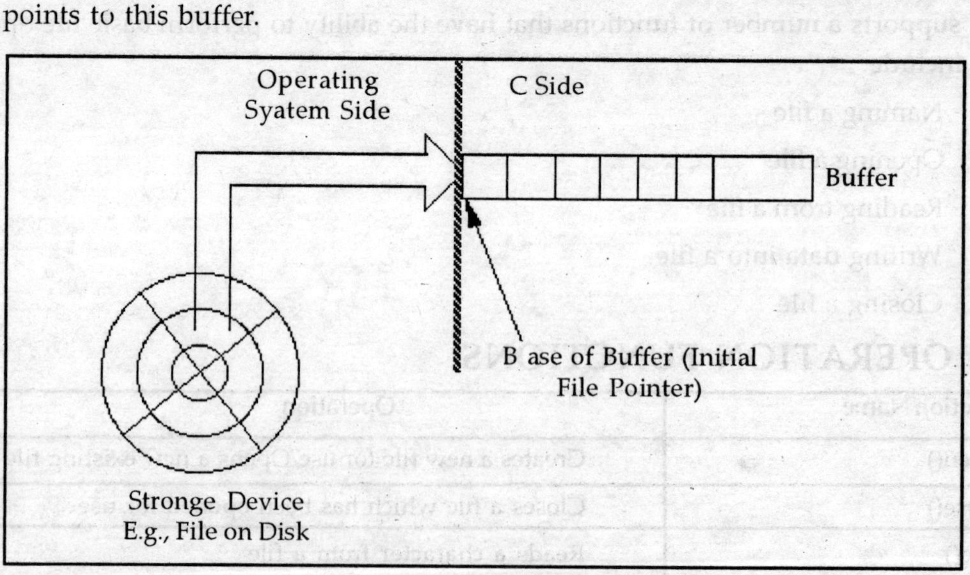

Fig. 9.1: Stream I/O Model

This leads to efficient I/O but be careful that the data written to a buffer does not appear in a file (or device) until the buffer is flushed or written out.

FILE OPERATIONS ON TEXT FILES

Defining and Opening a File

If we want to store data in the file into the secondary memory, we must specify certain things about the file to the operating system. They include the filename, data structure, purpose.

The general format of the function used for opening a file is:

```
FILE *fp;
fp = fopen("filename","mode");
```

The first statement declares the variable fp as a pointer to the data type FILE. As stated earlier, File is a structure that is defined in the I/O Library. The second statement opens the file named filename and assigns an identifier to the FILE type pointer fp. This pointer, which contains all the information about the file, is subsequently used as a communication link between the system and the program.

The second statement also specifies the purpose of opening the file. The mode does this job.

r	open the file for read only.
w	open the file for writing only.
a	open the file for appending data to it
r+	read & write, do not destroy file if it exists
w+	read & write, but overwrite file if it exists
a+	read & write, but append instead of overwrite

Consider the following statements:

```
FILE *p1, *p2;
p1=fopen("data","r");
p2=fopen("results","w");
```

In these statements, the p1 and p2 are created and assigned to open the file data and results respectively. The file data is opened for reading and result is opened for writing. In case the results file already exists, its contents are deleted and the files are opened as a new file. If data file does not exist, error will occur.

Closing a File

The input output library supports the function to close a file; it is in the following format.

```
fclose(file_pointer);
```

A file must be closed as soon as all operations on it have been completed. This would close the file associated with the file pointer.

Observe the following program.

```
....
FILE *p1 *p2;
p1=fopen("Input","w");
p2=fopen("Output","r");
....
...
fclose(p1);
fclose(p2)
```

The above program opens two files and closes them after all operations on them are completed, once a file is closed its file pointer can be reversed on other file.

The getc and putc functions are analogous to getchar and putchar functions and handle one character at a time. The putc function writes the character contained in character variable c to the file associated with the pointer fp1.

Example: putc(c,fp1);

Similarly, getc function is used to read a character from a file that has been open in read mode.

```
c=getc(fp2).
```

The program shown below displays use of file operations. The data enter through the keyboard and the program writes it, character by character, to the file input. The end of the data is indicated by entering an EOF character, which is control Z . The file input is closed at this signal.

/* Program for using fopen and fclose functions*/

```
#include <stdio.h>
#include <stdlib.h>
```

```
main(){
file *f1;
printf("Data input output");
f1=fopen("Input","w"); /*Open the file Input*/
while((c=getchar())!=EOF) /*get a character from keyboard*/
putc(c,f1); /*write a character to input*/
fclose(f1); /*close the file input*/
printf("\nData output\n");
f1=fopen("INPUT","r"); /*Reopen the file input*/
while((c=getc(f1))!=EOF)
printf("%c",c);
fclose(f1);
}
```

STANDARD INPUT/OUTPUT FILES

The getw and putw Functions

These are integer-oriented functions. They are similar to getc and putc functions and are used to read and write integer values. These functions would be useful when we deal with only integer data. The general forms of getw and putw are:

```
putw(integer,fp);
integer=getw(fp);
```

/*Program for using getw and putw functions*/

```
#include <stdio.h>
#include <stdlib.h>
main(){
FILE *f1,*f2,*f3;
int number I;
printf("Contents of the data file\n\n");
f1=fopen("DATA","w");
for(i=1;i< 30;i++){
```

```
scanf("%d",&number);
if(number = =-1)
break;
putw(number,f1);
}
fclose(f1);
f1=fopen("DATA","r");
f2=fopen("ODD","w");
f3=fopen("EVEN","w");
while((number=getw(f1))!=EOF)/* Read from data file*/
{
if(number%2==0)
putw(number,f3);/*write to even file*/
else
putw(number,f2);/*write to odd file*/
}
fclose(f1);
fclose(f2);
fclose(f3);
f2=fopen("ODD","r");
f3=fopen("EVEN","r");
printf("\n\nContents of the odd file\n\n");
while(number=getw(f2))!=EOF)
printf("%d%d",number);
printf("\n\nContents of the even file");
while(number=getw(f3))!=EOF)
printf("%d",number);
fclose(f2);
fclose(f3);
}
```

The fprintf and fscanf Functions

The fprintf and fscanf functions are identical to printf and scanf functions except that they work on files. The first argument of these functions is a file pointer which specifies the file to be used.

Syntax:

fprintf(fp,"control string", list);

Where fp is a file pointer associated with a file that has been opened for writing. The control string is file output specifications list may include variable, constant and string.

fprintf(f1,%s%d%f",name,age,7.5);

Here, name is an array variable of type char and age is an int variable.

Syntax:

fscanf(fp,"controlstring", list);

This statement would cause the reading of items in the control string.

Example:

fscanf(f2,"5s%d", item, &quantity");

Like scanf, fscanf also returns the number of items that are successfully read.

/*Program to handle mixed data types*/

```
#include <stdio.h>
#include <stdlib.h>
main(){
FILE *fp;
int num,qty,I;
float price,value;
char item[10],filename[10];
printf("Input filename");
scanf("%s",filename);
fp=fopen("filename","w");
printf("Input inventory data\n\n"0;
printf("Item namem number price quantity\n");
for (i=1;i< =3;i++) {
```

```
fscanf(stdin,"%s%d%f%d",item,&number,&price,&quality);
fprintf(fp,"%s%d%f%d",itemnumber,price,quality);
}
fclose (fp);
fprintf(stdout,"\n\n");
fp=fopen(filename,"r");
printf("Item name number price quantity value");
for(i=1;i< =3;i++) {
fscanf(fp,"%s%d%f%d",item,&number,&prince,&quality);
value=price*quantity");
fprintf(stdout,"%s%d%f%d%d\n",item,number,price,quantity,value);
}
fclose(fp);
}
```

RANDOM ACCESS FILES OR BINARY FILES

Random Access files are different from sequential text files in two important ways:

- You can jump instantly to any structure in the file, which provides random access as in an array.
- You can change the contents of a structure anywhere in the file at any time.

Once one opens a file one can read, write, or seek any arbitrary structure in the file. C maintains a "file pointer" to enable these functions. When the file is opened, the pointer points to record 0 (zero) (the first record in the file). Any read operation reads the currently pointed-to structure and moves the pointer to the next record or structure. A write is done at the currently pointed-to structure and moves the pointer down one structure. Sometimes it is required to access only a particular part and not the complete file.

This can be accomplished by using the following function: fseek moves the pointer to the specified record.

> fseek

fseek() Function

Syntax:

```
fseek(file pointer,offset, position);
```

This function is used to move the file position to a desired location within the file.

fileptr() Function

The Filter() is a pointer to the file concerned. Offset is a number or variable of type long, and position in an integer number. Offset specifies the number of positions (bytes) to be moved from the location specified by the position. The position can take the 3 values.

Value Meaning

(0) Beginning of the file

(1) Current position

(2) End of the file.

ftell() Function

ftell() function tells the current location of the file in bytes. The ftell takes file pointer as an argument and returns a long integer which corresponds to the current position in the file.

p = ftell(fp);

p – represents the relative offset, in bytes of the current position. This means that p bytes have already been read or return.

ftell() returns 0 when the file pointer position is at the end of the file, the value of p is equal to the size of the file in bytes.

rewind() Function

rewind() takes a file pointer and resets the position to the start of the file, i.e., the function repositions the filepointer to the beginning of the file.

Example: rewind(fp);

n = ftell(fp);

would assign 0 to n because the file position has been set to the start of the file by rewind. The first byte in the file is numbered as 0, second as 1 and so on.

It helps us in reading a file several times without having to close and open the file each time. Remember that whenever a file is opened for reading or writing, a rewind is done implicitly.

fread() and fwrite() Function

The fread() and fwrite() functions perform I/O on binary files. These functions are used to read data from a file into a structure variable or to write data from a structure variable to a file.

The fread and fwrite function takes four arguments:

- A memory address
- The number of bytes to read per block
- The number of blocks to read
- The file variable

C Program Examples

/* Program – Handling files with mixed data*/

```
#include <stdio.h>
# include <stdlib.h>
# include <conio.h>
# include <math.h>
# include <string.h>
# include <ctype.h>
main(){
FILE *fp;
int number,quantity,i;
float price,value;
char item[10],filename[10];
printf("input filename\n");
scanf("%s",filename);
fp=fopen("filename","w");
printf("input inventory data\n\n");
printf("item name number  price   quantity\n");
for(i=1;i<=3;i++)   {
fscanf(stdin, "%s%d%f%d", item,&number,&price,&quantity);
fprintf(fp,"%s%d%.2f%d", item,number,price,quantity);
}
fclose(fp);
fprintf(stdout,"\n\n");
```

```
fp=fopen("filename","r");
printf("item name NUMBER price quntity   value\n");
for(i=1;i<=3;i++){
fscanf(fp,"%s%d%f%d",item,&number,&price,&quantity);
value=price*quantity;
fprintf(stdout,"%-8s%7d%8.2f%8d%11.2f\n",item,number,price,quantity,value);
}
fclose(fp);
return(0);
}
```

/* Program for EOF Implementation*/

```
#include <stdio.h>
#include <stdlib.h>
main(){
int r,c;char name;
FILE *fp;
fp=fopen("test","w");
scanf("READ name %s%d",name,&r);
fprintf(fp,"%s\t%d",name,r);
fclose(fp);
name='\0';
r=0;
fp=fopen("test","r");
while((c=fscanf(fp,"%s%d",name,&r))!=EOF)
printf("print name %s%d",name,r);
fclose(fp);
return(0);
}
```

/* Program – getc and putc */

```
#include <stdio.h>
# include <conio.h>
#include <stdlib.h>
main(){
FILE *fp, *ft;
char ch;
clrscr();
fp=fopen("one.txt","r");
if(fp==0){
printf("cannot open source file");
exit();
}
else
{
ft=fopen("two.txt","w");
while(1){
ch=getc(fp);
if(ch==EOF)
break;
else
putc(ch,ft);
}
getch();
}
```

/*Program – fscanf and fprintf */

```
#include <stdio.h>
# include <stdlib.h>
# include <conio.h>
```

```
# include <math.h>
# include <string.h>
# include <ctype.h>
main(){
int price;
char name[10];
char con='y';
FILE *fp;
fp=fopen("book.dat","w+");
while(con=='y'){
printf("enter bookname and price");
scanf("%s%d",name ,&price);
fprintf("do you want to continue");
con=getchar();
}
fclose(fp);
fp=fopen(book.dat","r+");
while((fscanf(fp,"%s%d",name,&price))!=EOF){
printf("book name: %s",name);
printf("price: %d",price);
}
fclose(fp);
getch();
}
```

/*Program for demonstrating Binary files

```
#include <stdio.h>
#include <stdlib.h>
struct arec{
int x,y,z;
};
/* writes and then reads 5 records from the file "junk". */
```

```
int main(void){
int i,j;
FILE *f;
struct arec myrec;
/* create the file of 5 records */
f=fopen("junk","w");
if (!f)
return 1;
for (i=1;i<=5; i++){
myrec.x=i;
fwrite(&r,sizeof(struct arec),1,f);
}
fclose(f);
/* read the 5 records */
f=fopen("junk","r");
if (!f)
return 1;
for (i=1;i<=5; i++){
fread(&myrec,sizeof(struct arec),1,f);
printf("%d\n",.rx);
}
fclose(f);
 printf("\n");
/* use fseek to read the 5 records in reverse order */
f=fopen("junk","r");
if (!f)
return 1;
for (i=4; i>=0; i—){
fseek(f,sizeof(struct arec)*i,SEEK_SET);
fread(&myrec,sizeof(struct arec),1,f);
printf("%d\n",myrec.x);
```

```
}
fclose(f);
printf("\n");
/* use fseek to read 3rd record, change it, and write it back */
f=fopen("junk","r+");
if (!f)
return 1;
fseek(f,sizeof(struct arec)*2,SEEK_SET);
fread(&r,sizeof(struct arec),1,f);
myrec.x=100;
fseek(f,sizeof(struct arec)*3,SEEK_SET);
fwrite(&myrec,sizeof(struct arec),1,f);
fclose(f);
printf("\n");
return 0;
}
```

Review Questions

1. What is the primary advantage of using a data file?
2. What are streams? How they are useful in managing the data in a file?
3. What is meant by opening a data file? How is this accomplished?
4. What is the function of fclose function? Must a call to this function appear within a program that utilizes a data file?
5. Explain the significance of EOF.
6. Describe the use of getc() and putc() function.
7. How does an append mode differ from write mode?
8. Contrast on the use of fscanf and fprintf functions with the use of scanf and printf functions.
9. Explain the concept of error handling in file management.
10. Write a C program to copy the contents of one file into another.
11. What are text files? Explain with examples.
12. Discuss about the random access files with examples.

CHAPTER

10

Dynamic Memory Allocation

INTRODUCTION

When we declare an array, we need to reserve some memory to store the elements of this array. This memory allocation is stati, i.e., when we declare an array, we specify the number of elements in that array and a fixed memory is allocated. Once declared, the size of the array cannot be changed. But there are situations in which we may want to declare the variable and not allocate memory for it until we use that variable. We may also want to free the memory allocated for a variable after its use is over. So, data structures should be used to grow or shrink as elements are added or removed.

The dynamic allocation of memory during the program execution is achieved through two built-in functions malloc or calloc, realloc and free. There is also sizeof() function used to determine the number of bytes occupied by an entity in memory.

The operating system maintains a pool of free (unallocated) memory from which bytes of memory can be provided to an application, or to which an application can return unused memory; this process is called dynamic memory allocation.

DYNAMIC MEMORY ALLOCATION FUNCTIONS

C provides four standard routines of dynamic memory allocation functions:

- malloc( )
- calloc( )
- free( )
- realloc( )

MALLOC( )

- This function allocates the block of memory in bytes.
- This function is like a request to the RAM of the system to allocate the memory, if the request is granted, it returns a pointer to the first block of that block of memory and the type of pointer it returns is void. And if the request is not granted, then it returns a NULL.
- This function is available in the header file <stdlib.h> or <alloc.h>

Syntax:

```
malloc(number of elements*size of each element);
```

Example:

```
int * ptr;
ptr=malloc(10*sizeof(int));
```

Since type of ponter it returns is void, so type_casting is required to change the return pointer type.

Example of type_casting:

```
int * ptr;
ptr=(int*)malloc(10*sizeof(int));
```

CALLOC( )

- It works similar to the malloc() function except that it requires two arguments.
- This function is available in the header file <stdlib.h> or <alloc.h>
- The memory allocated by the malloc() contains garbage values and the memory allocated by calloc() contains all zeros.

Syntax:

```
ptr = calloc(number of elements, size of each element);
```

Example:

```
int * ptr;
ptr = (int*)calloc(10,2);
```

FREE( )

- This function is used to deallocate the previously allocated memory using malloc() or calloc() function.
- Free function is used to return the allocated memory block to the system memory RAM.

Syntax:

```
free(ptr);
```

REALLOC( )

- This function is used to resize the size of memory block, which is already allocated.
- This function is available in the header file <stdlib.h> or <alloc.h>
- Note that before using the realloc() function, the memory block to be resized should be allocated using the following statement:

```
ptr = malloc(size);
```

Syntax:

```
ptr = realloc(ptr, new_size);
```

Till now we have used variables which require all variables to be declared before we use it. So if we need to store 100 students roll nos., then we need to declare 100 individual integer variables. This problem can be solved with the help of array; a single array declaration can store 100 or more integer values. One of the biggest limitation is array size cannot be increased or decreased during the execution of a program. To get this better, consider the following C program statement:

```
int roll_no[100];
```

Suppose we want to store roll_no of 100 students (200 bytes of memory occupied due to above declaration) and above C language statement will do the same task. During C program execution, if we think to enter only 40 students' roll_no's instead of 100. This decision of entering only 40 students roll_no will use 80 bytes out of 200 bytes (2 bytes per integer*40 students) of memory and remaining 120 bytes of memory will be useless.

If we want to store 150 students' roll_no using same program, we cannot do so because we have already declared the array to store only 100 students' roll_no. To overcome this memory allocation problem, we need to dynamically allocate memory according to user input. We can do this with C's two in-built functions calloc, malloc and a pointer. Calloc and malloc are the two functions which help us to dynamically allocate memory at run time (during program execution) and this can reduce memory wastage problem.

/* Program to show Dynamic Memory Allocation using Malloc() */

```
#include <stdio.h>
#include <conio.h>
#include <stdlib.h>
void main(){
int no, *pt,i;
clrscr();
printf("Enter no of Students:");
scanf("%d",&no);
pt=(int *)malloc(no*2);
if(pt== NULL){
printf("\n\nMemory allocation failed!");
getch();
exit(0);
}
printf("* * * * Enter roll no of students. * * * *\n");
for (i=0;i<no;i++){
printf("—>");
scanf("%d",(pt+i));
}
printf("\n* * ** Entered roll no. * * * *\n");
for (i=0;i<no;i++){
printf("%d, ",*(pt+i));
}
getch();
}
```

EXPLANATION

The above program is a simple C program, which uses integer pointer to dynamically allocate memory according to user's input at runtime. We can do this either with malloc() or calloc(). In this example, we are using malloc() and calloc() functions. To use malloc() or calloc() function, we must include stdlib.h or alloc.h header file otherwise you will get malloc prototype error at compilation. Line no. 3 includes the stdlib.h header file. In line no. 7, an integer pointer pt and some other integer is declared which we will need later in input and loop. Line no. 11 stores integer number in no variable which is used as number of students whose roll number we are going to input. Next line (line no. 12) is most important one in this program; it does all allocation jobs. If malloc function is able to allocate memory, then it returns address of memory chunk that was allocated else it returns NULL.

```
pt = (int *)malloc(no*2);
```

malloc is a function that requires one parameter or argument, i.e., number of bytes to reserve. In our program, we provided no*2 as parameter. The variable no. holds the number of students whose roll no we are going to enter. But we are multiplying no with 2 because, we want to store roll numbers of 10 students. We stored 10 in no variable and passed this no variable in malloc function. The integer occupies 2 bytes and we wanted to store 10 students information. And if we pass 10 to malloc then compiler will reserve 10 bytes only which can store only 5 students' information. To solve this issue, we have multiplied no. with 2 so if you enter 10 then it will reserve 20 bytes of memory. If you don't remember which data type occupies how much memory, then you can use sizeof() which return data type size.

```
pt=(int *)malloc(no*sizeof(int));
```

Just before malloc() we have used (int *), this is called type casting (means converting from one data type to other compatible data type). If memory allocation is successful, then malloc() by default returns pointer to a void and we typecast that to integer pointer and stores the address in pt integer pointer variable. So, pt pointer contains starting address of memory allocated using malloc().

If, due to any reason, malloc() fails to allocate memory it returns NULL. Line no. 13-18 does the same job, if malloc() fails to allocate memory then it will show error and exit from program.

Line no 21-25 is used to take roll no. of student and store it in memory. Look at line no. 24 and particularly at (pt + i) statement. Integer pointer pt contains starting address of memory which is allocated by malloc() and by adding i variable value we are instructing it to move further to store value in that memory chunk. For example, if pointer starting address is 1002 then (pt+1) would mean 1004, (pt+2) = 1006 and so on.

Line no. 28-31 prints the value stored in the memory and thing is simple

/*Consider an example */

```
#include <math.h>
#include <stdio.h>
#include <alloc.h>
#define l 4
main(){
int *a, i,*p;
float *b,*c;
a=(int*) malloc(l);
for (i=0; i<l; i++){
*(a+i)=i;
}
for (i=0; i<l; i++){
printf ("a %d %d %u \n",i,*(a+i),(a+i));
}
p=(int*) calloc(l,4);
for (i=0; i<l; i++){
*(p+i)=i*2;
}
for (i=0; i<l; i++){
printf(" p %d %d %u %d\n",i,*(p+i),(p+i),sizeof(p));
}
b=(float*)malloc(l);
for(i=0;i<l+2;i++){
*(b+i)=i*4.0;
}
for(i=0;i<l+2;i++){
printf("b %d %f %u %d\n", i,*(b+i),(b+i),sizeof(b));
c=calloc(l,8);
```

```
for(i=0;i<l;i++){
*(c+i)=i*4.0;
}
for(i=0;i<l+1;i++){
printf(" c %d %f %u %d \n", i,*(c+i),(c+i),sizeof(c));
}
for(i=l+1;i<l+2;i++){
printf(" b %d %f %u \n", i,*(b+i),(b+i));
}
}
```

In the program above, we create an integer pointer ***a** two floating point pointers ***b**,***c**. Now we want to store a string of numbers using these pointers, instead of using a fixed size array, we first have to allocate enough space in the memory to which the pointers point to. We will allocate just enough memory to store the elements we want to. For example in the above program, we want to store 4 integer values. By using the malloc function, we will allocate memory for an integer array of size 4.

We invoke it by the statement

```
a=(int *) malloc(l);
```

We could also do the same with

```
p=(int *) malloc(l*sizeof(int)); or
p=(int *) malloc(l*size(a)); where l=4.
```

One important thing to note here is that since malloc returns a void pointer, we need to type cast it before equating it to the pointer we want. In the above case, **a** an integer so we have to use (int *) before malloc. Similarly, we see the use of a malloc to allocate memory for a float pointer **b**. We use the pointer p to demonstrate that we can do exactly the same using the function calloc. The function is exactly the same, except that we need not typecast it now and also that we have to give a second argument to **calloc**, which is the number of bytes need to store one variable. In most of the modern compilers, this value is ignored by the function.

So far, we have seen operations which are pretty much like that in the fixed size arrays. The only difference is that we assign the memory only just before the variable is used. This by itself is not very useful unless we can change this memory allocation, which increase it, if we want more and remove it, if we don't want to use the variable again in the program. This is what **realloc** and **free** will do for us. Let us look at the example.

/*Program–Dynamic memory allocation realloc and free functions*/

```
#include <math.h>
#include <stdio.h>
#include <alloc.h>
#define l 5
main(){
float *a;
int i;
a=(float *) malloc(l);
for(i=0;i<l;i++){
*(a+i)=i*3.0;
}
for(i=0;i<l;i++){
printf("a %d %f %u \n", i,*(a+i),(a+i));
}
a=(float *)realloc(a,sizeof(float)*(l+3));
for(i=0;i<l+3;i++){
*(a+i)=i*3.0;
}
for(i=0;i<l+3;i++){
printf("a %d %f %u \n", i,*(a+i),(a+i));
}
free(a);
}
```

In the above program, we have a pointer 'a' which is of type float. We then give it enough memory space to store 5 elements. After filling and printing out the address of those locations and the value stored in them, we increase the "size" of the memory allocated by the statement

"a=(float *)realloc(a, sizeof(float)*(l+3));".

This statement will increase the memory space to store 3 more floating points. You can see by yourself that if you remove this line and try to store more than 5 elements into 'a' you will get segmentation fault. The last statement in the program "free(a);" free all the space allotted to 'a'.

Thus, by using malloc, realloc and free we can change the memory taken up by the program as required by it. This is particularly useful when we have to use large temporary arrays in a calculation.

FUNCTIONS AND POINTERS TO FUNCTIONS – DYNAMIC MEMORY ALLOCATION

We hav e seen how to pass array to a function, return array from a function, and declare arrays, pointer arrays, pointers to arrays and also dynamic memory allocation. We will now see a different use of pointers that is to invoke function calls. Before we go on to the description of pointer to a function, let us have quick review of the structure of functions. All functions have the following components.

Definition

- type function name (arguments passed to the function)
- variable declaration of the arguments

ARGUMENT PASSING

Two ways of passing variables to a function are:

(1) Call by value

Here, the function works with a copy of the variable. Changes made in the function will not effect its value in the calling function

(2) Call by reference

Here the address of the variable is passed to the function. Changes made in the function will change its value in the calling function.

for example:

```
#include <math.h>
#include <stdio.h>
#include <alloc.h>
#define l 4
main(){
```

```
float b; int a[2],*c;
void myfunction();
c=(int*)malloc(1);
b=10.0;
*c=5;
a[0]=1;a[1]=2;
printf ("before function call %f %d  %d %d\n", b,a[1],a[2],*c);
myfunction (b,a,c);
printf ("after  function call %f %d %d %d\n", b,a[1],a[2],*c);
}
void myfunction (x,y,d)
float x;
int y[2],*d;
{
float z;
x=2*x;
y[0]=3*y[0];
y[1]=3*y[1];
*d=*d+2;
}
```

In this example, the main function is passing "b, a and c" to "myfunction", which receives it as "x, y and d ". Since 'a' is an array an 'c' is a pointer they are passed by "reference" while b is passed by value. Inside myfunction, all the values are altered. We print out the values of "b, a and c" in the main function before and after the call to myfunction. The output is:

```
before function call 10.000000 1 2 5
after function call 10.000000 3 6 7
```

We see that the variable that is passed by value does not get altered while any changes made to quantities that are passed by reference, in the sub-function will alter its value in the main function as well.

Review Questions

1. What is dynamic memory allocation? How does it help in building complex programs in C?
2. Differentiate the malloc() and calloc() functions.
3. How can you increase the size of a dynamically allocated array? Explain with an example.
4. Can you dynamically allocate arrays in expanded memory?

CHAPTER 11 Errors in C Programming

BEGINNER ERRORS

These are the errors that beginning C students often make.

Forgetting to put a break in a switch Statement

Remember that C does not break out of a switch statement if a case is encountered.

For example:

```
int x = 2;
switch(x){
case 2:   printf("Two\n");
case 3:   printf("Three\n");
}
```

prints out:

```
Two
Three
```

Put a break to break out of the switch:

```
int x = 2;
switch(x){
case 2:
printf("Two\n");
break;
case 3:
```

```
printf("Three\n");
break;  /* not necessary, but good if additional cases are added later */
}
```

Using = instead of ==

C's = operator is used exclusively for assignment and returns the value assigned.

The = = operator is used exclusively for comparison and returns an integer value (0 for *false*, not for *true*). Because of these return values, the C compiler often does not flag an error when '=' is used when one really wanted an = =.

For example:

```
int x = 5;
if (x = 6)
printf("x equals 6\n");
```

This code prints out x equals 6, because the assignment inside the if sets x to 6 and returns the value 6 to the if. Since 6 is not 0, this is interpreted as *true*.

One way to have the compiler find this type of error is to put any constants (or any r-value expressions) on the left side. Then if an = is used, it will be an error:

```
if (6 = x)
```

scanf() Errors

There are two types of common scanf() errors:

(1) Forgetting to Put an Ampersand (&) on Arguments

The scanf() must have the address of the variable to store input into. This means that often the ampersand address operator is required to compute the addresses. Here's an example:

```
int x;
char * st = malloc(31);
scanf("%d", &x);/* & required to pass address to scanf()*/
scanf("%30s", st);/* NO & here, st itself points to variable*/
```

As the last line above shows, sometimes no ampersand is correct!

(2) Using the Wrong Format for Operand

C compilers do *not* check that the correct format is used for arguments of a scanf() call. The most common errors are using the %f format for doubles (which must use the %lf format) and mixing up %c and %s for characters and strings.

Size of Arrays

Arrays in C always start at index 0. This means that an array of 10 integers defined as:

```
int a[10];
```

has valid indices from 0 to 9 *not* 10! It is very common for students go one too far in an array. This can lead to unpredictable behavior of the program.

Integer Division

Unlike Pascal, C uses the '/' operator for both real and integer division. It is important to understand how C determines which it will do. If both operands are of an integral type, integer division is used, else real division is used.

For example:

```
double half = 1/2;
```

This code sets half to 0 not 0.5! why because 1 and 2 are integer constants. To fix this, change atleast one of them to a real constant.

```
double half = 1.0/2;
```

If both operands are integer variables and real division is desired, cast one of the variables to double (or float).

```
int x = 5, y = 2;
double d = ((double) x)/y;
```

Loop Errors

In C, a loop repeats the very next statement after the loop statement. The code:

```
int x = 5;

while(x > 0);

x— —;
```

is an infinite loop, why because the semicolon after the while defines the statement to repeat as the null statement (which does nothing). Remove the semicolon and the loop works as expected.

Another common loop error is to iterate one too many times or one too few. Check loop conditions carefully!

Not Using Prototypes

Prototypes tell the compiler important features of a function: the return type and the parameters of the function. If no prototype is given, the compiler *assumes* that the function returns an int and can take any number of parameters of any type.

One important reason to use prototypes is to let the compiler check for errors in the argument lists of function calls. However, a prototype *must* be used if the function does not return an int. **For example,** the sqrt() function returns a double, not an int.

The following code:

```
double x = sqrt(2);
```

will not work correctly if a prototype:

```
double sqrt(double);
```

does not appear above it, because without a prototype, the C compiler assumes that sqrt() returns an int. Since the returned value is stored in a double variable, the compiler inserts code to convert the value to a double. This conversion is not needed and will result in the wrong value.

The solution to this problem is to include the correct C header file that contains the sqrt() prototype, math.h. For functions you write, you must either place the prototype at the top of the source file or create a header file and include it.

Not Initializing Pointers

Anytime you use a pointer, you should be able to answer the question: *What variable does this point to?* If you cannot answer this question, it is likely it doesn't point to *any* variable. This type of error will often result in a segmentation fault/core dump error on UNIX/LINUX or a general protection fault under Windows (anything could happen!).

Here's an example of this type of error.

```
#include <string.h>
int main(){
char * st;/* defines a pointer to a char or char array*/
strcpy(st, "abc"); /* what char array does st point to??*/
return 0;
}
```

The correct method of usage is using an array or dynamically allocating an array.

```
#include <string.h>
int main(){
char st[20];/* defines an char array*/
strcpy(st, "abc");/* st points to char array*/
return 0;
}
```

or

```
#include <string.h>
#include <alloc.h>
int main(){
char *st = malloc(20);  /* st points to allocated array*/
strcpy(st, "abc");  /* st points to char array */
free(st);           /* don't forget to deallocate when done! */
eturn 0;
}
```

Actually, the first solution is much preferred for what this code does. Dynamical allocation should only be used when it is required. It is slower and more error-prone than just defining a normal array.

STRING ERRORS

Confusing Character and String Constants

C considers character and string constants as very different things. Character constants are enclosed in single quotes and string constants are enclosed in *double quotes*. String constants act as a pointer to the actual string.

Consider the following code:

```
char ch = 'A';     /* correct */
char ch = "A";     /* error   */
```

The second line assigns the character variable ch to the address of a string constant. This should generate a compiler error. The same should happen if a string pointer is assigned to a character constant:

```
const char * st = "A";   /* correct */
const char * st = 'A';   /* error   */
```

Comparing Strings with ==

Never use the == operator to compare the value of strings! Strings are char arrays. The name of a char array acts like a pointer to the string (just like other types of arrays in C).

Consider the following code:

```
char st1[] = "abc";
char st2[] = "abc";
```

```
if ( st1 == st2 )
  printf("Yes");
else
  printf("No");
```

This code prints out No, because the == operator is comparing the *pointer values* of st1 and st2, not the data pointed to by them. The correct way to compare string values is to use the strcmp() library function (Be sure to include string.h). If the if statement above is replaced with the following:

```
if ( strcmp(st1,st2) == 0 )
  printf("Yes");
else
  printf("No");
```

the code will print out *Yes*. For similar reasons, don't use the other relational operators (<, >, *etc.*) with strings either. Use strcmp() here too.

Not Null Terminating Strings

C assumes that a string is a character array with a terminating null character. This null character has ASCII value 0 and can be represented as just 0 or '\0'. This value is used to mark the end of meaningful data in the string. If this value is missing, many C string functions will keep processing data past the end of the meaningful data and often past the end of the character array itself until it happens to find a zero byte in memory!

Most C library string functions that create strings will always properly null terminate them. Some do not use (*e.g.*, strncpy()). Be sure to read their descriptions carefully.

Not Leaving Room for the Null Terminator

A C string must have a null terminator at the end of the meaningful data in the string. A common mistake is to not allocate room for this extra character. For example, the string defined below:

```
char str[30];
```

only has room for only 29 (not 30) actually data characters, since a null *must* appear after the last data character.

This can also be a problem with dynamic allocation. Below is the correct way to allocate a string to the exact size needed to hold a copy of another.

```
char * copy_str = malloc( strlen(orig_str) + 1);
strcpy(copy_str, orig_str);
```

The common mistake is to forget to add one to the return value of strlen(). The strlen() function returns a count of the data characters which does *not* include the null terminator.

This type of error can be very hard to detect. It might not cause any problems or only problems in extreme cases. In the case of dynamic allocation, it might corrupt the *heap* (the area of the program's memory used for dynamic allocation) and cause the *next* heap operation (malloc(), free(), *etc.*) to fail.

INPUT/OUTPUT ERRORS

Using fgetc(), getc() and getchar() Incorrectly

The fgetc(), getc() and getchar() functions all return back an *integer* value. For example, the prototype of fgetc() is:

```
int fgetc(FILE *);
```

Sometimes, this integer value is really a simple character, but there is one very important case where the return value is **not** a character!

What is this value? **EOF.** A common misconception of students is that files have a special EOF character at the end. There is no special character stored at the end of a file. EOF is an *integer* error code returned by a function. Here is the **wrong** way to use fgetc():

```
int count_line_size(FILE * fp)
{
char ch;
int  cnt = 0;
while((ch = fgetc(fp)) != EOF && ch != '\n')
cnt++;
return cnt;
}
```

The problem occurs in the condition of the while loop. To illustrate, here is the loop rewritten to show what C will do behind the scenes.

```
while( (int) (ch = (char) fgetc(fp)) != EOF && ch != '\n')
cnt++;
```

The return value of fgetc(fp) is cast to char to store the result into ch. Then the value of ch must be cast back to an int to compare it with EOF. So, casting an int value to a char and then back to an int may not give back the original int value. This means in the example above that if fgetc() returns back the EOF value, the casting may change the value so that the comparison later with EOF would be false.

The solution is to make the ch variable an int as below:

```
int count_line_size(FILE * fp)
{
int  cnt = 0;
while((ch = fgetc(fp)) != EOF && ch != '\n')
cnt++;
return cnt;
}
```

Now the only hidden cast is in the second comparison.

```
while((ch = fgetc(fp)) != EOF &&  ch != '\n'))
cnt++;
```

This cast has no harmful effects at all! So, the moral of all this is: always use an int variable to store the result of the fgetc(), getc() and getchar().

Using feof() Incorrectly

There is a widespread misunderstanding of how C's feof() function works. Many programmers use it like Pascal's eof() function. However, C's function works differently! The difference is Pascal's function returns true if the *next* read will fail because of end of file. C's function returns true if the *last* function failed. Here's an example of a misuse of feof():

```
#include <stdio.h>
int main() {
FILE * fp = fopen("test.txt", "r");
char line[100];
while(! feof(fp)) {
fgets(line, sizeof (line), fp);
fputs(line, stdout);
}
fclose(fp);
return 0;
}
```

This program will print out the last line of the input file *twice*, why because after the last line is read in and printed out, feof() will still return 0 (false) and the loop will continue. The next fgets() fails and so the line variable holding the contents of the last line is not changed and is printed out again. After this, feof() will return true (since fgets() failed) and the loop ends.

For example:

```
#include <stdio.h>
int main(){
FILE * fp = fopen("test.txt", "r");
char line[100];
while(1){
fgets(line, sizeof(line), fp);
if (feof(fp))/* check for EOF right after fgets() */
break;
fputs(line, stdout);
}
fclose(fp);
return 0;
}
```

However, this is not the best way. There is really no reason to use feof() at all. C input functions return values that can be used to check for EOF. For example, fgets returns the NULL pointer on EOF. Here's a better version of the program:

```
#include <stdio.h>
int main(){
FILE * fp = fopen("test.txt", "r");
char line[100];
while(fgets(line, sizeof(line), fp) != NULL)
fputs(line, stdout);
fclose(fp);
return 0;
}
```

Leaving Characters in the Input Buffer

C input (and output) functions buffer data. Buffering stores data in memory and only reads (or writes) the data from (or to) I/O devices when needed. Reading and writing data in big chunks is much more efficient than a byte (or character) at a time. Often the buffering has no effect on programming.

One place where buffering is visible is input using scanf(). The keyboard is usually line buffered. This means that each line input is stored in a buffer. Problems can arise when a program does not process all the data in a line, before it wants to process the next line of input.

For example, consider the following code:

```
int x;
char st[31];
printf("Enter an integer: ");
scanf("%d", &x);
printf("Enter a line of text: ");
fgets(st, 31, stdin);
```

The fgets() will not read the line of text that is typed in. Instead, it will probably just read an empty line. In fact, the program will not even wait for an input for the fgets() call. Because the scanf() call reads the characters needed that represent the integer number read in, but it leaves the '\n' in the input buffer. The fgets() then starts reading data from the input buffer. It finds a '\n' and stops without needing any additional keyboard input.

The solution for this is one simple method to read and dump all the characters from the input buffer until a '\n' after the scanf() call. Since this is something that might be used in lots of places, it makes sense to make this a function. Here is a function that does just this:

function dump_line: This function reads and dumps any remaining characters on the current input line of a file.

Parameter: fp - pointer to a FILE to read characters from

Precondition: fp points to a open file

Postcondition: the file referenced by fp is positioned at the end of the next line or the end of the file. */

```
void dump_line(FILE * fp){
int ch;
while((ch = fgetc(fp)) != EOF && ch != '\n')
```

```
/* null body */;
}
```

Here is the code above fixed by using the above function:

```
int x;
char st[31];
printf("Enter an integer:");
scanf("%d", &x);
dump_line(stdin);
printf("Enter a line of text:");
fgets(st, 31, stdin);
```

One incorrect solution is to use the following:

```
fflush(stdin);
```

This will compile but its behavior is undefined by the ANSI C standard. The fflush() function is only meant to be used on streams open for output, not input. This method does seem to work with some C compilers, but is completely unportable! Thus, it should not be used.

Using the gets() Function

Do not use this function: It does not know how many characters can be safely stored in the string passed to it. Thus, if too many are read, memory will be corrupted. Many security bugs that have been exploited on the internet use this fact. Use the fgets() function instead (and read from stdin). But remember that unlike gets(), fgets() does *not* discard a terminating \n from the input.

The scanf() functions can also be used dangerously. The %s format can overwrite the destination string. However, it can be used safely by specifying a width. For example, the format %20s will not read more than 20 characters.

PART-II

Data Structures

CHAPTER 12

Introduction to Data Structures

INTRODUCTION

Data structure is a study of different methods of organizing the data and possible operations on structure. In a modern computer, data consists fundamentally of binary bits, but meaningful data is organized into primitive data types such as integer, real and boolean and into more complex data structures such as arrays and binary trees. These data types and data structures always come along with associated operations that can be done on the data. For example, the 32-bit int data type is defined both by the fact that a value of type int consists of 32 binary bits but also by the fact that two int values can be added, subtracted, multiplied, compared, and so on. An array is defined both by the fact that it is a sequence of data items of the same basic type, but also by the fact that it is possible to directly access each of the positions in the list based on its numerical index. So, the idea of a data type includes a specification of the possible values of that type together with the operations that can be performed on those values.

An algorithm is an abstract idea, and a program is an implementation of an algorithm. Similarly, it is useful to be able to work with the abstract idea behind a data type or data structure, without getting bogged down in the implementation details. The abstraction in this case is called an "abstract data type." An abstract data type specifies the values of the type, but not how those values are represented as collections of bits, and it specifies operations on those values in terms of their inputs, outputs, and effects rather than as particular algorithms or program code.

ABSTRACT DATA TYPE OR ADT

The idea of an Abstract Data Type (ADT) is to support this (the idea is generally considered good for program maintainability as well, but that is no great concern for this particular course). The specification of an ADT is a list of the operations that may be performed on it, together with the identities that they satisfy. This specification does not show how to implement anything in terms of any simpler data types. The user of an ADT is expected to view this specification as the complete description of how the data type and its associated functions will behave — no other way of interrogating or modifying data is available, and the response to any circumstances not covered explicitly in the specification is deemed undefined.

Abstract data type is also defined as a mathematical model which is a user-defined type along with the set of primitive operations that can be performed on that model. Basically abstract data type has two parts; the first part signifies the way in which the components are related to each other and the second part signifies the operations that can be operated on the components of the abstract data type.

Terminology

Data

Data is derived from a Latin word "Datum" which means collection. So, data can be defined as collection of facts and figures.

Data is classified into two types.

(1) Group data Item

(2) Elementary data Item

(1) Group Data Item

Data item that can be subdivided into different segments is called group data item.

For example: name is a group data item because it can be subdivided into different segments, i.e., First name, middle name and last name.

(2) Elementary Data Item

The data item that cannot be subdivided into different segments is called elementary data item.

For example: Account No., ID Number, etc.

Field

Field is the collection of related characters.

For example: Name, Roll No., Class, etc.

A single field cannot provide full information about any entity.

Record

Record is the collection of related fields.

For example: The record of student includes its Roll No, Name, Class and Registration No., etc.

Table/ Relation/File

Collection of related records is called a file or table.

For example

R.No.	Name	Class
1 Mohammad	3rd	Year
2 Ram	2nd	Year
3 Anthony	1st	Year

DATA STRUCTURE

Data structure is a mathematical way for storage of data in the computer memory. It is the way of storing and accessing the data from the computer memory, so that number of data is processed in small interval of time.

TYPES OF DATA STRUCTURES

There are two types of data structure:

(1) Linear Data Structure

(2) Non-linear Data Structure

(1) Linear Data Structure

When the data is to be stored in the memory in linear form, it is called linear data structure.

For example: Array, Stack, Queue, Linked List etc.

(2) Non-linear Data Structure

When the data is to be stored in the computer memory in dispersed order, it is called non-linear data structure.

For example: trees, files, graphs, etc.

CLASSIFICATION OF LINEAR DATA STRUCTURE

It can be classified into two types.

(1) Physical Data Structure

(2) Logical Data Structure

(1) Physical Data Structure

When the data is to be stored in the computer memory in proper order, it is called physical data structure.

Example: We insert the data in one-dimensional array, the data is stored in the memory in that way, as we insert the data in sequence.

(2) Logical Data Structure

The two-dimensional array is called logical data structure because we are not sure, that in which format data is stored in the memory, then we represent the data in the memory at row major order or column major order, so due to this reason it is called logical data structure.

OPERATIONS PERFORMED ON DATA STRUCTURE

When data is preceding, different types of operations are performed. Following are most important operations which play major role in data structures.

(1) Traversing: Accessing of records is called traversing. It is also known as visiting of records.

(2) Searching: Finding the location of record with given value is called searching.

(3) Sorting: The arrangement of data in ascending or descending order is called sorting.

(4) Insertion: Adding new record to structure is called inserting.

(5) Deletions: Removing a record or a set of records from data structure is called deleting process.

(6) Merging: When two or more than two records are combined it is called merging.

(7) Copying: The creation of duplicate data item is called copying process.

LISTS

The arrangement of elements in some sequence is called list. There are two types of lists.

(i) Ordered List

(ii) Unordered List

(i) Ordered List

The proper sequence of elements is called ordered list.

For example: The days of week, the month of year, seasons of year, etc.

(ii) Unordered List

In this type of list, the storage of elements does not take place in proper order.

For example: Stack, Queue, Dequeue, Circular Queue and Linked List.

Review Questions

1. What is a data structure? List out the areas in which data structures are applied extensively?
2. What does abstract data type means?
3. Define ADT? What are its advantages?
4. What are the different operations performed on data structures?

ঙ্গঙ্গঙ্গ

CHAPTER

13

Stack Operations

A stack is an ordered list in which all insertions and deletions are made at one end, called the top. The last element to be inserted into the stack will be the first to be removed. Thus, stacks are sometimes referred to as Last In First Out (LIFO) lists.

The insertion operation is referred to as 'push' and deletion operation refers to 'pop'.

Given a stack S=(a[1],a[2],.......a[n]) then we say that a[1] is the bottommost element and element a[i], is on top of element a[i-1], 1<i<=n.

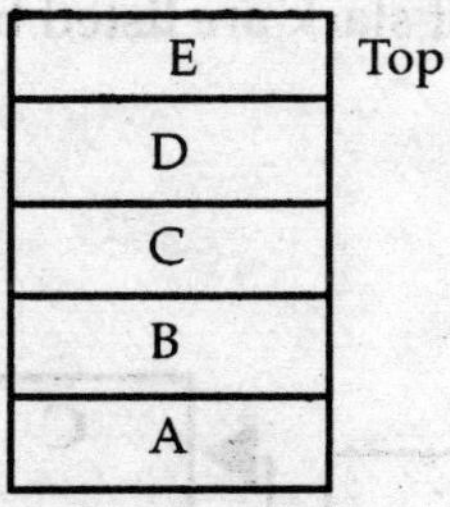

Fig.13.1: Stsck

The restrictions on a stack imply that if the elements A, B, C, D, E are added to the stack, in that order, then the first element to be removed/deleted must be E. Equivalently, we say that the last element to be inserted into the stack will be the first to be removed.

STACK INTERFACE

The following operations can be applied to a stack:

InitStack(Stack): creates an empty stack

Push (Item): pushes an item on the stack

Pop(Stack): removes the first item from the stack

Top(Stack): returns the first item from the stack without removing it

isEmpty(Stack): returns true is the stack is empty

OPERATIONS ON STACK

Different operation can be performed with stack.

(1)	Create Stack	:	The creation of stack structure
(2)	Push Operation	:	The insertion of element in the stack.
(3)	Pop Operation	:	The deletion of element from the stack
(4)	Full Stack	:	If stack is full, true value is returned, i.e., Boolean value
(5)	Empty Stack	:	If stack is empty, true value is returned, i.e., Boolean value

Two Major Operations of the Stack

(1) **Overflow:** When the stack is full and new element is inserted/pushed, then overflow condition occurs.

(2) **Underflow:** When the stack is empty and a deletion/pop process is performed, underflow condition occurs.

A stack is very useful in situations when data have to be stored and then retrieved in the reverse order. Some applications of stack are listed below:

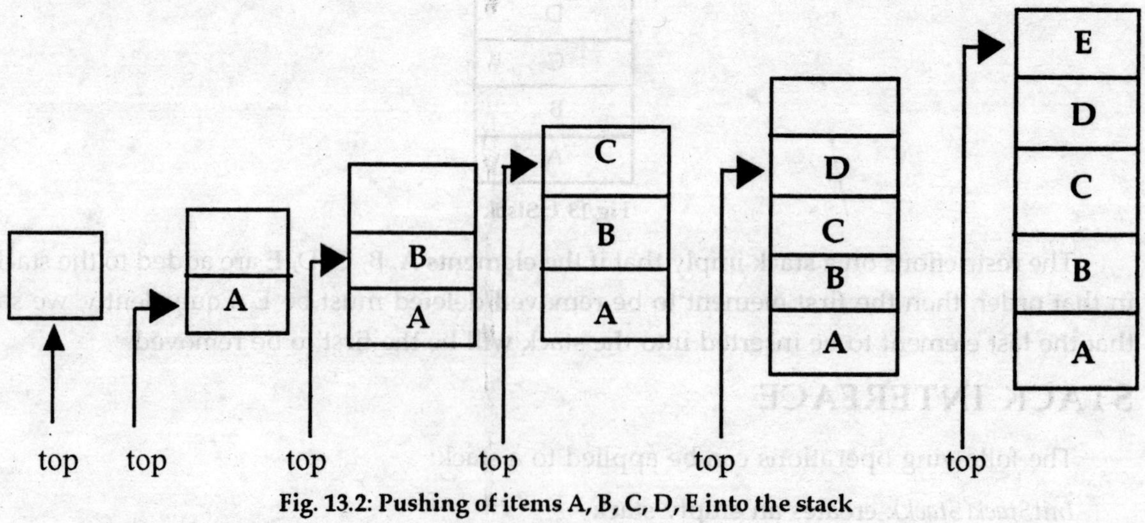

Fig. 13.2: Pushing of items A, B, C, D, E into the stack

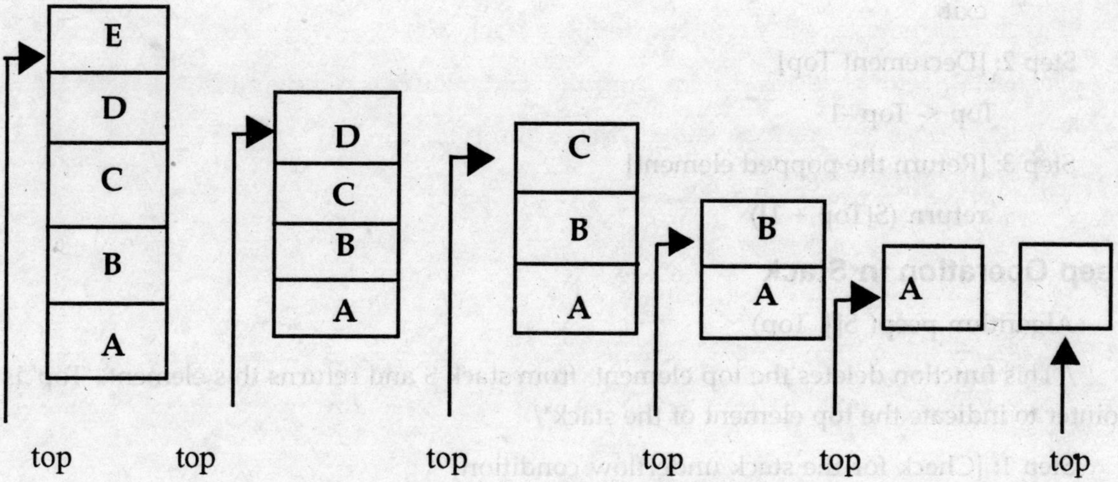

Fig. 13.3: Deleting or popping data items E, D, C, B, A

Adding or Pushing into Stack

Algorithm Push(S[], Top, item)

/* This function inserts an element 'item' to the top of stack which is represented by S, containing N elements with a pointer 'Top', denoting the top element of the stack*/

Step1: [Check for the stack overflow condition]

if (Top >= N) then

print "Stack Overflow"

return

Step 2: [Increment Top]

S[Top] <- item

Step 3: [Finished]

return

Deletion or Poping in Stack

Algorithm Pop(S[], Top)

/* This function deletes the top element from stack S and returns this element. 'Top' is a pointer to indicate the top element of the stack*/

Step 1: [Check for the stack underflow condition]

if (Top = = 0) then

print "Stack Underflow"

exit

Step 2: [Decrement Top]

Top <- Top -1

Step 3: [Return the popped element]

return (S[Top + 1])

Peep Operation in Stack

Algorithm peep(S[], Top)

/*This function deletes the top element from stack S and returns this element. 'Top' is a pointer to indicate the top element of the stack*/

Step 1: [Check for the stack underflow condition]

if (Top – i+1 < 0) then

print "Stack Underflow on peep operation"

exit

Step 2: [Return ith element from Top of stack]

return (S[Top – i - 1])

Change Operation

Algorithm Change(S[], Top, itemvalue, i)

/*Itemvalue to be palced in ith location of stack S, containing N elements. Top is a pointer variable to denote top of the stack*/

Step 1: [Check for the stack underflow condition]

if (Top – i +1 < =0) then

print "Stack Underflow on change operation"

return

Step 2: [Change the ith element with the value of item value]

S[Top – i + 1] <- itemvalue

Step 3: [Finished]

return

Display of Stack

Algorithm Display(S[])

/*To display the contents of stack S, containing N elements. Top is a pointer variable to denote top of the stack */

Step 1: [Check whether stack is empty or not]

if (Top = =0) then

print "Stack empty"

return

Step 2: [Display the stack elements]

Repeat for i = Top down to 1

print (S[i])

Step 3: [End]

Stop

APPLICATIONS OF STACKS

(1) Reversing the string.

(2) Converting Decimal to binary, Octal

(3) Polish Notation (conversion of Infix to Postfix/Prefix, Evaluation of Postfix/Prefix expression.

Example: Evaluation of arithmetic expressions:

Usually, arithmetic expressions are written in *infix* notations.

Example: A+B*C

An expression can as well be written in *postfix* notation (also called *reverse polish notation*):

A+B becomes AB+

A*C becomes AC*

A+B*C becomes ABC*+

(A+B)*C becomes AB+C*

Example:

Push()

5	
4	
3	21
2	12
1	5

Push(41)

5	
4	41
3	21
2	12
1	5

Pop()

5	
4	41
3	21
2	12
1	5

Pop(41)

5	
4	
3	21
2	12
1	5

LARGE NUMBER ARITHMETIC

As another example, consider adding very large numbers. Suppose, we wanted to add 353, 120, 457, 764, 910, 452, 008, 700 and 234, 765, 000, 129, 654, 080, 277. First of all, note that it would be difficult to represent the numbers as integer variables, as they cannot hold such large values. The problem can be solved by treating the numbers as strings of numerals, store them on two stacks and then perform addition by popping numbers from the stacks.

EVALUATION OF ARITHMETIC EXPRESSIONS

Stacks are useful in evaluation of arithmetic expressions.

Consider the expression

5 * 3 +2 + 6 * 4

The expression can be evaluated by first multiplying 5 and 3, storing the result in A, adding 2 and A, saving the result in A. We then multiply 6 and 4 and save the answer in B. We finish off by adding A and B and leaving the final answer in A.

A = 15 2 +

= 17

B = 6 4 *

= 24

A = 17 24 +

= 41

We can write this sequence of operations as follows:

5 3 * 2 + 6 4 * +

This notation is known as **postfix** notation and is evaluated as described above. We shall shortly show how this form can be generated using a stack.

Basically, there are three types of notations for expressions. The standard form is known as the **infix** form. The other two are **postfix** and **prefix** forms.

Infix: operator is between operands A + B

Postfix: operator follows operands A B +

Prefix: operator precedes operands + A B

Note that all infix expressions cannot be evaluated by using the left to right order of the operators inside the expression. However, the operators in a postfix expression are ALWAYS in the correct evaluation order. Thus, evaluation of an infix expression is done in two steps. The first step is to convert it into its equivalent postfix expression. The second step involves evaluation of the postfix expression. We shall see how stacks are useful in carrying out both the steps. Let us first examine the basic process of infix to postfix conversion.

CONVERTING AN INFIX EXPRESSION TO POSTFIX

A stack can be used to convert an infix expression in standard form into postfix form. Assume that the expression is a legal one (*i.e.*, it is possible to evaluate it). When an operand is read, it will be placed on output list (printed out straight away). The operators are pushed on a stack. However, if the priority of the top operator in the stack is higher than the operator being read, then it will be put on output list and the new operator pushed on to the stack. The priority is assigned as follows.

Order of precedence for operators:

(1) (Left parenthesis in the expression

(2) * /

(3) + –

(4) (Left parenthesis inside the stack

The left parenthesis has the highest priority when it is read from the expression, but once it is on the stack, it assumes the lowest priority.

To start with, the stack is empty. The infix expression is read from left to right. If the character is an OPERAND, it is not put on the stack. It is simply printed out as part of the postfix expression. The stack stores only the OPERATORS. The first operator is pushed on to the stack. For all subsequent operators, priority of the incoming operator will be compared with the priority of the operator at the top of the stack. If the priority of the incoming-operator is higher than the priority of topmost operator-on-thestack, it will be pushed on the stack.

If the priority of the incoming-operator is same or lower than the priority of the operator at the top of the stack, then the operator at top of the stack will be popped and printed on the output expression. The process is repeated if the priority of the incoming-operator is still same or lower than the next operator-on-the-stack.

When a right parenthesis is encountered, all operators up to the left parenthesis are popped from the stack and printed out. The left and right parentheses will be discarded. When all characters from the input infix expression have been read, the operators remaining inside the stack, are printed out in the order in which they are popped.

Infix to postfix conversion

Example 1:

a + b * c **Infix form**

(precedence of * is higher than of +)

Step 1: a + (b * c) Convert the multiplication

Step 2: a + (b c *) Convert the addition

Step 3: a (b c *) + Remove parentheses

Step 4: a b c * + **Postfix form**

Note that there is no need of parentheses in postfix forms.

Example 2:

(A + B) * C **Infix form**

Step 1: (A B +) * C Convert the addition

Step 2: (A B +) C * Convert multiplication

Step 3: A B + C * **Postfix form**

No need of parenthesis anywhere

Example 3:

a + ((b * c) / d)

Step 1: a + ((b c *) /d)

(Precedence of * and / are same and they are left associative)

Step 2: a + (b c * d /)

Step 3: a b c * d / +

Example 4:

Infix	**Postfix**
(a + b) * (c – d)	a b + c d - *
a – b / (c + d * e)	a b c d e * + / -
((a + b) * c – (d – e))/(f + g)	a b + c * d e - - f g + /

Converting Expression from Infix to Postfix using Stack

To convert an expression from infix to postfix, we are going to use a stack.

Algorithm

(1) Examine the next element in the input.

(2) If it is an operand, output it.

(3) If it is opening parenthesis, push it on stack.

(4) If it is an operator, then:

(i) If stack is empty, push operator on stack.

(ii) If the top of the stack is opening parenthesis, push operator on stack.

(iii) If it has higher priority than the top of stack, push operator on stack.

(iv) Else pop the operator from the stack and output it, repeat step 4.

(5) If it is a closing parenthesis, pop operators from the stack and output them until an opening parenthesis is encountered. Pop and discard the opening parenthesis.

(6) If there is more input, go to step 1.

(7) If there is no more input, unstack the remaining operators to output.

Example

Suppose we want to convert 2*3/(2-1)+5*(4-1) into Prefix form:

Char Scanned	Stack Contents (Top on right)	Postfix Expression
2	Empty	2
*	*	2
3	*	23
/	/	23*
(	/(	23*
2	/(	23*2
-	/(-	23*2
1	/(-	23*21

)	/	23*21-
+	+	23*21-/
5	+	23*21-/5
*	+*	23*21-/5
(	+*(	23*21-/5
4	+*(	23*21-/54
-	+*(-	23*21-/54
1	+*(-	23*21-/541
)	+*	23*21-/541-
	Empty	23*21-/541-*+

So, the final Prefix Expression is +/*23-21*5-41

Reversed Expression:)1-4(*5+)1-2(/3*2

Converting Expression from Infix to Prefix using Stack

It is a bit trickier algorithm, in this algorithm, we first reverse the input expression so that a+b*c will become c*b+a and then we do the conversion and then again the output string is reversed. Doing this has an advantage that except for some minor modifications the algorithm for Infix->Prefix remains almost same as the one for Infix->Postfix.

Algorithm

(1) Reverse the input string.

(2) Examine the next element in the input.

(3) If it is operand, add it to output string.

(4) If it is closing parenthesis, push it on stack.

(5) If it is an operator, then:

 (i) If stack is empty, push operator on stack.

 (ii) If the top of stack is closing parenthesis, push operator on stack.

 (iii) If it has same or higher priority than the top of stack, push operator on stack.

 (iv) Else pop the operator from the stack and add it to output string, repeat step 5.

(6) If it is an opening parenthesis, pop operators from stack and add them to output string until a closing parenthesis is encountered. Pop and discard the closing parenthesis.

(7) If there is more input, go to step 2.

(8) If there is no more input, unstack the remaining operators and add them to output string.

(9) Reverse the output string.

Example

Suppose we want to convert 2*3/(2-1)+5*(4-1) into Prefix form:

Reversed Expression:)1-4(*5+)1-2(/3*2

Reverse the output string : +/*23-21*5-41

Char Scanned	Stack Contents (Top on right)	Postfix Expression (Right to Left)
)	)	
1	)	1
-	)-	1
4	)-	14
(	Empty	14-
*	*	14-
5	*	14-5
+	+	14-5*
)	+)	14-5*
1	+)	14-5*1
-	+)-	14-5*1
2	+)-	14-5*12
(	+	14-5*12-
/	+/	14-5*12-
3	+/	14-5*12-3
*	+/*	14-5*12-3
2	+/*	14-5*12-32
	Empty	14-5*12-32*/+

POSTFIX EXPRESSION EVALUATION

We can use stack which helps to evaluate a postfix expression, while reading the expression elements (tokens) from left to right.

- Operands are pushed on the stack.
- Operators pop 2 operands and push results.
- Stack contains 1 element, the result, when a valid expression is fully evaluated.
- Algorithm is slightly more complex if we permit negative numbers (unary operator). Note we need a separate operator for this in postfix.

Algorithm

For each token in postfix expression

if operand, push its value;

if operator

pop operand2;

pop operand1;

result = operand1 operator operand2;

push result;

value at top of stack is result of expression;

For example: convert (a–b)/c*(d+e–f/g)

Char scanned	Action	Stack contents	Postfix expression
(	Push	*(	ab–c/
D	Output	*(	ab–c/d
+	Push	*(+	ab–c/d
E	Output	*(+	ab–c/de
-	Pop	*(	ab–c/de+
	Push	*(-	ab–c/de+
F	Output	*(-	ab–c/de+f
/	Push	*(- /	ab–c/de+f
G	Output	*(- /	ab–c/de+fg
)	pop to (	*	ab–c/de+fg/–
	pop until stack is empty		ab–c/de+fg/–*z

C Program Examples

/*Program – stack operations*/

```
#include <stdio.h>
#include <conio.h>
#include <process.h>
#include <stdlib.h>
#include <string.h>
int top=0,a[10];
```

```
int push(int a[10]);
int view(int a[10]);
int pop(int a[10]);
int peep(int a[10]);
int change(int a[10]);
void main(){
int a[10],i,opt;
do{
clrscr();
/* printf("1.push\n");
printf("2.pop\n");
printf("3.peep\n");
printf("4.list\n");
printf("5.exit\n");
printf("select"); */
printf("enter your option");
scanf("%d", &opt);
switch(opt){
case 1: push(a); getch();
break;
case 2: pop(a); getch(); break;
case 3: peep(a); getch(); break;
case 4: change(a); getch(); break;
case 5: printf("thank you");
break;
default :
printf("option entered is invalid");
}
}
```

```
while(opt<5);
getch();
}
int push(int a[10]){
int x;
if(top==10)
printf("stack is full");
if(top==0)
top=1;
else
top+=1;
printf("enter the element to be inserted");
scanf("%d",&x);
a[top]=x;
view(a);
return(0);
}
int view(int a[10]){
int i;
if (top==0)
printf ("the status of stack is null");
for (i=1; i<=top; i++)
printf ("the status of stack is%d", a[i]);
return(0);
}
int pop(){
int i;
if(top==0)
printf("stack is empty");
```

```
else
{
i=a[top];
top-=1;
printf("the element deleted is%d",i);
view(a);
}  return(0);
}
int peep(int a[50]){
int y;
printf("enter the element to view\n");
scanf("%d",&y);
if(y<=0)
printf("stack under flow");
else
printf("%d",a[y]);
return(0);
}
int change(int a[10]){
int j,r;
printf("enter the element to be changed");
scanf("%d",&r);
if(r<=0)
printf("stack under flow");
else
{
printf("enter the element to insert");
scanf("%d\n",j);
a[r]=j;
```

```
view(a);
} return(0);
}
```

/*Infix to Prefix Conversion*/

```
#include <stdio.h>
#include <conio.h>
#include <string.h>
#include <stdlib.h>
#define MAX 15
#define true 1
#define false 0
/*Structure Declaration*/
typedef struct
{
char data[MAX];
char top;
}STK;
/*Function Declarations*/
void input(char str[]);
void intopre(char str1[],char pre[]);
void intopost(char str1[],char post[]);
int isoperand(char sym);
int prcd(char sym);
void push(STK *s1,char elem);
int pop(STK *s1);
int empty(STK *s2);
int full(STK *s2);
void dis(char str[]);
void main(){
```

```
STK s;
int cs ,ans;
char str[MAX], pre[MAX], post[MAX];
clrscr();
do /*Using Do-while Loop*/
{
clrscr();
printf("    --Program for Expressions--");
printf("Input The String:");
printf("MENU: ");
printf("1.Infix to Prefix");
printf("2.Infix to Postfix");
printf("3.Exit");
cs=getche();
switch(cs)  /*Using Switch Case*/
{
case 1: intopre(str,pre);
break;
case 2: intopost(str,post);
break;
case 3: exit(0);
default: printf("Enter a Valid Choice!"); /*Default Case*/
}
printf("Do you wish to Continue?(y/n)");
ans=getche();
}while(ans=='y'||ans=='Y');   /*Condition for Do-while loop*/
getch();
}
/*To Input String*/
```

```
void input(char str){
printf("Enter the Infix String:");
scanf("%s",str);
}
/*To Covert Infix to Prefix*/
void intopre(STK s1,char str1[],char pre[]){
int len,flag;
len=strlen(str1);
int check=0,cnt=len-1,pos=0;
char elem;
while(cnt>=0)  /*while condition*/
{
flag=0;
if(isoperand(str1[cnt]))   /*Checking for Operand*/
{
printf("%c",str1[cnt]);
cnt–;
pos++;
}
else
{
check=prcd(str1[cnt]);
while(check==false){
pre[pos]=str1[cnt];
flag=1;
pos++;
cnt–;
}
if(flag==0){
```

```
elem=pop(&s1);
printf("%c",elem);
}
}
}
}
/*To Convert Infix to Postfix*/
void intopost(STK s1,char str1[],char post[]){
int len;
len=strlen(str1);
int check=0,cnt=len-1,pos=0;
}
/*To Check for Operand*/
int isoperand(char sym){
if('A'<sym<'Z'||'a'<sym<'z')
return(true);
return(false);
}
/*To Check the Precedence*/
int prcd(char sym){
-----
}
/*To Display String*/
void dis(char str[])
{
------------
}
/*Push Function Definition*/
void push(STK *s1,char elem){
```

```
if(!full(s1)){
s1->top++;                 /*Incrementing top*/
s1->data[s1->top]=elem;    /*Storing element*/
}
else
printf("Stack is Full!");
}
/*Full Function Definition*/
int full(STK *s2){
if(s2->top==MAX)    /*Condition for Full*/
return(true);
return(false);
}
/*Pop Function Definition*/
int pop(STK *s1){
char elem;
if(!empty(s1)){
elem=s1->data[s1->top]; /*Storing top stack element in elem*/
s1->top--;           /*Decrementing top*/
return(elem);
}
return(false);
}
/*Empty Function Definition*/
int empty(STK *s2){
if(s2->top==-1)       /*Condition For Empty*/
return(true);
return(false);
}
```

/*Program – stack operations using arrays*/

```
#include <stdio.h>
#include <conio.h>
#include <process.h>
#include <stdlib.h>
#define size 5
int a[size],top=-1,i;
main(){
int ch;
do{
clrscr();
printf("1.push\n");
printf("2.pop\n");
printf("3.peep\n");
printf("4.list\n");
printf("5.exit\n");
printf("select");
scanf("%d",&ch);
switch(ch){
case 1: push();
break;
case 2: pop();break;
case 3: peep();break;
case 4: list();break;
case 5: exit();
}
getch();
}while(1);
}
```

```
push(){
if(top==size-1)
printf("stack is full");
else
{
top++;
printf("enter the value:\n");
scanf("%d",&a[top]);
}return(a[top]);
}
pop(){
if(top==-1)
printf("stack is empty");
else
{
printf("%d\n",a[top]);
top—;
} return(a[top]);
}
peep(){
printf("enter the value of i:\n");
scanf("%d",&i);
if(top-i+1<0)
printf("stack is empty");
else
printf("%d",a[top-i+1]);
return(a[top-i+1]);
}
list(){
```

```
if(top==-1)
printf("stack is empty");
else
{
for(i=0;i<=top;i++)
printf("%d\n",a[i]);
}return(a[i]);
}
exit(){
printf("the entered chioce is exited");
return(0);
}
```

/*Program – conversion of infix to postfix*/

```
#include <stdio.h>
#include <conio.h>
#include <alloc.h>
#include <string.h>
//#define NULL \0
struct node{
char data;
struct node *next;
};
main(){
struct node *top=NULL;
char s[80],t[80],r;
int i,j;
clrscr();
puts("enter any infix expression");
gets(s);
```

```
for(i=0,j=0;i<strlen(s);i++){
if(s[i]>=48 && s[i]<=57)
t[j++]=s[i];
else{
if(s[i]!='>')
push(&top,s[i]);
else
{
r=pop(&top);
t[j++]=r;
r=pop(&top);
if(r!='<')
t[j++]=r;
}
}
}
while(top!=NULL){
r=pop(&top);
if(r!='<'){ t[j++]=r;}
t[j]='\0';
puts(t);
}
push(struct node **t,char d){
struct node *q;
q=malloc(size of(struct node));
q->data=d;
q->next= (*t);
*t=q;
}
```

```
pop(struct node **t){
char ch;
ch=(*t)->data;
*t=(*t)->next;
return ch;
}
}
}
```

/*Program – evaluation of postfix expression*/

```
#include <stdio.h>
#include <conio.h>
#include <alloc.h>
#include <string.h>
//#define NULL \0
struct node{
char data;
struct node *next;
};
void main(){
struct node *top=NULL;
char s[80];
int op1,op2,i,r;
clrscr();
puts("enter any postfix expression");
gets(s);
for(i=0;i<strlen(s);i++){
if(s[i]>=48 && s[i]<=57)
push(&top,s[i]%48);
else{
```

```
op2=pop(&top);
op1=pop(&top);
switch(s[i]){
case'+': r=op1+op2; break;
case '-':r=op1-op2; break;
ase'*': r=op1*op2; break;
case '/':r=op1/op2; break;
case'%': r=op1%op2; break;
}
push(&top,r);
}
}
r=pop(&top);
printf("the result is %d",r);
}
push(struct node **t,char d){
struct node *q;
q=malloc(sizeof(struct node));
q->data=d;
q->next= (*t);
*t=q;
}
pop(struct node **t){
int d=(*t)->data;
*t=(*t)->next;
return(d);
}
}
}
```

Review Questions

1. What are stacks? How they are used to push or pop a data item into a stack?
2. Write an algorithm to push an item into a stack.
3. Which data structure is used to perform recursion?
4. Write an algorithm to pop an item from a stack.
5. What are the notations used in evaluation of arithmetic expressions using prefix and postfix forms?
6. Convert the expression ((A + B) * C – (D – E) ^ (F + G)) to equivalent prefix and postfix notations.
7. How is it possible to insert different type of elements in stack?
8. Which data structure is needed to convert infix notations to post fix notations?
9. Can a stack be described as a pointer? Explain.
10. What are the applications of stacks?
11. Write a C program using pointers to implement a stack with all the operations.

CHAPTER 14
Queue Operations

A Queue is an ordered collection of items from which items may be deleted at one end (called the *front* of the queue) and into which items may be inserted at the other end (the *rear* of the queue). The basic concept is that the elements in queues are "First Come, First Serve" or "First In First Out", i.e., FIFO.

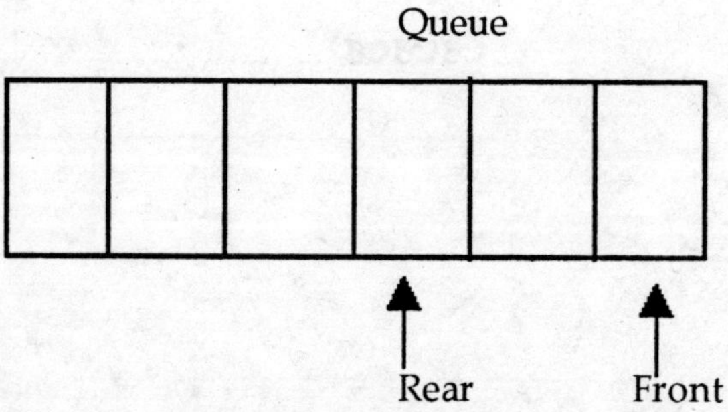

Fig.14.1: Representation of Queue

QUEUE INTERFACE

The following operations can be applied to a queue:

InitQueue(Queue): creates an empty queue

Join(Item): inserts an item to the rear of the queue

Leave(Queue): removes an item from the front of the queue

IsEmpty(Queue): returns true if the queue is empty

OPERATIONS ON QUEUE

Different operations can be performed at queue as:

(1) **Create Queue:** By using this operation, the structure of the queue is generated.

(2) **Enqueue:** The insertion of element in the queue is called enqueue.

(3) **Dequeue:** The deletion of element from the queue is called dequeue.

(4) **Empty Queue:** It returns Boolean value true, if queue is empty.

(5) **Full Queue:** It returns Boolean value false, if queue is full.

(6) **Destroy Queue:** This operation deletes all the elements of the queue and also deletes the structure of queue from the computer memory.

Insertion of a Data Element at the Rear

Example

Queues (FIFO-lists)

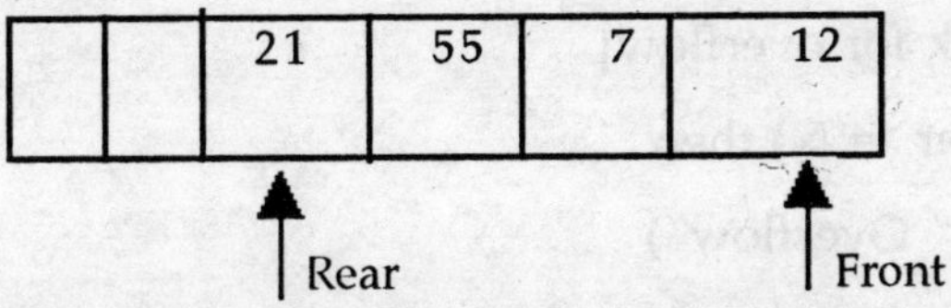

Insert (36);

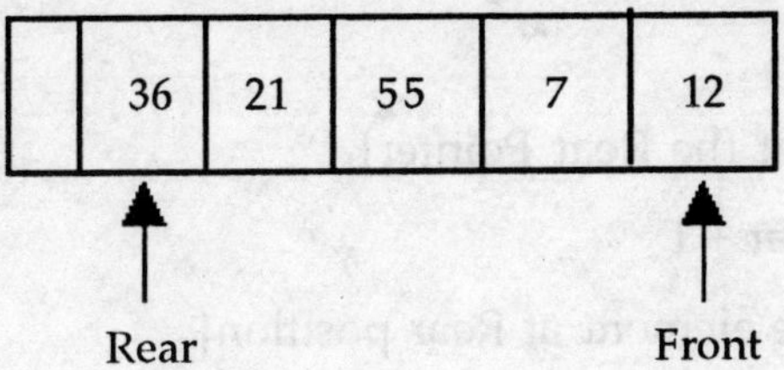

Elements can only be added to the rear of the queue and removed from the front of the queue.

Deletion of a Data Element from the Front

Delete (12);

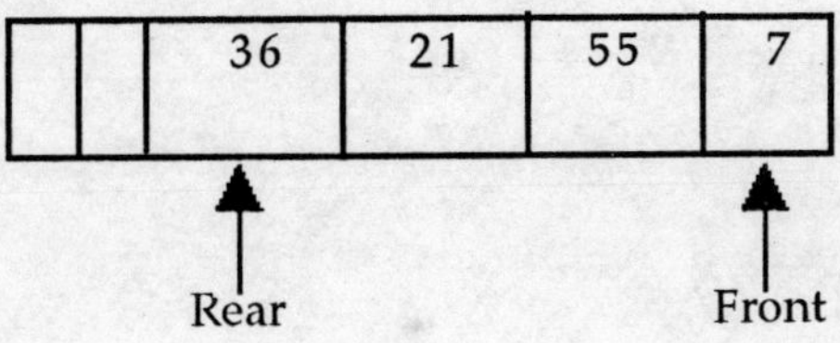

MAJOR OPERATIONS ON QUEUE

(1) **Overflow Condition:** When no more elements can be inserted in the queue, this condition is called overflow condition.

(2) **Underflow Condition:** When queue is empty and no more elements can be deleted from the queue, this condition is called underflow condition.

Algorithm for the Insertion of an Element in the Queue

```
Algorithm enqueue (Q, N, item, Rear, Front)
[This algorithm is used to insert the element in the queue where
Q = Queue Array
N  = Total number of elements
item  = which is to be inserted
Front, Rear =  Deletion and Insertion pointers
Step 1:[Check for overflow]
        if (Rear >= N) then
        print(" Overflow")
        goto step 5
        end if
Step 2:[Increment the Rear Pointer]
        Rear = Rear + 1
Step 3:[Insert the element at Rear position]
        Q [Rear] = item
Step 4:[Reset Pointer]
        if (Front = 0) then
        set Front = 1
        end if
        goto Step 1
Step 5:[Finished]
        exit
```

Algorithm for the Deletion of Element from the Queue

Algorithm DelQueue (Q, item, Front, Rear)

[This algorithm is used for the deletion of element from the queue where

Q = Array

item = which is to be deleted]

Step 1:[Check for underflow]

```
    if ((Front = 0) or (Front > Rear)) then
    print ("UnderFlow")
    goto Step 4
    end if
```

Step 2:[Delete the item from queue]

```
    item←Q[Front]
```

Step 3:[Set Front Pointer]

```
    if (Front = Rear) then
    Front←Rear ← 0
    else
    Front←Front + 1
    end if
    goto step 1
```

Step 4:[Finished]

```
    exit
```

Algorithm for Display of a Queue

Algorithm Qdisplay(Q)

[Front Pointer and Rear Pointer are the pointers to the Front and Rear elements of a queue, Q. It is going to display the Q array contents]

Step 1:[Display the Q contents]

```
    repeat for i = Front Pointer to Rear Pointer
    print(Q(Front Pointer))
```

Step 2:[End]

```
    stop
```

APPLICATIONS OF QUEUES

CIRCULAR QUEUE

Removing an element from the queue is an expensive operation because all remaining elements have to be moved by one position. A more efficient implementation is obtained if we consider the array as being 'circular'. Circular queue provide flexible way for the insertion of element in a circular way.

In queue, we are not sure that when the rear pointer goes to an end, i.e., Rear = N, overflow condition occur, may be the same element from the front are deleted, it is the major drawback of queue. This drawback can be overcome with the help of circular queue. In circular queue, the insertion can takes place by using this sequence 0, 1, 2, 3, ...11.

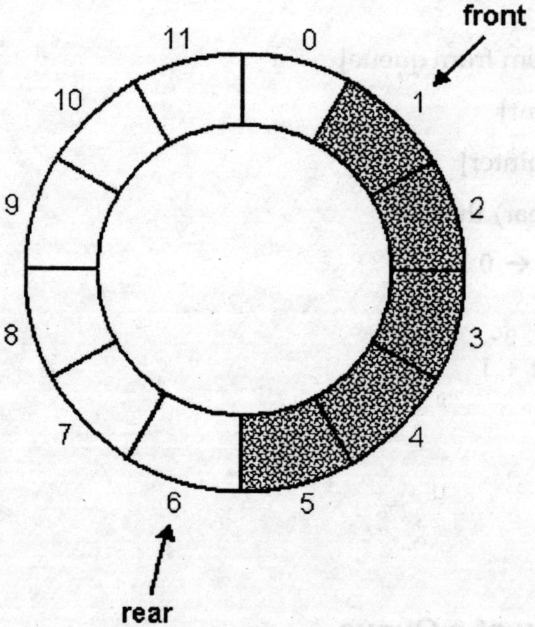

Fig.14.2: Representation of a Circular Queue

Check for Underflow

When the front and rear pointer become equal, i.e., Front ←←0 underflow condition may arise.

Check for Overflow

When Front = 1 and Rear = N, an overflow condition may arise.

OR

When Front ← + 1, an overflow condition may arise.

Algorithm for the Insertion of Element in Circular Queue

Algorithm Circularinsertion (CQ, N, item, Rear, Front)

[This algorithm is used to insert the element in CQ, where

CQ = Array

N = Final Limit

item = which is to be inserted

Front, Rear = Deletion and Insertion pointers]

Step 1:[Check for overflow]

    if ((Front = 1) && (Rear = N) or (Front = Rear + 1) then

    print ("Overflow")

    goto step 4

    end if

Step 2:[Reset Rear Pointer]

    if (Front = Rear = 0) then

    Rear = Front = 1

    else if (Rear = N) then

    Rear = 1

    else

    Rear = Rear + 1

    end if

Step 3:[Insert the element]

    CQ [Rear] = item

    goto Step 1

Step 4:[Finished]

    exit

Algorithm for the Deletion of Element from the Circular Queue

Algorithm DeleteCQ (CQ, item, N, Front, Rear)

[This algorithm is used for the deletion of element from Circular queue where

CQ = Array

item = which is to be deleted

N = Total number of element

Step 1: [Check for underflow]

if ((Front = Rear = 0)) then

print ("Underflow")

goto step 4

end if

Step 2: [Delete the item from Circular queue]

item ← [Front]

Step 3: [Set Front Pointer]

if (Front = Rear) then

Front ← Rear ← item

else if (Front = N) then

Front = 1

else

Front ←Front + 1

end if

goto Step 1

Step 4:[Finished]

exit

Algorithm for the Display of a Circular Queue

Algorithm displayCQ (CQ)

[Front and Rear are the pointers to the Front and Rear elements of a circular queue, CQ. It is going to display the CQ array contents]

Step 1: [Display the CQ contents]

repeat for i = Front to Rear

print(Q(Front))

Step 2: [End]

stop

DEQUEUE

It is a linear data structure. This queue is called double-ended queue. In this type of queue, insertion and deletion of elements can be take place from both ends.

In queue, insertion and deletion of elements from Rear and Front can take place on the principal of Right and Left pointer.

There are two types of dequeue:

(1) Input restricted queue

In this type of queue, insertion can take place only from one end and deletion can take place from both ends.

(2) Output restricted queue

In this type of queue, insertion can take place from both ends and deletion can take place from one end.

Principle for Insertion

When the elements are inserted from Rear/Right, Rear pointer is incremented and when elements are inserted from Front/Left, Front pointer decremented.

Algorithm for the Insertion of Element to Right in Dequeue

Algorithm DQInsertRight (DQ, N, item, Rear, Front)

[This algorithm is used to insert the element to the right of DQ, where

DQ = Array

N = Final Limit

item = which is to be inserted

Front, Rear = Deletion and Insertion pointers]

Step 1: [Check for overflow]

if ((Front = 1) && (Rear = N) or (Front = Rear + 1) then

print ("Overflow")

goto Step 4

end if

Step 2: [Reset Rear Pointer]

if (Rear =0) then

Rear = Front = 1

else if (Rear = N) then

Rear = 1

else

Rear = Rear + 1

end if

Step 3: [Insert the element]

DQ [Rear] = item

goto Step 1

Step 4: [Finished]

exit

Algorithm for the Insertion of Element to Left in Dequeue

Algorithm DQInsertLeft (DQ, N, item, Rear, Front)

[This algorithm is used to insert the element to the left of DQ, where

DQ = Array

N = Final Limit

item = which is to be inserted

Front, Rear = Deletion and Insertion of pointers]

Step 1: [Set the Front Pointer]

if (Front = 1 or Front = 0) then

Front = N

else

Front = Front - 1

end if

Step 2: [Check for overflow]

if (Front = Rear) then

print ("Overflow")

goto Step 5

end if

Step 3: [Insert the element]

DQ [Front] = item

Step 4: [Set the Rear Pointer]

if (Rear = 0) then

Rear = N

end if

goto step 1

Step 5: [Finished]

exit

PRIORITY QUEUES

Like a (normal) queue, a priority queue contains a collection of items that are waiting to be processed. In a queue, items are removed for processing in the same order in which they were added to the queue. In a priority queue, however, each item has a priority, and when it's time to select an item, the item with the highest priority is the one that is chosen. The priority might have nothing to do with the time at which the item was added to the data structure.

Another way to describe a queue is as an implementation of a first come, "first served" policy. The items in the queue wait in line in order of arrival. This is the right policy when all the items in the queue are of equal importance. In many situations, however, some items are more important than others, and in that case the more important items should be moved up in the line, ahead of the other items. A priority queue is an implementation of this idea. The priority of an item represents its importance, so items of higher priority should be selected before items of lower priority.

The operations on a Priority Queue are:

- create an empty Priority Queue
- insert an element having a certain priority to the Priority Queue
- remove that element having the highest priority

C Program Examples

/*Program – queue operations using arrays*/

```
#include <stdio.h>

#include <conio.h>

#include <stdlib.h>

int a[size], rear=-1,front=0;
```

```
main(){
int ch;
do{
clrscr();
printf("1.insert\n");
printf("2.delete\n");
printf("3.list\n");
printf("4.exit\n");
printf("select");
scanf("%d",&ch);
switch(ch){
case 1: insert();
break;
case 2: delete();break;
case 3: list();break;
case 4: exit(0);
}
getch();
}while(1);
}
insert(){
if(rear>=size-1)
printf("queue is full");
else
{
rear++;
printf("enter the value:\n");
scanf("%d",&a[rear]);
}//return(a[top]);
}
```

```
delete(){
if(front>rear)
printf("queue is underflow");
else
{ if(front==rear){
printf("%d\n",a[front]);
front=0;
rear--;
} //return(a[top]);
else
printf("popped element is %d\n",a[front]);
a[front]=NULL;
frontt++;
}
}
list(){
for(i=front;i<=rear;i++){
printf("%d\n",a[i]);
}
}
/*exit(){
printf("the entered chioce is exited");
return(0);
} */
```

/* Program – Circular queue implementation*/

```
#include <stdio.h>
#include <conio.h>
#include <stdlib.h>
#define size 5
struct cqueue{
int front, rear;
```

```
int a[10];
};
typedef struct cqueue cqueue;
void insert(cqueue *q,int item){
q->rear = ((q->rear)+1)%size;
if(q->rear==q->front){
printf("cqueue is full");
if(q->rear==0)
q->rear=size-1;
else
(q->rear)—;
}
else
q->a[q->rear]=item;
}
int delete(cqueue *q){
if(q->front==q->rear){
printf("cqueue is empty");
return(-1);
}
else
return(q->a[++(q->front))%size]);
}
void display(cqueue *q){
int i;
if(q->front==q->rear)
printf("cqueue is empty");
else{
printf("elements of cqueue");
if(q->rear<q->front){
```

```
for(i=(q->front)+1;i<=size-1;i++)
printf("%d\t",q->a[i]);
printf("\n");
}
}
main(){
cqueue *qu;
int ch,item,d;
qu->front=0;
qu->rear=0;
do{
printf("\n 1.insert\n2.delete\n3.display\n4.exit\n");
printf("enter your choice");
scanf("%d",&ch);
switch(ch){
case 1: printf("\nenter element to insert");
scanf("%d"&item);
insert(qu,item);break;
case 2: d=delete(qu);
printf("%delement is deleted",d);
break;
case 3: display(qu);break;
case 4: exit(0);
}
printf("\n");
}
while(1);
getch();
}
```

Review Questions

1. What are queues? Explain how to insert or delete a data item in a queue.
2. What is the difference between a stack and a queue?
3. Write an algorithm to insert a data item into a queue.
4. Write an algorithm to delete an item from the queue.
5. What are the applications of queues?
6. Are queues more advantageous than stacks? Why?
7. What are the different types of queues? Explain in detail.
8. What are circular queues? Explain with an example.
9. Are circular queues better than linear queues? Why?
10. Minimum number of queues needed to implement the priority queue?

CHAPTER 15

Linked Lists

INTRODUCTION

A linked list is a data structure that can hold an arbitrary number of data items and can easily change its size to add or remove items. A linked list, at its simplest is a pointer to a data node. Each data node is then composed of data (possibly a record with several data values), and a pointer to the next node. At the end of the list, the pointer is set to NULL.

Each item in a list is called a node and contains two fields, an information field and a next address field. The information field holds the actual element on the list. The next address field contains the address of the next node in the list. Such an address, which is used to access a particular node is known as a pointer. The entire linked list is accessed from an external pointer *list* that points to first node in the list. The next address field of the last node in the list contains a special value called null value.

Linear linked list is a data structure of explicit ordering of items and each item contains two portions; one is information portion and the other one is next address portion. In explicit ordering of items, each item contained within itself the address of another item. Such an explicit ordering gives rise to a data structure which is known as a linear linked list.

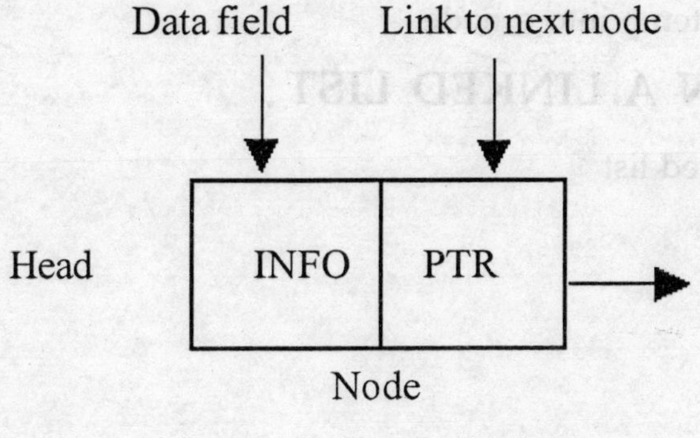

Each element in the queue is called 'Node,' which consists of:

Node

Data	Pointer to the node next to it

Structure

Head{frontPtr/*pointer*/count/ *int*/rearPtr/*pointer*/}	Node{data/*any type of variable*/ nextLink/*pointer*/}

Terminology

Node: The components which form the list.

Temp: Contains the temporary address which is pointer variable.

Head/Header: Contains the address of first node.

c_node: Contains the address of current node.

Next: Contains the address of next node. If there is only one node in the list, then it holds 'NULL'.

In linked lists, the following steps are required.

- Creation of memory [using malloc()].
- Collecting the base address returned by malloc() into a temporary pointer variable.
- Storing own data into the information part of the node.
- Now store data into the node.

  Store 'NULL' into the next part of the node.
- If head contains 'Null', then

  Head=temp

  else c_node -> next = temp
- And at last store temp into c_node.

OPERATIONS ON A LINKED LIST

- Creation of a linked list
- Display
- Traversing
- Insertion

- Deletion
- Searching
- Concatenation
- Merging

TYPES OF LINKED LISTS

(1) Singly Linked List

(2) Circular Linked List

(3) Doubly Linked List

(4) Circular Doubly Linked List

SINGLY LINKED LIST

The singly linked list is the most basic of all the pointer based data structures. A singly linked list is simply a sequence of dynamically allocated storage elements, each containing a pointer to its successor. The figure below gives a simple illustration.

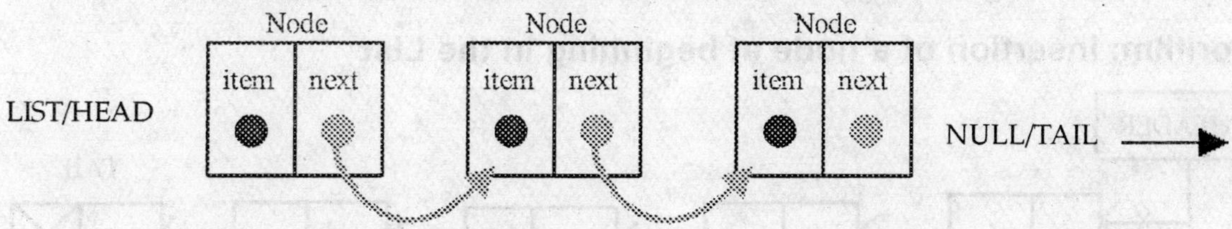

Fig. 15.1: Representation of a Singly Linked List

Each node of the list has two elements:

(1) the item being stored in the list *and*

(2) a pointer to the next item in the list

The last node in the list contains a NULL pointer to indicate that it is the end or *tail* of the list. As items are added to a list, memory for a node is dynamically allocated. Thus, the number of items that may be added to a list is limited only by the amount of memory available. Inspite of its simplicity, there are many variations of its implementation. The above figures show several of the most common singly-linked list variants.

Each element of the list contains a pointer to its successor; the last element contains a null pointer. A pointer to the first element of the list, labelled **head** in the above Figure, is used to keep track of the list.

Inserting a Node into a Singly Linked List

To insert a new node (say X) after the node (say N),

Create the node X (Allocate memory for the new node X, update the node's data field properly and set the link-field for the node to NULL)

Set the link-field of node X to the same as that of node N's link-field

Set the link-field of node N to point to X

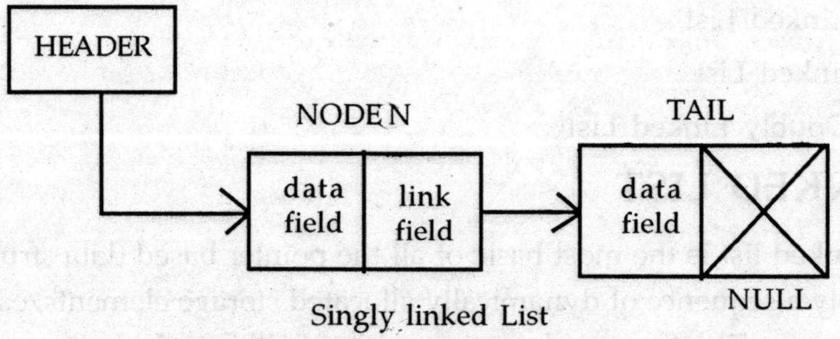

Fig. 15.2: Singly Linked List Representation with Header Node

Algorithm: Insertion of a node at beginning in the List

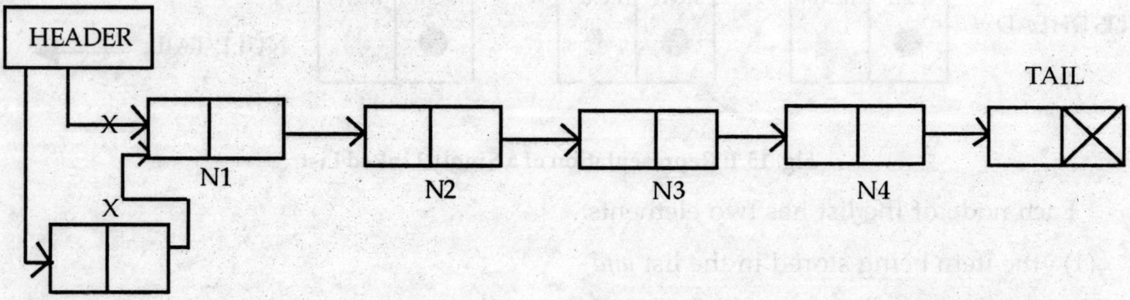

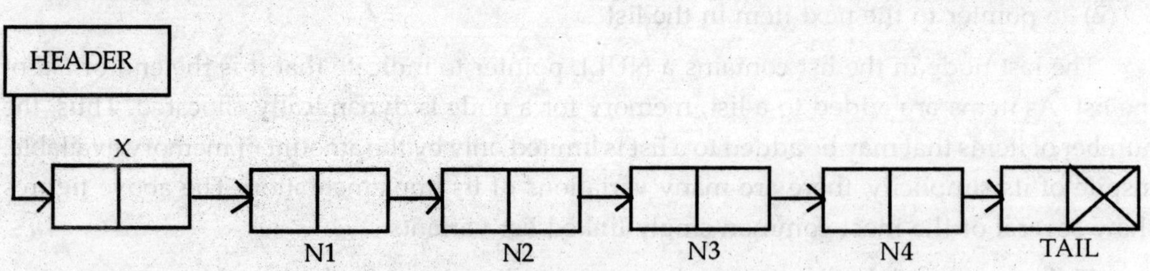

/* Newnode is a node to be inserted. Nodeptr is a pointer to indicate the first element of linked list, a node contains Info and Link fields. This algorithm inserts a new node at the beginning of the list*/

Step 1: [Check the availability of free space from the Avail list]

if Avail = NULL

then

print("there is no free space available for a new node")

return

Step 2: [Obtain a node from free list and name it New]

New = Avail

Step 3: [Adjust Avail pointer]

Avail = Link(Avail)

Step 4: [Store the information and insert at the beginning of the list]

Info (New) <- Newnode

Link (New) <- Nodeptr

Step 5: [Return the modified linked list address]

return(New)

Algorithm: Insertion of a Node at the Middle in the List

/* Newnode is a node to be inserted. Nodeptr is a pointer to indicate the first element of linked list, a node contains Info and Link fields. This algorithm inserts a new node in the given order */

Step 1: [Check the availability of free space from the Avail list]

if Avail = NULL

then

print(" there is no free space available for a new node")

return

Step 2: [Obtain a node from free list and name it New]

New = Avail

Step 3: [Adjust Avail pointer]

Avail = Link(Avail)

Step 4: [Store the information and insert at the beginning of the list]

Info (New) <- Newnode

Step 5: [Check whether the list id empty]

if Nodeptr = NULL

then

Link (new) <- NULL

Return (New)

Step 6: [Does the new node precede all others in the list]

if Info (New) <= Info (Nodeptr)

then

Link (New) <- Nodeptr

return (New)

Step 7: [initialize temporary pointer]

Tempptr <- Nodeptr

Step 8: [Search for precedence of new nodes]

Repeat

while Link (Tempptr)<= NULL and Info (Link (Tempptr))<=Info (Nodeptr)

Tempptr <- Link (Tempptr)

Step 9: [Set link fields of new node and its predeceddor]

Link (Nodeptr) <- Link (Tempptr)

Link (Tempptr) <- Nodeptr

Step 10: [Return first node pointer]

return (Nodeptr)

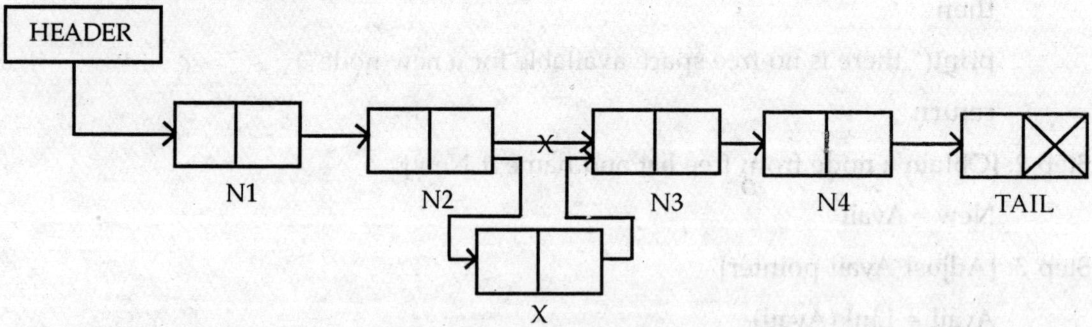

Algorithm: Insertion of a Node at the End of the List

/* Newnode is a node to be inserted. Nodeptr is a pointer to indicate the first element of linked list, a node contains Info and Link fields. This algorithm inserts a new node at the end of the list */

Step 1: [Check the availability of free space from the Avail list] if Avail = NULL

then

print(" there is no free space available for a new node")

return

Step 2: [Obtain a node from free list and name it New]

New = Avail

Step 3: [Adjust Avail pointer]

Avail = Link (Avail)

Step 4: [Store the information and insert at the beginning of the list]

Info (New) <- Newnode

Link (New) <- Nodeptr

Step 5: [Check whether the list id empty]

if Nodeptr = NULL

then

return (New)

Step 6: [Initiate search for the last node in the list]

Tempptr <- Nodeptr

Step 7: [Search the end of the list]

Repeat

while Link (Nodeptr) <= NULL

Tempptr <- Link (Tempptr)

Step 8: [Set link fields of last node to new node]

Link (Tempptr) <- Nodeptr

Step 9: [Return the modified linked list address]

return (Nodeptr)

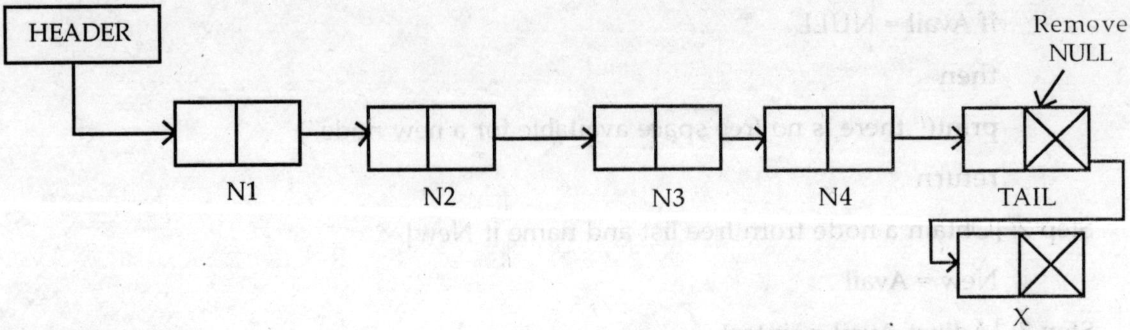

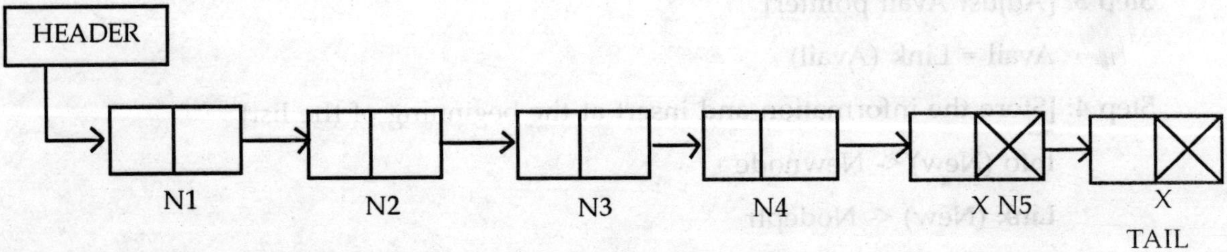

Deleting a Specified Node in a Singly Linked List

To delete a node (say X)

Determine the previous node of the node X to be deleted by traversing the linked list.

Set the link field of the previous node to the same as the node X's link field

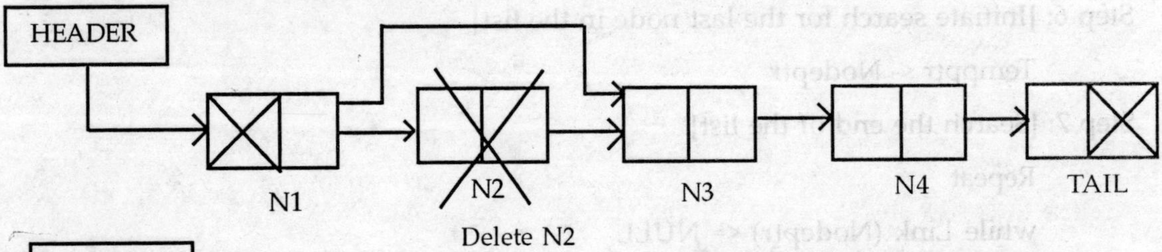

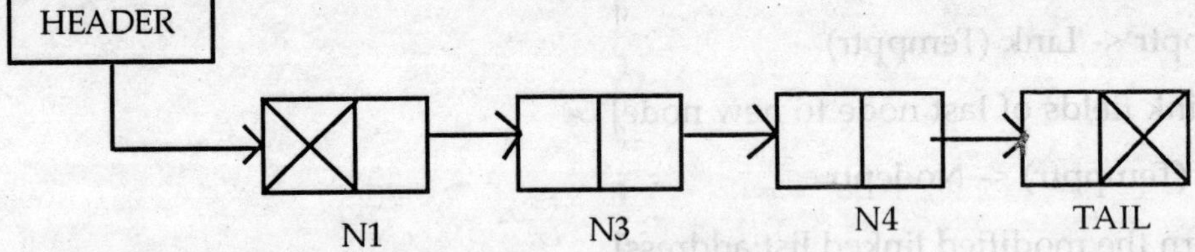

Algorithm: Deletion of a Node in the List

/* Delete the node whose value is Newnode. Nodeptr is a pointer to indicate the first element of linked list, a node contains Info and Link fields. Tempptr is a pointer used to find the desired node and Predptr indicates the predecessor of the Tempptr. */

Step 1: [Check for the Underflow condition]

if Nodeptr = NULL

then

print("there is no nodes to delete from the list")

return

Step 2: [initialize the search for node whose value is Newnode]

Tempptr = Nodeptr

Step 3: [Finding Newnode]

Repeat through 5

while Info (Tempptr) <= Newnode and Link (Tempptr) <= NULL

Step 4: [Update the Predecessor pointer]

Predptr <- Tempptr

Step 5: [Move to the next node]

Tempptr <- Link (Tempptr)

Step 6: [End of the List]

if Tempptr =Newnode

then

print ("Node not found")

return

Step 7: [Delete Newnode]

if Newnode = Info (Nodeptr)

then

Nodeptr <- Link (Nodeptr)

else

Link (Predptr) <- Link (Tempptr)

Step 8: [Return node to the available space]

Link (Newnode) <- Avail

Avail <- Newnode

return

The following C code represents the List.

```
typedef struct{
int info; // information portion
```

```
struct Node *next; // next address portion
}Node;
typedef Node *Nodeptr;
```

Implementing Various Operations like insert, remove and list traversal

```
Nodeptr getNode(){
return ((Nodeptr) malloc (sizeof(Node)));
}
void insert(Nodeptr List, int value){
Nodeptr p = getNode();
p -> info = value;
p -> next = List;
List = p;
}
int remove(Nodeptr List){
int x;
Nodeptr p = List;
List = p -> next;
x = p->info;
free(p);
return x;
}
void list_traversal(Nodeptr List){
Nodeptr p = List;
for(;p!=NULL;){
int x = p -> info;
printf("%d", x);
p = p -> next;
}
}
```

Although a circularly linked list has advantages over a linear list, it still has several drawbacks.

Implementation on Stacks

```
struct node{
int info;
node *next;
};
typedef struct node *Nodeptr;
int isEmpty(Nodeptr &list){
if(list == NULL)
return 1;
else
return 0;
}
void push(Nodeptr &list, int value){
Node p;
p = (Nodeptr)malloc(sizeof(node));
if(p==NULL){
printf("Can't allocate memory.");
getch();
exit(0);
}
p -> next = list;
list = p;
list -> info = value;
}
int pop(Nodeptr &list){
int info;
if(isEmpty(list)){
printf("Underflow");
```

```
getch();
exit(0);
}
Nodeptr p;
p = list;
info = p -> info;
list = p -> next;
free(p);
return info;
}
```

Implementation on Queues

```
struct node{
int info;
struct Node *next;
};
typedef struct Node* nodeptr;
int isEmpty(nodeptr& front){
if(front==NULL)
return 1;
else
return 0;
}
void insert(nodeptr& front, nodeptr& rear, int v){
nodeptr p= (nodeptr)malloc(sizeof(Node));
p->next = NULL;
p->info = v;
if(front==NULL)
front = p;
if(rear == NULL)
```

```
rear = p;
else
{
rear->next = p;
rear = rear->next;
}
}
int remove(nodeptr &front){
if(isEmpty(front)){
printf("Underflow");
getch();
exit(1);
}
nodeptr p;
p = front;
int x = p->info;
front = p->next;
free(p);
return x;
}
```

Example for Implementation of Singly Linked List

/*Program to Create a Singly Linked List*/

```
#include <stdio.h>
#include <alloc.h>
void main(){
char ch;
Struct node{
int info;
struct node *next;
```

```
};
struct node *head, *temp, *c_node;
int data;
head=NULL;
do{
printf("Enter data into list:\n");
scanf("%d",&data);
if(head==NULL){
temp=(struct node*)malloc(sizeof(struct node));
temp->info=data;
temp->next=NULL;
head=temp;
c_node=temp;
}
else
{
temp=(struct node *)malloc(sizeof(struct node));
temp->info=data;
temp->next=NULL;
c_node->next=temp;
c_node=temp;
}
printf("Enter Y to Continue.........\n");
}while(ch=='y'||ch=='Y');
printf("Linked List successfully Created\n");
/*Code for Display*/
c_node=head;
while(c_node!=NULL){
printf("%d\n",c_node->info);
```

```
c_node=c_node->next;
}
```

/*Code for Traversal*/

```
int n;
c_node=head;
printf("Enter a Element To search\n ");
scanf("%d\n",&n);
printf("The List Elements are at %dth no. \n",n);
while(c_node!=NULL){
printf("%d\n",c_node->info);
if(c_node->info==n)
 break;
c_node=c_node->next;
}
```

/*Code for Insertion of a Data*/

```
printf("Enter Data To Be Inserted\t");
scanf("%d",&data);
```

/*Code for Insertion of a Data at the Beginning of Linked List*/

```
temp=(struct node *)malloc(sizeof(struct node));
temp->info=data;
temp->next=head;
head=temp;
}
```

/*Code for Insertion of a Data at the End of Linked List*/

```
temp=(struct node *)malloc(sizeof(struct node));
struct node *cnode=head;
while(cnode->next!=NULL){
Cnode=cnode->next;
}
```

```
temp->info=data;
temp->next=NULL;
cnode->next=temp;
}
```

/*Code for Insert a Data at Special Position of Linked List*/

```
printf("Enter Data and The Position No. where You want to insert the Data\n");
int i,k;
struct node *p;
for(i=0,temp=head;k<pos;k++){
temp=temp->next;
if(temp==NULL){
printf("node in the list at less than ONE\n");
return;
}
}
p=(struct node *)malloc(sizeof(struct node));
p->info=data;
p->next=pos->next;
pos->next=p;
}
```

/*Code for Delete a Data at the Beginning of Linked List*/

```
struct node *ptr;
ptr=head;
head=head->next;
printf("U have Deleted %d This\n",ptr->info);
free(ptr);
}
```

/*Code for Delete a Data at the Beginning of Linked List*/

```
struct node *add,*pnode;
add=head;
pnode=NULL;
while(add->next!=NULL){
pnode=ptr;
add=add->next;
}
pnode->next=NULL;
free(add);
}
```

/*Code for Delete a Data from Specified Position of Linked List*/

```
struct node *ptr,*temp;
int i,pos;
printf("Enter Position to Delete\n");
scanf("%d",&pos);
ptr=head;
for(i=1;i<=pos;i++){
temp=ptr;
ptr=ptr->next;
}
printf("The NUMBER Which U have deleted is %d",ptr->info);
temp->next=ptr->next;
free(ptr);
}
```

/*Code for Searching a Data in SINGLY Linked List*/

```
(In particular Function body)
void search(){
printf("Which Data do U wanna SEARCH:\n");
```

```
scanf("%d",&data);
struct node *cnode=head;
int i=0,flag=0;
while(cnode!=NULL){
i++;
if(cnode->info==data){
flag=1;
printf("UR DATA FOUND ON NODE NO %d",i);
break;
}
cnode=cnode->next;
}
if(flag==0)
printf("SORRY DATA NOT FOUND\N");;
}
```

/*Code for CONCATENATION Two Linked Lists*/

```
void concat(struct node *head1,struct node *head2){
struct node *cnode;
cnode=head1;
while(cnode->next!=NULL){
printf("%d",cnode->info);
cnode=cnode->next;
}
while(cnode!=NULL){
printf("%d",cnode->info);
cnode=cnode->next;
}
}
```

/*Code for SORTING a Singly Linked List*/

```
void sort(struct node *head){
struct node *temp,*cnode,*curr;
int c=0;
```

```
cnode=head;
while(cnode!=NULL){
c++;
cnode=cnode->next;
}
temp=head;
for(i=0;i<c-1;i++){
curr=temp->next;
for(j=i+1;j<c;j++){
if(temp->info>curr->info){
t=temp->info;
temp->info=curr->info;
curr->info=t;
}
temp=temp->next;
}
curr=curr->next;
}
}
```

Problems with Singly Linked List

- Singly Linked list allows traversal of the list in only one direction.
- Deleting a node from a list requires keeping track of the previous node, i.e., the node whose link points to the node to be deleted.
- If the link in any node gets corrupted, the remaining nodes of the list become unusable.

The problems of singly linked lists can be overcome by adding one more link to each node, which points to the previous node. This type of linked list is called a Doubly Linked List.

CIRCULARLY LINKED LISTS

Although a linear linked list is a useful data structure, it has several shortcomings. Given a pointer p to a node in a linear list, we cannot reach any of the nodes that precede node p. If a list is traversed, the external dummy pointer to the list must be preserved to be able to reference the list again. Suppose that a small change is made to the structure of a linear list, so that the next field in the last node contains a pointer back to the first node rather than the null pointer. Such a list is called a *Circularly Linked List.*

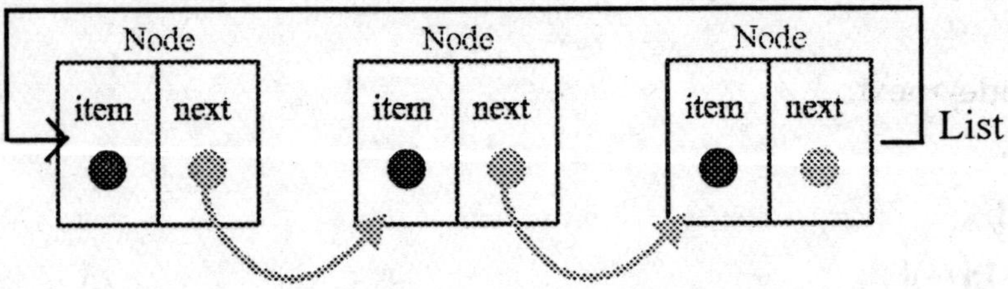

Fig. 15.3: Representation of a Circularly Linked List

A Circular List is a linked list in which the node at the last of the list, instead of having a null pointer, points back to the node at the head of the list. We then need only one pointer (dummy) to access both ends of the list, since we know that last->next points back to the first node in the list.

Application of Circular Linked List

Circular linked list is used to represent arrays that are naturally circular.

- For a pool of buffers that are used and released in FIFO order
- For a set of processes that should be time-shared in round robin order
- Applications that require access to both ends of the list, (e.g., implementation of a queue)

Stacks as a Circular List

The following diagram illustrates the sequences of push operation.

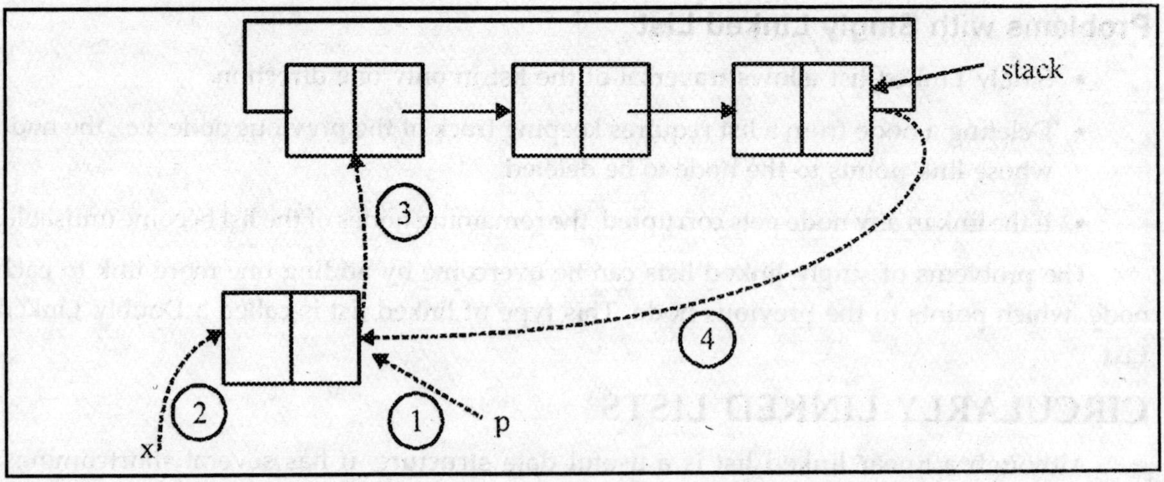

Fig. 15.4: Representation of Sequences of Push Operation in a Stack

```
int isEmpty(Nodeptr &stack){
if(stack == NULL)
return 1;
else
return 0;
}
void push(Nodeptr &stack, int x){
Nodeptr p = (Node)malloc(sizeof(Node));
p->info = x;
if(stack==NULL){
stack = p;
}
else
{
p->next = stack->next;
}
stack->next = p;
}
```

The following diagram illustrates the sequences of pop operation.

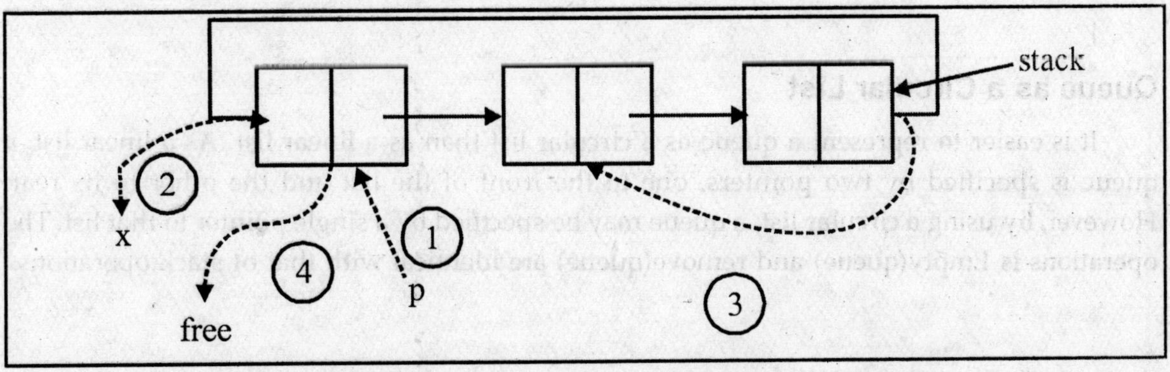

Fig. 15.5: Representation of Sequences of Pop Operation in a Stack

```
int pop(Nodeptr &stack){
int info;
Nodeptr p;
if(stack == null){
printf("Underflow");
getch();
exit(0);
}
p = stack->next;
info = p->info;
if(p==stack){ // in case of one node only
stack = null;
}
else
{
stack->next = p->next;
}
free(p);
return info;
}
```

Queue as a Circular List

It is easier to represent a queue as a circular list than as a linear list. As a linear list, a queue is specified by two pointers, one to the front of the list and the other to its rear. However, by using a circular list, a queue may be specified by a single pointer to that list. The operations is Empty(queue) and remove(queue) are identical with that of stack operations.

The following diagram illustrates the sequences of insert operation.

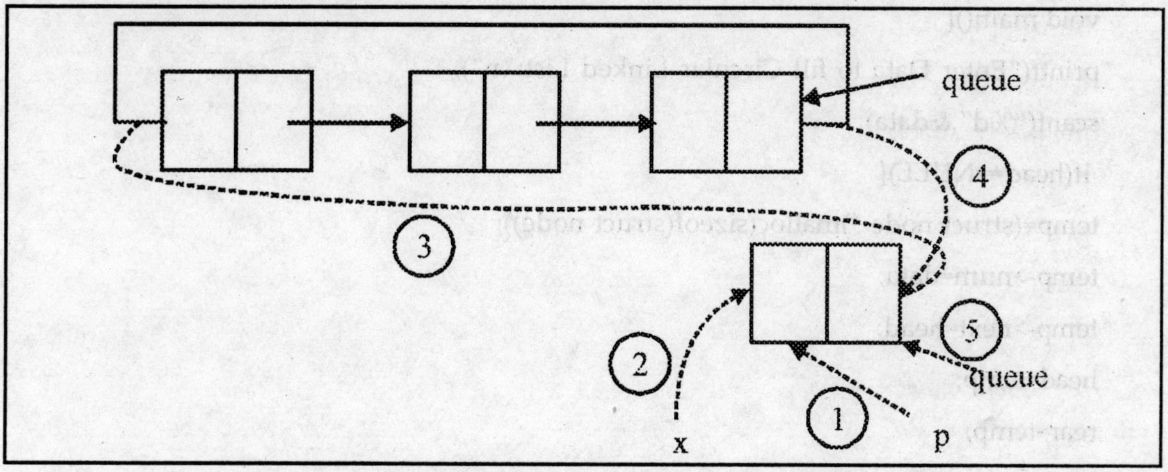

Fig. 15.6: Representation of Sequences of Insertion Operation in a Queue

```
void insert(Nodeptr &queue, int x){
Nodeptr p = (Node)malloc(sizeof(Node));
p->info = x;
if(queue==NULL){
queue = p;
}
else
{
p->next = queue->next;
}
queue->next = p;
queue = p;
}
```

/*Program for Creation of a Circular Linked List*/

```
#include <stdio.h>
#include <alloc.h>
struct node{
int num;
struct node *next;
```

```
}*head,*temp,*rear;
void main(){
printf("Enter Data to fill Circular Linked List:\n");
scanf("%d",&data);
 if(head==NULL){
temp=(struct node *)malloc(sizeof(struct node));
temp->num=data;
temp->next=head;
head=temp;
rear=temp;
}
else
{
temp=(struct node *)malloc(sizeof(struct node));
temp->num=data;
temp->next=head;
rear->next=temp;
rear=temp;
}
}
```

/*Inserting a Node at the Beginning in a Circular Linked List*/

```
void insert_beg(){
struct node *temp;
temp=(struct node *)malloc(sizeof(struct node));
printf("Enter a Number to INSERT it at the beginning of CCL:");
scanf("%d",&temp->info);
temp->next=head;
head=temp;
rear->next=head;
}
```

/*Inserting Node at a Given Position in a Circular Linked List*/

```
void main(){
int n;
printf("Enter Position Number:");
scanf("%d",&n);
n——;
specifiedpos(n);
}
void specifiedpos(int j){
int c=0,k=j-2;
struct node *num,*prev;
printf("Linked List Upto %d element=",j);
do{
printf("%d",head->info);
head=head->next;
if(k==c)prv=head;
c++;
}while(c<j);
num=(struct node *)malloc(sizeof(struct node));
printf("Enter a Element:");
scanf("%d",&num->info);
num->next=head;
prv->next=num;
head=temp;
}
```

/*Deleting the frist node from a Circular Linked List*/

```
void del_beg(){
struct node *cnode;
cnode=temp;
temp=head=head->next;
free(cnode);
```

```
rear->next=head;
c—;
}
```

/*Deleting the Last Node from a Circular Linked List*/

```
void del_end(){
int k=0;
while(k++<(c-2)){
head=head->next;
}
free(rear);
rear=head;
rear->next=temp;
head=temp;
c—;
}
```

/*Deleting a Node from Specified Position in a Circular Linked List*/

```
prinft("Enter a position no:\n");
scanf("%d",&n);
del_spe();
}
void del_spe(int x){
struct node *prv,*temp1;
int k=0,p;
p=x-2;
while(k++<x){
head=head->next;
if(k==x)
prv=head;
if(k==(x+1))temp1=head;
```

```
}
c—;
prv->next=head;
head=temp;
free(temp1);
}
```

/*Code for Displaying a Circular Linked List*/

1st Method

```
void show(){
printf("Linked List Elements are:");
do{
printf("%d",head->info);
head=head->next;
if(rear->next==head)Break;
}while(1);
head=temp;
}
```

2nd Method

```
void show2(){
node *p=head;
while(p->next=head){
printf("%d",p->info);
p=p->next;
}
}
```

DOUBLY LINKED LISTS

One cannot traverse such a list backward, nor can a node be deleted from a circularly linked list, given only a pointer to that node. In cases, where these facilities are required, the appropriate data structure is a doubly linked list. Each node in such a list contains two pointers, one to its predecessor and another to its successor. It is thus possible to move either direction through the list while keeping only one pointer. With a doubly linked list, traversals in direction, insertions and deletions from arbitrary positions in the list can be programmed without difficulty. The cost of a doubly linked list, of course, is the extra space required in each node for a second link.

The node structure is:

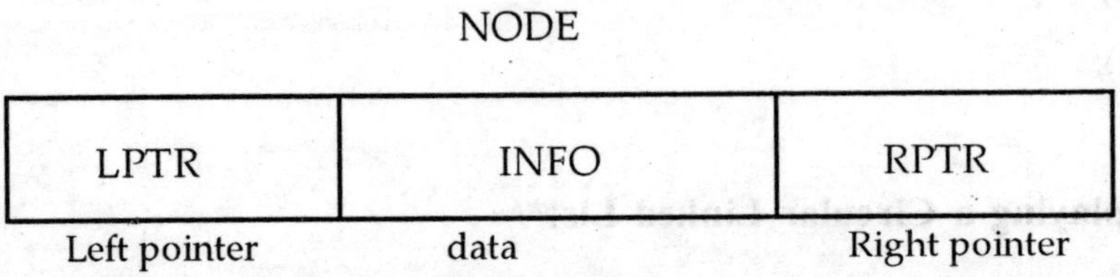

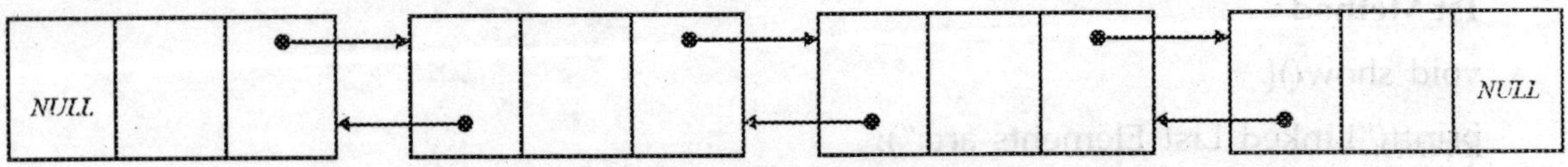

Fig. 15.7: Linearly Double Linked List

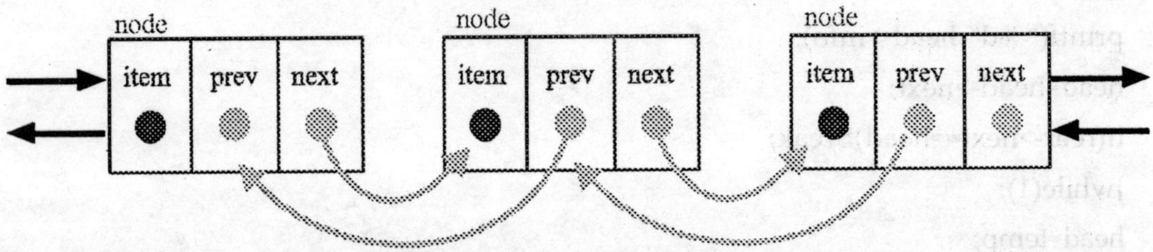

Fig. 15.8: Representation of Doubly Linked List

Doubly linked lists have a pointer to the preceding item as well as one to the next.

In doubly linked list, each structure type node contains three parts: Info, Next and Prev. 'Prev' contains the address of just previous node. 'Next' contains the address of just next node and 'Item' contains the information (variable).

Algorithm for Inserting a Node in a Doubly Linked List

Algorithm Doublelinkedlistinsertion(previous, next, nodeptr, x)

/* previous, p and next, n are the pointer variables which holds the addresses of the first and last nodes. 'new' is a pointer variable to hold the new node address. 'lptr' and 'rptr' are the left and right links of a node. 'nodeptr' is a pointer variable used to hold the address of a specified node and the information is to entered in 'x'*/

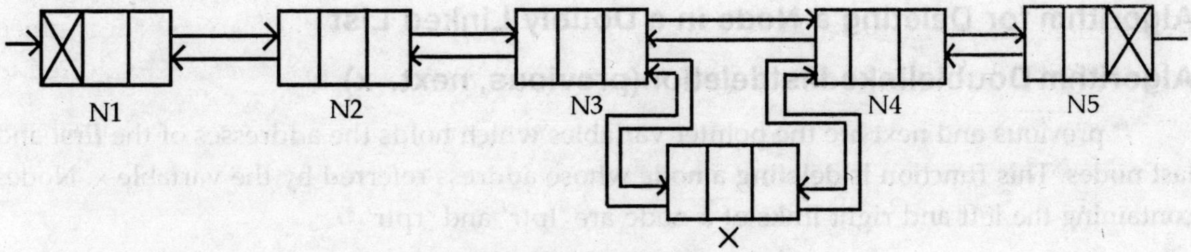

Fig. 15.9: Before inserction of node

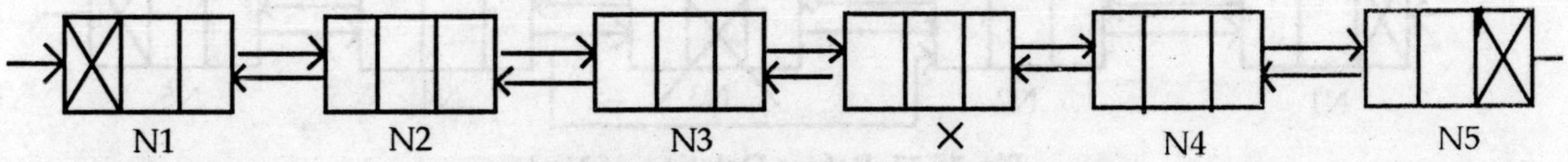

Fig. 15.10: After inserction of node

Step 1: [Obtain a node from the available space]

new <- node

Step 2: [Place the information into the info field of the node]

info(new) <- x

Step 3: [Insertion into the empty list]

if previous = NULL

then

lptr(new) <- rptr(new) <- NULL

previous <- next <- new

return

Step 4: [Left insertion]

lptr(new) <- NULL

rptr(new) <- previous

lptr(previous) <- new

previous < - new

return

Step 5: [Right insertion]

lptr(new) <- next

rptr(next) <- new

rptr(new) <- NULL

next < - new

return

Algorithm for Deleting a Node in a Doubly Linked List

Algorithm Doublelinkedlistdeletion(previous, next, x)

/* previous and next are the pointer variables which holds the addresses of the first and last nodes. This function is deleting a node whose address referred by the variable x. Nodes containing the left and right links of a node are 'lptr' and 'rptr' */

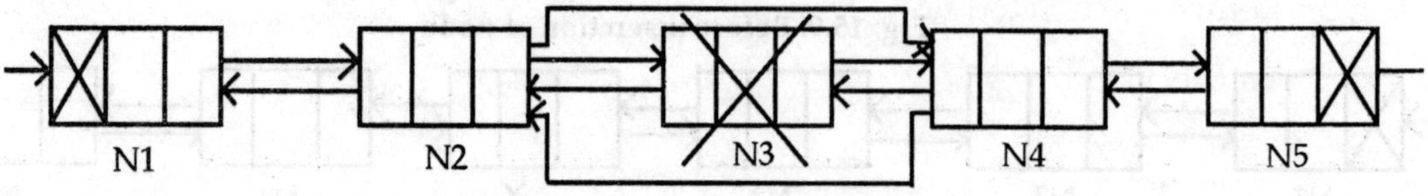

Fig. 15.11: Before Deletion of Node

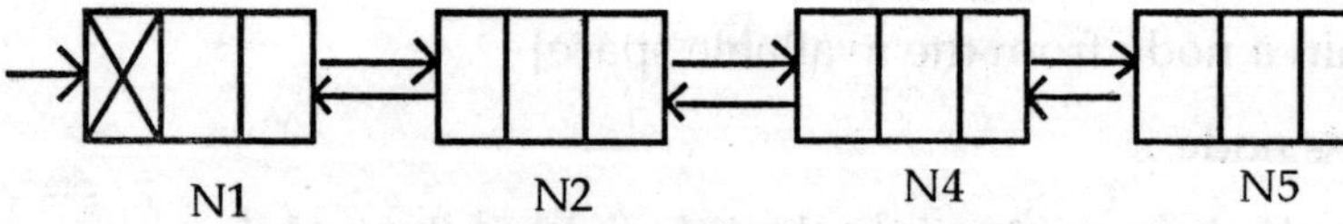

Fig. 15.12: After Deletion of Node

Step 1: [Check for underflow condition]

if previous = NULL

then

print ("List is empty")

return

Step 2: [Delete specified node]

if previous = next

then

previous <- next <- NULL

else

if x = previous

then

previous <- rptr(previous)

lptr(previous) <- NULL

else

if x = next

then

next <- lptr(next)

```
rptr(next) <- NULL
else
rptr(lptr (x)) <- rptr(x)
lptr(rptr(x)) <- lptr(x)
```

Step 3: [Return the deleted node from the list]

```
restore(x)
return
```

Applications of Doubly Linked List

- In memory management, a doubly linked list is used to maintain both the list of allocated blocks and the list of free blocks by the memory manager of the operating system.
- A doubly linked list can be traversed in both directions.
- Having 2 pointers in a doubly linked list provides safety, because even if one of the pointers get corrupted the node still remains linked.
- Deleting a particular node from a list does not require keeping track of the previous node.

Implementing Some Operations

```
void insertNodeInRight(nodeptr &p, int x){
nodeptr n, r = p-> next;
n = (nodeptr)malloc(sizeof(node));
n-> previous = r-> previous;
n-> next = p->next;
p-> next = n;
r-> previous = n;
n-> info = x;
}
```

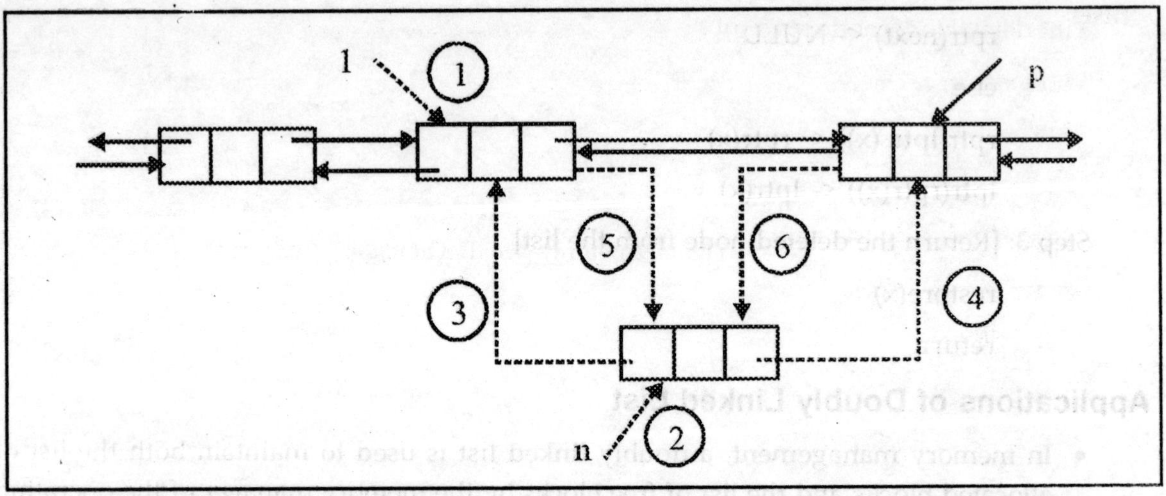

Fig. 15.13: Representation of inserting a node in the right position of a doubly linked list

```
void insertNodeInLeft(nodeptr &p, int x){
nodeptr n, l;
n = (nodeptr)malloc(sizeof(node));
n-> previous = p-> previous;
n-> next = l-> next;
l-> next = n;
p-> previous = n;
n-> info = x;
}
```

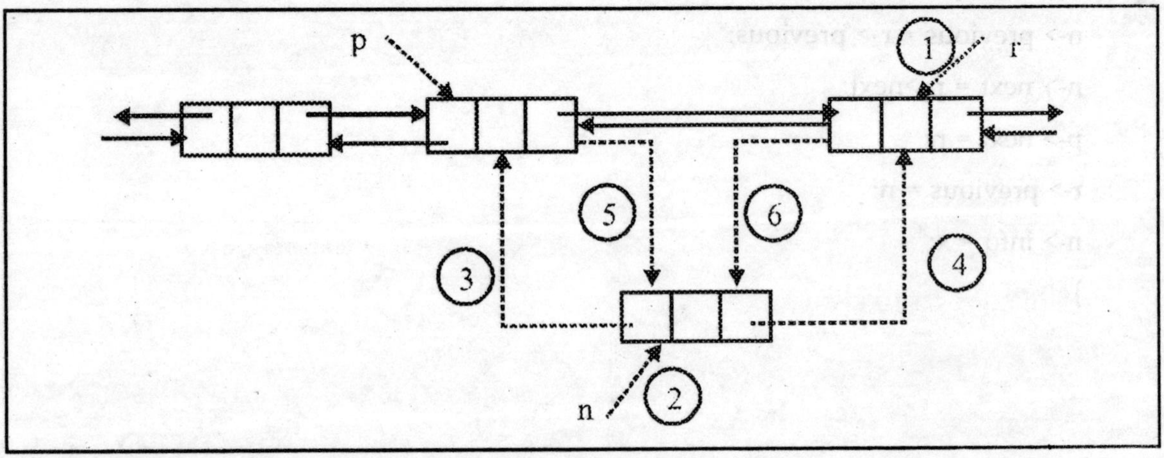

Fig. 15.14: Representation of inserting a node in the left position of a doubly linked list

```
int deleteNode(nodeptr &p){
nodeptr q, r;
int res;
if(p==null){
printf("void deletion");
exit(0);
}
res = p-> info;
q = p-> previous;
r = p-> next;
q-> next = r;
r-> previous = q;
free(p);
return res;
}
```

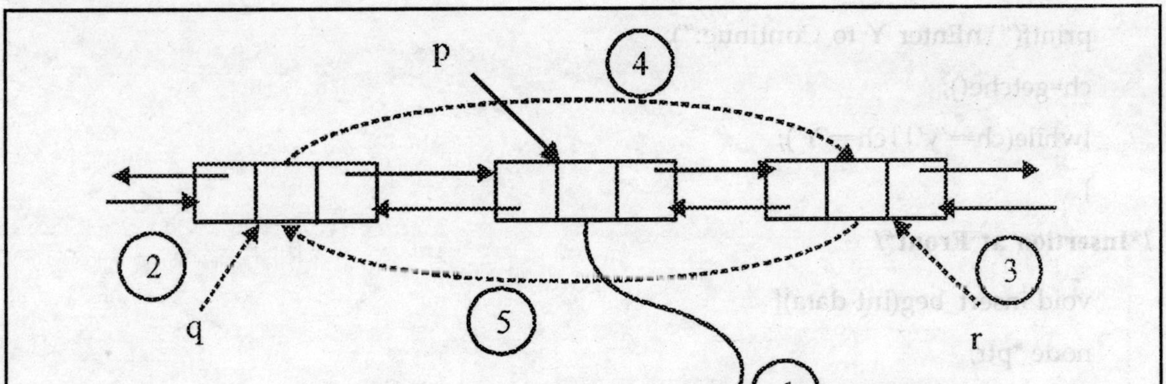

Fig. 15.15: Representation of deleting a node from doubly linked list

/*Creation of Doubly Linked List*/

```
void create(){
do{
temp=(struct node *)malloc(sizeof(struct node));
printf("\nEnter Ur Data");
```

```
scanf("%d",&temp-> info);
if(front==NULL){
temp-> next=NULL;
temp-> prv=NULL;
rear=front-> temp;
cnode=temp;
}
else
{
temp-> next=NULL;
temp-> prv=cnode;
cnode-> next=temp;
cnode=cnode-> next;
rear=temp;
}
printf("\nEnter Y to Continue:");
ch=getche();
}while(ch=='y'||ch=='Y');
}
```

/*Insertion at Front*/

```
void insert_beg(int data){
node *ptr;
prt=(node *)malloc(sizeof(node));
ptr->info=data;
ptr-> prv=NULL;
ptr-> next=front;
front-> prv=ptr;
front=ptr;
}
```

/*Insertion at the End*/

```
void insert_end(int data){
node *ptr;
ptr=(node *)malloc(sizeof(node));
ptr-> info=data;
ptr-> next=NULL;
ptr-> prv=rear;
rear-> next=ptr;
rear = ptr;
}
```

/*Deletion of a Node from Specified Position in Doubly Linked List*/

(i) First Method

```
void del_spe(){
struct node *case1,*yahoo,*ali,*ptr;
int data,c=0;
printf("\nEnter Position of node");
scanf("%d",&data);
case1=front;
if(data==0){
ptr=front;
free(ptr);
front=front->next;
front->prv=NULL;
}
else
{
while(case1!=NULL){
c++;
if(c==(data-1)){
```

```
ptr=case1;
}
if(c==data){
yahoo=case1;
free(yahoo);
}
if(c==(data+1))
ali=case1;
case1=case1->next;
}
ptr->next=ali;
}
}
```

(ii) Second Method

```
cnode=front;
while(cnode!=NULL){
if(cnode->info==data)Break;
node=node->next;
}
cnode->next->prv=cnode->prv;
cnode->prv->next=cnode->next;
free(cnode);
```

/*Searching Data in Doubly Linked List*/

```
fnode=front;
rnode=rear;
flag=0,f=0,l=0,data=10;
while(fnode!=NULL||rnode!=NULL){
f++;
l++;
```

```
if(fnode->info==data){
printf("Data found At %d from starting",f);
flag=1;
break;
}
if(rnode->info==data){
printf("Data is found At %d from last",l);
flag=1;
break;
}
fnode=fnode->next;
rnode=rnode->prv;
}
if(flag==0)
   printf("\nTry Again Data Not Found:");
}
```

CIRCULARLY DOUBLE LINKED LISTS

In a doubly-circularly-linked list, each node has two links, similar to a *doubly-linked list*, except that the previous link of the first node points to the last node and the next link of the last node points to the first node. As in a doubly-linked list, insertions and removals can be done at any point with access to any nearby node.

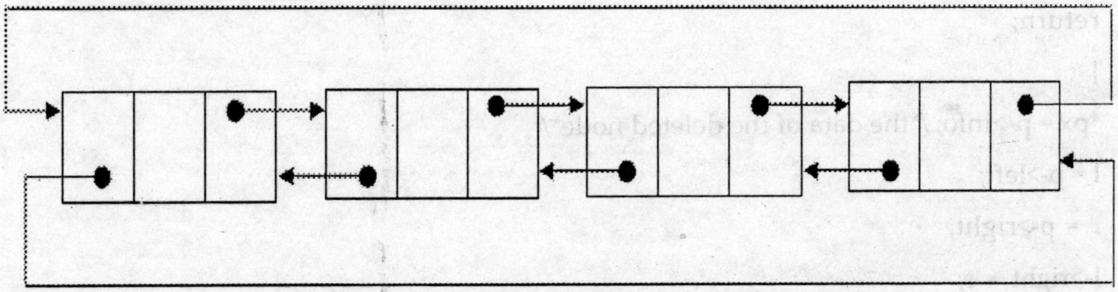

Fig. 15.16: Representation of circularly double linked list

Insert a node: The following function ***insertright*** inserts a node with information field x to the right of a node pointed by p in a doubly circular linked list. ***Insertleft*** function can be written similarly.

Example:

```
void insertright(nodeptr *p, int x){
nodeptr *q,*r;
if(p == NULL){
printf("void insertion\n");
return;
}
q = getnode();
q->info = x;
r = p->right;
r->left = q;
q->right = r;
q->left = p;
p->right = q
}
```

Delete a Node: The following function can be used to delete a node pointed by a node pointercan be deleted in a doubly circular linked list.

```
void delete(nodeptr *p, int *px){
nodeptr *l,*r;
if(p == NULL){
printf("void deletion\n");
return;
}
*px = p->info; /*the data of the deleted node*/
l = p->left;
r = p->right;
l->right = r;
r->left = l;
freenode(p);
}
```

/*Creation of Circular Doubly Linked List*/

1st method

```
#include <stdio.h>
#include <conio.h>
#include <alloc.h>
struct node{
int info;
struct node *left,*right;
}*head;
head=(struct node *)malloc(sizeof(struct node));
head->left=head->right=head;
head->info=0;
```

2nd method with rear and front concept

```
front=rear=NULL;
do{
temp=(struct node *)malloc(sizeof(struct node));
scanf("%d",&temp->info);
if(front==NULL){
fornt=temp;
temp->prv=NULL;
temp->next=front;
rear=temp;
cnode=temp;
}
else
{
temp->next=front;
temp->prv=cnode;
cnode->next=temp;
```

```
rear=temp;
cnode=cnode->next;
}
printf("\n Press Y to continue");
ch=getche();
}while(ch=='y'||ch=='Y');
```

/*Insertion at beginning*/

```
void insert_beg(){
node *ptr,*temp;
int item;
ptr=(node *)malloc(sizeof(node));
printf("\nEnter the No:");
scanf("%d",&item);
ptr->info=item;
temp=head->right;
head->right=ptr;
ptr->left=head;
ptr->right=temp;
temp->left=ptr;
}
```

/*Insertion at Last*/

```
void insert_end(){
node *ptr,*temp;
int item;
ptr=(node *)malloc(sizeof(node));
scanf("%d",&ptr->info);
temp=head->left;
temp->right=ptr;
ptr->left=temp;
```

```
ptr->right=head;
head->left=ptr;
}
```

/*Deletion from Beginning*/

```
void del_beg(){
node *temp;
if(head->right==head){
return;
}
else
{
temp=head->right;
printf("\deleted element is =%d \n", temp->info);
head->right=temp->right;
temp->right=temp->left=head;
free(temp);
}
}
```

/*Delete from Last*/

```
void del_end(){
node *temp;
if(head->right==head){
return;
}
else
{
temp=head->left;
printf("\nDeleted element is %d \n",temp->info);
head->left=temp->left;
```

```
free(temp);
}
```

/*Program for Reversal of a Singly Linked List by Recursion*/

```
#include<stdio.h>
#include<conio.h>
#include<alloc.h>
struct node
{
int data;
struct node *next;
};
void insert(struct node **p,int num)   /*Function for inserting an element into a list */
{
if(*p==NULL){
(*p)=(struct node *)malloc(sizeof(struct node));
(*p)->next=NULL;
(*p)->data=num;
}
else
{
insert(&((*p)->next),num);
}
}
void display(struct node *p) /*Function for displaying the list*/
{
while(p!=NULL) {
printf("%d ",p->data);
p=p->next;
}
```

```
}
void reverse(struct node **p) /*Function for reversing the list by recursion */
{
struct node*q,*r,*x;
int d;
q=(*p);     /*stores the address of the first element */
x=q;        /*also stores the element of the first element for counter purpose */
d=q->data;  /*stores the data of the first element*/
r=q->next;  /*stores the address of the second element in the list*/
free(q);  /*deletes the first element of the list*/
if(x==NULL)
return
else
{
reverse(&(r));/*Recursive call*/
insert(p,d);  /*This function is put in the stack so the first
will be taken as last element for the new list */
}
}
void main(){
clrscr();
struct node *p=NULL;
int n, d, i=0;
printf("How many...?");
scanf("%d", &n);
while(i++!=n){
scanf("%d",&d);
insert(&p,d);
}
```

```
display(p);
reverse(&p);
printf("The reversed list is...");
display(p);
getch();
}
```

Review Questions

1. If you are using C language to implement the heterogeneous linked list, what pointer type will you use?
2. Whether Linked List is linear or non-linear data structure?
3. Explain in brief a linked list. Explain about the types of linked lists.
4. Write the programs for Linked List (Insertion and Deletion) operations.
5. Describe the steps to insert data into a singly linked list.
6. What is the difference between linked list and an array?
7. Construct a doubly linked list using a single pointer in each node.
8. Define circular linked list. Write an algorithm for insertion and deletion of a data item into a circularly linked list.
9. Explain the implementation of stacks as linked lists.
10. Explain the implementation of queues as linked lists.
11. What are the different types of linked lists? Explain each with an example.
12. What are the advantages and disadvantages of doubly linked lists.
13. Represent a circularly linked list using an array. Write routines to insert and delete elements for this representation.
14. What is circular doubly linked list? Explain the various operations on circular doubly linked lists with suitable algorithms.

CHAPTER

16

Trees

INTRODUCTION

A tree is a widely used data structure that emulates a tree structure with a set of linked nodes. Tree structures support various basic dynamic set operations including Search, Predecessor, Successor, Minimum, Maximum, Insert and Delete in time proportional to the height of the tree. Ideally, a tree will be balanced and the height will be log n where n is the number of nodes in the tree. To ensure that the height of the tree is as small as possible and therefore provide the best running time, a balanced tree structure like a red-black tree, AVL tree or b-tree must be used.

When working with large sets of data, it is often not possible or desirable to maintain the entire structure in primary storage (RAM). Instead, a relatively small portion of the data structure is maintained in primary storage and additional data is read from secondary storage as needed. Unfortunately, a magnetic disk, the most common form of secondary storage is significantly slower than random access memory (RAM). In fact, the system often spends more time retrieving data than actually processing data.

TERMINOLOGY

Nodes

A node may contain a value or a condition which represents a separate data structure or a tree of its own. Each node in a tree has zero or more child nodes, which are below it in the tree (by convention, trees grow down, not up as they do in nature). A node that has a child is called the child's parent node (or ancestor node, or superior). A node has at most one parent. Nodes that share the same parent are called as siblings.

The height of a node is the length of the longest downward path to a leaf from that node. The height of the root is the height of the tree.

The depth of a node is the length of the path to its root (i.e., its root path).

Root Nodes

The topmost node in a tree is called the root node. Being the topmost node, the root node will not have parents. It is the node at which operations on the tree commonly begin (although some algorithms begin with the leaf nodes and work up ending at the root). All other nodes can be reached from it by following edges or links. (In the formal definition, each such path is also unique). In diagrams, it is typically drawn at the top. In some trees, such as heaps, the root node has special properties. Every node in a tree can be seen as the root node of the subtree rooted at that node.

Leaf Nodes

Nodes at the bottommost level of the tree are called leaf nodes. Since they are at the bottommost level, they do not have any children.

Internal Nodes

An internal node or inner node is any node of a tree that has child nodes and is thus not a leaf node.

Subtrees

A subtree is a portion of a tree data structure that can be viewed as a complete tree in itself. Any node in a tree T, together with all the nodes below it, comprises a subtree of T. The subtree corresponding to the root node is the entire tree; the subtree corresponding to any other node is called a proper subtree (in analogy to the term proper subset).

Definition of a Tree

(1) A data structure accessed beginning at the root node. Each node is either a leaf or an internal node. An internal node has one or more child nodes and is called the parent of its child nodes. All children of the same node are siblings. Contrary to a physical tree, the root is usually depicted at the top of the structure, and the leaves are depicted at the bottom.

(2) A connected, undirected, acyclic graph. It is rooted and ordered unless otherwise specified.

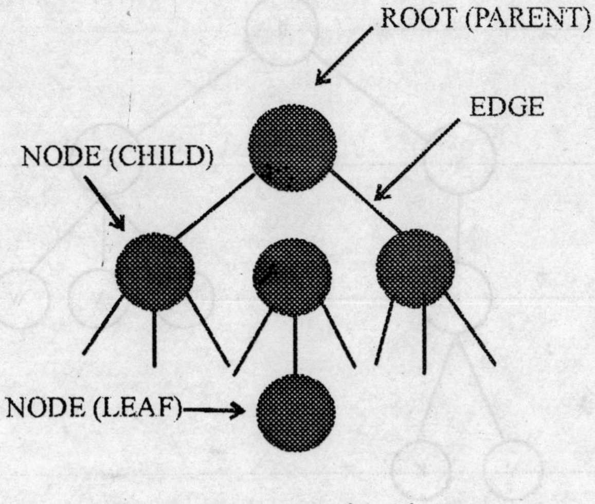

Fig. 16.1: Representation of a Tree

Paths and Levels

A path is a sequence of nodes n1, n2, ..., nk such that node ni is the parent of node ni+1 for all 1 <= i <= k.

The length of a path is the number of edges on the path (one less than the number of nodes).

The descendents of a node are all the nodes that are on some path from the node to any leaf.

The ancestors of a node are all the nodes that are on the path from the node to the root.

The depth of a node is the length of the path from root to the node. The depth of a node is sometimes called its level.

The height of a node is the length of the longest path from the node to a leaf.

The height of a tree is the height of its root.

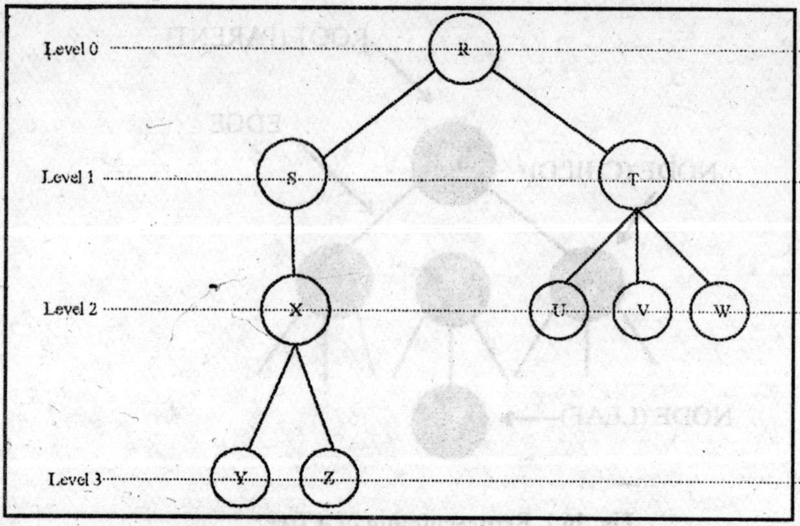

Fig. 16.2: A General Tree Showing Node Depth Levels

In the example above

The nodes Y, Z, U, V, and W are leaf nodes.

The nodes R, S, T, and X are internal nodes.

The degree of node T is 3. The degree of node S is 1.

The depth of node X is 2. The depth of node Z is 3.

The height of node Z is zero. The height of node S is 2. The height of node R is 3.

The height of the tree is the same as the height of its root R. Therefore, the height of the tree is 3.

The sequence of nodes R,S,X is a path.

The sequence of nodes R, X, Y is not a path because the sequence does not satisfy the "parenthood" property (R is not the parent of X).

BINARY TREE

A binary tree is an important type of structure which occurs very often. It is characterized by the fact that any node can have at most two branches, i.e., there is no node with degree greater than two. For binary trees, we distinguish between the subtree on the left and on the right, whereas for trees the order of the subtree is irrelevant. Also a binary tree may have zero nodes. Thus, a binary tree is really a different object than a tree.

Definition: A binary tree is a finite set of nodes which is either empty or consists of a root and two disjoint binary trees called the left subtree and the right subtree.

FORMAL DEFINITION

A binary tree is:

- either empty, or
- it is a node that has a left and a right subtree, each of which is a binary tree.

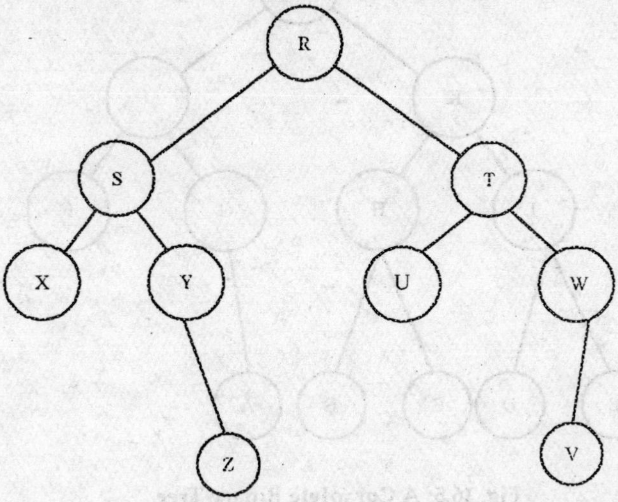

Fig. 16.3: A Binary Tree. As Usual, the Empty Children are Not Explicitly Shown

Full Binary Tree

A full binary tree (FBT) is a binary tree in which each node has exactly two non-empty children or exactly two empty children, and all the leaves are on the same level.

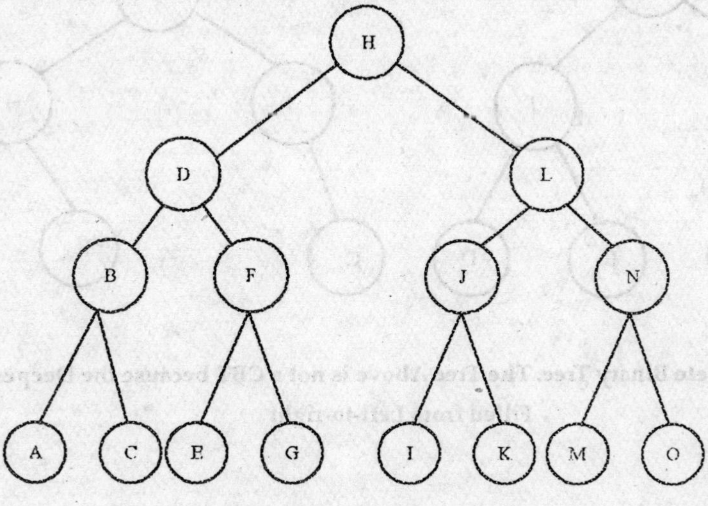

Fig. 16.4: A Full Binary Tree. In a FBT, the Number of Nodes at Level i is 2i

Complete Binary Tree

A complete binary tree (CBT) is a FBT except, perhaps, that the deepest level may not be completely filled. If not completely filled, it is filled from left-to-right.

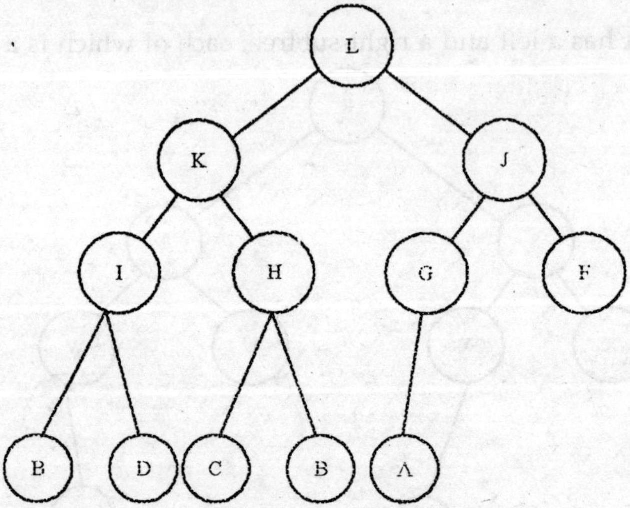

Fig. 16.5: A Complete Binary Tree

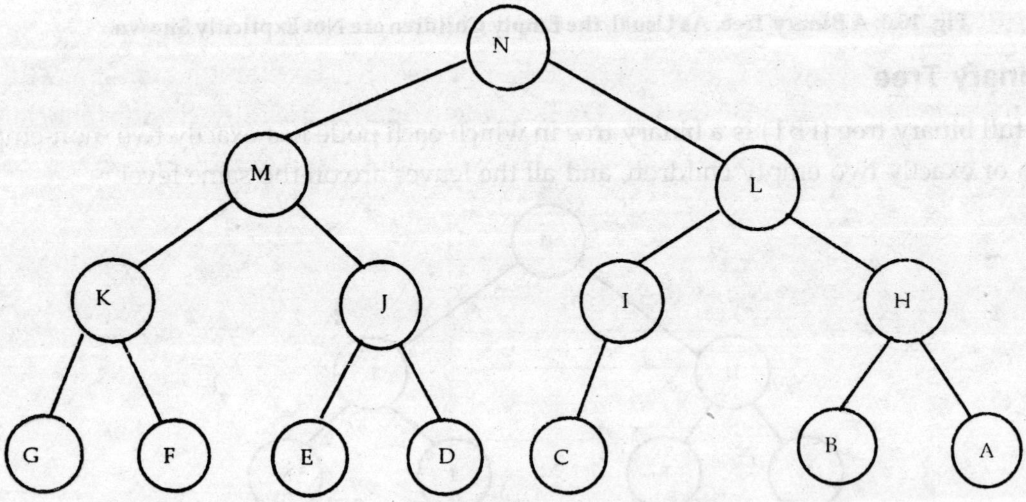

Fig. 16.6: Not a Complete Binary Tree. The Tree Above is not a CBT because the Deepest Level is not Filled from Left-to-right

BINARY TREE REPRESENTATION

A binary tree can be represented in two ways:

- Sequential representation
- Linked representation

Consider an example of a binary tree:

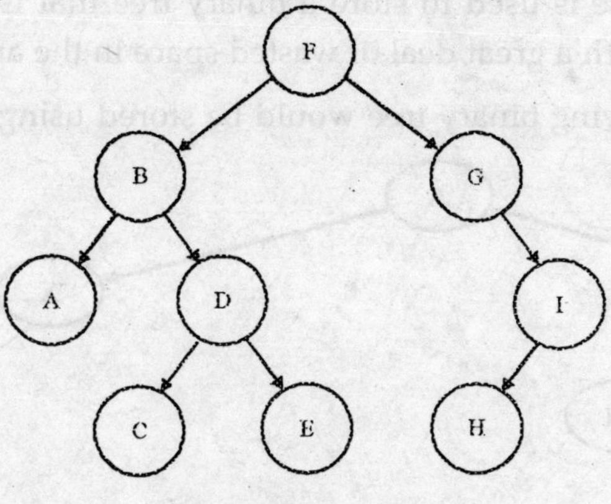

Fig. 16.7: Binary Tree

Sequential representation

In sequential representation, only one linear array is used. The root R is stored at TREE [1]. If the node occupies TREE[K], then its left child is stored at in TREE[K*2] and right child is stored in TREE[K*2 + 1].

TREE

1	F
2	B
3	G
4	A
5	D
6	NULL
7	I
8	NULL
9	NULL
10	C
11	E
12	NULL
13	NULL
14	H
15	NULL

For example, the almost complete binary tree shown in below figure can be stored in an array like so:

[0]	[1]	[2]	[3]	[4]	[5]	[6]	[7]	[8]	[9]
A	C	X	E	M	S	O	K	W	N

However, if this scheme is used to store a binary tree that is not complete or almost complete, we can end up with a great deal of wasted space in the array.

For example, the following binary tree would be stored using this technique like so:

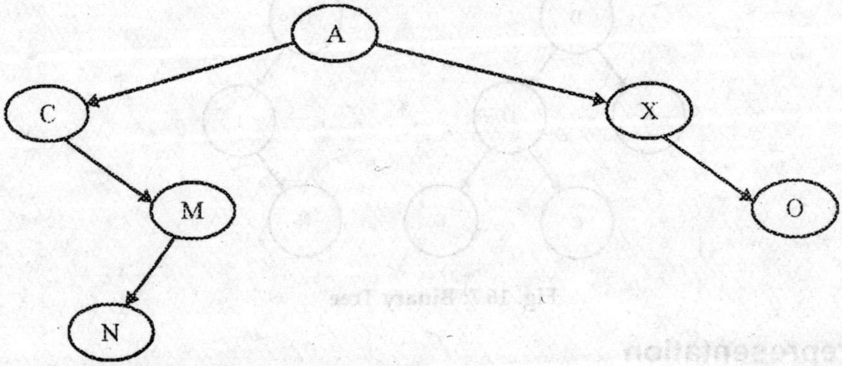

[0]	[1]	[2]	[3]	[4]	[5]	[6]	[7]	[8]	[9]
A	C	X		M		O			N

Linked Representation

Linked representation uses three parallel arrays, INFO, LEFT and RIGHT and a pointer variable ROOT. Each node N of T will correspond to a location K such that –

INFO[K] contains the data at node N

LEFT[K] contains the location of left child node N

RIGHT[K] contains the location of right child node N

ROOT will contain the location of root R of T

Root 5

	INFO	LEFT	RIGHT
1	A	NULL	NULL
2	B	1	10
3	H	NULL	NULL
4	G	NULL	6
5	F	2	7
6	I	3	NULL
7	G	3	4
8	C	NULL	NULL
9	E	NULL	NULL
10	D	8	9

If a binary tree is not complete or almost complete, a better choice for storing it is to use a linked representation similar to the linked list structures.

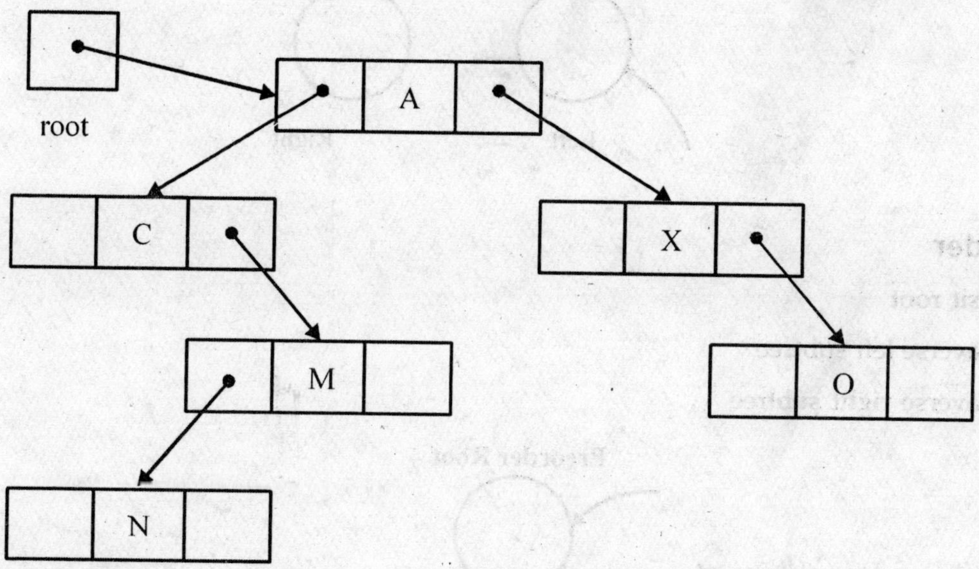

Each tree node has two pointers (usually named left and right). The tree class has a pointer to the root node of the tree (labelled root in the diagram above).

Any pointer in the tree structure that does not point to a node will normally contain the value NULL. A linked tree with N nodes will always contain N + 1 null links.

BINARY TREE TRAVERSALS

Inorder

Traverse left subtree

Visit root

Traverse right subtree

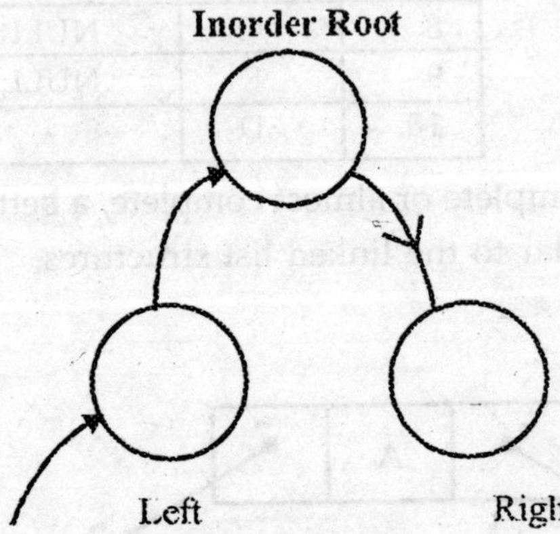

Preorder

Visit root

Traverse left subtree

Traverse right subtree

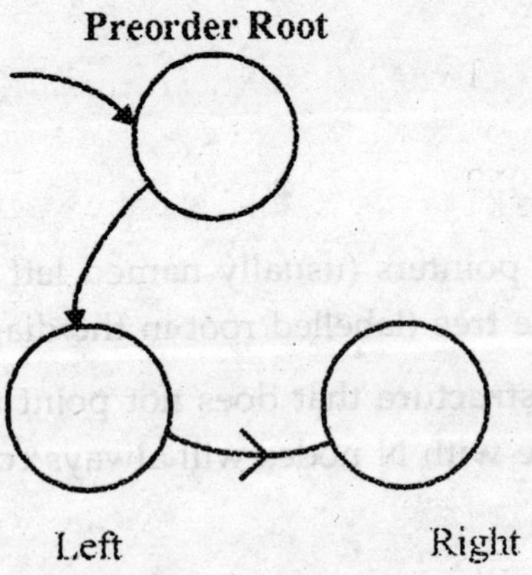

Postorder

Traverse left subtree

Traverse right subtree

Visit root

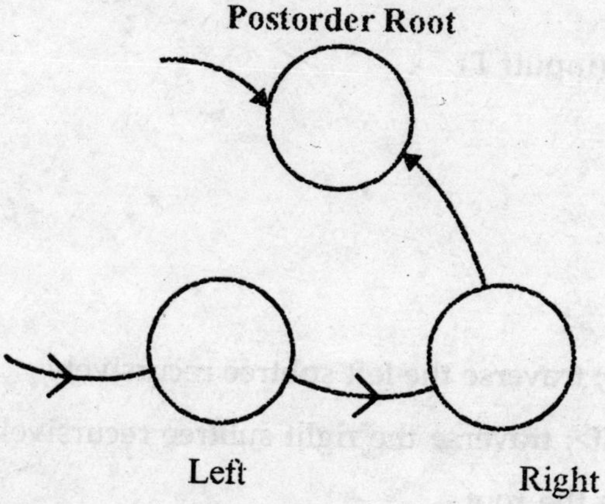

Tree Travesal Techniques — Algorithms

Inorder Traversal

Procedure inorder(input: T)

begin

if T = nil then

return;

endif

inorder(T —> left>; traverse the left subtree recursively

visit(T); visit/process the root

inorder(T —> right>; traverse the right subtree recursively

end

Preorder Traversal

Procedure preorder(input: T)

begin

if T = nil then

return;

endif

visit(T); visit/process the root

preorder(T —> left>; traverse the left subtree recursively

preorder(T —> right>; traverse the right subtree recursively

end

Postorder Traversal

Procedure postorder(input: T)

begin

if T = nil then

return;

endif

postorder(T —> left>; traverse the left subtree recursively

postorder(T —> right>; traverse the right subtree recursively

visit(T); visit/process the root

end

BINARY SEARCH TREES

Binary search trees are binary trees with an additional property, which holds for the binary tree and for all of the subtrees it contains. This property is that all the elements in the left subtree are less than or equal to the root node value and all elements in the right subtree are greater than the root node value. This property assumes that the concepts of 'less than or equal to' and 'greater than' are meaningful for the type of element stored in the tree. For Java implementations, we use the standard meanings of '<=' and '>' for primitive types. Otherwise we assume that objects stored in the tree implement the comparable interface.

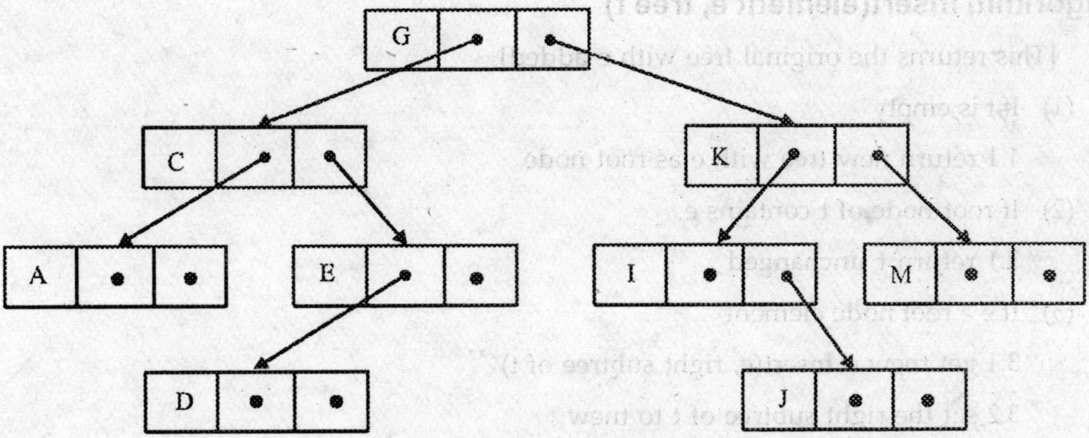

Fig. 16.8: A Binary Search Tree

Binary search trees are particularly useful for storing sets and similar data types. This is because, for a balanced tree, the number of operations required to search for, remove, or insert an element is O(log n), where n is the size of the set. This is much better than the O(n) result for array or linked list implementations of sets.

Binary Search Tree Algorithms

The three basic algorithms are: search for an element, insert an element and remove an element. Usually, these are implemented as mutative methods for maximum efficiency.

The Search Algorithm

This can be defined recursively or non-recursively. The recursive algorithm is as follows.

Algorithm FindNode(element e, tree t)

[Returns the node containing e in t, or null]

(1) If t is empty then return null

(2) If root node of t contains e

2.1 Return root node

(3) If e > root node element

3.1 Return FindNode(right subtree of t)

(4) Return FindNode(left subtree of t)

The Insert Algorithm

The following defines a recursive algorithm. It assumes that an element should be included at most once (the extension to multiple occurrences is straight forward). It is also possible to define a non-recursive algorithm.

Algorithm Insert(element e, tree t)

[This returns the original tree with e added]

(1) If t is empty

1.1 return new tree with e as root node

(2) If root node of t contains e

2.1 return t unchanged

(3) If e > root node element

3.1 get tnew = Insert(e, right subtree of t)

3.2 set the right subtree of t to tnew

3.3 return t

(4) Else

4.1 get tnew = Insert (e, left subtree of t)

4.2 set the left subtree of t to tnew

4.3 return t

The following diagram shows the result of inserting "F" into the binary search tree shown above.

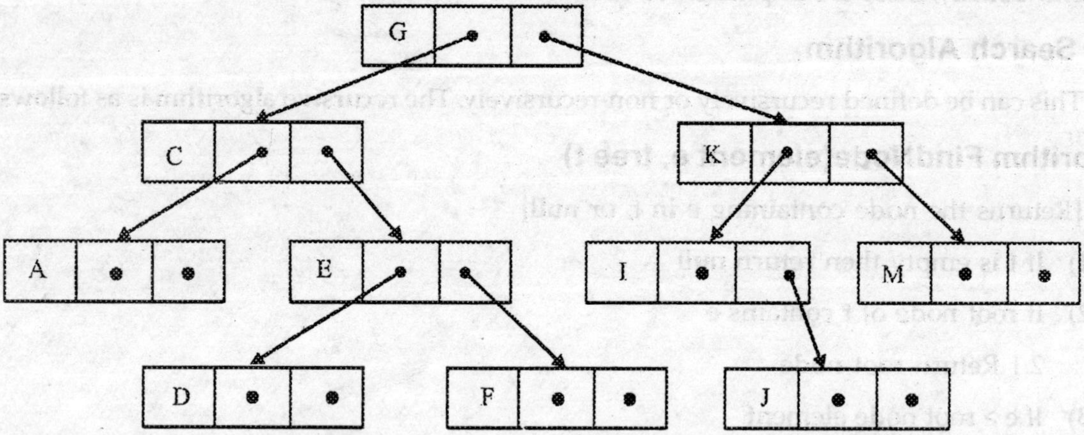

Fig. 16.9: Binary Search Tree after Inserting "F"

The Delete Algorithm

This is the most complex of the three algorithms. The main problem is that the element we wish to delete may well be in a node which has two child nodes. If this is the case, then some re-organization of the nodes in the tree will be needed. Even so, this re-organization can be achieved quite straightforwardly.

There are three cases to consider.

(1) Node to be deleted is a leaf node. Make link from parent null instead.

(2) Node to be deleted has no left (or right) subtree. Make link from parent refer to right (or left) subtree instead.

(3) Node to be deleted has non-empty left and right subtrees. Change node value to the smallest value in right subtree, then delete smallest value from right subtree. (This deletion of the smallest must be either case 1 or 2.)

The following diagram shows the result of deleting "G" from the above tree.

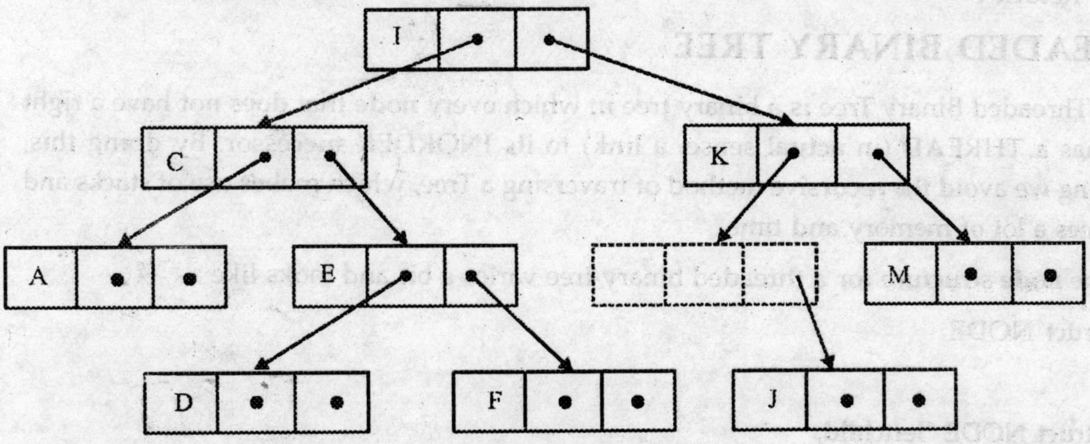

Fig. 19.10: Tree after deleting "G"

Algorithm Delete(element e, tree t)

[This returns the original tree with e removed]

(1) If t is empty return t

(2) If e > root node element

2.1 Set tnew = Delete(e, right subtree of t)

2.2 Set the right subtree of t to tnew

(3) If e < root node element

3.1 Set tnew = Delete(e, left subtree of t)

3.2 Set the left subtree of t to tnew

(4) (e equals root node element)

If left subtree of t is empty

4.1 Return right subtree of t

(5) If right subtree of t is empty

5.1 Return left subtree of t

(6) (Both subtrees are non-empty)

Get smallest element, s, in right subtree

(7) Change root node element from e to s

(8) Set tnew = Delete(s, right subtree of t)

(9) Set the right subtree of t to tnew

(10) Return t

THREADED BINARY TREE

A Threaded Binary Tree is a binary tree in which every node that does not have a right child has a THREAD (in actual sense, a link) to its INORDER successor. By doing this, threading we avoid the recursive method of traversing a Tree, which makes use of stacks and consumes a lot of memory and time.

The node structure for a threaded binary tree varies a bit and looks like –

```
struct NODE
{
 struct NODE *leftchild;
 int node_value;
 struct NODE *rightchild;
 struct NODE *thread;
}
```

Let's make the Threaded Binary tree out of a normal binary tree...

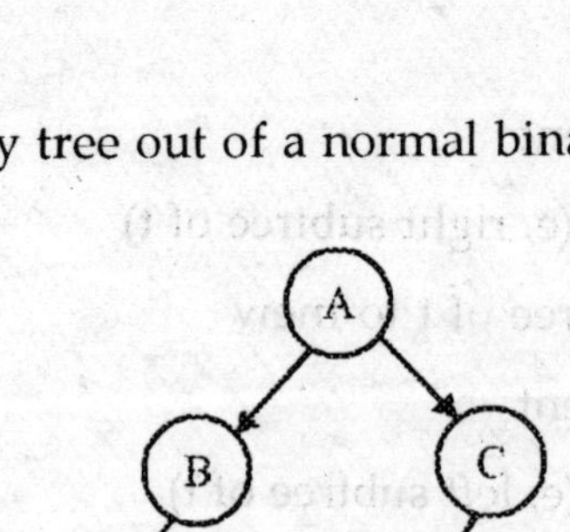

The INORDER traversal for the above tree is — D B A E C. So, the respective Threaded Binary tree will be –

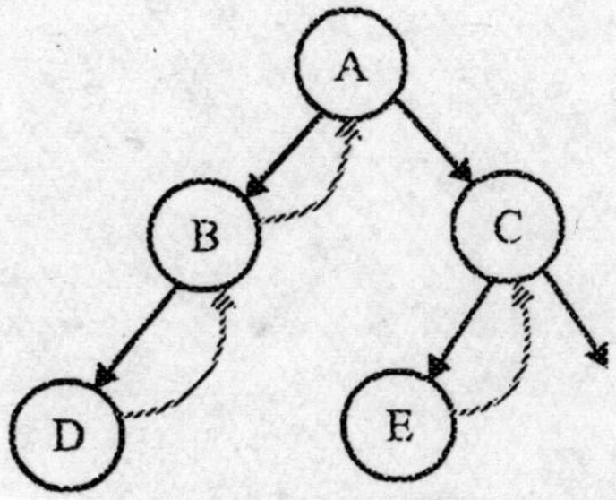

B has no right child and its inorder successor is A and so a thread has been made in between them. Similarly, for D and E. C have no right child but it has no inorder successor even, so it has a hanging thread.

C Program Examples

/* Program – Tree Implementation*/

```
#include <stdio.h>
#include <conio.h>
#include <alloc.h>
struct tree{
int a;
struct tree *left;
struct tree *right;
};
struct tree *ins(int p,int x);
struct tree *p;
int x;
{
if(p==NULL){
p=(struct tree *)malloc(sizeof(struct tree));
p->a=x;
p->left=NULL;
p->right=NULL;
return(p);
}
```

```
if(x<p->a)
p->left=ins(p->left, x);
else
p->right=ins(p->right, x);
return(p);
}
void prn(x, level);
struct tree *x;
int level;
{
int i;
if(x)x->right,level+1);
printf('\n');
for(i=0;i<level;i++)
printf("");
printf("%d",x->a);
prn(x->left,level+1);
}
}
struct tree *delete(g,h)
struct tree *g,*h;
{
struct tree *f;
if(g->right!=NULL)
g->right=delete(g->right,h);
else{
f=g;
h->a=g->a;
free(f);
}
```

```
return(g);
}
void copy(t,d)
struct tree *t,**d;{
int i;
if(t){
*d=(struct tree *)malloc(sizeof(struct tree));
(*d)->a=t->a;
copy(t->left,&(*d)->left);
copy(t->right,&(*d)->right);
}
else
*d=NULL;
}
struct tree *del(t, x)
struct tree *t;
int x;
{
struct tree *q;
if(x<t >a)
t->left=del(t->left, x);
else
t->right=del(t->right, x);
else{
q=t;
if(q->right==NULL){
t=q->left;
free(q);
}
else if(q->left==NULL){
```

```
t=q->right;
free(q);
}
else
q->left=delete(q->left, q);
}
return(t);
}
main(){
struct tree *t=NULL,*d=NULL;
int a,b;
clsrcr();
while(1){
printf("\n enter value -1 to stop");
scnaf("%d"&a);
if(a==-1)
break;t=ins(t,a);
}
prn(t,1);
print("\nenter value to be deleted");
t=del(t,b);
printf("\n');
printf(t,l);
getch();
}
```

/*Implementation of Binary Tree using Linked List*/

```
#include <stdio.h>
#include <conio.h>
#include <alloc.h>
```

```
#include <stdlib.h>
struct btree{
int n;
struct btree *left;
struct btree *right;
}typedef btree,node;
btree *root,*ptr,*prev,*bfor,*x,*y;
int num;
char ch;
void main(){
 int c;
void create(node *);
void print(node *);
void insert(node *);
void modify(node *);
void delet(node *);
while(c!=7){
clrscr();
printf("1. CREATE<BR>");
printf("2. PRINT<BR>");
printf("3. SEARCH<BR>");
printf("4. INSERT<BR>");
printf("5. MODIFY<BR>");
printf("6. DELETE<BR>");
printf("7. EXIT<BR>");
printf("Enter your choice : ");
scanf("%d",&c);
switch(c){
case 1:{
```

```
root=(node *)malloc(sizeof(node));
printf("Enter number:");
scanf("%d",&root->n);
ptr=root;
root->left=root->right=NULL;
printf("Enter more(y/n)?");
ch=getch();
create(root);
break;
}
case 2:{
print(root);
getch();
break;
}
case 3:{
printf("<BR>);
search(root);
getch();
break;
}
case 4:{
printf("<BR>);
insert(root);
getch();
break;
}
case 5:{
printf("<BR>);
```

```
modify(root);
getch();
break;
}
case 6:{
printf("<BR>);
delet(root);
getch();
break;
}
case 7:
exit(0);
default:{
printf("Invalid choice");
getch();
break;
}
}
}
getch();
}
void create(node *ptr){
while(ch == 'y'){
printf("<BR>");
ptr=prev=root;
printf("Enter number:");
scanf("%d",&num);
do
{
```

```
if(num < ptr->n){
prev=ptr;
ptr=ptr->left;
}
else if(num > ptr->n){
prev=ptr;
ptr=ptr->right;
}
else
{
prev=NULL;
break;
}
}while(ptr);
if(prev){
ptr=(node *)malloc(sizeof(node));
ptr->n=num;
ptr->left=ptr->right=NULL;
if(ptr->n < prev->n){
prev->left=ptr;
if(prev == root)
root=prev;
}
if(ptr->n > prev->n){
prev->right=ptr;
ptr->left=ptr->right=NULL;
if(prev == root)
root=prev;
}
```

```
}
else
printf("'%d' is already present.. <BR>",num);
printf("Enter more(y/n)?");
ch=getch();
}
}
void print(node *ptr){
void inprint(node *);
void preprint(node *);
void postprint(node *);
if(!ptr){
printf("Tree is empty...");
return;
}
printf("Root is '%d'<BR>",root->n);
printf("INORDER:");
inprint(root);
printf("PREORDER:");
preprint(root);
printf("POSTORDER:");
postprint(root);
}
void inprint(node *ptr){
if(!ptr)
return;
inprint(ptr->left);
printf("%2d ",ptr->n);
inprint(ptr->right);
```

```
return;
}
void preprint(node *ptr){
if(!ptr)
return;
printf("%2d ",ptr->n);
preprint(ptr->left);
preprint(ptr->right);
return;
}
void postprint(node *ptr){
if(!ptr)
return;
postprint(ptr->left);
postprint(ptr->right);
printf("%2d ",ptr->n);
return;
}
void search(node *ptr){
if(!ptr){
if(ptr == root){
printf("Tree is empty... You can't search anything...");
return;
}
}
printf("Enter the number to search: ");
scanf("%d",&num);
while(ptr){
if(ptr->n == num){
printf("Success... You found the number...");
```

```
return;
}
else if(ptr->n < num)
ptr=ptr->right;
else
ptr=ptr->left;
}
printf("Tree don't contain  %d'...",num);
}
void insert(node *ptr){
if(!ptr){
printf("Tree is empty...First create & then insert... ");
return;
}
printf("<BR>);
ptr=prev=root;
printf("Enter number to be inserted:");
scanf("%d",&num);
do{
if(num < ptr->n){
prev=ptr;
ptr=ptr->left;
}
else if(num > ptr->n){
prev=ptr;
ptr=ptr->right;
}
else
{
prev=NULL;
```

```
break;
}
}while(ptr);
if(prev){
ptr->n=num;
ptr->left=ptr->right=NULL;
if(ptr->n < prev->n){
prev->left=ptr;
if(prev == root)
root=prev;
}
if(ptr->n > prev->n){
prev->right=ptr;
ptr->left=ptr->right=NULL;
if(prev == root)
root=prev;
}
printf("'%d' is inserted...",num);
}
else
printf("'%d' is already present...",num);
return;
}
void modify(node *ptr){
int mod;
if(!ptr){
if(ptr == root){
printf("Tree is empty... You can't modify anything...");
return;
```

```
}
}
printf("Modification of particular number can't create a binary tree...");
getch();
printf("Enter the number to get modified:");
scanf("%d",&num);
prev=ptr;
while(ptr){
if(ptr->n == num){
x=ptr;
mod=x->n;
printf("Then enter new number:");
scanf("%d",&num);
bfor=ptr=root;
while(ptr){
if(ptr->n == num){
printf("'%d' already present...Modification denied...,",num);
return;
}
else if(ptr->n < num){
bfor=ptr;
ptr=ptr->right;
}
else
{
bfor=ptr;
ptr=ptr->left;
}
}
```

```
if(x==root){
y=x->right;
root=y;
while(y->left)
y=y->left;
y->left=x->left;
free(x);
}
else if(!(x->left) && !(x->right)){
if(prev->left == x){
prev->left=NULL;
free(x);
}
else if(prev->right == x){
prev->right=NULL;
free(x);
}
}
else if(!(x->left)){
if(prev->left == x){
prev->left=x->right;
free(x);
}
else if(prev->right == x){
prev->right=x->right;
free(x);
}
}
else if(!(x->right)){
```

```
if(prev->left == x){
prev->left=x->left;
free(x);
}
else if(prev->right == x){
prev->right=x->left;
free(x);
}
}
else
{
y=x->right;
while(y->left)
y=y->left;
y->left=x->left;
if(prev->left == x)
prev->left=y;
else if(prev->right == x)
prev->right=y;
free(x);
}
ptr=(node *)malloc(sizeof(node));
ptr->n=num;
ptr->left=ptr->right=NULL;
if(ptr->n < bfor->n){
bfor->left=ptr;
if(bfor == root)
root=bfor;
}
```

```
if(ptr->n > bfor->n){
bfor->right=ptr;
ptr->left=ptr->right=NULL;
if(bfor == root)
root=bfor;
}
printf("'%d' is modified by '%d'",mod,ptr->n);
return;
}
else if(ptr->n < num){
prev=ptr;
ptr=ptr->right;
}
else
{
prev=ptr;
ptr=ptr->left;
}
}
printf("Tree don't contain '%d'...",num);
}
void delet(node *ptr){
if(!ptr){
if(ptr == root){
printf("Tree is empty... You can't delete anything...");
return;
}
}
printf("Enter the number to get deleted: ");
```

```
scanf("%d",&num);
prev=ptr;
while(ptr){
if(ptr->n == num){
if(ptr==root){
x=ptr->right;
root=x;
while(x->left)
x=x->left;
x->left=ptr->left;
free(ptr);
printf("'%d' is deleted...",num);
return;
}
else if(!(ptr->left) && !(ptr->right)){
if(prev->left == ptr)
prev->left=NULL;
else
prev->right=NULL;
free(ptr);
printf("'%d' is deleted...",num);
return;
}
else if(!(ptr->left)){
if(prev->left == ptr){
prev->left=ptr->right;
free(ptr);
}
else if(prev->right == ptr){
```

```
prev->right=ptr->right;
free(ptr);
}
printf("'%d' is deleted...",num);
return;
}
else if(!(ptr->right)){
if(prev->left == ptr){
prev->left=ptr->left;
free(ptr);
}
else if(prev->right == ptr){
prev->right=ptr->left;
free(ptr);
}
printf("'%d' is deleted...",num);
return;
}
else
{
x=ptr->right;
while(x->left)
x=x->left;
x->left=ptr->left;
if(prev->left == ptr)
prev->left=ptr->right;
else if(prev->right == ptr)
prev->right=ptr->right;
free(ptr);
```

```
printf("'%d' is deleted...",num);
return;
}
}
else if(ptr->n < num){
prev=ptr;
ptr=ptr->right;
}
else
{
prev=ptr;
ptr=ptr->left;
}
}
printf("Tree don't contain '%d'...",num);
}
```

/*Program for Demonstration of Tree Operations – Insertion. Inorder. Preorder. Postorder Traversal*/

```
# include <stdio.h>
# include <conio.h>
# include <alloc.h>
struct node
{
struct node *left;
int data;
struct node *right;
};
void main(){
void insert(struct node **,int);
void inorder(struct node *);
```

```
void postorder(struct node *);
void preorder(struct node *);
struct node *ptr;
int will,i,num;
ptr = NULL;
ptr->data=NULL;
clrscr();
printf("Enter the number of terms you want to add to the tree");
scanf("%d",&will);
/* Getting Input */
for(i=0;i<will;i++){
printf("Enter the item");
scanf("%d",&num);
insert(&ptr,num);
}
getch();
printf("INORDER TRAVERSAL");
inorder(ptr);
getch();
printf("PREORDER TRAVERSAL");
preorder(ptr);
getch();
printf("POSTORDER TRAVERSAL");
postorder(ptr);
getch();
}
void insert(struct node  **p,int num){
if((*p)==NULL){
 printf("Leaf node created.");
```

```
(*p)=malloc(sizeof(struct node));
(*p)->left = NULL;
(*p)->right = NULL;
(*p)->data = num;
return;
}
else
{
if(num==(*p)->data){
printf("REPEATED ENTRY ERROR VALUE REJECTED");
return;
}
if(num<(*p)->data){
printf("Directed to left link.");
insert(&((*p)->left),num);
}
else
{
printf("Directed to right link.");
insert(&((*p)->right),num);
}
}
return;
}
void inorder(struct node *p){
if(p!=NULL){
inorder(p->left);
printf("Data :%d",p->data);
inorder(p->right);
```

```
}
else
return;
}
void preorder(struct node *p){
if(p!=NULL){
printf("Data :%d",p->data);
reorder(p->left);
preorder(p->right);
}
else
return;
}
void postorder(struct node *p){
if(p!=NULL){
postorder(p->left);
postorder(p->right);
printf("Data :%d",p->data);
}
else
return;
}
```

/*Program for Insertion, Deletion and Traversal in Binary Search Tree*/

```
# include <stdio.h>
# include <conio.h>
# include <stdlib.h>
struct node
{
int info;
```

```
struct node *lchild;
struct node *rchild;
}*root;
main(){
int choice,num;
root=NULL;
while(1){
printf("\n");
printf("1.Insert\n");
printf("2.Delete\n");
printf("3.Inorder Traversal\n");
printf("4.Preorder Traversal\n");
printf("5.Postorder Traversal\n");
printf("6.Display\n");
printf("7.Quit\n");
printf("Enter your choice : ");
scanf("%d",&choice);
switch(choice){
case 1:
printf("Enter the number to be inserted:");
scanf("%d",&num);
insert(num);
break;
case 2:
printf("Enter the number to be deleted:");
scanf("%d",&num);
del(num);
break;
case 3:
```

```
inorder(root);
break;
case 4:
preorder(root);
break;
case 5:
postorder(root);
break;
case 6:
display(root,1);
break;
case 7:
exit(0);
default:
printf("Wrong choice\n");
}/*End of switch */
}/*End of while */
}/*End of main()*/
find(int item,struct node **par,struct node **loc){
struct node *ptr,*ptrsave;
if(root==NULL){ /*tree empty*/
*loc=NULL;
*par=NULL;
return;
}
if(item==root->info){ /*item is at root*/
*loc=root;
*par=NULL;
return;
```

```
}
/*Initialize ptr and ptrsave*/
if(iteminfo)
ptr=root->lchild;
else
ptr=root->rchild;
ptrsave=root;
while(ptr!=NULL){
if(item==ptr->info){
 *loc=ptr;
*par=ptrsave;
return;
}
ptrsave=ptr;
if(iteminfo)
ptr=ptr->lchild;
else
ptr=ptr->rchild;
}/*End of while */
*loc=NULL; /*item not found*/
*par=ptrsave;
}/*End of find()*/
insert(int item){
struct node *tmp,*parent,*location;
find(item,&parent,&location);
if(location!=NULL){
printf("Item already present");
return;
}
```

```
tmp=(struct node *)malloc(sizeof(struct node));
tmp->info=item;
tmp->lchild=NULL;
tmp->rchild=NULL;
if(parent==NULL)
root=tmp;
else
if(iteminfo)
parent->lchild=tmp;
else
parent->rchild=tmp;
}/*End of insert()*/
del(int item){
struct node *parent,*location;
if(root==NULL){
printf("Tree empty");
return;
}
find(item,&parent,&location);
if(location==NULL){
printf("Item not present in tree");
return;
}
if(location->lchild==NULL && location->rchild==NULL)
case_a(parent,location);
if(location->lchild!=NULL && location->rchild==NULL)
case_b(parent,location);
if(location->lchild==NULL && location->rchild!=NULL)
case_b(parent,location);
```

```
if(location->lchild!=NULL && location->rchild!=NULL)
case_c(parent,location);
free(location);
}/*End of del()*/
case_a(struct node *par,struct node *loc ){
if(par==NULL) /*item to be deleted is root node*/
root=NULL;
else
if(loc==par->lchild)
par->lchild=NULL;
else
par->rchild=NULL;
}/*End of case_a()*/
case_b(struct node *par,struct node *loc){
struct node *child;
/*Initialize child*/
if(loc->lchild!=NULL) /*item to be deleted has lchild */
child=loc->lchild;
else /*item to be deleted has rchild */
child=loc->rchild;
if(par==NULL ) /*Item to be deleted is root node*/
root=child;
else
if( loc==par->lchild) /*item is lchild of its parent*/
par->lchild=child;
else /*item is rchild of its parent*/
par->rchild=child;
}/*End of case_b()*/
case_c(struct node *par,struct node *loc){
```

```
struct node *ptr,*ptrsave,*suc,*parsuc;
/*Find inorder successor and its parent*/
ptrsave=loc;
ptr=loc->rchild;
while(ptr->lchild!=NULL){
ptrsave=ptr;
ptr=ptr->lchild;
}
suc=ptr;
parsuc=ptrsave;
if(suc->lchild==NULL && suc->rchild==NULL)
case_a(parsuc,suc);
else
case_b(parsuc,suc);
if(par==NULL) /*if item to be deleted is root node*/
root=suc;
else
if(loc==par->lchild)
par->lchild=suc;
else
par->rchild=suc;
suc->lchild=loc->lchild;
suc->rchild=loc->rchild;
}/*End of case_c()*/
preorder(struct node *ptr){
if(root==NULL) {
printf("Tree is empty");
return;
}
```

```
if(ptr!=NULL){
printf("%d ",ptr->info);
preorder(ptr->lchild);
preorder(ptr->rchild);
}
}/*End of preorder()*/
inorder(struct node *ptr){
if(root==NULL){
printf("Tree is empty");
return;
}
if(ptr!=NULL){
inorder(ptr->lchild);
printf("%d ",ptr->info);
inorder(ptr->rchild);
}
}/*End of inorder()*/
postorder(struct node *ptr){
if(root==NULL){
printf("Tree is empty");
return;
}
if(ptr!=NULL){
postorder(ptr->lchild);
postorder(ptr->rchild);
printf("%d ",ptr->info);
}
}/*End of postorder()*/
display(struct node *ptr,int level){
```

```
int i;
if ( ptr!=NULL ){
display(ptr->rchild, level+1);
printf("\n");
for (i = 0; i < level; i++)
printf(" ");
printf("%d", ptr->info);
display(ptr->lchild, level+1);
}/*End of if*/
}/*End of display()*/
```

/*Program – Basic Binary Search Tree Routines*/

```
#include <stdio.h>
#include <stdlib.h>
# include <alloc.h>
struct tnode{
int data;
struct tnode *left;
struct tnode *right;
};
/*insert, swap, search value, search minimum and search maximum values*/
struct tnode *tnode_insert(struct tnode *p, int value);
struct tnode *tnode_swap(struct tnode *p);
struct tnode *tnode_search(struct tnode *p, int key);
struct tnode *tnode_searchmin(struct tnode *p);
struct tnode *tnode_searchmax(struct tnode *p);
/*destroy, count tree nodes*/
void tnode_destroy(struct tnode *p);
int tnode_count(struct tnode *p);
/*print binary tree inorder, preorder, postorder [recursive]*/
```

```
void print_inorder(struct tnode *p);
void print_preorder(struct tnode *p);
void print_postorder(struct tnode *p);
int main(void){
int demo_nr[] = {1, 3, 4, 7, 2, 9, 9, 0, 5, 6, 8, 7, 1, 2, 4};
struct tnode *root = NULL;
struct tnode *searchval = NULL;
int querry = 0;
int i = 0;
/*insert some nr's into the binary tree*/
for(i = 0; i < 15; i++)
root = tnode_insert(root, demo_nr[i]);
printf("=-=-=\n");
printf("Total number of tree nodes: %d\n", tnode_count(root));
printf("inorder:");
print_inorder(root);
printf("\n");
printf("preorder:");
print_preorder(root);
printf("\n");
printf("postorder:");
print_postorder(root);
printf("\n");
printf("=-=-=\n");
printf("Enter integer, find:");
scanf("%d", &querry);
searchval = tnode_search(root, querry);
if(searchval == NULL)
printf("* %d Not! found in btree\n", querry);
```

```
else
printf("* Found! %d in btree\n", searchval->data);
searchval = NULL;
printf("Searching for Minimum value\n");
searchval = tnode_searchmin(root);
if(searchval == NULL)
printf("* Minimum Not! found in btree?\n");
else
printf("*Found! minimum value %d in btree\n", searchval->data);
searchval = NULL;
printf("Searching for Maximum value\n");
searchval = tnode_searchmax(root);
if(searchval == NULL)
printf("*Maximum Not! found in btree ?\n");
else
printf("*Found! Maximum value %d in btree\n", searchval->data);
printf("=-=-=\n");
printf("Exchanging all tree nodes: left <-> right\n");
root = tnode_swap(root);
printf("inorder:");
print_inorder(root);
printf("\n");
printf("preorder:");
print_preorder(root);
printf("\n");
printf("postorder:");
print_postorder(root);
printf("\n");
printf("=-=-=\n");
```

```
printf("Destroying btree... bye!\n");
tnode_destroy(root);
return 0;
}
/* insert a tnode into the binary tree */
struct tnode *tnode_insert(struct tnode *p, int value) {
struct tnode *tmp_one = NULL;
struct tnode *tmp_two = NULL;
if(p == NULL) {
/* insert [new] tnode as root node */
p = (struct tnode *)malloc(sizeof(struct tnode));
p->data = value;
p->left = p->right = NULL;
} else {
tmp_one = p;
/*Traverse the tree to get a pointer to the specific tnode*/
/*The child of this tnode will be the [new] tnode*/
while(tmp_one! = NULL){
tmp_two = tmp_one;
if(tmp_one ->data > value)
tmp_one = tmp_one->left;
else
tmp_one = tmp_one->right;
}
If(tmp_two->data > value){
/*insert [new] tnode as left child*/
tmp_two->left = (struct tnode*)malloc(sizeof(struct tnode));
tmp_two = tmp_two->left;
tmp_two->data = value;
```

```
tmp_two->left = tmp_two->right = NULL;
} else {
/*insert [new] tnode as left child*/
tmp_two->right = (struct tnode *)malloc(sizeof(struct tnode));
tmp_two = tmp_two->right;
tmp_two->data = value;
tmp_two->left = tmp_two->right = NULL;
}
}
return(p);
}
/*print binary tree inorder*/
void print_inorder(struct tnode *p){
if(p != NULL) {
print_inorder(p->left);
printf("%d ", p->data);
print_inorder(p->right);
}
}
/* print binary tree preorder */
void print_preorder(struct tnode *p){
if(p != NULL) {
printf("%d ", p->data);
print_preorder(p->left);
print_preorder(p->right);
}
}
/*print binary tree postorder*/
void print_postorder(struct tnode *p){
if(p != NULL) {
```

```
print_postorder(p->left);
print_postorder(p->right);
printf("%d ", p->data);
}
}
/*returns the total number of tree nodes*/
int tnode_count(struct tnode *p){
if(p == NULL)
return 0;
else {
if(p->left == NULL && p->right == NULL)
return 1;
else
return(1 + (tnode_count(p->left) + tnode_count(p->right)));
}
}
/*exchange all left and right tnodes*/
struct tnode *tnode_swap(struct tnode *p){
struct tnode *tmp_one = NULL;
struct tnode *tmp_two = NULL;
If(p != NULL){
tmp_one = tnode_swap(p->left);
tmp_two = tnode_swap(p->right);
p->right = tmp_one;
p->left = tmp_two;
}
return(p);
}
/*locate a value in the btree*/
struct tnode *tnode_search(struct tnode *p, int key){
struct tnode *temp;
temp = p;
while(temp != NULL){
if(temp->data == key)
```

```
return temp;
else if(temp->data > key)
temp = temp->left;
else
temp = temp->right;
}
return NULL;
}
/*locate a minimum value in the btree*/
struct tnode *tnode_searchmin(struct tnode *p){
if(p == NULL)
return NULL;
else
if(p->left == NULL)
return p;
else
return tnode_searchmin(p->left);
}
/*locate a maximum value in the btree*/
struct tnode *tnode_searchmax(struct tnode *p){
if(p != NULL)
while(p->right != NULL)
p = p->right;
 return p;
}
/*destroy the binary tree*/
void tnode_destroy(struct tnode *p){
if(p != NULL){
tnode_destroy(p->left);
tnode_destroy(p->right);
free(p);
}
}
```

Review Questions

1. What is a tree? What do you understand by leaf, root, siblings and child of a tree?
2. Explain the following: (a) level of a tree and (b) depth of a tree.
3. What is a binary tree? Explain the relationship between total number of nodes and depth of a tree.
4. How are binary trees represented in memory? What are the uses of binary trees?
5. What are the three traversal technique for binary trees.
6. Draw the binary tree structure for the following expression: (a) E = (a + b)/[(c * d) - e] and (b) (2x + y)(a - 7b)3.
7. How many different trees are possible with 10 nodes?
8. List out few of the Application of tree data structure?
9. Differentiate between full binary tree and complete binary tree.
10. What is the maximum total number of nodes in a tree that has N levels? Note that the root is level (zero) .
11. How many different binary trees and binary search trees can be made from three nodes that contain the key values 1, 2 and 3?
12. How will inorder, preorder and postorder traversals print the elements of a tree?
13. How do you find the depth of a binary tree?
14. Formulate an algorithm for Postorder traversal of binary tree.
15. Write a C program to implement binary tree traversals.

CHAPTER 17

Graphs

INTRODUCTION TO GRAPHS

Graphs are similar to trees except that, they do not have as many restrictions. We have studied previously at the binary tree data structure, which provides a useful way of storing data for efficient searching. In a binary tree, each node can have up to two child nodes. More general tree structures can be created in which different numbers of child nodes are allowed for each node.

All tree are structures. Tthis means that each node can have one parent node. Trees can be used to store data which has a definite hierarchy; for example a family tree or a computer files system. Some data need to have connections between items which not fit into a hierarchy like this. Data structures can be useful in these situations. A graph consists of a number of data items, each of which is called an edge A vertex, it may be connected to any other and these connections are called an edge

TERMINOLOGY

Graphs: A graph is a set of vertices and edges which connect them. We write:

$G = (V,E)$

where V is the set of vertices and E is the set of edges,

$E = \{(V_i, V_j)\}$

where V_i and V_j are in V.

Vertex: A simple object that can have a name and other properties

Edge: A connection between two vertices

Paths: A list of vertices in which successive vertices are connected by edges in the graph.

A path (p) of length (k) through a graph is a sequence of connected vertices:

$p = < v_0, v_1, ..., v_k >$

for all i in (0,k-1) or (v_i,v_i+1) is in E.

Connected Graph: A graph in which there is a path from every node to every other node in the graph.

Connected Component: A set of vertices within a graph in which:

- there is a path from every vertex within the set to every other vertex in the set, and
- there is not a path from any vertex within the set to any vertex not in the set

If a graph is not connected, then it has at least two connected components.

Cycle: A path in which the first and last vertices are the same (i.e., a path from a vertex back to itself). A graph contains no cycles if there is no path of non-zero length through the graph, $p = < v_0, v_1, ..., v_k >$ such that $v_0 = v_k$.

Undirected Graph: A graph in which the edges are undirected (i.e., bidirectional).

Directed Graph: A graph in which the edges are directed (i.e., unidirectional). If edges are directed, then we speak of the edge as going from one vertex to another vertex.

Dense Graph: Roughly speaking, a graph in which the number of edges is greater than or equal to V log V, where V is the number of vertices.

Sparse Graph: Roughly speaking, a graph in which the number of edges is < V log V, where V is the number of vertices.

GRAPHS

A graph G = (V,E) consists of finite non-empty set of objects V,

where V(G) = {V_1, V_2, V_3,......V_n} called vetices, and

another set E, where E(G) = {e_1, e_2, e_3,.......e_m}, 1 d" k d" m, is identified with an unordered pair (V_i, V_j) of vertices. The vertices of 'ek'. The pictorial representation of graph is shown in figure in which the vertices are represented as points and each edge as a line segment joining its end vertices.

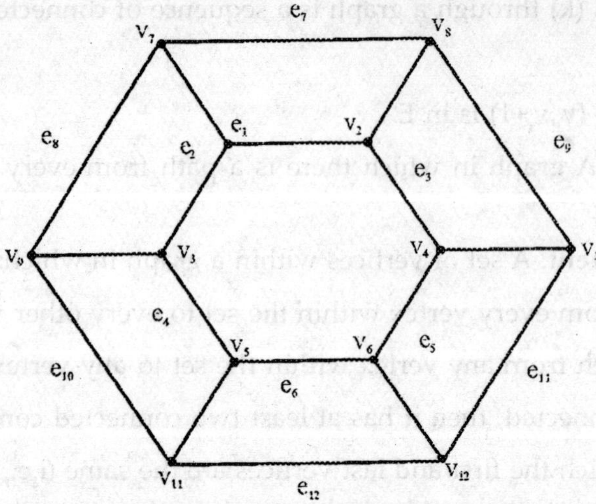

Fig. 17.1: Graph with Twelve Vertices and Twelve Edges

$V(G) = \{V_1, V_2, V_3, V_4, V_5, V_6, V_7, V_8, V_9, V_{10}, V_{11}, V_{12}\}$

$E(G) = \{e_1, e_2, e_3, e_4, e_5, e_6, e_7, e_8, e_9, e_{10}, e_{11}, e_{12}\}$

End-vertices for each 'e_k' are:

$e_1 = \{V_1, V_2\}$

$e_2 = \{V_1, V_3\}$

$e_3 = \{V_2, V_4\}$

$e_4 = \{V_3, V_5\}$

$e_5 = \{V_4, V_6\}$

$e_6 = \{V_5, V_6\}$

$e_7 = \{V_7, V_8\}$

$e_8 = \{V_7, V_9\}$

$e_9 = \{V_8, V_{10}\}$

$e_{10} = \{V_9, V_{11}\}$

$e_{11} = \{V_{10}, V_{12}\}$

$e_{12} = \{V_{11}, V_{12}\}$

Undirected graph

If the edges in a graph are undirected or 'two-way", then the graph is known as undirected graph. In this, the edges are unordered pairs, which means, the order in which the vertex V_i and V_j occur in the pair of vertices (V_i, V_j) and (V_j, V_i) both represent the same edge e_k that connects the vertices V_i and V_j.

Example:

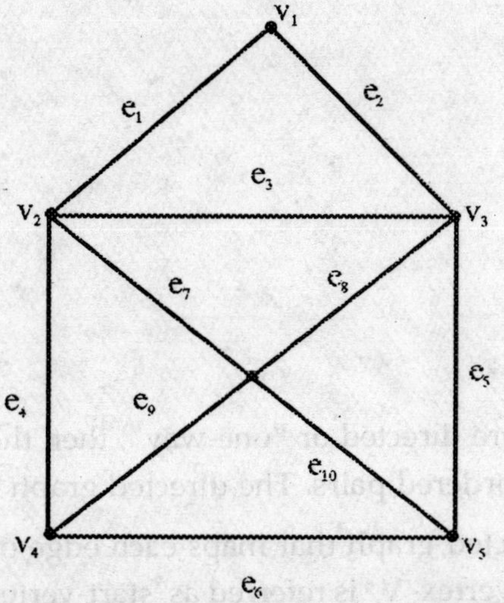

Fig. 17.2: An undirected Graph with 5 Vertices and 10 Edges

$V(G) = \{V_1, V_2, V_3, V_4, V_5\}$

$E(G) = \{e_1, e_2, e_3, e_4, e_5, e_6, e_7, e_8, e_9, e_{10}\}$

End vertices for each 'e_k' are:

$e_1 = \{V_1, V_2\}$

$e_2 = \{V_1, V_3\}$

$e_3 = \{V_2, V_3\}$

$e_4 = \{V_2, V_4\}$

$e_5 = \{V_3, V_5\}$

$e_6 = \{V_4, V_5\}$

$e_7 = \{V_2, V_6\}$

$e_8 = \{V_3, V_6\}$

$e_9 = \{V_4, V_6\}$

$e_{10} = \{V_5, V_6\}$

and from definition, for (V_i, V_j) and (V_j, V_i) the same edge 'e_k' is associated, thus

$e_1 = \{V_1, V_2\} = \{V_2, V_1\}$

$e_2 = \{V_1, V_3\} = \{V_3, V_1\}$

$e_3 = \{V_2, V_3\} = \{V_3, V_2\}$

$e_4 = \{V_2, V_4\} = \{V_4, V_2\}$

$e_5 = \{V_3, V_5\} = \{V_5, V_3\}$

$e_6 = \{V_4, V_5\} = \{V_5, V_4\}$

$e_7 = \{V_2, V_6\} = \{V_6, V_2\}$

$e_8 = \{V_3, V_6\} = \{V_6, V_3\}$

$e_9 = \{V_4 V_6\} = \{V_6, V_4\}$

$e_{10} = \{V_5, V_6\} = \{V_6, V_5\}$

Directed Graphs

If the edges in a graph are directed or "one-way", then the graph is known as directed graph. In this, the edges are ordered pairs. The directed graph is also referred as Digraph.

A mapping exist in directed graph that maps each edge of a graph onto some ordered pair of vertices (V_i, V_j). Here, vertex 'V_i' is referred as 'start-vertex', and 'V_j' is referred as 'end-vertex', for every (V_i, V_j) pair.

Thus, the pair of vertices $(V_i, V_j) \neq (V_j, V_i)$ as $V_i \rightarrow V_j$ represent direct edge from V_i to V_j and $V_j \rightarrow V_i$ represent direct edge from V_j to V_i.

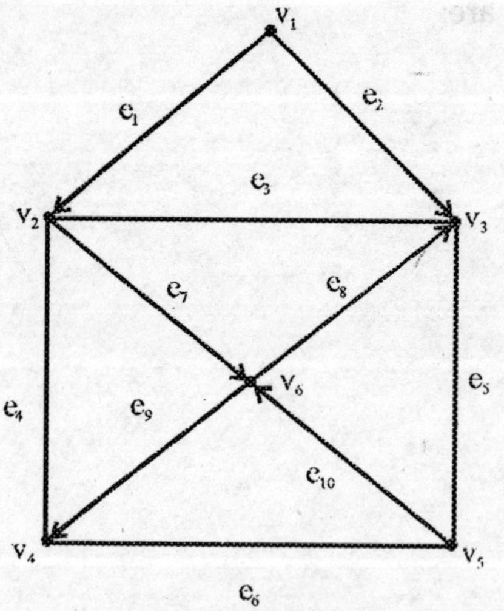

Fig. 17.3: Directed Graph with 5 Vertices and 10 Edges

$V(G) = \{V_1, V_2, V_3, V_4, V_5\}$

$E(G) = \{e_1, e_2, e_3, e_4, e_5, e_6, e_7, e_8, e_9, e_{10}\}$

But from the definition, an edge 'e$_k$' is different for both (V_i, V_j) and (V_j, V_i), thus

$$e_1 = \{V_1, V_2\} \neq \{V_2, V_1\} \text{ as } V_1 \xrightarrow{e_1} V_2$$

$$e_2 = \{V_1, V_3\} \neq \{V_3, V_1\} \text{ as } V_1 \xrightarrow{e_2} V_3$$

$$e_3 = \{V_2, V_3\} \neq \{V_3, V_2\} \text{ as } V_3 \xrightarrow{e_3} V_2$$

$$e_4 = \{V_2, V_4\} \neq \{V_4, V_2\} \text{ as } V_2 \xrightarrow{e_4} V_4$$

$$e_5 = \{V_3, V_5\} \neq \{V_5, V_3\} \text{ as } V_3 \xrightarrow{e_5} V_5$$

$$e_6 = \{V_4, V_5\} \neq \{V_5, V_4\} \text{ as } V_5 \xrightarrow{e_6} V_4$$

$$e_7 = \{V_2, V_6\} \neq \{V_6, V_2\} \text{ as } V_2 \xrightarrow{e_7} V_6$$

$$e_8 = \{V_3, V_6\} \neq \{V_6, V_3\} \text{ as } V_6 \xrightarrow{e_8} V_3$$

$$e_9 = \{V_4, V_6\} \neq \{V_6, V_4\} \text{ as } V_4 \xrightarrow{e_9} V_6$$

$$e_{10} = \{V_5, V_6\} \neq \{V_6, V_5\} \text{ as } V_5 \xrightarrow{e_{10}} V_6$$

Weighted Graph

A graph G is said to be weighted graph if for every edge 'e$_k$' weight 'w$_k$' is associated. Thus, a weighted graph can be represented by 3 tuple G = {V, e, w}.

Where V(G) is a finite non-empty set of vertices

e(G) is the set of edges

w(G) is the set of weights such that for each 'e$_k$' weight 'w$_k$' is available.

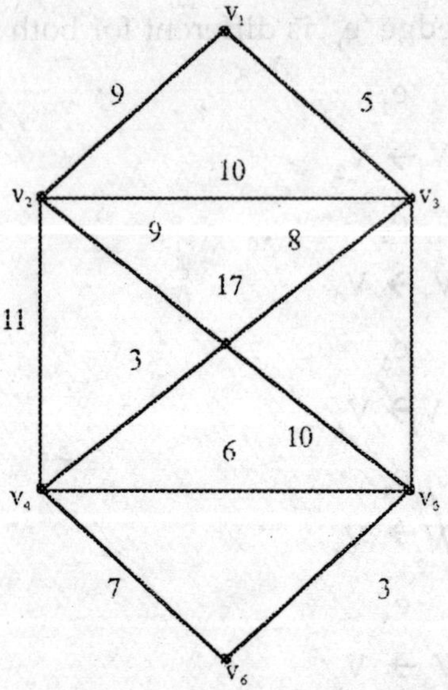

Fig. 17.4: Representation of Weighted Graph

The graph of the above figure is a weighted graph where vertices represent the cities and edges set up the link between cities. Each edge has weight, where each weight in a graph denotes distance between the cities connected by the corresponding edges.

EXPLICIT REPRESENTATIONS OF GRAPHS

There are two common data structures used to explicitly represent graphs: *adjacency matrices* and *adjacency lists*. The representation methods are applicable to both undirected graphs and directed graphs.

Adjacency matrix

The adjacency matrix representation for the graph is explained as: "the adjacency matrix A = [1] of the graph 'G' is an n by n binary matrix, where 'G' is a graph with 'n' vertices, containing no parallel edges". The element of matrix 'A' is as follows:

a_{ij} = 1 if there is an edge between i^{th} and j^{th} vertices

= 0 if there is no edge between them

Consider the examples of both directed and undirected graphs.

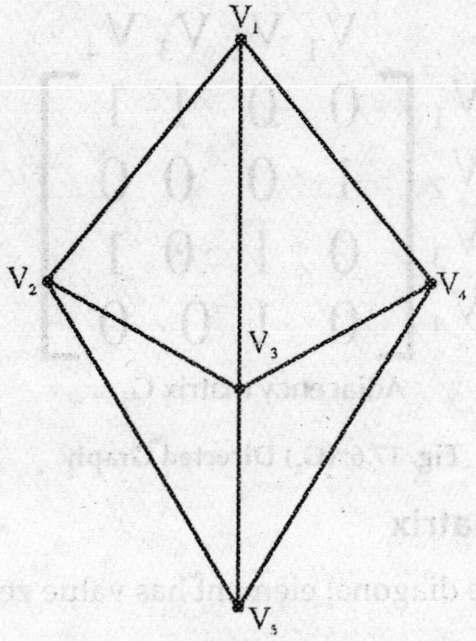

$$A = \begin{array}{c c} & \begin{array}{ccccc} V_1 & V_2 & V_3 & V_4 & V_5 \end{array} \\ \begin{array}{c} V_1 \\ V_2 \\ V_3 \\ V_4 \\ V_5 \end{array} & \begin{bmatrix} 0 & 1 & 1 & 1 & 0 \\ 1 & 0 & 1 & 0 & 1 \\ 1 & 1 & 0 & 1 & 1 \\ 1 & 0 & 1 & 0 & 1 \\ 0 & 1 & 1 & 1 & 0 \end{bmatrix} \end{array}$$

Adjacency matrix (G_1)

Fig. 17.5: (G_1) Undirected Graph

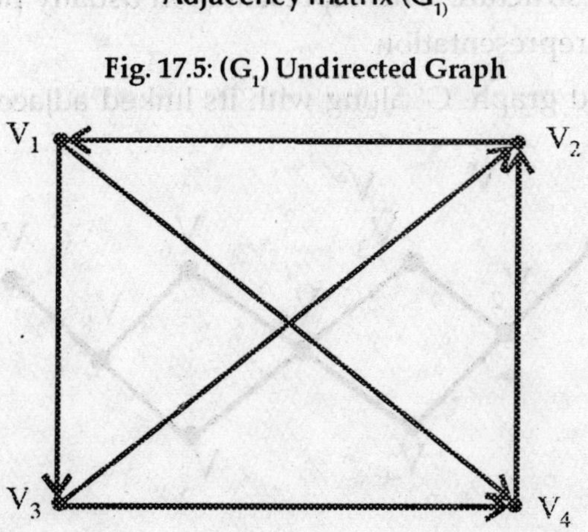

$$A = \begin{array}{c} \\ V_1 \\ V_2 \\ V_3 \\ V_4 \end{array} \begin{array}{c} \begin{array}{cccc} V_1 & V_2 & V_3 & V_4 \end{array} \\ \begin{bmatrix} 0 & 0 & 1 & 1 \\ 1 & 0 & 0 & 0 \\ 0 & 1 & 0 & 1 \\ 0 & 1 & 0 & 0 \end{bmatrix} \end{array}$$

Adjacency matrix G_2

Fig. 17.6: (G_2) Directed Graph

Properties of Adjacency Matrix

Except for the self-loops, the diagonal element has value zero. A self-loop at the ith vertex corresponds to a_{ii} =1.

And adjacency matrix of an undirected graph is symmetric, as $a_{ij} = a_{ji} = 1$

If the graph has no parallel edges and self-loops, then in an undirected graph the degree of the vertex is the number of 1's corresponding to row or column of A. For the directed graph, the sum of each row is equal to out degree of the corresponding vertex and the sum of each column is equal to in degree of the corresponding vertex.

The non-zero elements in the matrix represent the number of edges in a matrix.

Adjacency Lists

Also called as linked adjacency list representation, where each vertex of the graph is represented by a linked list structure. This representation usually proves to be more efficient than the adjacency matrix representation.

Consider an undirected graph 'G' along with its linked adjacency lists.

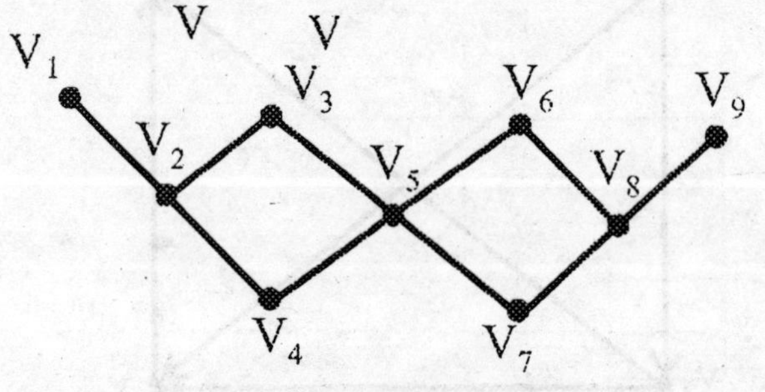

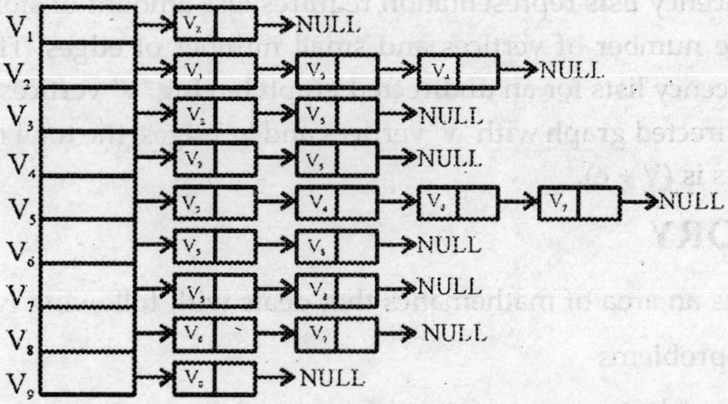

Fig. 17.7: (G) Undirected Graph

Linked Adjacency Lists

Consider the directed graph 'G' along with its linked adjacency list representation.

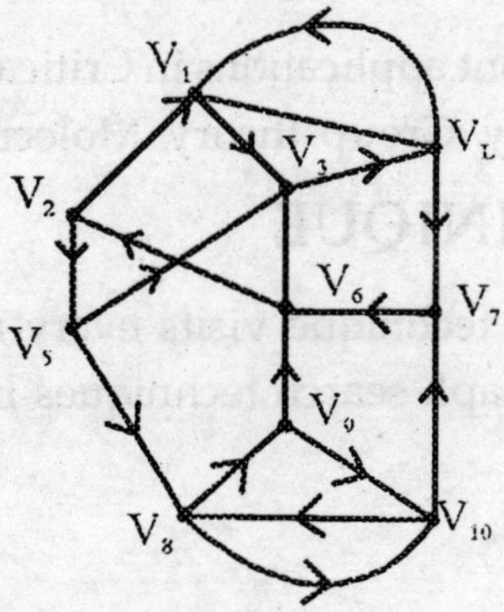

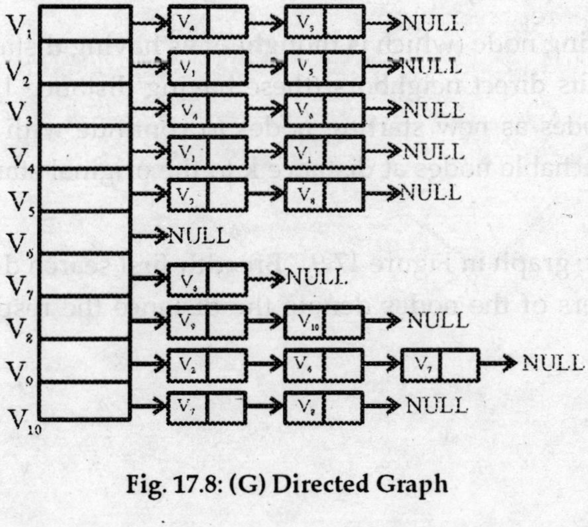

Fig. 17.8: (G) Directed Graph

The linked adjacency lists representation requires less amount of storage when a graph 'G' consists of large number of vertices and small number of edges. The total number of nodes in linked adjacency lists for an undirected graph having 'V' vertices and 'e' edges is (V + 2e). Similarly, for directed graph with 'V' vertices and 'e' edges, the total number of nodes in linked adjacency lists is (V + e).

GRAPH THEORY

Graph Theory is an area of mathematics that deals with following types of problems:

- Connection problems
- Scheduling problems
- Transportation problems
- Network analysis
- Games and Puzzles

The Graph Theory has important applications in Critical path analysis, Social psychology, Matrix theory, Set theory, Topology, Group theory, Molecular chemistry, and Searching.

GRAPH SEARCH TECHNIQUE

A graph search (or traversal) technique visits every node exactly one in a systematic fashion. There are two standard graph search techniques have been widely used:

- Breadth-First Search (BFS)
- Depth-First Search (DFS)

Breadth-First Search (BFS)

Beginning at a starting node (which is thought of as having distance 0 to itself) breadth-first search visits all of its direct neighbors (these having distance 1) before it in turn uses these already visited nodes as new starting nodes to continue with their direct neighbors. That way, it visits all reachable nodes at distance k to the original starting node before those at distance k+1.

Look at the example graph in Figure 17.9, "Breadth-first search distances". The numbers at the upper-right corners of the nodes denote the distance the respective node has to the starting node.

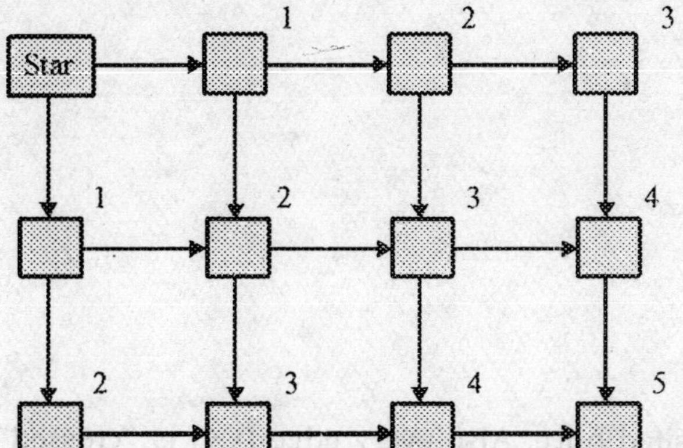

Fig. 17.9: Breadth-first Search Distances

BFS follows the following rules:

Select an unvisited node s, visit it, have it be the root in a BFS tree being formed. Its level is called the current level.

From each node x in the current level, in the order in which the level nodes were visited, visit all the unvisited neighbors of x. The newly visited nodes from this level form a new level that becomes the next current level.

Repeat the previous step until no more nodes can be visited.

If there are still unvisited nodes, repeat from Step 1.

Algorithm

```
Procedure BFS(input: graph G)
begin
Queue Q;
Integer s,x;
while (G has an unvisited node) do
s := an unvisited node;
visit(s);
Enqueue(s,Q);
While (Q is not empty) do
x := Dequeue(Q);
For (unvisited neighbor y of x) do
```

visit(y);

Enqueue(y,Q);

end for

end while

end while

end

Time Complexity

Every node is visited once. Also every edge (x,y) is "crossed" once when node y is checked from x to see if it is visited (if not visited, then y would be visited from x).

Therefore, the time of BFS is O (n+|E|).

Applications of BFS

Connectivity and spanning trees are easily done with BFS much as with DFS. The details are left as an exercise.

Depth-First Search (DFS)

Beginning at a starting node depth-first search (DFS) recursively visits the first yet undiscovered direct neighbor of every reached node before continuing in the same manner with the remaining neighbors at this node.

Look at the graph example in Figure 17.10, "Depth-first search graph traversal". The numbers at the upper-right corners of the nodes denote the visiting sequence with directed DFS. Additionally, the emphasized edges show the path of the DFS run. Observe that the "Start" node is visited first and accordingly is assigned the first index (not shown).

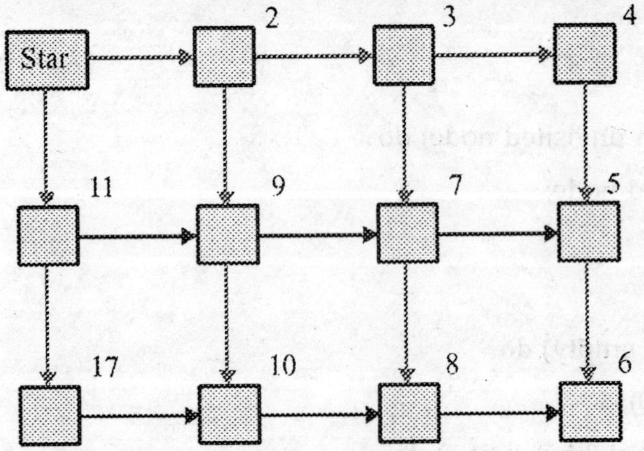

Fig. 17.10: Depth-first search graph traversal

DFS follows the following rules:

Select an unvisited node s, visit it and treat it as the current node;

Find an unvisited neighbor of the current node, visit it, and make it the new current node;

If the current node has no unvisited neighbors, backtrack to its parent, and make the new current node;

Repeat the above two steps until no more nodes can be visited.

If there are still unvisited nodes, repeat from step 1.

Algorithm

```
Procedure DFS(input: graph G)
begin
Stack S;
Integer s,x;
while (G has an unvisited node) do
s:= an unvisited node;
visit(v);
push(v,S);
While (S is not empty) do
    x := top(S);
    if (x has an unvisited neighbor y) then
            visit(y);
            push(y,S);
else
            pop(S);
        end if
    end while
  end while
end
```

Every node is visited once. Also, every edge (x,y) is "crossed" twice: one time when node y is checked from x to see if it i; s visited (if not visited, then y would be visited from x), and another time, when we back track from y to x.

Therefore, the time of DFS is O (n+|E|).

If the graph is connected, the time is O (|E|) because the graph has atleast n-1 edges, and so n+|E| <= 2|E| -1, implying that n+|E|) is O(|E|).

APPLICATIONS OF DFS

First Application of DFS: Connectivity

By having a counter count, the number of time the outer while-loop iterates in the DFS algorithm, the counter value at the end will be equal to the number of connected components of the input graph G.

This is because the body of the outer loop, i.e., every iteration, fully traverses the connected component that contains the node v.

If the counter value is 1, then the graph is connected, i.e., the DFS algorithm becomes a connectedness-testing algorithm that tells if a graph is connected, in O(n+|E|) time.

If the counter value is > 1, the algorithm will indicate that the graph is disconnected and the nodes visited in each iteration constitute a separate connected component. In other terms, the DFS algorithm identifies the various connected components.

Second Application of DFS: Minimum spanning trees in uniformly weighted graphs.

Assume that a graph is weighted but all the weights are equal. In that case, all spanning trees are of the same weight (because all trees of n nodes have exactly n-1 edges). Thus, to find a minimum spanning tree in such graphs, it suffices to find any spanning tree.

DFS yields a spanning tree (if the input graph is connected, otherwise, it is a spanning forest). That tree is then a minimum spanning tree. The time to compute the tree is O(|E|), which is better than the O(|E| log |E|) time MST algorithm for general weighted graphs.

Third Application of DFS: Biconnectivity

A node in a connected graph is called an articulation point if the deletion of that node disconnects the graph.

A connected graph is called biconnected if it has no articulation points, i.e., the deletion of any single node leaves the graph connected. In the case of networks, an articulation point is referred to as a single point of failure.

MINIMUM SPANNING TREE

If a weighted graph is considered, then the weight of the spanning tree (T) of graph 'G' can be calculated by summing all the individual weights in the spanning tree. But for any graph, there can be many spanning trees and also in the case of weighted graphs from which we can get different spanning trees having different weights. A minimum spanning tree (MST) is a spanning tree of minimum weight.

For computing the minimum cost spanning tree, we have two algorithms: Kruskal's and Prim's algorithm. Consider G = (V, E, W) to be an undirected connected weighted graph. The weights of the edges are numeric, maybe positive, zero or negative. Let 'M' be feasible subset of EεG and (V_s, V-V_s) be any cut that respect M. Also, an edge (V_i, V_j) be a light crossing the cut. Then the edge (V_i, V_j) is a safe edge for the subset M.

Kruskal Algorithm

Kruskal's Algorithm finds a minimum spanning tree for a connected weighted graph. It finds a subset of edges that forms a tree that includes every vertex, where total weight of all the edges in the tree is minimized. For non-connected graph, it finds a minimum spanning forest.

Algorithm of Kruskal (G)

Step 1: [Initially M is empty]

set M <- { Ø }

print("Set is empty")

Step 2: [For each vertex create a set]

repeat through step 4 for V_i <- V_1, V_2,……V

V-> V_i ε V

call to create-set(V_i)

Step 3: [Set E is sorted in increasing order by weight]

for each (V_i, V_j) from the sorted list

if (Find (V_i) ≠ Find (Vj)) then

Vi and V_j are in different trees

set M <- {call to addedge (V_i, V_j)}

add edge to M

call to Union (V_i, V_j)

Step 4: [Return M, at the point of call]

return (M)

Prim-Jarnik Algorithm

Prim-Jarnik algorithm finds a minimum spanning for a connected weighted graph. It finds a subset of edges that form a tree and includes every vertex of the graph. This algorithm continuously increases the size of the tree starting with a single vertex until it spans all the vertices.

Algorithm of Prim-Jarnik(G, W, S)

Step 1: [Initialization]

for a <- V_1, V_2, ...V_n , a ε V

set key [a] <- +

set color [a] <- white

Step 2: [Start at root vertex]

set key [S] <-0

set pre [S] <-NULL

set Q <- call to priority queues (V)

put vertices in Q

Step 3: [Searches until all vertices in MST]

while (non-empty) (Q)

set a <- Extract-minimum (Q)

vertex with light edge

for V<- V_1, V_2.... Adj [a], V ε Adj [a]

if (color [V] = white) && (W(a,V) < key[V]) then

set key [V] <- W(a, V)

new lighter edge out of V

call to decrease key (Q, V, key [V])

set color [a] <- a

set color [a] <- black

Step 4: [Return at the point of call]

return

Consider an example of both a graph and a weighted graph:

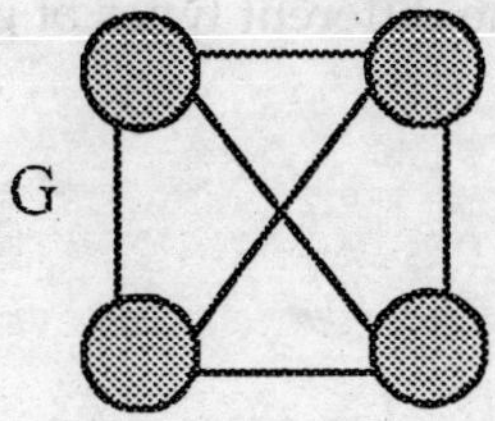

Fig. 17.12: A Graph, G

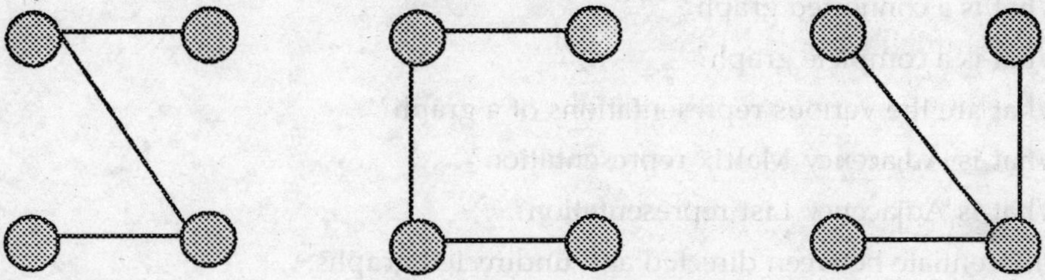

There are many possible spanning of trees from graph, G.

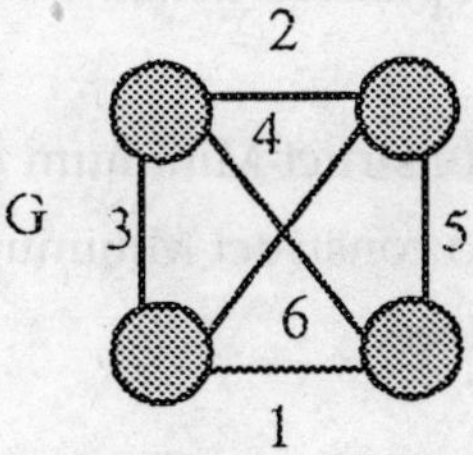

Fig. 17.13: A Weighted Graph, G

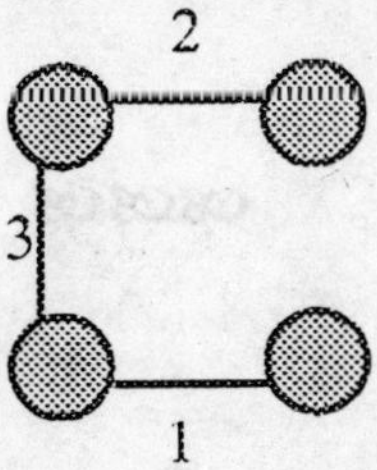

The minimum spanning tree from a weighted graph, G.

Review Questions

1. What are graphs? What are the different types of graphs?
2. What is a Path in a graph?
3. What is the length of a path?
4. What is a loop?
5. What is a cycle?
6. What is a Cyclic graph?
7. What is a Acyclic graph?
8. What is a connected graph?
9. What is a complete graph?
10. What are the various representations of a graph?
11. What is Adjacency Matrix representation?
12. What is Adjacency List representation?
13. Differentiate between directed and undirected graphs.
14. What are graph search techniques?
15. What are weighted graphs? Explain in detail.
16. What are spanning of trees.
17. Explain Prim's algorithm to construct Minimum cost spanning tree.
18. Explain Kruskal's algorithm to construct Minimum cost spanning tree.
19. Explain Minimum Spanning Tree.
20. What is DFS?
21. What are the applications of DFS?

CHAPTER 18

Sorting Techniques

SORTING

The process of getting data elements into order is called sorting. The order may be either ascending or descending order for numbers or alphabetical order for strings.

Sorting methods can be classified into two types based on the size of the data to be sorted, i.e., internal sorting and external sorting.

Internal Sorting

Internal sorting methods are applied on small sets of data which is sufficient to store in the main memory.

Examples: bubble sort, insertion sort, selection sort, etc.

External Sorting

External sorting methods are applied on large sets of data which reside on secondary storage devices and can't completely fit in the main memory.

Examples: merge sort, etc.

There are several different sorting techniques. But no one algorithm is best for all cases. We should select the particular sorting technique depending upon the size of the data, degree of order (partially sorted or almost sorted) of data to be sorted.

Complexity of Sorting Algorithms

We can decide the complexity of different algorithms by calculating its order based on the number of loops and number of iterations the algorithm contains. The complexity can be represented as O (n) (order of n), $O(n^2)$ (order of n^2) etc.

Sorting methods can be classified into two types based on the complexity of algorithms, i.e., simple algorithms and sophisticated algorithms.

Simple Algorithms

The algorithms having complexity of O (n), O (n^2) are known as simple algorithms.

Sophisticated Algorithms

The algorithms having complexity of O (n $\log_2 n$) are known as sophisticated algorithms.

STABLE SORT

A stable sort is one where two records will retain their order when sorted according to a particular field, even when the two fields have the same contents. Thus those two records come out in the same relative order that they were in before sorting, although their positions relative to other records may change.

Two examples of differing sorting algorithms are Quick Sort and Merge. Quick Sort is not stable while Merge Sort is stable. (A Bubble Sort, as typically implemented, is also stable.)

Suppose that you have the following records and you sort on the Last_Name field only:

Original Records

Record	Last_Name	First_Name
1	Davis	John
2	Davis	Mark
3	Curtner	Fred

Merge sort results

Record	Last_Name	First_Name
3	Curtner	Fred
1	Davis	John
2	Davis	Mark

Quick sort results

Record	Last_Name	First_Name
3	Curtner	Fred
2	Davis	Mark
1	Davis	John

As you see from the above, the Quicksort algorithm is not stable; the records 1 and 2 are not in the same order they were in before sorting.

DETERMINISTIC SORT

A deterministic sort is a sort algorithm that returns the same results each time. The key concept is that these sorting algorithms are deterministic when two records have unequal fields, but they may return different results at different times when two records have equal fields.

For example, a classic Quick Sort algorithm works recursively on ranges of records. For any given range of records, it takes the first element as the pivot element, but that algorithm performs badly with input data that happens to be sorted. A randomized Quick Sort, which picks a random element as the pivot, can on average be faster. The results it gets are not deterministic; from exactly the same input, different results can be output:

Record	Last_Name	First_Name
3	Curtner	Fred
1	Davis	John

As another example, multiprocessor sorting algorithms can be non-deterministic. The work of sorting different blocks of data are farmed out to different processors and then merged back together. The ordering of records with equal fields might be different according to when different processors finish different tasks.

The deterministic sort is weaker than a stable sort. A stable sort is always deterministic, but not *vice versa*. And typically when people say they want a deterministic sort, they really mean that they want a stable sort.

BUBBLE SORT

The bubble sort is the easiest of all the sorting techniques but the slowest one also. It compares the adjacent elements in a list of data elements and swaps them if they are not in order. Each pair of adjacent elements are compared and swapped until the smallest/largest element "bubbles up" to the top of array, thus the name bubble sort. This process should be repeated until all the elements are in sorting order. This technique is also called as exchange sort, adjacent sort or sinking sort.

Algorithm

Let us know the algorithm to sort a set of numbers in ascending order:

(1) Compare two numbers at a time, starting with the first two numbers.

(2) If the first number is larger than second number, then exchange two numbers.

(3) Go down one number and compare that number to the number that follows it. These two form a new pair.

(4) Continue this process until no exchanges has been made in the entire pass through the list.

```
Procedure bubblesort (A[1..n])
begin
for i<-1 to n-1 do
for j<-1 to (n-i) /* in each iteration, one less number of elements is taken into consideration
i.e., why j varies upto only (n-i)*/
A[j] > A[j+1] then
Interchange A[j] and A[j+1]
end
A[1..n] is in increasing order
end
```

Example:

Let us take a set of 7 numbers to sort them in ascending order

2 6 5 4 1 7 3

Pass 1:

2 6 5 4 1 7 3

Comparison 1:

Compare 2 with 6, no exchange

2 6 5 4 1 7 3

Comparison 2:

Compare 6 with 5, exchange

2 5 6 4 1 7 3

Comparison 3:

Compare 6 with 4, exchange

2 5 4 6 1 7 3

Comparison 4:

Compare 6 with 1, exchange

2 5 4 1 6 7 3

Comparison 5:

Compare 6 with 7, no exchange

2 5 4 1 6 7 3

Comparison 6:

Compare 7 with 3, exchange

2 5 4 1 6 3 7

Observations in pass 1:

Totally, 6 comparisons are needed in one pass to a set of 7 elements, so for the first pass N-1 iterations are needed. 7 is the largest of all the given numbers and is placed in the correct position after 1st pass. So ith element will be placed in the correct position in the ith pass. If we place the 6 elements in their correct positions, then the 7th element will automatically be placed in the correct order. So, to place all the 7 elements in the correct positions, we need 6 passes. In other words, a set of N elements can be sorted in N-1 passes.

Pass 2:

2 5 4 1 6 3 7

Comparison 1:

Compare 2 with 5, no exchange

2 5 4 1 6 3 7

Comparison 2:

Compare 5 with 4, exchange

2 4 5 1 6 3 7

Comparison 3:

Compare 5 with 1, exchange

2 4 1 5 6 3 7

Comparison 4:

Compare 5 with 6, no exchange

2 4 1 5 6 3 7

Comparison 5:

Compare 6 with 3, exchange

2 4 1 5 3 6 7

Observations in pass 2:

As the last element is already sorted in the first pass, we need not compare it again. So now comparisons should be among N-1 elements, so N-2 iterations are needed. After 2nd pass, last but one element is placed in its correct position.

Pass 3:

2 4 1 5 3 6 7

Comparison 1:

Compare 2 with 4, no exchange

2 4 1 5 3 6 7

Comparison 2:

Compare 4 with 1, exchange

2 1 4 5 3 6 7

Comparison 3:

Compare 4 with 5, no exchange

2 1 4 5 3 6 7

Comparison 4:

Compare 5 with 3, exchange

2 1 4 3 5 6 7

Observations in pass 3:

As the last two elements are already sorted in the two passes, we need not compare them again. So now comparisons should be among N-2 elements, so N-3 iterations are needed. After 3rd pass, 3rd element from last is placed in its correct position.

Pass 4:

2 1 4 3 5 6 7

Comparison 1:

Compare 2 with 1, exchange

1 2 4 3 5 6 7

Comparison 2:

Compare 2 with 4, no exchange

1 2 4 3 5 6 7

Comparison 3:

Compare 4 with 3, exchange

1 2 3 4 5 6 7

Observations in pass 4:

Only 3 comparisons are needed and 4th element from last is placed in the correct position.

Pass 5:

1 2 3 4 5 6 7

Comparison 1:

Compare 1 with 2, no exchange

1 2 3 4 5 6 7

Comparison 2:

Compare 2 with 3, no exchange

1 2 3 4 5 6 7

Observations in pass 5:

Only 2 comparisons are needed and 5th element from last is placed in the correct position.

Pass 6:

1 2 3 4 5 6 7

Comparison 1:

Compare 1 with 2, no exchange

1 2 3 4 5 6 7

Observations in pass 6:

Only 1 comparison is needed and 6th element from last is placed in the correct position.

Note

In the above example, all the elements are in sorted order in pass 4 and hence there is no exchange in last two passes. These unnecessary passes can be avoided by introducing a simple check: when there are no exchanges in a particular pass, the sorting is completed and the process can be terminated.

Summary

A set of elements can be sorted through bubble sort by comparing the adjacent elements. If different successive pairs of elements are compared once throughout the set, then one element will get sorted. Next time we need not consider that element. So the number of comparisons will get decreased as the number of passes increases in the series N-1, N-2, etc. (where N is number of elements). Totally N-1 passes are needed and the ith pass makes N-i comparisons where i =1,2,...N-1.

Complexity

As we know, the algorithm requires N-1 passes and the ith pass makes N-i comparisons. So, the time required can be calculated as.

$$T(N) = (N-1) + (N-2) + (N-3) + \dots + 2 + 1$$

$$\sum_{i=1}^{N-1} i = (N(N-1))/2 = O(N^2) \quad \text{(roughly equal)}$$

Thus, the complexity of bubble sort is $O(N^2)$.

Bubble sort should be avoided when the number of elements to be sorted is very large.

Suitability

It can be used when the input data is already nearly in order before the sorting starts. In such cases, one or two passes may be sufficient to complete the ordering. Thus, the bubble sort may be good choice in situations where a few elements have to be added to an already sorted list of elements. It is a stable sort.

Example: Program to illustrate bubble sort

```
#include <stdio.h>
void swap(int *a,int *b){
int iTemp;
iTemp=*a;
*a=*b;
*b=iTemp;
}
void BubbleSort(int arr[], int size){
bool bIsSwap=false;
for(int pass=0;pass<size-1;pass++){
bIsSwap=false;
for(int j=0;j<size-pass-1;j++){
if(arr[j]>arr[j+1]) //ascending order
```

```
{
swap(&arr[j],&arr[j+1]);
bIsSwap=true;
}
}
if(!bIsSwap)
break;
}
}
void main(){
int arr[7]={2, 6, 5, 4, 1, 7, 3};
printf("numbers before sorting:");
for(int i=0;i<7;i++){
printf("%d",arr[i]);
}
BubbleSort(arr,7);
printf("numbers after sorting:");
for(int i=0;i<7;i++){
 printf("%d",arr[i]);
}
}
```

Explanation

In the bubble sort, we have to make a set of comparisons in a single pass and several different passes to sort the whole set. For that, we need two loops called as inner and outer loops. Outer loop represents the number of passes and the inner loop represents the comparisons within a pass. As we discussed above, passes required are N-1 and comparisons within a pass are N-pass-1 (where pass starts from 0) where N is the size of the array. The two loops are:

```
for(int pass=0;pass<size-1;pass++) //outer loop running N-1 times representing passes
{
bIsSwap=false;
```

```
for(int j=0;j<size-pass-1;j++) //inner loop running N-pass-1 times for each pass
{
}
}
```

In the inner loop, we have to compare the adjacent elements and swap them if necessary. bIsSwap variable tracks whether any exchanges are made or not. If no exchanges are made in any pass, then we can come out of loop thinking that items have been sorted.

INSERTION SORT

In insertion sort, we pick up each element and insert them in the correct position by comparing that element with the elements prior to it. Insertion sort is similar to card game. In card game, you might have observed the following sequence of events: The first card is taken and placed in the hand as this is first one. The second card, is taken and placed in the hand before or after the first card. With the third card the decision that must be made is whether we should place it in first or second or third position. This sequence repeats for each card. Just similar to card game, we have to arrange numbers also to sort a set of numbers.

Algorithm

Procedure Insertionsort(A[1..n]:real)

Begin

if n=1 then

Print " a list of one element is already sorted"

else

Begin

for j<-2 to n do /*to find the correct relative position for A[j] and insert it there among the already sorted elements A[1] to A[j-1]*/

begin

if A[j]< A[j-1] then begin /*we shift entries only if A[j] < A[j-1]*/

i<- j-1;

m<- A[j]

/*in order to find the correct relative position we store A[j] in m and start with the last element A[j-1] of the already sorted part. If m is less than A[j-1], then we move towards left, compares again with the new element of the array. The process is repeated until either m>= some element of the array or we reach the leftmost element A[1]*/

```
while(i>0 and m < A[i]) do
begin
A[i+1] <- A[i]
i<- i-1
end
```

/*after finding the correct relative position, we move all the elements of the array found to be greater than m =A[j], one place to the right so as to make a vacancy at correct relative position for A[j]*/

```
end;
A[i+1]<- m   /*m=A[j] is stored at the correct relative position*/
end;
end;
end;
end;
return
```

Example:

Let us take a set of 7 numbers to sort them in ascending order

2 6 5 4 1 7 3

Pass 1:

2 6 5 4 1 7 3

As the first element requires no sorting, start with the second element and place it in the correct position. Compare 6 with 2, as they are in the correct order no need to change the order.

2 6 5 4 1 7 3

Pass 2:

2 6 5 4 1 7 3

Now take the 3rd element and compare it with first two elements. First, compare it with 2nd element and place in the correct position and then with first element and place in the correct position. Comparing 5 with 6 needs exchange, then the set will become

2 5 6 4 1 7 3

Now compare 5 with 2, no exchange is needed.

Pass 3:

2 5 6 4 1 7 3

Now take 4th element, compare it with first 3 elements. Comparing 4 with 6 needs exchange, the set will be

2 5 4 6 1 7 3

Now 4 should be compared with 5, needs exchange.

2 4 5 6 1 7 3

Now compare 4 with 2, no exchange is needed.

Pass 4:

2 4 5 6 1 7 3

Now take 5th element which is 1 and place it in the correct position by comparing it with first 4 elements. Finally, the set will be

1 2 4 5 6 7 3

Pass 5:

1 2 4 5 6 7 3

Now take 6th element which is 7 and place it in the correct position by comparing it with first 5 elements. Finally, the set will be

1 2 4 5 6 7 3

Pass 6:

1 2 4 5 6 7 3

Now take 7th element which is 3 and place it in the correct position by comparing it with first 6 elements. Finally, the set will be

1 2 3 4 5 6 7

Summary

A set of elements can be sorted in insertion sort by comparing each element with the elements prior to it and placing it in the correct position. As the first element need not be sorted, we have to start from the second element. Totally, N-1 passes should be there. Within each pass, the number of comparisons and moves will be equal to number of passes. In the first pass, 1 comparison and 1 move (if necessary), in the second pass 2 comparisons and 2 moves and so on.

Complexity

Insertion sort needs N-1 passes. First pass needs 1 comparison and 1 move (if necessary), the second pass needs 2 comparisons and 2 moves and so on. Thus, the number of comparisons can be sum of N-1 elements (1+2+3+.....+N-1).

$T(N) = 1+2+.....+(N-2)+(N-1)$

$= \sum_{i=1}^{N-1} i = (N(N-1))/2 = O(N^2)$ (roughly equal)

So, the complexity of insertion sort is $O(N^2)$.

Worst case: When the elements to be sorted are in the exact reverse order. For example, if we want to sort 1, 2, 3, 4, 5, 6, 7 set of elements in descending order.

Best case: When the list of elements to be sorted is already sorted. For example, if we want to sort 1, 2, 3, 4, 5, 6, 7 set of elements in ascending order.

Advantage

The insertion sort has the main advantage in case of incremental data sorting. Consider the situation of having a sorted list and a set of new items that need to be sorted. For example,

5 8 13 17 19 2 7 3 1

In the above array, all the elements upto 19th are sorted. Now, we can start sorting from 2 by giving the value of array element 6 to the outer loop.

Disadvantage

This is also the slowest sorting technique.

Example: Program to illustrate insertion sort

```
void InsertionSort(int arr[], int size){
int temp, position;
for(int i=1;i<size;i++){
temp=arr[i];
position=i;
while(position>0 && temp<arr[position-1]){
arr[position]=arr[position-1];
position—;
}
```

```
arr[position]=temp;
}
}
void main(){
int arr[7]={2, 6, 5, 4, 1, 7, 3};
printf("numbers before sorting:");
for(int i=0;i<7;i++) {
printf("%d", arr[i]);
}
InsertionSort(arr, 7);
printf("numbers after sorting:");
for(i=0; i<7; i++) {
printf("%d", arr[i]);
}
}
```

Explanation

The outer for loop runs for N-1 times. It starts from second element whose array index is 1. The element which is to be compared is stored in temp variable. The current position of the element is stored in position value. The inner while loop compares that element with the previous elements by decrementing position value. When the while loop completes, the position value will become equal to the value where the element present in the temp has to be placed. The same process repeats for N-1 times.

SELECTION SORT

The selection sort searches all of the elements in a list until it finds the smallest/largest element. It swaps that element with the first element in the list. Next time, it finds the smallest/largest of remaining elements and swaps it with the second element. The same process will be repeated until the last two elements in the list are compared. As we are selecting the smallest/largest element by searching the entire list, the name is selection sort.

Algorithm

(1) Find the minimum value in the list.

(2) Swap it with the value in the first position.

(3) Repeat the steps above for the remainder of the list (starting at the second position and advancing each time).

```
Procedure SelectionSort(A, N)
for index = 1 to N-1 do
begin
minposition <- index
for j = index+1 to N do begin
if A[j] < A[minposition])
minposition <- j;
end;
swap(A[index], A[minposition])
end;
return
```

Example:

Let us take a set of 7 numbers to sort them in ascending order

2 6 5 4 1 7 3

Pass 1:

2 6 5 4 1 7 3

First, search for the smallest element in the list. Here, 1 is the smallest element. Swap it with the first element of the list. The list will be:

1 6 5 4 2 7 3

Pass 2:

1 6 5 4 2 7 3

Now, we have search for the smallest element from 2nd element onwards. The smallest element is 2 and has to be swapped with 2nd element of the list, i.e., 6. The list will be:

1 2 5 4 6 7 3

Pass 3:

1 2 5 4 6 7 3

Now, we have to search for the smallest element from 3rd element onwards. The smallest element is 3 and has to be swapped with 3rd element of the list, i.e., 5. The list will be:

1 2 3 4 6 7 5

Pass 4:

1 2 3 4 6 7 5

Now, we have to search for the smallest element from 4th element onwards. The smallest element is 4 and has to be swapped with 4th element of the list, i.e., 4. As it is in the correct place no need to swap.

Pass 5:

1 2 3 4 6 7 5

Now, we have to search for the smallest element from 5th element onwards. The smallest element is 5 and has to be swapped with 5th element of the list, i.e., 6. The list will be:

1 2 3 4 5 7 6

Pass 6:

1 2 3 4 5 7 6

Now, we have to search for the smallest element from 6th element onwards. The smallest element is 6 and has to be swapped with 6th element of the list, i.e., 7. The list will be:

1 2 3 4 5 6 7

Summary

Totally, N-1 passes are needed to sort all the elements where N is the number of elements in the list. In each pass, we need to search for the smallest/largest element in the list and should be swapped with the element in the position equal to the number of passes.

Complexity

The number of comparisons is N-1 in the first pass, N-2 in the second pass, N-3 in the third pass and N-i in the ith pass. The complexity will be:

$$T(N) = (N-1)+(N-2)+(N-3)+\dots\dots\dots+2+1$$

$$= \sum_{i=1}^{N-1} i = (N(N-1))/2 = O(N^2) \text{ (roughly equal)}$$

The complexity of selection sort is O(N2).

Advantage

Selection sort is efficient than bubble sort and insertion sort because there are no more than N-1 actual exchanges, (i.e., roughly proportional to N rather N^2). Thus, selection sort is very much suitable in the applications in which excessive swapping is a problem.

Best Case and Worst Case

Since the number of comparisons can't be limited in a particular pass, there is no significance if the input data is completely sorted or unsorted. That is, performance for both worse case and best case is same.

Example: Program to illustrate selection sort

```
void swap(int *a,int *b){
int iTemp;
iTemp=*a;
*a=*b;
*b=iTemp;
}
void SelectionSort(int arr[], int size){
int smallest_pos;
for(int i=0;i<size-1;i++){
smallest_pos=i;
for(int j=i+1;j<size;j++){
if(arr[j]<a[smallest_pos]){
smallest_pos=j;
}
}
swap(&arr[smallest_pos],&arr[i]);
}
}
void main(){
int arr[7]={2, 6, 5, 4, 1, 7, 3};
printf("numbers before sorting:");
for(int i=0;i<7;i++) {
printf("%d",arr[i]);
}
```

```
SelectionSort(arr,7);
printf("numbers after sorting:");
for(i=0;i<7;i++) {
printf("%d\t",arr[i]);
}
}
```

Explanation

As the selection sort needs N-1 passes, the outer loop runs upto size-1 times. In each pass, a set of comparisons have to be made to find the smallest element. So, the inner loop runs for each pass to find the smallest element and getting swapped with the element in the position equal to the number of passes.

QUICK SORT

Quick sort is a fast algorithm invented by C.A.R. Hoare. It follows the divide and conquer method for sorting. It divides the array into two parts and calls the quick sort on both the parts recursively. To divide the array into two parts, we select an item as a pivot and arrange all the items less than the pivot to left side of pivot and all the items greater than the pivot are to the right side of it.

Consider an array A of N elements. Select a pivot element among the N elements. The selection of pivot is some what arbitrary; usually it is the first element of the array. The array will be partitioned based on the pivot element as shown below:

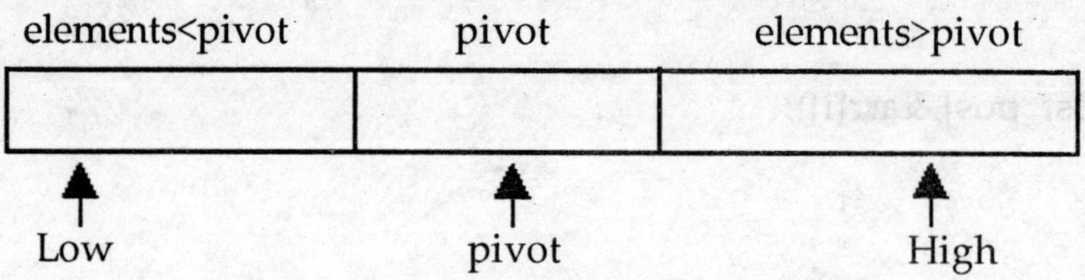

Thus, the entire array will be divided into two parts as shown above based on pivot element. The two arrays are again divided using the same algorithm until a single element is present in each part of array.

Algorithm

(1) Select the first element of array A as pivot

(2) Initialize i and j to first and last elements of the array respectively

(3) Increment i, until A[i]>pivot; stop

(4) Decrement j, until A[j]<pivot; stop

(5) If i<j, exchange A[i]>A[j]

(6) Repeat steps 3, 4 and 5 until i > j, i.e., when i and j cross each other

(7) Exchange the pivot element with the element pointed to by j which is the correct place for pivot

(8) Now pivot is in the place of j which is in the correct position. We have to apply steps from 1 to 7 on each part of the left and right arrays of pivot element. Now lower bound (low) to j-1 forms one array and j+1 to upper bound (high) forms another array. 1 to 7 steps have to be repeated on these two arrays.

(9) Repeat 1 to 8 steps until all the elements are in sorted order

```
Procedure QuickSort (A, lowerbound, upperbound)
if lowerbound < upperbound then begin
i <- lowerbound
j <- upperbound
pivot <- lowerbound
while (i < j) do begin
while ((A[i]<=A[pivot] && (i < upperbound)) do
i <- i+1
while(A[j]>A[pivot]) do
j <- j-1
if i < j then
swap(A[i],A[j])
end;
swap(A[pivot], A[j])
call QuickSort(A, lowerbound, j-1)
call QuickSort(A, j+1, upperbound)
end;
return
```

Example:

Let us take an array of elements as shown below:

5 7 1 2 10 4 9 6 3 8

Pass 1:

Step 1:

5 7 1 2 10 4 9 6 3 8

↑i (at 5) ↑j (at 8)

Let us consider first element 5 as pivot element. As per step 3, we have to increment i until A[i]>5. As 7>5, i will stop at 7. Now the i and j positions in the array will be

5 7 1 2 10 4 9 6 3 8

↑i (at 7) ↑j (at 8)

Step 2:

As per step 4, we have to decrement j until A[j]<5. As 3 < 5, j will stop at 3. Now the i and j positions in the array will be

5 7 1 2 10 4 9 6 3 8

↑i (at 7) ↑j (at 3)

Step 3:

As per step 5 in algorithm, we have to exchange A[i] and A[j] as i<j. Now the array will be

5 3 1 2 10 4 9 6 7 8

↑i (at 3) ↑j (at 7)

Step 4:

Now, increment i as per step 3, the i position in array will be

5 3 1 2 10 4 9 6 7 8

↑i (at 10) ↑j (at 7)

Step 5:

Now decrement j as per step 4, the j position in array will be

```
5   3   1   2   10   4   9   6   7   8
                 ↑    ↑
                 i    j
```

Step 6:

As per step 5 in algorithm, we have to exchange A[i] and A[j] as i < j. Now the array will be

```
  5   3   1   2   4   10   9   6   7   8
↑   ↑
i   j
```

Step 7:

Now increment i as per step 3, the i position in array will be

```
5   3   1   2   4   10   9   6   7   8
                    ↑↑
                    i j
```

Step 8:

Now decrement j as per step 4, the j position in array will be

```
5   3   1   2   4   10   9   6   7   8
                ↑    ↑
                j    i
```

Step 9:

As per step 7 in algorithm, we have exchange pivot element with element in j[th] position as i>j. So swapping 5 (pivot) and 4 (j[th] element). Then the array will be

```
4   3   1   2   5   10   9   6   7   8
                ↑    ↑
                j    i
```

After pass 1, all the elements before pivot element (5) are less than it and all the elements after pivot element are greater than it.

Pass 2:

```
4   3   1   2   5   10   9   6   7   8
↑               ↑                    ↑
Low             j                    high
```

In this pass, we have to divide the array into two parts low to j-1 and j+1 to high as j[th] element is in already correct position.

[4 3 1 2] 5 [10 9 6 7 8]

↑ Low ↑ high

[4 3 1 2] 5 [10 9 6 7 8]

↑ i ↑ j

Step 1:

[2 3 1] 4 5 [10 9 6 7 8]

Step 2:

[1] 2 [3] 4 5 [10 9 6 7 8]

Step 3:

1 2 [3] 4 5 [10 9 6 7 8]

Step 4:

1 2 3 4 5 [10 9 6 7 8]

Step 5:

1 2 3 4 5 [8 9 6 7] 10

Step 6:

1 2 3 4 5 [8 9 6 7] 10

Step 7:

1 2 3 4 5 [6 7] 8 [9] 10

Step 8:

1 2 3 4 5 6 [7] 8 [9] 10

Step 9:

1 2 3 4 5 6 7 8 [9] 10

Step 10:

1 2 3 4 5 6 7 8 9 10

Summary

We have to partition an array of elements based on the pivot element. First element is selected as pivot element usually. After partitioning all the elements less than the pivot should be on the left of the pivot and the element greater than the pivot should be on the right of it. The pivot element is placed in the correct position after one partition. The same procedure should be applied on these sub arrays also until all the elements get sorted.

Complexity

The time requirement to sort N elements using quick sort procedure involves 3 components

(a) Time taking for partitioning array which is roughly proportional to N

(b) Time required for sorting lower sub array

(c) Time required for sorting upper sub array

Let's assume that K elements are there in lower sub array.

So,

T(N)=T(K)+T(N-K-1)+cN where c is proportional constant

Worst Case Analysis

In the worst case, one of the sub arrays will be always empty. Then,

T(N)=T(N-1)+cN for N>1

We can get equations for recursive calls by replacing N with N-1, N-2,......2

T(N-1)=T(N-2)+c(N-1)

T(N-2)=T(N-3)+c(N-2)

....

....

T(2)=T(1)+c(2)

T(1)=T(0)+c(1)=c(1)

By combining all of the above equations, we can write it as

$$T(N) = c \sum_{i=1}^{N} i = c.(N(N+1))/2 = O(N^2) \text{ (roughly equal)}$$

The complexity of quick sort in worst case is $O(N^2)$.

Best Case Analysis

The best case can be viewed when the partition takes place exactly at half the original array. Then,

$T(N)=2.T(N/2)+cN$

Assume the total number of elements N is a power of 2, such that N=2M (i.e., M=log2 N), there are M steps to add since the array is divided into exactly half. So,

$T(N)/N = T(1)/1 + C \log_2 N$

$T(N) = N + CN \log_2 N = O(N \log_2 N)$

The complexity of quick sort in best case is $O(N \log_2 N)$

The complexity of quick sort in average case is also $O(N \log_2 N)$

Advantages

It is very fast. It can be used when the number of elements to be sorted is very large. Because it uses element exchange, it also requires relatively small amount of memory.

Disadvantages

As it works with the concept of recursion, it can't use in the applications running on the systems with limited memory. It is not a stable sort.

Example: Program to illustrate Quick sort

```
void swap(int *a,int *b){
int iTemp;
iTemp=*a;
*a=*b;
*b=iTemp;
}
void QuickSort(int arr[],int lb,int ub){
int i,j,pivot;
if(lb<ub){
i=lb;
j=ub;
pivot=lb;
while(i<j){
while((arr[i]<=arr[pivot]) && (i<ub)){
i++;
}
```

```
while(arr[j]>arr[pivot]) {
j--;
}
if(i<j){
swap(&arr[i],&arr[j]);
}
}
swap(&arr[j],&arr[pivot]);
QuickSort(arr,lb,j-1);
QuickSort(arr,j+1,ub);
}
}
int main(){
int arr[7]={2, 6, 5, 4, 1, 7, 3};
printf(“numbers before sorting:”);
for(int i=0;i<7;i++) {
printf(“%d”,arr[i]);
}
QuickSort(arr,0,6);
printf(“numbers after sorting:”);
for(i=0;i<7;i++) {
printf(“%d\t”,arr[i]);
}
}
```

Explanation

Two while loops run to increment i and decrement j values until the required conditions are satisfied. After that if i < j, the two elements will be swapped. If i becomes greater than j, the pivot element is swapped with element in position j. The same quick sort algorithm gets called recursively for the sub arrays also.

HEAP SORT

Heap sort algorithm was invented by Floyd. This method sorts the elements by building heap and then repeatedly extracting the maximum item.

Heap is a complete binary tree with the property that a parent is always greater than or equal to either of its children (if they exist). Thus, the root node always contains the largest element.

Sample binary tree

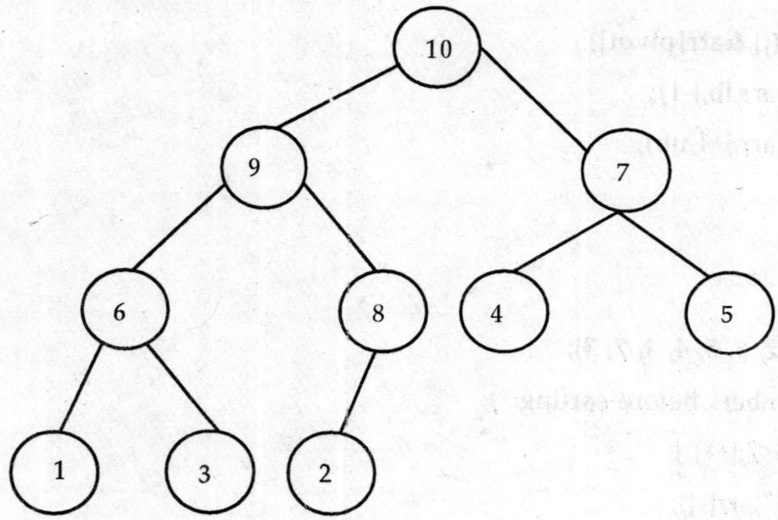

Binary trees can represented as arrays by numbering their nodes from left to right. The above binary tree can be represented in array as shown below

10	9	7	6	8	4	5	1	3	2
1	2	3	4	5	6	7	8	9	10

The relationship between parent and child nodes can be understood from this array representation. If a node is at position j, its left and right children will be at positions 2j and 2j+1, respectively. Also, its parent will be at position j/2. There is no parent node for root node. For instance, consider the node having key value 7. It is at the position 3. Its parent node is therefore at position 3/2 = 1, i.e., the parent is 10. Its left and right children are at the positions 2×3 = 6 and (2×3) + 1 = 7 respectively, i.e., the nodes 4 and 5 are its children. The heap supports 2 operations delete and insert. Delete operation removes the root node and replace it with the last rightmost leaf. After this, the tree might not be in ordered. Then we have to migrate the root down the tree until we find its correct position, by swapping it with one of the two children as to preserve the heap property.

Insert operation inserts the new element as the last rightmost node in binary tree. At this point, the new node might not be in the correct position, so we move it up the tree structure by swapping it with its parent node until the correct position is attained. The heap sort algorithm consists of two phases:

(1) Building a heap tree

(2) Sorting

Building a heap tree

To build a heap tree, start with one element and insert next element into the existing heap by calling the insert operation (as discussed above) recursively, so that a heap is constructed.

Sorting

Once the heap is constructed, the largest element must be the root of the heap. In the sorting phase, the root is placed into the correct position, swapping it with the last rightmost element of binary tree (or last element of the array). After swapping, we have to construct the heap again. The same process of removing root by swapping it with rightmost element and constructing heap should be repeated until heap is empty.

Example

Let us consider a set of elements 4,8,3,9,5,6,7.

Building heap

First take element 4. Next take 8 and place it as left child to 4. As parent has to be larger than its children, exchange both 8 and 4. Now, take third element 3 and place it as right child. No exchanges are needed as it is satisfying heap property. The same process continues until all the elements are constructed in a heap. Following is the pictorial representation of building heap.

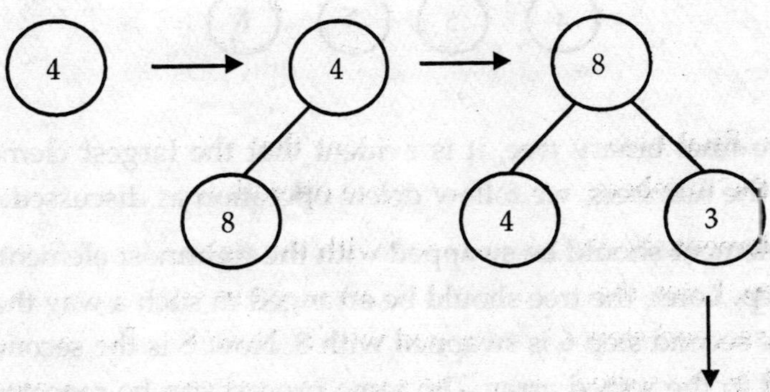

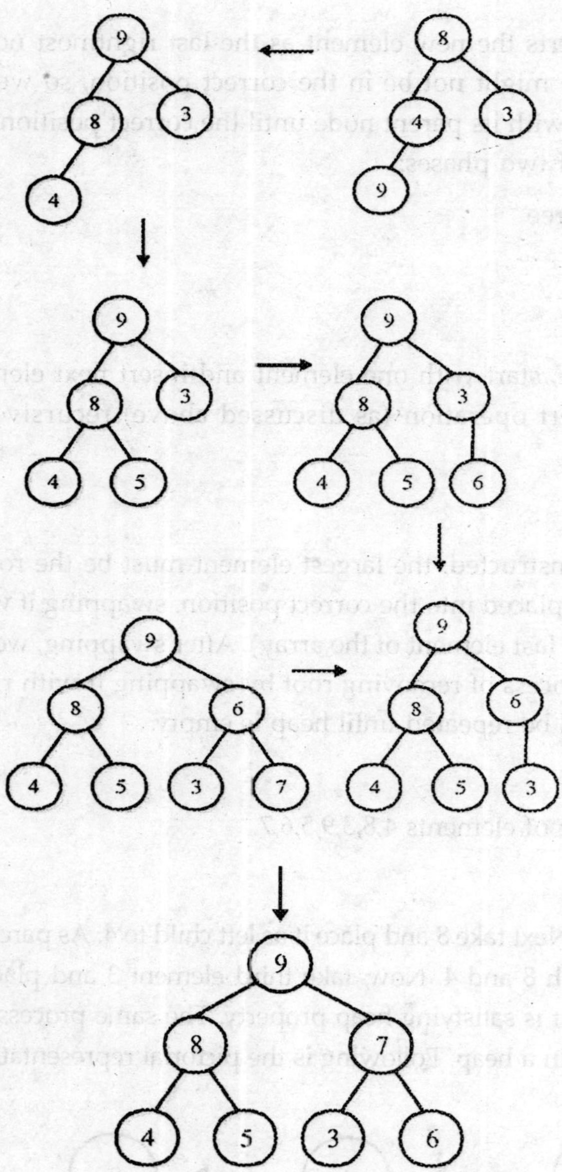

Sorting

From the above final binary tree, it is evident that the largest element is in the root position. To sort all the numbers, we follow delete operation as discussed.

First, the root element should be swapped with the rightmost element, so 9 is swapped with 6 in the first step. Later, the tree should be arranged in such a way that it satisfies heap properties. So, in the second step 6 is swapped with 8. Now, 8 is the second biggest element which can be placed in the sorted array. The same process can be repeated until the tree is empty.

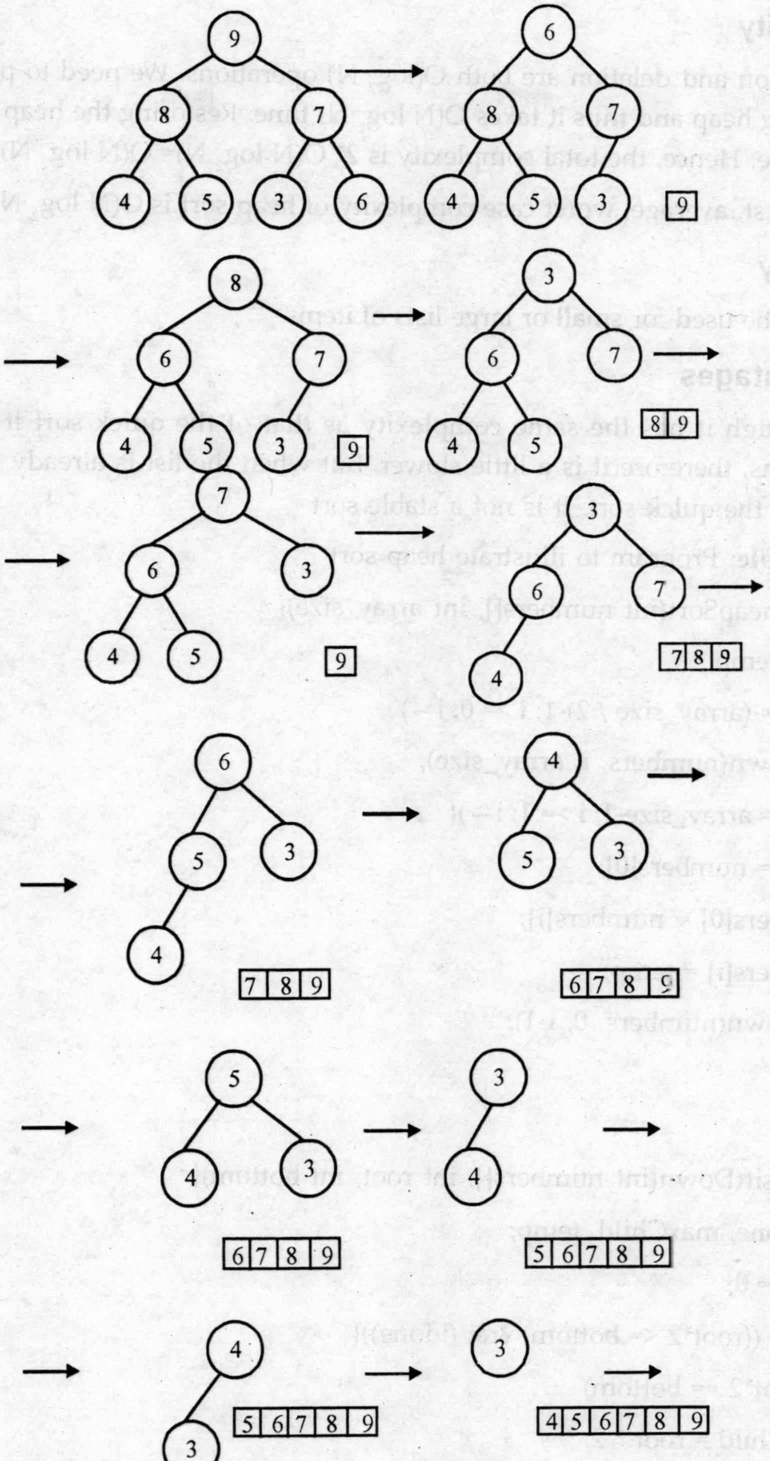

Complexity

Addition and deletion are both O($\log_2$ N) operations. We need to perform n additions for building heap and thus it takes O(N $\log_2$ N) time. Restoring the heap N times takes O(N $\log_2$ N) time. Hence, the total complexity is 2* O(N $\log_2$ N)= O(N $\log_2$ N).

The best, average, worst case complexity of heap sort is O(N $\log_2$ N).

Suitability

It can be used for small or large lists of items.

Disadvantages

Although it has the same complexity as that of the quick sort it needs a few more comparisons, therefore it is a little slower. But when the list is already sorted, heap sort is faster than the quick sort. It is not a stable sort.

Example: Program to illustrate heap sort

```
void heapSort(int numbers[], int array_size){
int i, temp;
for (i = (array_size / 2)-1; i >= 0; i—)
siftDown(numbers, i, array_size);
for (i = array_size-1; i >= 1; i—){
temp = numbers[0];
numbers[0] = numbers[i];
numbers[i] = temp;
siftDown(numbers, 0, i-1);
}
}
void siftDown(int numbers[], int root, int bottom){
int done, maxChild, temp;
done = 0;
while ((root*2 <= bottom) && (!done)){
if (root*2 == bottom)
maxChild = root * 2;
else if (numbers[root * 2] > numbers[root * 2 + 1])
```

```
maxChild = root * 2;
else
maxChild = root * 2 + 1;
if (numbers[root] < numbers[maxChild]){
temp = numbers[root];
numbers[root] = numbers[maxChild];
numbers[maxChild] = temp;
root = maxChild;
}
else
done = 1;
}
}
int main(){
const int size=16
int arr[size]={10,14,13,25,23,33,27,25,59,39,65,74,45,94,82,94};
int temparr[size];
printf("numbers before sorting:");
for(int i=0;i< size;i++){
printf("%d",arr[i]);
}
heapSort(arr,size);
printf("numbers after sorting:");
for(i=0;i< size;i++){
printf("%d\t",arr[i]);
}
}
```

MERGE SORT

Merge sort also follows divide and conquer algorithm just like quick sort. In this, the array of elements will be divided into two equal halves, and placed them in separate arrays. Each array is recursively sorted, and then merged back together to form the final sorted list.

In order to place the final sorted list, merge sort requires one additional array with size equal to the total number of elements to be sorted. That is the main disadvantage of merge sort.

Algorithm

(1) If the list is of length 0 or 1, then it is already sorted.
Otherwise

(2) Divide the unsorted list into two sublists of about half the size.

(3) Sort each sublist recursively by re-applying merge sort.

(4) Merge the two sublists back into one sorted list.

Example

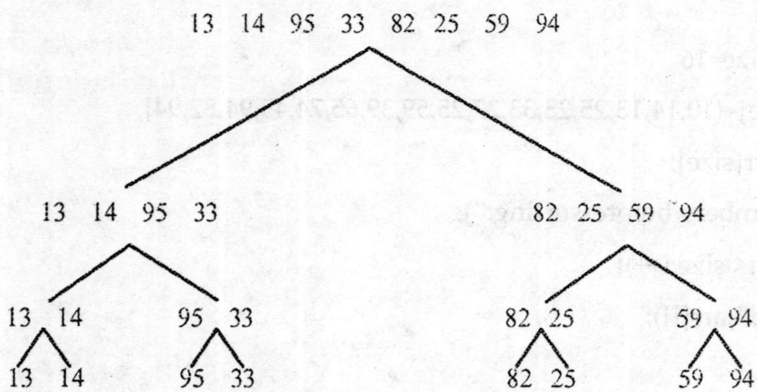

Let us take a set of element to be sorted as shown below:

Once the array is recursively split into single elements (13, 14, 94, 33, 82, 25, 59 and 94), the recursion algorithm will sort the individual arrays and combine them. An array {13} is sorted, because it has only one element. When the recursion is rolling backwards (after expanding), it merges the two branched columns together. Here, 13 and 14 are sorted and 94 and 33 are sorted as 33 and 95. Now it will combine these two arrays to form a single array as 13 14 33 94. In the similar way, another array will also be formed from the elements on the right hand side as 25 59 82 94.

Graphical representation of this process is as shown below:

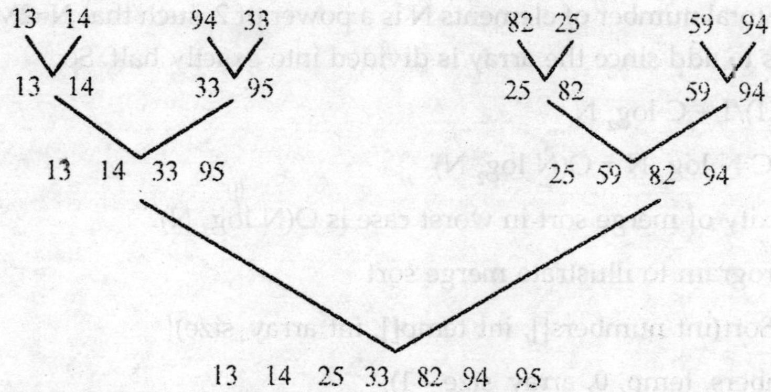

The merging continues as explained while both arrays have elements. As soon as one of the arrays becomes empty, all the elements of the other array are blindly (without any comparisons) appended onto our final array. Those elements are already in ascending (sorted) order and are higher than all of the elements presently in the final array. The final array is the array which contains the sorted elements.

Suitability

Merge sort is good for data that's too big to have in memory at once, because its pattern of storage access is very regular. It uses even fewer comparisons than heap sort, and is especially suited for data stored as linked lists.

Advantages

- Slightly faster than the heap sort for larger sets
- It is a stable sort.

Disadvantages

It requires twice the memory of the heap sort because of the second array used to store the sorted list. Like the quick sort, the merge sort is recursive which can make it a bad choice for applications that run on machines with limited memory.

Complexity

The sorting method in merge sort involves sorting of two equal parts of array and combining two sorted lists into one sorted list. Let T(N/2) be the time taken to sort each half part of array and N is time required to combined two sorted lists into a single sorted list. Then,

$$T(N) = T(N/2)+T(N/2)+N$$

$$= 2T(N/2)+N$$

$$T(N)/N = T(N/2)/(N/2) + 1$$

$T(N)/N = T(N/2)/(N/2) + 1$

Assume the total number of elements N is a power of 2, such that N=2M (i.e., $M=\log_2 N$), there are M steps to add since the array is divided into exactly half. So,

$T(N)/N = T(1)/1 + C \log_2 N$

$T(N) = N + C N \log_2 N = O(N \log_2 N)$

The complexity of merge sort in worst case is $O(N \log_2 N)$.

Example: Program to illustrate merge sort

```
void mergeSort(int numbers[], int temp[], int array_size){
m_sort(numbers, temp, 0, array_size - 1);
}
void m_sort(int numbers[], int temp[], int left, int right){
int mid;
if (right > left){
mid = (right + left) / 2;
m_sort(numbers, temp, left, mid);
m_sort(numbers, temp, mid+1, right);
merge(numbers, temp, left, mid+1, right);
}
}
void merge(int numbers[], int temp[], int left, int mid, int right){
int i, left_end, num_elements, tmp_pos;
left_end = mid - 1;
tmp_pos = left;
num_elements = right - left + 1;
while ((left <= left_end) && (mid <= right)){
if (numbers[left] <= numbers[mid]){
temp[tmp_pos] = numbers[left];
tmp_pos = tmp_pos + 1;
left = left +1;
}
```

```
else
{
temp[tmp_pos] = numbers[mid];
tmp_pos = tmp_pos + 1;
mid = mid + 1;
}
}
while (left <= left_end){
temp[tmp_pos] = numbers[left];
left = left + 1;
tmp_pos = tmp_pos + 1;
}
while (mid <= right){
temp[tmp_pos] = numbers[mid];
mid = mid + 1;
tmp_pos = tmp_pos + 1;
}
for (i=0; i <= num_elements; i++){
numbers[right] = temp[right];
right = right - 1;
}
}
int main(){
const int size=16
int arr[size]={10,14,13,25,23,33,27,25,59,39,65,74,45,94,82,94};
int temparr[size];
printf("numbers before sorting:");
for(int i=0;i< size;i++){
printf("%d",arr[i]);
```

```
}
mergeSort(arr,temparr,size);
printf("numbers after sorting:");
for(i=0;i< size;i++){
printf("%d\t",arr[i]);
}
}
```

SHELL SORT

It is invented by Donald shell; it is very fast and easy to code. This is the old algorithm. The shell sort is a "diminishing increment sort", better known as a "comb sort". It improves the performance of insertion sort by considering a group of elements for sorting.

The idea of shell sort is the following:

(a) Arrange the data sequence in a two-dimensional array

(b) Sort the columns of the array

Sort the each column of the two dimensional array. Repeat this process, each time with smaller number of longer columns. At the end, the table has only one column. We can sort each column of the table by using either insertion sort or bubble sort.

Procedure mergesort(m, start, end)

```
if length(m) d ≤ 1
return m
else
middle = start+end / 2
left = mergesort(m, start, middle)
right = mergesort(m, middle,end)
result = merge(left, right)
return result
```

Example:

Let us consider an array of elements

13 14 94 33 82 25 59 94 65 23 45 27 73 25 39 10

Pass 1:

We can arrange it as 2-D array consisting of 5 columns (5-gap sequence) as shown below:

13 14 94 33 82

25 59 94 65 23

45 27 73 25 39

10

After sorting each column, the array will look like this:

10 14 74 25 23

13 27 94 33 39

25 59 94 65 82

45

Now the number 10 is in right position. We have to sort them again by arranging them in 3 columns (3-gap sequence)

10 14 74

25 23 13

27 94 33

39 25 59

94 65 82

45

After sorting each column, the array will look like this:

10 14 13

25 23 33

27 25 59

39 65 74

45 94 82

94

Now, the array will be [10 14 13 25 23 33 27 25 59 39 65 74 45 94 82 94]. Now, it can be sorted using 1-gap sequence, in other words it's a normal insertion sort.

Note:

The first gap sequence should be calculated as Prev gap=size of the array/2. The next gap sequences should be calculated as gap=Prev gap/2.2. Some analyses showed that these calculations will give best results.

Complexity

Best and Average case complexity is O(N logN).

Worst case complexity is $O(N^2)$

Advantages

Shell sort is faster than an insertion sort and a heap sort. It is faster than a quick sort for small arrays (less than 50 elements), it is slower for bigger arrays.

Disadvantages

It is not a stable sort.

Example: Program to illustrate shell sort

```
void ShellSort(int arr[],int size){
int cols_num=size/2,j,temp;
while(cols_num>0){
for(int i=cols_num;i<size;i++){
j=i;
temp=arr[i];
while(j>=cols_num && arr[j-cols_num]>temp){
arr[j]=arr[j-cols_num];
j=j-cols_num;
}
arr[j]=temp;
}
if(cols_num==2)
cols_num=1;
else
cols_num=(int)(cols_num/2.2);
}
}
int main(){
const int size=16
```

```
int arr[size]={10,14,13,25,23,33,27,25,59,39,65,74,45,94,82,94};
printf("numbers before sorting:");
for(int i=0;i< size;i++){
printf("%d",arr[i]);
}
QuickSort(arr,0, size);
printf("numbers after sorting:");
for(i=0;i< size;i++){
printf("%d\t",arr[i]);
}
}
```

C Program examples

/*Program – sorting – bubble, insert, quick*/

```
#include <stdio.h>
#include <conio.h>
#include <process.h>
#include<stdlib.h>
#include <string.h>
#include <ctype.h>
void insort(int a[10],int n);
void bubsort(int a[10],int n);
void qusort(int list[10],int m,int n1);
void main(){
int i,n,ch,a[10];
clrscr();
printf("enter the number of element in the array");
scanf("%d",&n);
for(i=0;i<n;i++)
scanf("%d",&a[i]);
```

```
do{
printf("1. insertion sort");
printf("2. bubble sort");
printf("3. quick sort");
printf("4. exit");
printf("enter the choices");
scanf("%d",&ch);
switch(ch){
case 1: insort(a,n);getch();
break;
case 2: bubsort(a,n);getch();break;
case 3: qusort(a,n,i);
printf("the array is sorted order using quick sort is\n");
for(i=0;i<n;i++)
printf("%d",a[i]);getch();break;
case 4: printf("thank you");
break;
default :
printf("option entered is invalid");
}
}
while(ch<4);
getch();
}
void insort(int a[10],int n){
int i,temp,j;
for(i=0;i<n;i++){
if(a[i]>a[i+1]){
temp=a[i+1];
```

```
j=1;
while((j>=0)&&(a[i]>temp)){
a[j+1]=a[j];
j--;}
a[j+1]=temp;
}
}
printf("the array in the sorted order using insertion sort is:");
for(i=0;i<n;i++)
printf("%d",a[i]);
return;
}
void bubsort(int a[10],int n){
int j,temp;
for(i=0;i<n-1;i++){
for(j=0;j<n-1;j++){
temp=a[j];
a[j]=a[j+1];
a[j+1]=temp;
}
}
}
printf("the array is the sorted order using bubble sort is \n");
for(i=0;i<n;i++)
printf("%d",a[i]);
return;
}
void qusort(int list[10],int m, int n1){
int temp, i,j,k;
```

```
i=m;
j=n1;
k=list[m];
if(m=n1){
do{
do{
i++;
while(list[i]<k
do
j− −;
while(list[j]>k);
if(i<j){
temp=list[i];
list[i]=list[j];
list[m]=temp;
}
}
while(i<j);
temp=list[j];
list[j]=list[m];list[m]=temp;
qusort(list,m,j);
qusort(list,j+1,n1);
}
return;
}}
```

/*Program – Implementation of Selection Sort*/

```
#include <stdio.h>
#include <conio.h>
main() {
```

```
int a[100],i,j,n,p,temp;
clrscr();
printf("Enter the no. of elements\n");
scanf("%d",&n);
for(i=0;i<n;i++){
printf("Enter a[%d] element",i);
scanf("%d",&a[i]);
}
for(i=0;i<n-1;i++){
temp=a[i];
p=i;
for(j=i+1;j<n;j++){
if(a[j]<temp){
temp=a[j];
p=j;
}
}
a[p]=a[i];
a[i]=temp;
}
for(i=0;i<n;i++){
printf("%d\t",a[i]);
}
getch();
}
```

/*Program – Implementation of Heap Sort*/

```
#include <stdio.h>
crheap(int k[20],int n){
int i,j,q,key;
```

```
for(q=2;q<=n;++q){
i=q;
key=k[q];
j=(int)(i/2);
while((i>1)&&(key>k[j])){
k[i]=k[j];
i=j;
j=(int)(i/2);
if(j<1)
j=1;
}
k[i]=key;
}
}
heapsort(int k[20],int n){
int q,i,j,key,temp;
crheap(k,n);
for(q=n;q>=2;--q){
temp=k[1];
k[1]=k[q];
k[q]=temp;
i=1;
key=k[1];
j=2;
if((j+1)<q)
if(k[j+1]>k[j])
j=j+1;
while(j<=(q-1)&&(k[j]>key)){
k[i]=k[j];
```

```
i=j;
j=2*i;
if((j+1)<q)
if(k[j+1]>k[j])
j=j+1;
else
if(j>n)
j=n;
k[i]=key;
}
}
}
main(){
int k[20],n,i;
printf("Enter the number of elements of the list: \n");
scanf("%d",&n);
printf("Enter the elements of the list: \n");
for(i=1;i<=n;++i)
scanf("%d",&k[i]);
printf("\n");
heapsort(k,n);
printf("The sorted elements of the list is: \n");
for(i=1;i<=n;++i)
printf("\t%d",k[i]);
printf("\n");
}
```

/*Program – Implementation Quick Sort*/

```
#include <stdio.h>
void main(){
```

```
int a[100],n,i;
void quicksort(int a[],int,int);
printf(“Enter N value:”);
scanf(“%d”,&n);
for(i=0;i<n;i++)
scanf(“%d”,&a[i]);
quicksort(a,0,n-1);
printf(“Sorted Data is \n”);
for(i=0;i<n;i++)
printf(“\t %d”,a[i]);
}
void quicksort(int a[],int lb, int ub){
int i,j,temp,key;
if(lb>=ub)
return;
i=lb;
j=ub+1;
key=a[lb];
while(1){
i++;
while(key>a[i]&&i<=ub)
i++;
j—;
while(key<a[j]&&j>=lb)
j—;
if(i<j){
temp=a[i];
a[i]=a[j];
a[j]=temp;
```

```
}
else
break;
}
temp=a[lb];
a[lb]=a[j];
a[j]=temp;
quicksort(a,lb,j-1);
quicksort(a,j+1,ub);
}
```

Review Questions

1. A list is ordered from smaller to largest when a sort is called. Which sort would take the longest time to execute?
2. Define time and space complexity.
3. Explain quick sort and merge sort algorithms.
4. Explain the algorithm for bubble sort with a suitable example.
5. Explain the algorithm for selection sort and give a suitable example.
6. What are the best and worst cases for quick sort?
7. Explain about the time complexity of the sorting algorithms.
8. Compare the different sorting techniques with respect to the time and space complexities.
9. What is divide and conquer technique?

CHAPTER 19

Searching Techniques

The task of searching is one of the most frequent operations in computer programming. It also provides an ideal ground for application of the data structures so far encountered. There exist several basic variations of the theme of searching, and many different algorithms have been developed on this subject. The basic assumption in the following presentations is that the collection of data, among which a given element is to be searched, is fixed. We shall assume that this set of N elements is represented as an array, say as:

Example: ARRAY N of Item

Typically, the type item has a record structure with a field that acts as a key. The task then consists of finding an element of whose key field is equal to a given search argument x. The resulting index i, satisfying a[i].key = x, then permits access to the other fields of the located element. Since we are here interested in the task of searching only, and do not care about the data for which the element was searched in the first place, we shall assume that the type *Item* consists of the key only, i.e., is the key.

COMMON SEARCHING ALGORITHMS

- Linear or Sequential Search
- Binary Search
- Fibonacci Search
- Hash tables

Important Points

- Searching requires a key field (e.g., name, ID, code) which is related to the target item.
- When the key field of a target item is found, a *pointer* to the target item is returned. The pointer may be an address, an index into a vector or array, or some other indication of where to find the target.
- If a matching key field isn't found, the user is informed.
- Important factor: Speed! How long does it take to find the target? What is the response time?
- Response time may depend on:
    - ❖ size of the list (number of records and record size)
    - ❖ data structure used (vector, linked list, binary tree, etc.)
    - ❖ data organization (key ordered, random, etc.)
    - ❖ search strategy (linear, binary, other)
    - ❖ location of the list
        - – external (on a disk or other device)
        - – internal (in memory)
- Search time can be measured with *big-O* notation:

O(n) linear time

O($\log_2$n) logarithmic time

O(1) constant time

Assume you have **n** items in list.

Linear time: It takes about **n** probes to find target. Double the size of the list and you double the number of probes.

Logarithmic time: It takes about **$\log_2$(n)** probes. Double the list size and increase the number of probes by one. Double it again and increase the probes by only one.

Constant time: The search time is independent of the size of the list. Double the list size and the number of probes remains the same.

LINEAR SEARCH

A simple algorithm that search for a specific item inside a list. It operates looping on each element $O(n)$ until a match occurs or the end is reached.

Linear Search – Array Based List

Scan the list until:

(1) last record is searched, or

(2) target record is found.

Return:

(3) index of found target or other useful information (e.g., find a name and return the phone number), or

(4) flag (e.g., -1) indicating target record not found:

Suppose that the given array was not necessarily sorted. This might correspond, for example, to a collection exams which have not yet been sorted alphabetically. If a student wanted to obtain her exam score, how could she do so? She would have to search through the entire collection of exams, one by one, until her exam was found. This corresponds to the unordered linear search algorithm.

Algorithm

Unordered-Linear-Search[A, n, x]

(1) for i 1 to n

(2) do if A[i] = x

(3) then return i

(4) else i i + 1

(5) return "x not found"

Note that in order to determine that an object does not exist in the collection, one needs to search through the entire collection.

Now consider the following array:

i	1	2	3	4	5	6	7	8
A	34	16	12	11	54	10	65	37

Consider executing the pseudocode Unordered-Linear-Search[A, 8, 54]. The variable i would initially be set to 1, and since A[1] (i.e., 34) is not equal to x (i.e., 54), i would be incremented by 1 in Line 4. Since A[2] = 6 = x, i would again be incremented, and this would continue until i = 5.

At this point, A[5] = 54 = x, so the loop would terminate and 5 would be returned in Line 3.

Now consider executing the pseudocode Unordered-Linear-Search[A, 8, 53]. Since 53 does not exist in the array, i would continue to be incremented until it exceeded the bounds of the for loop, at which point the for loop would terminate. In this case, "x not found" would be returned in Line 5.

Ordered Linear Search

Now suppose that the given array is sorted. In this case, one need not necessarily search through the entire list to find a particular object or determine that it does not exist in the collection. For example, if the collection of exams were sorted by name, one need not search beyond the "P"s to determine that the exam for "Peterson" does or does not exist in the collection. A simple modification of the above algorithm yields the ordered linear search algorithm.

Algorithm

Ordered-Linear-Search[A, n, x]

(1) for i 1 to n

(2) do if A[i] = x

(3) then return i

(4) elseif A[i] < x

(5) then i i + 1

(6) else return "x not found"

(7) return "x not found"

Note that the search can now be terminated early if and when it is determined that A[i] > x in Line 6.

Now consider the following array, the sorted version of the array used in our previous example:

i	1	2	3	4	5	6	7	8
A	10	11	12	16	34	37	54	65

Consider executing the pseudocode Ordered-Linear-Search[A, 8, 54]. The variable i would initially be set to 1, and since A[1] (i.e., 10) is not equal to x (i.e., 54), a test would be performed in Line 4 to see if A[1] is less than x. Since A[1] is less than x, i would be incremented by 1 in Line 5. Since A[2] < x, i would again be incremented, and this would continue until i = 7. At this point, A[7] = 54 = x, so the loop would terminate and 7 would be returned in Line 3.

Now consider executing the pseudocode Ordered-Linear-Search[A, 8, 53]. Since 53 does not exist in the array, i would continue to be incremented until i = 7, at which point A[i] (i.e., 54) is no longer less than x (i.e., 53) so the loop would terminate in Line 6 returning "x not found."

/*Program – Linear Search*/

```
#include <stdio.h>
#include <conio.h>
main(){
int a[20],i,n,x,f=1;
clrscr();
printf("Enter the number of elements present in the list\n");
scanf("%d",&n);
printf("Enter the elements of the list:\n");
for(i=0;i<n;i++){
scanf("%d",&a[i]);
}
printf("Enter the searching Elements:\n");
scanf("%d",&x);
for(i=0;i<n;i++){
if(a[i]==x){
printf("The element is present in the list");
f=0;
break;
}
}
if(f==1){
printf("The element is not present in the list");
}
getch();
}
```

BINARY SEARCH

Now consider the following idea for a search algorithm using our phone book example. Select a page roughly in the middle of the phone book. If the name being sought is on this page, you're done. If the name being sought occurs alphabetically before this page, repeat the process on the "first half" of the phone book; otherwise, repeat the process on the "second half" of the phone book.

Note that in each iteration, the size of the remaining portion of the phone book to be searched is divided in half; the algorithm applying such a strategy is referred to as binary search. While this many not seem like the most "natural" algorithm for searching a phone book (or any ordered list), it is provably the fastest. This is true for many algorithms in computer science: the most natural algorithm is not necessarily the best!

Binary search is fast, but the list **must** be ordered.

We can call this an O(N) algorithm and not be wrong because the time complexity will never exceed O(N). But because the array is split in half each time, the number of steps is always going to be equal to the base-2 logarithm of N, which is considerably less than O(N). So an even better choice would be to set the upper bound to log N, which is the upper limit that we know we're guaranteed never to cross. Therefore, a more accurate claim is that binary search is a logarithmic, or O($\log_2$ N), algorithm.

Binary Search – Array Based List

(1) Probe middle of list

(2) If target equals list[mid], FOUND.

(3) If target < list[mid], discard 1/2 of list between list[mid] and list[last].

(4) If target > list[mid], discard 1/2 of list between list[first] and list[mid].

(5) Continue searching the shortened list until either the target is found, or there are no elements to probe.

Algorithm

Binary-Search[A, n, x]

(1) low <- 1

(2) high <- n

(3) while low < high

(4) do mid [(low + high)/2]

(5) if A[mid] = x

(6) then return mid

(7) elseif A[mid] < x

(8) then low <- mid + 1

(9) else high <- mid - 1

(10) return "x not found"

Consider executing the pseudocode Binary-Search[A, 8, 34].

The variable high is initially set to 8, and since low (i.e., 1) is less than or equal to high, mid is set to b(low + high)/2c = b9/2c = 4.

Since A[mid] (i.e., 16) is not x (i.e., 34), and since A[mid] < x, low is reset to mid + 1 (i.e., 5) in Line 8. Since low _ high, a new mid = b(5 + 8)/2c = 6 is calculated, and since A[mid] (i.e., 37) is greater than x, high is now reset to mid "1 (i.e., 5) in Line 9. It is now the case that low and high are both 5; mid will then be set to 5 as well, and since A[mid] (i.e., 34) is equal to x, mid = 5 will be returned in Line 6.

Now consider executing the pseudocode Binary-Search[A, 8, 33]. Binary-Search will behave exactly as described above until the point when mid = low = high. Since A[mid] (i.e., 34) is greater than x (i.e., 33), high will be reset to mid " 1 = 4 in Line 9. Since it is no longer the case that low _ high, the while loop terminates, returning "x not found" in Line 10.

Again consider the following array:

i	1	2	3	4	5	6	7	8
A	10	11	12	16	34	37	54	65

/*Program – Binary Search*/

```
#include <stdio.h>
#include <conio.h>
main(){
int a[100],low,high,mid,i,x,found=1,n;
clrscr();
printf("Enter the size of the list:");
scanf("%d",&n);
printf("Enter the elements of the list in a sorted order:\n");
for(i=0;i<n;i++){
scanf("%d",&a[i]);
```

```
}
printf("Enter the Search element: \n");
scanf("%d",&x);
low=0;
high=n-1;
while(low<=high){
mid=(low+high)/2;
if(x<a[mid])
high=mid-1;
else
if(x>a[mid])
low=mid+1;
else
if(x==a[mid]){
printf("The element is present in the list");
found=0;
break;
}
}
if(found==1){
printf("The element is not present in the list");
}
getch();
}
```

FIBONACCI SEARCH

The Fibonacci search technique is a method of searching a sorted array using a divide and conquer algorithm that narrows down possible locations with the aid of Fibonacci numbers. Compared to binary search, Fibonacci search examines locations whose addresses have lower dispersion. Therefore, when the elements being searched have non-uniform access memory storage (i.e., the time needed to access a storage location varies depending on the location previously accessed), the Fibonacci search has an advantage over binary search in slightly reducing the average time needed to access a storage location. The typical example of non-uniform access storage is that of a magnetic tape, where the time to access a particular element is proportional to its distance from the element currently under the tape's head. Note, however, that large arrays not fitting in cache or even in RAM can also be considered as non-uniform access examples. Fibonacci search has a complexity of O(log(x)).

$F_0 = 0, F_1 = 1$

$F_n = F_n\text{-}1+F_{n-2}$ for n>=2.

```
function fibonacci_search(item: integer; arr: sort_array)return index is
l: index:= arr'first;— first element of array
u: index:= arr'last;— last element of array
m: index:= (u+l)/2;
x,a,b: integer;
begin
a: = (F_n-3);
b: = (F_n-2)-(F_n-3);
discrete (f_2,f_1): = (F_n-2,F_n-3)
new (f_2,f_1): = (f_2-f_1,2*f_1-f_2) | (a,b)
with i: = u-l+1
new i=i/2loop
loop
if item < arr(m)then
m: = m-f_1;— compute new position of compared element
f_2: = f_2-f_1;
f_1: = f_1-f_2;
elsif item > arr(m)then
m: = m+f_1;— compute new position of compared element
x: = f_1;
f_1: = f_2-f_1;
f_2: = x;
a: = f_2; b: = f_1;
```

```
else
return m;— return index of found item
end if;
i: = i/2;
end loop;
end fibonacci_search;
```

Notes on design

Since the present implementation of the preprocessor does not allow more than one identifier in the discrete-loop, our example is not executable at the moment. Let's assume that our array has the length F_{n-1} ($N=F_{n-1}$). Now, we divide the array into two subsets according to the both preceding fibonacci numbers and compare 'item' to the element at the position F_{n-2}. If 'item' is greater than the element, we continue in the right subset, otherwise in the left subset. In this algorithm we don't have to make a division to calculate the middle element, but we get along only with additions and subtractions. In our implementation, we assumed that the fibonacci numbers are given explicitly, (e.g., as constants in the frame program).

Worst Case Performance

Beginning with an array containing Fj-1 elements, the length of the subset is bounded to Fj-1-1 elements. To search through a range with a length of F_{n-1} at the beginning, we have to make n comparisons in the worst case.

Fn=(1/sqrt(5))*((1+sqrt(5))/2)n, that's approximately c*1,618n (with a constant c).

For N+1 = c*1,618n elements we need n comparisons, i.e., the maximum number of comparisons is O (logN).

HASHING TABLES

Hash Tables are used in computer software as a data structure for storing and retrieving data very quickly. Data to be stored in a hash table require a key. For example, a key for a person's data record might be their social security number.

Given the key, the hash table data structure can find a piece of data in one or at most a few key comparisons (O(1) time independent of the size of the table or the number of entries in the table.)

At its heart, a hash table consists of an array of entries. The number of entries in the hash table is usually bigger than the expected number of entries. Each entry can be a linked list of the data (this is the normal case) or just the data you wish to access (rarer, this is known as an open address hash table).

To insert a data entry in the hash table, the hash function for the key of the data is run to generate an integer called a hash. The hash is then used modulo — the length of the table and is used to index into the array. The key and data is then placed in the linked list (or in the case of an open addressed table, inserted in the hash table at that point – or as near as possible).

Similarly, to retrieve the entry the key is used, and hashed to determine the position to search for the entry. Once the entry is found, it is searched until the correct one is found. There's usually only 1 or a very few data records around or at that point in the table, so this is very fast.

As we saw with binary search, certain data structures such as a binary search tree can help improve the efficiency of searches. From linear search to binary search, we improved our search efficiency from O(n) to O(logn) . We now present a new data structure, called a hash table, that will increase our efficiency to O(1), or constant time.

A hash table is made up of two parts: an array (the actual table where the data to be searched is stored) and a mapping function, known as a hash function. The hash function is a mapping from the input space to the integer space that defines the indices of the array. In other words, the hash function provides a way for assigning numbers to the input data such that the data can then be stored at the array index corresponding to the assigned number.

Hash Table is a data structure in which keys are mapped to array positions by a hash function. This table can be searched for an item in O(1) time using a hash function to form an address from the key. The easiest way to conceptualise a hash table is to think of it as an array. When a program stores an element in the array, the elements key is transformed by a hash function that produces array indexes for that array.

Hash Function is a function which, when applied to the key, produces an integer which can be used as an address in a hash table. The intent is that elements will be relatively randomly and uniformly distributed. In the example above, the code for the hash function would look like this (assuming TABLE_SIZE was defined 100):

```
int Hashtable::hash_function(int id_num)
{
return (id_num % TABLE_SIZE);
}
```

Then, for example, to find an element in the table, a program applies hash function to the element's key, producing the array index at which the element is stored.

```
Type* Hashtable::find (char* key)
```

```
{
int index;
index = hash_function(key);
//finding the element
}
```

Unfortunately, this is not quite simple. For example, we have already stored several employees' records, and our table looks something like this:

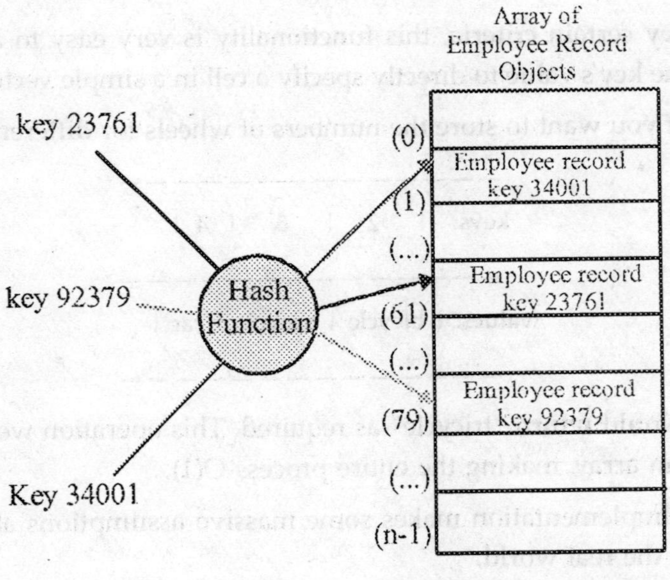

Fig. 19.1: Representation of Hash Table and Hash Function

Suppose, our next employee's key is 57879. Then our hash function will produce array index 79. But the array element with index 79 already has a value. As the array begins to fill, keys will inevitably produce the same array index when transformed by the hash function. When more than one element tries to occupy the same array position, we have a collision.

One complication with hash functions is known as a collision. A collision occurs when two hashes resolve down to the same array location (which usually happens somewhat unless a perfect hash can be employed). With the linked list concept, the key/data pair just gets added to the end of the same list. If open addressing is used, then the key/data pair is just placed in the next free hole in the array.

Because the hash function typically runs quickly and an array lookup is also a fast operation, inserting, deleting and retrieving from a hash table is very fast; the hash function is often the slowest operation performed. However, the comparison can be slow too. Note that issues such as paging and cache limitations can occur on large tables.

In practice, open addressing is rarely employed – the open addressed hash table has a maximum size, whereas linked list hash tables have no limit to their capacity except available memory; also the performance degrades much more slowly with linked lists as more entries are added (open addressed tables basically crawl to a halt as the table fills). Still, open addressed tables have certain advantages, and sometimes the extra space and extra indirection used by linked lists is bothersome.

The hash table belongs to the abstract type of data structures called the table or dictionary. In tables, information as stored in (key, value) pairs, in which the key is the 'handle' used to get to the useful data stored as the value.

If the keys obey certain criteria, this functionality is very easy to acheive. All that is required is to use the key's value to directly specify a cell in a simple vector.

For example, if you want to store the numbers of wheels for different vehicles:

```
        ________________
keys:   |   2   |   3    | 4 |
        ________________
values: | bicycle | tricycle | car |
        ________________
```

So that get(3) would return "tricycle" as required. This operation would only require a single lookup into an array, making the entire process O(1).

However, this implementation makes some massive assumptions about the keys that are unreasonable in the real world.

- The criteria that need to be met are:
- The keys are integers. As only integers can be used to index an array.

The keys are strictly between zero and some predefined upper limit. If a key is outside these boundaries, the table would attempt to read from outside the array. The keys are densely packed over the predefined range. Otherwise, most of the cells in the array are unused, and the table is very space inefficient.

These requirements are so restrictive as to make this implementation impractical in all but a very limited set of cases.

An alternative approach keeps the pairs in a vector, sorted according to the keys' values. This means that the keys can be any comparable type – a much less strict requirement than those detailed above.

If the inverse of the above table was to be created, the sorted vector would look like this:

```
 _ _ _ _ _ _ _ _ _ _ _ _ _ _ _ _
keys: | bicycle | car | tricycle |
 _ _ _ _ _ _ _ _ _ _ _ _ _ _ _ _
values: |   2   | 4 |   3   |
```

So that get("tricycle") returns the value 3, as required.

This lookup would be performed using a binary chop on the vector, making the operation O(log (n)).

However, hash tables boast even better performance than this, but through a totally different method: while sorted arrays rely on order, a hash table relies on chaos.

The reason why hash tables work so well is because the key is converted very simply and neatly from any sort of object into an integer obeying the three requirements listed before.

To do this, the key is fed into a hash function, which returns a integer which is effectively unique to that key. This integer is then used to index an array directly, as in the example outlined above. The beauty of this system is that the hash function is very cheap to compute, as is the array lookup, so a get(key) or set(key, value) operation is O(1) on average!

If a hash table is being used to map the type of vehicle onto the values "zero", "one", "two", etc., this is how it would look:

```
          (key, value)
               |
               |
         Hash Function
               |
               |
 _ _ _ _ _ _ _ _ _ _ _ _ _ _ _ _
      |        |        |
      V        V        V
 _ _ _ _ _ _ _ _ _ _ _ _ _ _ _ _
keys: | bicycle | tricycle | car |
 _ _ _ _ _ _ _ _ _ _ _ _ _ _ _ _
values: |  two  | three  four |
 _ _ _ _ _ _ _ _ _ _ _ _ _ _ _ _
```

When an operation is called, the key is converted by the hash function into a hash value which is then used to access a cell in the vector, or bucket, all in O(1) time (on average).

However, this is a much simplified overview of the workings of a hash table. There are a few 'gotchas' and glitches which need to be sorted out.

Collision

Collision is a condition resulting when two or more keys produce the same hash location.

can We generate the hash function that never produces a collision, i.e., in some cases it is possible to generate such a function. This is known as a perfect hash function.

Perfect Hash Function

Perfect Hash Function is a function which, when applied to all the members of the set of items to be stored in a hash table, produces a unique set of integers within some suitable range. Such function produces no collisions.

Good Hash Function

Good Hash Function minimizes collisions by spreading the elements uniformly throughout the array.

There is no magic formula for the creation of the hash function. It can be any mathematical transformation that produces a relatively random and unique distribution of values within the address space of the storage. Although the development of a hash function is trial and error, here are some hints that may make process easier:

Set the size of the storage space to a prime number. This will help generate a more uniform distribution of addresses.

Use modulo arithmetic (%). Transform a key in such a way that you can perform X % TABLE_SIZE to generate the addresses

To transform a numeric key, try something like adding the digits together or picking every other digit.

To transform a string key, try to add up the ASCII codes of the characters in the string and then perform modulo division.

There are two different methods employed here, giving rise to two types of hash table:

(1) Open HashTable

Open hash tables don't simply store the (key, value) pairs in an array, they store an array of pointers, each leading to a linked list. Each element in the list contains a (key, value) pair and a pointer to the next list element.

The hash table's array of pointers:

```
                 _ _ _ _ _ _ _ _ _ _
        ... pointer | pointer | pointer ...
                 _ _ _ _ _ _ _ _ _ _
                        |
                        |
                        V
              _ _ _ _ _ _ _ _ _ _ _ _ _ _
      L     | key1 | value1 | pointer1 |
      I   _ _ _ _ _ _ _ _ _ _ _ _ _ _ _ _
             N                 |
             K                 |
             E                 V
      D   _ _ _ _ _ _ _ _ _ _ _ _ _ _ _ _
            | key2 | value2 | pointer2 |
      L   _ _ _ _ _ _ _ _ _ _ _ _ _ _ _ _
             I                 |
             S                 |
             T                 V
                      null
```

When an operation is performed, the pointer is followed into the linked list, which is searched linearly for the relevant (key, value) pair.

This approach has the advantage that the hash table has not got a maximum capacity. As more and more entries are added, and more and more collisions occur, the linked lists just grow in size. This means performance will degrade, but the hash table won't die.

(2) Closed Hash Table

This implementation of a hash table has a fixed size, but will offer better performance when sparsely filled.

Instead of having a list of pairs for each bucket, when a collision occurs, some algorithm is employed to work out an alternative bucket for this key. One simple, and quite inefficient, method is to traverse the vector linearly until a free bucket is found, and use that one; i.e., if a bucket is full already, the next empty one is used instead.

If a malicious user or cracker learns what your hash function is, then both the open and closed hash tables' pathological case can easily be created by constructing keys that all hash to the same value. If this happens, operations are O(n) instead of O(1); a disastrous performance hit, which could have massive importance for the effectiveness of the entire system.

As the open hash table offers better performance, on average, and are guaranteed not to saturate, they are chosen more often than closed hash tables.

The Uses of Hash Tables

Although the general idea behind hash tables is simple, there are a number of tricky implementation details that must be adequately handled to achieve an acceptable level of robustness.

Why use hash tables?

There exists a common, erroneous attitude that because modern computers are so fast, high-performance data structures and algorithms are becoming unnecessary. However, if one program runs 10 times faster than another on an 8086, it will probably run 10 times faster on modern CPU. The absolute difference is smaller, but the relative speed will remain fairly constant. As modern processing jobs are much larger than jobs 8086's were expected to do, the relative speed of a bad programme to a good one is just as relevant now as it was back then.

For this reason, the most efficient data structures and algorithms should be used in all but the simplest cases.

Although hash tables boast O(1) operations, this does not mean they are as fast as O(1) array lookups or even some small O(log(n)) sorted vector or binary tree lookups. The invisible constant factor in big-O notation is increased by the need for computing the hash function every time an operation is performed. For reasons discussed below, when the pattern and type of use of a data structure is well known at design time, it may well be that slighly more exotic data structures offer better performance. That said, a well implemented hash table guarantees excellent scalability, relaxed key requirements and, above all, efficiency. They are a good choice for a general-purpose yet functional data structure.

There are many different algorithms used in hash tables. Some of them are:

Separate Chaining

Every entry in the hash table's array is actually a linked-list. We perform lookups by taking the modulus of the ID and the length of the array, to get an index. Then, if two entries collide, (ie: they try to use the same index) the second entry is simply added into the linked list. This algorithm is very simple, and good for small databases. However, if many objects are added to the table, lookups will stop being O(1), and will begin looking more like O(log n) searches, or worse.

Non-linked List Methods

These algorithms use vectors with wrap-around that will resize them once they get too full. Most implementations will say a hash table is "too full" when the table is 50% filled.

Linear Probing

Every entry in the array contains a "status" field, which can either be EMPTY, FULL, or DELETED.

When inserting, we take the modulus of the ID and the array length, and if it collides, then we simply increment by 1, until we get to a spot with an EMPTY or a DELETED flag.

When looking-up, we take the modulus of the ID and the array length, and if it collides, we increment the index until we either find the value, we get to an EMPTY slot, or until we have traversed the entire array.

When deleting, we perform a lookup, and if we find the value, we set the "status" to DELETED.

Quadratic Probing

This method is very similar to the Linear probing example. The main difference, is that instead of incrementing by 1, we increment by perfect squares, (i.e., 1, 4, 9, ...). This is done, because it can be mathematically proven that if we increment by perfect squares, keep the table under 50% full, and make the table size a prime number, then we will always be able to find an EMPTY or a DELETED spot to insert into, (i.e., We will never enter an infinite loop).

Note: When doing lookups in quadratic probing, we want to test the original spot, then test the (original spot)+1, then the (original spot)+4, etc.

In all situations, the length of the array is a prime number. If the hash table needs more room, the hash table will find its new size by doubling its current size, and then increasing this number until it is prime. This way, it will avoid situations where various IDs will collide often, because they are multiples of the table size.

If we need to "re-hash," we resize the old table using the method described in the previous paragraph. We then go item-by-item through the old table, and insert them into the new one.

/*Program – Basic Hash Example*/

```
#include <stdio.h>
#include <stdlib.h>
#include <alloc.h>
#define HASHSIZE    1000
#define MAXLINE     1024
typedef struct tnode{
char *data;
struct tnode *next;
} node;
void htable_init(node *hashtable);                          // fire up hashtable
void htable_insert(node *hashtable, char *str);             // insert data into hashtable
void htable_resolve(node *hashtable, int loc, char *str); // resolve collisions in hashtable
void htable_display(node *hashtable);                       // display hashtable
int  htable_delete(node *hashtable, char *str);             // delete an entry from hashtable
int  htable_hash(char *str);                                // hash data for hashtable
int main(void){
char line[MAXLINE];
node *hashtable;
hashtable = (node *)malloc(HASHSIZE * sizeof(node));
htable_init(hashtable);
while((fgets(line, MAXLINE, stdin)) != NULL)
htable_insert(hashtable, line);
 htable_display(hashtable);
return 0;
}
/*free up hashtable*/
void htable_init(node *hashtable){
int i = 0;
```

```
for(i = 0; i < HASHSIZE; i++)
hashtable[i].data = NULL, hashtable[i].next = NULL;
}
/*insert data into hashtable*/
void htable_insert(node *hashtable, char *str){
 int index = 0;
 /* determine hash function*/
 index = htable_hash(str);
 if(hashtable[index].data != NULL){
  /*gcollision occurs - resolve by chaining*/
 htable_resolve(hashtable, index, str);
 }
else{
hashtable[index].data = calloc(strlen(str) + 1, sizeof(char));
strcpy(hashtable[index].data, str);
}
}
/*hash data for hashtable*/
int htable_hash(char *str){
 int index = 0;
 char *tmp = NULL;
 tmp = calloc(strlen(str) + 1, sizeof(char));
 strcpy(tmp, str);
 while(*tmp){
index += *tmp;
tmp++;
 }
index = index % HASHSIZE;
return index;
```

```
}
/*resolve collisions in hashtable*/
void htable_resolve(node *hashtable, int loc, char *str){
node *tmp;
tmp = hashtable + loc;
while(tmp->next != NULL)
tmp = tmp->next;
tmp->next = (node *)malloc(sizeof(node));
tmp->next->data = calloc(strlen(str) + 1, sizeof(char));
strcpy(tmp->next->data, str);
tmp->next->next = NULL;
}
/*display hashtable*/
void htable_display(node *hashtable){
int i = 0;
node *target;
for(i = 0; i < HASHSIZE; i++){
if(hashtable[i].data != NULL){
target = hashtable + i;
while(target)
/* printf("location: %d, data: %s", i, target->data), target = target->next;*/
printf("%s", target->data), target = target->next;
} /* if */
} /* for */
}
/*delete an entry from hashtable•*/
int htable_delete(node *hashtable, char *str){
node *bla;
node *blb;
```

```
char *tmp = NULL;
int index = 0;
index = htable_hash(str);
/*no item at this location*/
if(hashtable[index].data == NULL)
 return 1;
/*only one item at this location*/
if(hashtable[index].next == NULL){
 if(strcmp(hashtable[index].data, str) == 0){
/*item found*/
tmp = hashtable[index].data;
hashtable[index].data = NULL;
free(tmp);
}
else{
/*there is a chaining case*/
bla = hashtable + index;
/*linked list similar*/
while(bla->next != NULL){
if(strcmp(bla->next->data, str) == 0){
blb = bla->next;
if(bla->next->next)
bla->next = bla->next->next;
else
bla->next = NULL;
free(blb);
} /* if */
} /* while */
} /* else */
 return 0;
}
```

Review Questions

1. What are the searching techniques? How they are used for searching an element?
2. The element being searched for is not found in an array of 100 elements. What is the average number of comparisons needed in a sequential search to determine that the element is not there, if the elements are completely unordered?
3. What is the average number of comparisons needed in a sequential search to determine the position of an element in an array of 100 elements, if the elements are ordered from largest to smallest?
4. Which one is faster? A binary search of an ordered set of elements in an array or a sequential search of the elements.
5. Write and explain non-recursive algorithm for binary search with suitable example and discuss the various time complexities of binary search.
6. Suppose that the list contains the integers 10, 20, 30.......100 in this order. Trace through the steps of binary search to determine, what comparisons of keys are done in searching: (a) to locate 40 and (b) to locate 90.
7. Write and explain linear search procedure with a suitable example.
8. Formulate an algorithm for binary search with its timing analysis.
9. Write a C program that searches a value in a stored array using linear search. What is the time complexity of linear search.
10. What are binary search and Fibonacci search?
11. What are hash tables and explain its uses?
12. What is hashing?
13. What is collision?
14. What is open addressing?
15. What is a hash function?
16. What is separate chaining?
17. What is linear probing?
18. What are the advantages and disadvantages of various collision resolution techniques?

CHAPTER 20

C Programming Examples

1. **/*The atoi() function: read numeric values from the keyboard The atoi() function converts a string into an integer value*/**

```
#include <stdio.h>
#include <stdlib.h>
int main(){
int age;
char years[8];
printf("Age:");
gets(years);
age=atoi(years);
printf("Age was %d years old.\n",age);
return(0);
}
```

INPUT : Age:1

OUTPUT: Age was 1 years old.

2. **/*Display the ASCII characters and their corresponding codes, from Code 32 on up to Code 127*/**

```
#include <stdio.h>
int main(){
unsigned char a;
```

```
for(a=32;a<128;a=a+1)
printf("%3d = '%c'\t",a,a);
return(0);
}
```

OUTPUT: Displays ASCII characters on to the screen

3. **/*The putchar() function**
putchar() displays a character on the screen*/

```
#include <stdio.h>
int main(){
puts("Press Enter:");
getchar();
putchar('H');
putchar('e');
putchar('l');
putchar('l');
putchar('o');
putchar('!');
putchar('\n');
return(0);
}
```

INPUT: Press Enter 1

OUTPU: Hello!

4. **/*The getchar() function**
The getchar() function is used to read a single character from the keyboard*/

```
#include <stdio.h>
int main(){
char key;
puts("Type your favorite keyboard character:");
key=getchar();
printf("Your favorite character is %c!\n",key);
```

```
return(0);
}
```

INPUT: Type your favorite keyboard character: 1

OUTPUT: Your favorite character is 1!

5. **/*All letters of the alphabet, symbols, and number keys on the keyboard have ASCII codes values range from 0 to 127*/**

```
#include <stdio.h>
int main(){
char key;
printf("Press a key on your keyboard:");
key=getchar();
printf("You pressed the '%c' key.\n",key);
printf("Its ASCII value is %d.\n",key);
return(0);
}
```

INPUT: Press a key on your keyboard: 1

OUTPUT: You pressed the '1' key.

Its ASCII value is 49.

6. **/*Converting uppercase to lowercase*/**

```
#include <stdio.h>
int main(void){
char letter = 'B';
if(letter >= 'A')
if (letter <= 'Z'){
letter = letter - 'A'+ 'a';
printf("You entered an uppercase %c\n", letter);
}
else
printf("Try using the shift key, Buddy! I want a capital letter.\n");
return 0;
```

```
}
```

OUTPUT: You entered an uppercase b

7. **/*Using an enumeration type*/**

```
#include <stdio.h>
enum months{
JAN = 1, FEB, MAR, APR, MAY, JUN, JUL, AUG, SEP, OCT, NOV, DEC};
int main(){
enum months [illegible]
const char *monthName[] = {"", "January", "February", "March", "April", "May", "June",
"July", "August", "September", "October","November", "December"};
for(month = JAN; month <= DEC; month++){
printf("%2d%11s\n", month, monthName[month]);
}
return 0;
}
```

OUTPUT:

```
1  January
2  February
3  March
4  April
5  May
6  June
7  July
8  August
9  September
10 October
11 November
12 December
```

8. **/*Data type cast: from int to float*/**

```
#include <stdio.h>
int main(void){
```

```
int count = 110;
long sum = 10L;
float average = 0.0f;
 average = (float)sum/count;
 printf("\nAverage of the ten numbers entered is: %f\n", average);
return 0;
}
```

OUTPUT: Average of the ten numbers entered is: 0.090909

9. **/*Program to convert digits into numbers*/**

```
#include <stdio.h>
#include <conio.h>
void f20(int);
void f1to19(int);
void main(){
unsigned long int a,c,d,di,b=1000;
clrscr();
printf("Enter the Amount in digit:");
scanf("%ld",&di);
printf("\n\n");
for(;di>=1;){
if(di>=1000){
for(a=0;b<=di;a++){
b=b*100;
}
b=b/100;
for(;b>=1000;b=b/100,a—){
d=di/b;
if(d>19){
c=d/10;
f20(c);
```

```
c=d%10;
f1to19(c);
}else f1to19(d);
if(d!=0){
if(a>=3) printf("Carror");
else if(a>=2&&a<3) printf("Lakh");
else if(a<2) printf("Thousand");
}
di=di%b;
}
}else if(di>=100&&di<1000)
{
c=di/100;
f1to19(c);
printf(" Hundred");
di=di%100;
}
else if(di<100){
if(di>19){
c=di/10;
f20(c);
c=di%10;
f1to19(c);
}
else f1to19(di);
di=di/100;
}
}
getch();
```

```
}
void f1to19(int n){
if(n==1) printf("One");
else if(n==2) printf("Two");
else if(n==3) printf("Three");
else if(n==4) printf("Four");
else if(n==5) printf("Five");
else if(n==6) printf("Six");
else if(n==7) printf("Seven");
else if(n==8) printf("Eight");
else if(n==9) printf("Nine");
else if(n==10) printf("Ten");
else if(n==11) printf("Eleven");
else if(n==12) printf("Twelve");
else if(n==13) printf("Thirteen");
else if(n==14) printf("Forteen");
else if(n==15) printf(" Fifteen");
else if(n==16) printf("Sixteen");
else if(n==17) printf("Seventeen");
else if(n==18) printf("Eighteen");
else if(n==19) printf("Ninteen");
}
void f20(int n){
if(n==2) printf("Twenty");
else if(n==3) printf("Thirty");
else if(n==4) printf("Forty");
else if(n==5) printf("Fifty");
else if(n==6) printf("Sixty");
else if(n==7) printf("Seventy");
```

```
else if(n==8) printf("Eighty");
else if(n==9) printf("Ninty");
}
```

10. /*Working with complex numbers*/

```
#include <complex.h>
#include <stdio.h>
int main(void){
double complex cx = 1.0 + 3.0*I;
double complex  cy = 1.0 - 4.0*I;
printf("Working with complex numbers:");
printf("\nStarting values: cx = %.2f%+.2fi  cy = %.2f%+.2fi", creal(cx), cimag(cx), creal(cy),
Cimag(cy));
double complex  sum = cx+cy;
printf("\n\nThe sum cx + cy = %.2f%+.2fi", creal(sum), cimag(sum));
double complex  difference = cx-cy;
printf("\n\nThe difference cx - cy = %.2f%+.2fi", creal(difference), cimag(difference));
double complex product = cx*cy;
printf("\n\nThe product cx * cy = %.2f%+.2fi",creal(product), cimag(product));
double complex quotient = cx/cy;
printf("\n\nThe quotient cx / cy = %.2f%+.2fi", creal(quotient), cimag(quotient));
double complex conjugate = conj(cx);
printf("\n\nThe conjugate of cx =  %.2f%+.2fi", creal(conjugate), cimag(conjugate));
return 0;
}
```

OUTPUT:

```
Working with complex numbers:
Starting values: cx = 1.00+3.00i  cy = 1.00-4.00i
The sum cx + cy = 2.00-1.00i
The difference cx - cy = 0.00+7.00i
The product cx * cy = 13.00-1.00i
The quotient cx / cy = -0.65+0.41i
```

The conjugate of cx = 1.00-3.00i

11. /*Arithmetic operators in action*/

```
#include <stdio.h>
main(){
int a = 1,b = 2,c = 3,d = 4;
int sum,sub,mul,rem;
float div;
sum = b+c;
sub = b-c;
mul = b*c;
div = b/c;
rem = b%d;
a = b/c * d;
printf("\n sum = %d, sub = %d, mul = %d, div = %f",sum,sub,mul,div);
printf("\n remainder of division of b & d is %d",rem);
printf("\n a = %d",a);
}
```

12. /* Program to print the given shape

```
* * * *
* * * *
* * * *
* * * * */
#include <stdio.h>
#include <conio.h>
void main(){
int a,b,c;
clrscr();
printf("Enter the No:");
scanf("%d",&a);
```

```
printf("\n");
for(b=1;b<=a;b++){
for(c=1;c<=a;c++)
printf("*");
printf("\n");
}
getch();
}
```

13. /* Program to print the given shape

```
        *
      * * *
    * * * * *
  * * * * * * *
* * * * * * * * *
  * * * * * * *
    * * * * *
      * * *
        *     */
```

```
include <stdio.h>
include <conio.h>
void main(){
int a,i,j;
clrscr();
printf("Enter the no. of rows in odd no.s");
scanf("%d",&a);
a=a/2+1;
for(i=1;i<=a;i++){
for(j=1;j<=a-i;j++){
printf(" ");
}
```

```
for(j=1;j<=2*i-1;j++){
printf("*");
}
printf("\n");
}
for(i=1;i<a;i++){
for(j=1;j<=i;j++){
printf(" ");
}
for(j=2*a-2*i-1;j>=1;j— —){
printf("*");
}
printf("\n");
}
getch();
}
```

14. **/* Program to print**

```
1
2 2
3 3 3
4 4 4 4
5 5 5 5 5*/
#include <stdio.h>
main(){
int n, i,j;
clrscr();
printf("Enter an integer number:");
scanf("%d", &n);
for(i=1;i<=n;i++){
```

```
for(j=1;j<=i;j++)
printf("%d",i);
printf("\n");
}
}
```

15. **/* Program to print**

```
            1
          2   2
        3   3   3
      4   4   4   4
    5   5   5   5   5*/
#include <stdio.h>
main(){
int n, i,j,k;
clrscr();
printf("Enter an integer number:");
scanf("%d", &n);
for(i=1;i<=n;i++){
for(k=1;k<=40-4*i/2;k++)
printf(" ");
for(j=i;j>=1;j—)
printf("%d",i);
printf("\n");
}
}
```

16. **/*Initializing multidimensional arrays*/**

```
#include <stdio.h>
void printArray(const int a[][3]);
int main(){
int array1[2][3] = {{1, 2, 3}, {4, 5, 6}};
```

```
int array2[2][3] = {1, 2, 3, 4, 5};
int array3[2][3] = {{1, 2}, {4}};
printf( "Values in array1 by row are:\n");
printArray(array1);
printf("Values in array2 by row are:\n");
printArray(array2);
printf("Values in array3 by row are:\n");
printArray(array3);
return 0;
}
void printArray(const int a[][3]){
int i;
int j;
for (i = 0; i <= 1; i++){
for (j = 0; j <= 2; j++){
printf("%d ", a[i][j]);
}
printf("\n");
}
}
```

Output

```
Values in array1 by row are:
1 2 3
4 5 6
Values in array2 by row are:
1 2 3
4 5 0
Values in array3 by row are:
1 2 0
4 0 0
```

17. **/* Program to print**

```
            1
          2   3
        4   5   6
      7   8   9   10
    11  12  13  14   15*/
#include <stdio.h>
#include <conio.h>
void main(){
int i,j,t, rows;
clrscr();
printf("Enter number of rows");
scanf("%d", &rows);
for(i=0;i<rows;i++){
for(j=0;j<=i;j++){
if(t<10)
printf("%d",t);
else
printf("%d",t);
t++;
}
printf("\n");
}
getch();
}
```

18. /* Program to print pyramid of numbers

```
                1
              2 3 4
            5 6 7 8 9
        10 11 12 13 14 15 16
    17 18 19 20 21 22 23 24 25*/
```

```
#include <stdio.h>
#include <conio.h>
void main(){
int i,j,k,t, s, rows;
clrscr();
printf("Enter number of rows");
scanf("%d", &rows);
for(i=0;i<rows;i++){
for(j=0;j<=rows-i;j++){
printf(" ");
s=(2*i)-1;
for(k=0;k<s;k++){
if(t<10)
printf("%d",t);
else
printf("%d",t);
t++;
}
printf("\n\n");
}
getch();
}
```

19. /* Program to print Pascal's triangle

```
        1
      1   1
    1   2   1
  1   3   3   1
1   4   6   4   1 */
```

```
#include<stdio.h>
#include <conio.h>
```

```
void main(){
int  p,q, s, t, rows;
clrscr();
printf("Enter number of rows");
scanf("%d", &rows);
s=1;
q=0;
printf(" Pascals Triangle\n");
while(q<rows){
for(p=30-3*q;p>0;p--){
printf("  ");
for(t=0;t<=q;t++){
if(t==0!! q ==0 )
s=1;
   else
s=(s*q-t+1)/s);
printf("%6d",s);
}
printf("\n");
q++;
}
getch();
}
```

20. /*Program – Swapping of two strings*/

```
#include <stdio.h>
#include <conio.h>
#include <string.h>
main(){
char ch[20],st[20],temp[20];
clrscr();
```

```
printf("enter any two strings");
scanf("%s%s", ch,st);
printf("\n\n");
printf("entered strings are");
printf("\n%s\t%s",ch,st);
strcpy(temp,ch);
strcpy(ch,st);
strcpy(st,temp);
printf("\n\n");
printf("after swapping");
printf("\n%s\t%s",ch,st);
getch();
}
```

21. /*Function calls function*/

```
#include <stdio.h>
f1 (void){
printf ("f1-1 \n");
f2 ( );
printf ("f1-2 \n");
}
f2 (){
printf ("f2 \n");
}
main ( ){
printf ("1 \n");
f1 ( );
printf ("2 \n");
}
```

OUTPUT:

1

```
f1-1
f2
f1-2
2
```

22. **/*Program – Recursion*/**

```
#include <stdio.h>
int add(int k,int m);
main(){
int k ,i,m;
m=2;
k=3;
i=add(k,m);
printf("The value of addition is %d\n",i);
}
int add(int pk,int pm){
if(pm==0)
return(pk);
else
return(1+add(pk,pm-1));
}
```

OUTPUT: The value of addition is 5

23. **/*Calculate factorials using recursion*/**

```
#include <stdio.h>
unsigned long factorial(unsigned long);
int main(void){
unsigned long number = 0L;
printf("\nEnter an integer value:");
scanf(" %lu", &number);
printf("\nThe factorial of %lu is %lu\n", number, factorial(number));
return 0;
```

```
}
unsigned long factorial(unsigned long n){
if(n < 2L)
return n;
else
return n*factorial(n - 1L);
}
```

24. /*Recursive fibonacci function*/

```
#include <stdio.h>
long fibonacci(long n);
int main(){
long result;
long number;
printf("Enter an integer:");
scanf("%ld", &number);
result = fibonacci(number);
printf("Fibonacci(%ld) = %ld\n", number, result);
return 0;
}
long fibonacci(long n){
if (n == 0 || n == 1){
return n;
}
else{
return fibonacci(n - 1) + fibonacci(n - 2);
}
}
```

INPUT: Enter an integer: 3

OUTPUT: Fibonacci(3) = 2

25. **/*Write a function that takes the time as three integer arguments (for hours, minutes, and seconds) and returns the number of seconds since the last time the clock "struck 12." Use this function to calculate the amount of time in seconds between two times, both of which are within one 12-hour cycle of the clock*/**

```
#include <stdio.h>
#include <conio.h>
long int sec(long int,long int,long int);
void main(){
long int diff,t1,t2,h1,m1,s1,h2,m2,s2;
clrscr();
printf("Enter the 1st Time \n");
printf("\n Hours:");
scanf("%ld",&h1);
printf("Minutes:");
scanf("%ld",&m1);
printf(" Seconds:");
scanf("%ld",&s1);
t1=sec(h1,m1,s1);
printf("\nEnter the 2nd Time \n");
printf("\n Hours:");
scanf("%ld",&h2);
printf("Minutes:");
scanf("%ld",&m2);
printf("Seconds:");
scanf("%ld",&s2);
t2=sec(h2,m2,s2);
if(t1>t2)
diff=t1-t2;
if(t2>=t1)
diff=t2-t1;
```

```
printf("\nThe amount of Seconds between two times is %ld sec.s",diff);
getch();
}
long int sec(long int h,long int m,long int s){
while(h>12){
h=h-12;
}
h=h*3600;
m=m*60;
s=s+m+h;
return s;
}
```

26. /*Program: The greatest common divisor (GCD) of two integers is the largest integer that evenly divides each of the two numbers. Write function gcd that returns the greatest common divisor of two integers*/

```
#include <stdio.h>
#include <conio.h>
int gcd(int,int);
void main(){
int n1,n2,Gcd;
clrscr();
printf("Enter the 1st No:");
scanf("%d",&n1);
printf("Enter the 2nd No:");
scanf("%d",&n2);
Gcd=gcd(n1,n2);
printf("\nGreatest Common Divisor is %d",Gcd);
getch();
}
int Gcd(int n1,int n2){
```

```
int a,gcd=1;
for(a=2;n1>0&&n2>0;a++){
if(n1%a==0||n2%a==0){
if(n1%a==0)
n1=n1/a;
if(n2%a==0)
n2=n2/a;
gcd=gcd*a;
a--;
}
}
return gcd;
}
```

27. **/*Implement the following integer functions:**

(a) Function celsius returns the Celsius equivalent of a Fahrenheit temperature.

(b) Function fahrenheit returns the Fahrenheit equivalent of a Celsius temperature.

(c) Use these functions to write a program that prints charts showing the Fahrenheit equivalents of all Celsius temperatures from 0 to 100 degrees, and the Celsius equivalents of all Fahrenheit temperatures from 32 to 212 degrees. Print the outputs in a neat tabular format that minimizes the number of lines of output while remaining readable*/

```
#include <stdio.h>
#include <conio.h>
void ftoc(int);
void ctof(int);
void main(){
int f,c=0;
clrscr();
printf("Farenheit to Centigrade: Centigrade to Farenheit\n");
for(f=32;f<=212;f++){
ftoc(f);
```

```
if(c<=100)
ctof(c);
c++;
printf("\n");
}
getch();
}
void ftoc(int f){
float cf;
cf=(f-32)* 0.555555555;
printf(" %d %f",f,cf);
}
void ctof(int c){
float fc;
fc=1.8*c+32;
printf(" %d %f",c,fc);
}
```

28. **/* Program – Local Variables*/**

```
#include <stdio.h>
#include <conio.h>
void fun1();
void fun2();
main(){
int t;
clrscr();
t=1000;
fun2();
printf("\n");
printf("%d",t);
getch();
```

```
}
void fun1(){
int t;
t=10;
printf("%d",t);
}
}
void fun2(){
int t;
t=100;
fun1() ;
printf(("\n");
printf("%d",t);
        }
```

OUTPUT:

10

100

1000

29. /*Program – Global Variables*/

```
#include <stdio.h>
#include <conio.h>
void fun1();
void fun2();
void fun3();
main(){
clrscr();
b=10;
fun1();
fun2();
```

```
fun3();
b=b+10 ;
printf("%d\n",b);
getch();
}
void fun1(){
b=b+10;
printf("%d\n",b);
}
}
void fun2(){
int b;
b=1000;
fun1() ;
printf("%d\n",b);
}
void fun3(){
b=b+100;
printf("%d\n",b);
}
```

OUTPUT:

```
10
1000
120
130
```

30. /*Program – Static Variables*/

```
#include <stdio.h>
#include <conio.h>
main(){
int c;
```

```
clrscr();
for(c=1 ;c<=3 ;c++)
stat() ;
getch();
}
stat(){
static int sv=0;
sv=sv+1;
printf("%d",sv);
}
```

OUTPUT:

1

2

3

31. **/*Program – Memory Allocation*/**

```
#include <stdio.h>
#include <malloc.h>
main(){
int *base;
int i,j;
int cnt=0;
int sum=0;
printf("how many integers you have to store \n");
scanf("%d",&cnt);
base = (int *)malloc(cnt * sizeof(int));
printf("the base of allocation is %16lu \n",base);
if(!base)
printf("unable to allocate size \n");
else{
```

```
for(j=0;j<cnt;j++)
*(base+j)=5;
}
sum = 0;
for(j=0;j<cnt;j++)
sum = sum + *(base+j);
printf("total sum is %d\n",sum);
free(base);
printf("the base of allocation is %16lu \n",base);
base = (int *)malloc(cnt * sizeof(int));
printf("the base of allocation is %16lu \n",base);
base = (int *)malloc(cnt * sizeof(int));
printf("the base of allocation is %16lu \n",base);
base = (int *)calloc(10,2);
printf("the base of allocation is %16lu \n",base);
}
```

OUTPUT: how many integers you have to store

```
1234
the base of allocation is      4016352
total sum is                      6170
the base of allocation is      4016352
the base of allocation is      4016352
the base of allocation is      4021296
the base of allocation is      4007120
```

32. **/*Deallocate the memory by using the function free*/**

```
#include <stdio.h>
#include <malloc.h>
main(){
int *base;
int i,j;
```

```
int cnt=0;
int sum=0;
printf("how many integers you have to store \n");
scanf("%d",&cnt);
base = (int *)malloc(cnt * sizeof(int));
printf("the base of allocation is %16lu \n",base);
if(!base){
printf("unable to allocate size \n");
}
else
{
for(j=0;j<cnt;j++)
*(base+j)=5;
}
sum = 0;
for(j=0;j<cnt;j++)
sum = sum + *(base+j);
printf("total sum is %d\n",sum);
free(base);
printf("the base of allocation is %16lu \n",base);
base = (int *)malloc(cnt * sizeof(int));
printf("the base of allocation is %16lu \n",base);
base = (int *)malloc(cnt * sizeof(int));
printf("the base of allocation is %16lu \n",base);
base = (int *)calloc(10,2);
printf("the base of allocation is %16lu \n",base);
}
```

OUTPUT: how many integers you have to store

4321

the base of allocation is	4016352
total sum is	21605
the base of allocation is	4016352
the base of allocation is	4016352
the base of allocation is	4033648
the base of allocation is	4007120

33. /*Program to calculate the sum of $n^4+(n-1)^4+.........+2^4+1^4$*/

```
#include <stdio.h>
#include <conio.h>
void main(){
int i,f,n,sum=0;
clrscr();
printf("enter the n value");
scanf("%d",&n);
for(i=i;i<=n;i++){
f=i*i*i*i;
sum=sum+f;
}
printf("the required sum is %d",sum);
getch();
}
```

OUTPUT:

Enter the n value 3

The required sum is 98

34. /*Program to calculate the sum of $n^4-(n-1)^4-(n-2)^4-.........-2^4-1$*/

```
#include <stdio.h>
#include <conio.h>
#include <math.h>
void main(){
int i,j,n,sum=0,p,x,f;
```

```
clrscr();
printf("enter a number");
scanf("%d",&n);
x=pow(n,4);
for(i=n-l;i>=l;i--){
p=pow(i,4);
sum=sum+p;
}
f=x-sum;
printf("required sum is %d\n",f);
getch();
}
```

OUTPUT:

Enter a number 2

Required sum is 15

35. **/*Program to find (1^5+2^5+……+n^5)–(1^3+2^3+……+n^3)*/**

```
#include <stdio.h>
#include <conio.h>
void main(){
int n,sum=0,s=0,i,j,x;
clrscr();
printf("enter the n value");
scanf("%d",&n);
for(i=l;i<=n;i++){
sum=sum+i*i*i*i*i;
}
printf ("\nsum=l^5+2^5+..........+n^5=%d\n\n", sum);
for(j=l;j<=n;j++){
s=s+j*j*j;
```

```
}
printf ("s=1^3+2^3+.......... +n^3=%d\n\n", s);
{
x=sum-s;
printf("x=%d",x) ;
}
getch();
}
```

OUTPUT :

Enter the n value 4

Sum = 1^5+2^5+.........+n^5 = 1786

S = 1^3+2^3+.........+n^3 = 100

X = 1686.

36. **/*Program to enter 5, five digit numbers and find out the largest of all at the same it has to sum up all the digits of the largest 5 digit number*/**

```
#include <stdio.h>
#include <conio.h>
void main(){
int a[5], large, c=0,i,b,n;
printf("enter the nos\n") ;
for(i=0;i<5;i++)
scanf("%d\t",&a[i]);
large = a[0];
for(i=1; i<5; i++){
if (a[i]>large)
large = a[i];
printf("largest no=%d", large);
n=large;
while(n!=0){
b=n%10;
```

```
c=c+b;
n=n/10;
printf("sum of digits=%d", c);
getch();
}
}
```

OUTPUT:

```
Enter the No.s
10345
11345
12345
13345
14345
Largest No = 14345
Sum of digits = 17.
```

37. /*Program to print the required pattern

```
    5 4 3 2 1
    4 3 2 1
    3 2 1
    2 1
    1       */
#include <stdio.h>
#include <conio.h>
void main(){
int i,j;
clrscr();
printf("required pattern\n");
for(i=5;i>=1;i--){
for(j=i;j>=1;j--){
```

```
printf("\t%d",j);
}
printf("\n");
getch();
}
}
```

38. /* **Program to print the required pattern**

```
    1
    1 2
    1 2 3
    1 2
    1          */
#include <stdio.h>
#include <conio.h>
void main(){
int i,j,n;
printf("enter an integer number");
scanf("%d",&n);
for(1=1;i<=n;i++){
for(j=l;j<=i;j++)
pnintf(%d",j);
printf("\n");
}
for(i=n-l;i>=l;i—){
for(j=i;j<=i;j—)
printf("%d",j);
printf("\n");
}
getch();
}
```

39. **/*Program to find the sum of elements of fibonacci series*/**

```
#include <stdio.h>
#include <conio.h>
void main(){
int i=l, a=0, b=l, c=0, sum=l,n;
clrscr ();
printf ("enter n value\n");
scanf ("%d\n",&n);
printf("fibonacci series............... \n");
printf ("%d\n%d",a,b);
for (i=l;i<n-l;i++){
c=a+b;
printf("\n");
printf ("%d",c);
a=b;
b=c;
sum+=c;
}
printf ("\n");
printf ("the sum of %d terms of fibonacci series is %d\t", n, sum)
getch();
}
```

OUTPUT:

```
Enter n value
8
fibonacci series. . ..
0
1
1
2
```

3

5

8

13

The sum of 8 terms of fibonacci series is 33.

40. /*Program to print numbers in reverse pyramid*/

```
#include <stdio.h>
#include <conio.h>
void main(){
int i, j, k, n, a, x;
clrscr();
printf("enter number of rows\n");
scanf("%d",&i);
a=(i*(i-l)/2)+l;
n=i-l;
x=i;
for(; i>=l; i--){
for(j=x ;j>l; j--)
printf("");
for(k=l;i<=l;k++){
printf("%d",a);
a++;
}
a=a-1;
printf("\n");
a=a-(2*n);
n--;
}
getch();
}
```

OUTPUT:

```
Enter number of rows 3
4 5 6
 3 2
  1
```

41. **/*Program to execute given pattern**

```
0 0 0 0 *
0 0 0 * *
0 0 * * *
0 * * * *
* * * * *
*/
#include<stdio.h>
#include<conio.h>
void main(){
int i,p,s,r;
clrscr();
printf("enter the number of rows:");
scanf("%d",&r);
for(i=l;i<=r;i++){
for(s=r; s>=i; s—)
printf("0");
}
for(p=l;p<=i;p++){
printf("*");
printf("\n");
}
getch();
}
```

42. **/* Program to print the required shape**

```
*

*   *

*   *    *

*   *

*            */

#include <stdio.h>

#include <conio.h>

void main(){

int i,j,n;

printf("enter maximum number of stars in a row");

scanf("%d",&n);

for(i=l;i<=n;i++){

for(j=l;j<=i;j++)

printf("*\t");

printf("\n\n");

}

for(i=1;i<=n;i++){

for(j=i;j<n;j++)

printf("*\t");

printf("\n\n");

}

}
```

43. **/*Program to display numbers in descending order in pyramid form*/**

```
#include<stdio.h>

#include <conio.h>

void main(){

int i,j,k,a,n;

clrscr();

printf("enter no. of lines\n");
```

```
scanf("%d",&i);
a=((i*(i-l))/2)+l;
n=i-1;
for(;i>=l;i--){
for(j=4;j>i;j--)
printf(" ");
for(k=l;k<=i;k++){
printf("%d",a);
a++;
}
a=a-l;
printf("\n");
a=a-(2*n);
n--;
}
getch();
}
```

OUTPUT:

```
Enter no. of lines 4
7 8 9 10
 4 5 6
  2 3
   1
```

44. /*Program to Print

```
          1
      2       3
    4     5      6
  7     8    9      10
11    12   13  14    15
```

and add the pyramid edges on both sides, also which adds all the diagonal elements*/

```
#include <stdio.h>
void main(){
int i, j, u, y, x, k, z, n, r, c;
clrscr();
printf("Enter n value");
scanf("%d",&n);
c=40;
r=l;
y=0;
x=0;
k=l;
for(i=l;i<=n;i++){
u=0;
x = x + k;
gotoxy(c,r);
for(j=l;j<=i;j++){
u=u+k;
printf("%3d",k);
k++;
}
r = r+l;
c=c-l;
y=y+(k-l);
printf("\n");
}
z=x+y;
printf("\nX=%d",x);
printf("\nY=%d",y);
printf("\nZ(x+y)=%d",x+y);
printf("\nSum(Z+U)=%d",z+u);
```

```
getch();
}
```

45. /*Program to enter any number, reverse it in the following form

```
 Ex : 12345
   1
 + 20
 + 300
 + 4000
 + 50000
 - 54321
 ————
   45679              /* CHECK THIS ONCE  54321 – 54321=0*/
 ———— */
#include <stdio.h>
#include <conio.h>
#include <math.h>
void main(){
int i,r;
long int u,a,n,s=0,b=0,t;
printf("enter any number\n");
scanf("%ld",&n);
a=n;
while(n!=0){
r=n%10;
n=n/10;
s=s*10+r;
}
printf("reverse of the no is %ld\n",s);
for(i=0;s!=0;i++)    {
r=s%10;
```

```
s=s/10;
u=pow(10,i);
printf("%u\n",u*r);
b=b-(r*u);
}
printf("%ld\n",b);
t=2*((a%10)*pow(10,i-1))+b;
printf("%ld\n",t);
getch();
}
int pow(int b,int p){
int r=l,i;
for(i=l;i<=p;i++)
r=r*b;
return(r);
}
```

46. /*Program to search integer in an array and find its occurrence*/

```
#include <stdio.h>
#include <conio.h>
void main(){
int a[10],i,s, p, m=0;
clrscr();
printf("enter the elements\n);
for(i=0;i<10;i++){
scanf("%d",&a[i]);
}
printf("enter a searching element\t");
scanf("%d",&s);
for(i=l;i<=10;i++){
if(a[i]==s)
```

```
m++;
}
printf("the frequency of %d is %d",s,m);
if(a[i]==p)
printf("enter the elements\n");
for(i=0;i<10;i++){
scanf("%d",&a[i]);
}
printf("enter a searching element\t");
scanf("%d",&s);
for(i=l;i<=10;i++){
if(a[i]==s)
m++;
printf("frequency is %d%d",s,m);
}
getch();
}
```

OUTPUT:

```
Given elements
2
3
4
6
5
8
9
1
3
Searching element 3
Frequency 2
```

p=4

Frequency

1

47. **/*Program to arrange the given matrix in ascending order*/**

```
#include <stdio.h>
#include <conio.h>
void main(){
int i,j,m,n,a[3][3],b[9],t,p,k;
clrscr();
printf("\n enter the matrix elements");
for(i=0;i<3;i++){
for(j=0;j<3;j++)
 scanf("%d",&a[i][j]);
}
for(i=0;i<3;i++){
printf("\n");
for(j=0;j<3;j++)
printf("    %d",a[i][j]);
}
k=0;
for(i=0;i<3;i++){
for(j=0;j<3;j++){
b[kl=a[i][j];
k++;
}
}
for(i=0;i<9;i++){
printf("\n");
for(j=i+l;j<9;j++){
if(b[i]>b[j]){
```

```
t=b[i];
b[i]=b[j];
b[j]=t;
}
}
}
k=0;
for(i=0;i<3;i++){
for(j=0;j<3;j++){
a[i][j]=b[k];
k++;
}
}
printf("\n the sorted matrix is:");
for(i=0;i<3;i++){
printf("\n");
for(j=0;j<3;j++){
printf(" %d",a[i][j]);
}
}
printf("\n enter the position of element:");
scanf("%d %d", &m, &n);
printf("enter the number to be deleted:");
scanf("%d",&p);
i =m-l;
j = n-l;
a[i][j] = a[i][j] - p;
printf("\n after deletion:");
for(i=0;i<3;i++){
printf("\n\t");
```

```
for(j=0;j<3;j++){
printf(" %d",a[i][j]);
}
}
getch();
}
```

OUTPUT:

Enter the elements:

3

5

4

7

8

6

2

1

9

The sorting matrix is:

1 2 3

4 5 6

7 8 9

Enter the position of element:

2

3

Enter the number:

3

After deletion:

1 2 3

4 5 3

7 8 9

48. **/*Program to find resultant matrix [5 x 5], diagonal sum and difference*/**

```
#include <stdio.h>
#include <conio.h>
void main(){
int a[5][5], b[5][5], c[5][5], ar, ac, br, bc, i, j, k, x=0, y=0, z=0;
clrscr();
printf("enter the rows of matrix A:\n");
scanf("%d",&ar);
printf("enter the columns of matrix of A:\n");
scanf("%d",&ac);
printf("enter the rows of matrix B:\n");
scanf("%d",&br);
printf("enter the columns of matrix B:\n");
scanf("%d",&bc);
if(ac!=br)
printf("matrix cannot be multiplied:\n");
else
printf("enter the elements of matrix A:\n");
for(i=0; i<ar; i++){
for(j=0; j<ac; j++)
scanf("%d",&a[i][j]);
}
printf("\n matrix A is:\n");
for(i=0; i<ar; i++){
for(j=0; j<ac; j++)
printf("\t%d",a[i][j]);
printf("\n");
}
printf("\n enter the elements of matrix B:");
for(i=0; i<br; i++){
```

```
for(j=0;j<bc;j++)
scanf("%d", &b[i][j]);
}
printf("matrix B is:\n");
for(i=0;i<br;i++){
for(j=0;j<bc;j++)
printf ("\t%d",b[i][j]);
printf("\n");
}
for(i=0;i<ar;i++){
for(j=0;j<ac;j++){
c[i][j]=0;
for(k=0;k<ac;k++)
c[i][j]=c[i][j]+a[i][k]*b[k][j];
}
}
printf("\n the resultant matrix C is:\n");
for(i=0;i<ar;i++){
for(j=0;j<bc;j++)
printf("\t %d",c[i][j]);
printf("\n");
}
for(i=0;i<ar; i++){
for(j=0;j<bc; j++){
if(i==j)
x = x+c[i][j];
}
}
for(i=0;i<ar;i++){
```

```
for(j=0;j<bc;j++)
if(j==(bc-i-l))
y = y+c[i][j];
}
}
printf("\n  sum of the diagonal elements are %d and %d",x,y);
z =x-y;
printf("\n the difference sum is %d",z);
getch();
}
```

OUTPUT :

```
Enter the rows of the matrix A: 5
Enter the columns of the matrix A: 5
Enter the rows of the matrix B: 5
Enter the columns of the matrix B: 5
Enter the elements of the matrix A:
0
1
2
3
4
5
6
7
8
9
0
1
2
3
```

4

5

6

7

8

9

0

1

2

3

4

Matrix A is:

0 1 2 3 4

5 6 7 8 9

0 1 2 3 4

5 6 7 8 9

0 1 2 3 4

Enter the elements of matrix B:

9

8

7

6

5

4

3

2

1

0

9

8

7

6

5

4

3

2

1

0

9

8

7

6

5

Matrix B is:

9 8 7 6 5

4 3 2 1 0

9 8 7 6 5

4 3 2 1 0

9 8 7 6 5

The resultant matrix C is:

70	60	50	40	30
245	210	175	145	105
70	60	50	40	30
245	210	175	145	105
70	60	50	40	30

Sum of the diagonal elements are 500 and 500

The difference of sum is '0'.

49. /*Program to Replace the row matrix with first matrix*/

```
#include <stdio.h>
#include <conio.h>
```

```
void main(){
int a[3][3], b[1][3],ar,ac,br,bc;
int i,j,k,l;
clrscr();
printf("enter the number of rows and columns in both matrices\n");
scanf("%d%d%d%d",&ar,&ac,&br,&bc);
printf("enter the %d values of first matrix",ar*ac);
for(i=0;i<3;i++){
for(j=0;j<3;j++)
scanf("%d",&a[i][j]);
}
printf("the entered matrix is:");
for(i=0;i<3;i++){
for(j=0;j<3;j++)
printf("%d\t",a[i][j]);
}
printf("\n");
printf("enter the %d values of second matrix", br*bc);
for(k=0;k<1;k++){
for (l=0;l<3;l++)
scanf("%d", &b[k][l]);
}
printf("the matrix is:");
for(k=0;k<1;k++){
for(l=0;l<3;l++)
printf("%d\t",b[k][l]);
}
printf("\n");
printf("the replaced matrix is \n");
for(i=0;i<1;i++){
```

```
for(j=0;j<3;j++){
a[i][j]=b[i][j];
}
}
for(i=0,i<3;i++){
for (j=0;j<3;j++)
printf("%d\t",a[i][j]);
printf("\n");
}
getch();
}
```

OUTPUT:

```
Enter the number of rows and columns in both matrices:
3 3
1 3
Enter the 9 values of first matrix:
1 2 3 4 5 6 7 8 9
The matrix is:
   1      2      3
   4      5      6
   7      8      9
Enter the 3 values of second matrix:
   2      2      2
The matrix is:
   2      2      2
The replaced matrix is:
   2      2      2
   4      5      6
   7      8      9
```

50. **/*Program to sort the elements of matrix of order 3 * 3*/**

```
#include <stdio.h>
#include <conio.h>
void main(){
int a[10][10], i, j, l, k, temp, m, n, r =0, p, q;
clrscr();
printf("enter the  no of rows and no of columns");
scanf("%d%d",&p,&q);
printf("enter  the  matrix  elements\n");
for(i=0;i<p;i++){
for(j=0;j<q;j++){
scanf("%d",&a[i][j]);
}
}
for(i=0;i<p;i++){
for(j=0;j<q;j++){
for(k=0;k<p;k++){
for(l=0;l<q;l++){
if(a[i][j]<a[k][1]){
temp=a[i][j];
a[i][j]=a[k][l];
a[k][l]=temp;
}
}
}
}
}
printf("the sorted matrix  is\t");
for(i=0;i<p;i++){
printf("%d\t",a[i][j]);
```

```
}
printf("\n");
}
getch();
}
```

OUTPUT:

```
Enter the elements of matrix
  2 4 3 5 7 8 6 9 1
the sorted matrix is:
  1     2     3
  4     5     6
  7     8     9
```

51. /*Program to print a 3* 3 matrix. Find the sum of each diagonal. At last prints the difference of the two diagonals*/

```
#include <stdio.h>
#include <conio.h>
void main(){
int i,j,l,m,n,a[5][5],d1=0,d2=0,g;
clrscr();
printf("Enter the order\n");
scanf("%d",&n);
printf("Enter the elements\n");
for(i=0;i<n;i++){
for(j=0;j<n;j++)
scanf("%d",&a[i][j]);
}
printf("Given matrix is\n");
for(i=0;i<n;i++){
for(j=0;j<n;j++)
printf("%d\t",a[i][j]);
```

```
printf("\n");
}
for(i=0;i<n;i++){
for(j=0;j<n;j++){
if(i==j){
d1=d1+a[i][j];
}
}
}
printf("Sum of diagonal 1 is %d\n",d1);
for(i=0,j=n-l ;i<n,j>=0;i++,j—){
d2=d2+a[i][j];
}
printf("Sum of diagonal 2 is %d\n",d2);
g=dl-d2;
printf("DIFFERENCE=%d\n",g);
getch();
}
```

OUTPUT :

```
Enter the order
3
Enter the elements
1 2 3 4 5 6 7 8 9
Sum of diagonal 1 is 15
Sum of diagonal 2 is 15
DIFFERENCE = 0
```

52. **/*Program to print a matrix and replace an element from it*/**

```
#include <stdio.h>
#include <conio.h>
void main(){
```

```
int i, j, m, n, a[3][3],p;
clrscr();
printf("Enter the matrix Values\n");
for(i=0;i<3;i++){
for(j=0;j<3;j++)
scanf("%d", &a[i][j]);
}
printf("The given matrix is ...\n");
for(i=0;i<3;i++){
for(j=0;j<3;j++)
printf("%d\t",a[i][j]);
printf("\n");
}
printf("Enter the position to be deleted in rows and columns");
scanf("%d%d",&m,&n);
printf("Enter new element in  position");
scanf("%d",&p);
for(i=0;i<3;i++){
for(j=0;j<3;j++){
if(i==m && j==n){
a[i][j]=p;
}
}
}
printf("New matrix is ...\n");
for(i=0;i<3;i++){
for(j=0;j<3;j++)
printf("%d\t",a[i][j]);
printf("\n");
```

```
}
getch();
}
```

OUTPUT:

```
Enter the matrix values
1
2
3
4
5
6
7
8
9
The given matrix is....
1 2 3
4 5 6
7 8 9
Enter the position to be deleted
3
3
Enter the new element in position
45
new matrix is
1 2 3
4 5 6
7 8 45
```

53. /*Write a program to sort the elements in descending order into a matrix and it has to delete one element*

```
#include <stdio.h>
```

```
#include<conio.h>
void main(){
int a[10][10],i,j,k,l,m,n,r=0,p,q,temp;
clrscr();
printf("Enter the no. of rows and columns\n");
scanf("%d%d",&p,&q);
printf("Enter the matrix elements\n");
for(i=0;i<p;i++){
for(j=0;j<q;j++){
scanf("%d",&a[i][j]);
}
}
for(i=0;i<p;i++){
for(j=0;j<q;j++){
for(k=0;k<p;k++){
for(l=0;l<q;l++){
if(a[i][j]>a[k][l]){
temp=a[i][j];
a[i][j]=a[k][l];
a[k][l]=temp;
}
}
}
}
}
printf("The sorted matrix is\n");
for(i=0;i<p;i++){
for(j=0;j<q;j++){
printf("%d\t",a[i][j]);
```

```
printf("\n");
}
printf("Enter the position of the element\n");
scanf("%d%d",&m,&n);
for(i=0;i<p;i++){
for(j=0;j<q;j++){
if(i==m&&j==n)
printf("%d\t",r);
else
printf("%d\t",a[i][j]);
}
printf("\n");
}
getch();
}
```

OUTPUT:

```
Enter the no. of rows and columns  3 3
Enter the matrix elements          45 78 67 90 87 32 12 34 76
The sorted matrix is               90 87 78
                                   76 67 45
                                   34 32 12
Enter the position of element:  1     2
90        87        78
76        67        0
34        32        12
```

54. /*Program to replace the first row of a matrix with a set of row elements in other matrix*/

```
#include <stdio.h>
#include <conio.h>
void main(){
```

```
int a[3][3], b[1][3], ar, ac, br, bc;
int i,j,k,l;
clrscr();
printf("enter the number of rows and columns in both matrices \n");
scanf("%d%d%d%d",&ar,&ac,&br,&bc);
printf("enter the %d values of first matrix", ar*ac);
for(i=0;i<3;i++){
for(j=0;j<3;j++)
scanf("%d",&a[i][j]);
}
printf("the matrix is:");
for(i=0;i<3;i++){
for(j=0;j<3;j++)
printf("%d\t",a[i][j]);
}
printf("\n");
printf("enter the %d values of second matrix", br*bc);
for(k=0;k<1;k++){
for (l=0;l<3;l++)
scanf("%d",&b[k][l]);
}
printf("the matrix is:");
for(k=0;k<1;k++){
for(l=0;l<3;l++)
printf("%d\t",b[k][l]);
}
printf("\n");
printf("the replaced matrix is \n");
for(i=0;i<1;i++){
```

```
for(j=0;j<3;j++){
a[i][j]=b[i][j];
}
}
for(i=0;i<3;i++){
for (j=0;j<3;j++)
printf("%d\t",a[i][j]);
printf("\n");
}
getch();
}
```

OUTPUT:

Enter the number of rows and columns in both matrices:

3 3

1 3

Enter the 9 values of first matrix:

1 2 3 4 5 6 7 8 9

The matrix is:

1 2 3

4 5 6

7 8 9

Enter the 3 values of second matrix:

2 2 2

The matrix is:

2 2 2

The replaced matrix is:

2 2 2

4 5 6

7 8 9

55. /* Program to arrange the given elements in ascending order in a given matrix and to find the sum of diagonal elements */

```
#include <stdio.h>
#include <conio.h>
void main(){
int i,j, a[3][3], b[9], k=0, m, n, t, s=0;
clrscr();
printf("\n enter the elements of the matrix");
for(i=0;i<3;i++){
for(j=0;j<3;j++)
scanf("%d",&a[i][j]);
}
for(i=0;i<3;i++){
printf("\n\t");
for(j=0;j<3;j++)
printf("%d",a[i][j]);
}
for(i=0;i<3;i++){
for(j=0;j<3;j++){
b[k]=a[i][j];
k++;
}
}
for(i=0;i<8;i++){
for(j=i+1;j<9;j++){
if(b[i]>b[j]){
t = b[i];
b[i]=b[j];
b[j]=t;
}
```

```
}
}
k=0;
for(i=0;i<3;i++){
for(j=0;j<3;j++){
a[i][j]=b[k];
k++;
}
}
printf("\n\t sorted matrix is");
for(i=0; i<3; i++){
printf("\n\t");
for(j=0;j<3;j++)
printf(" %d",a[i][j]);
}
for(i=0;i<3;i++){
for(j=0;j<3;j++){
if(i==j)
s = s + a[i][j];
}
printf("\nsum of diagonal elements is%d", s);
}
getch();
}
```

OUTPUT: Enter the matrix elements

```
7 3 6
2 1 9
4 8 5
```

Sorted matrix

1 2 3

4 5 6

7 8 9

Sum of diagonal elements = 15

56. **/*Program to delete and insert elements in the given array list*/**

```
#include <stdio.h>
#include <conio.h>
void main(){
int a[20], i, j, k, n, s;
clrscr();
printf("\t OUTPUT:");
printf("\n\n ENTER THE NUMBER OF ELEMENTS IN THE GIVEN LIST\n");
scanf("%d",&n);
printf("\n ENTER THE ELEMENTS IN GIVEN LIST\n");
for(i=0;i<n;i++){
scanf("%d",&a[i]);
}
printf("\n\t—————————        \n");
printf("\n\t GIVEN LIST IS        \n");
printf("\n\t—————————        \n");
for(i=0;i<n;i++){
prinif("%d\t",a[i]);
}
printf("\n ENTER THE NUMBER OF ELEMENT TO BE DELETED \n");
scanf("%d",&k);
j=k-l;
for(i=j;i<n;i++){
a[i]=a[i+l];
}
```

```
printf("\n NOW THE LIST IS \n");
for(i=0;i<n-l;i++){
printf("%d\t",a[i]);
}
printf("\n ENTER THE VALUE OF DELETED ELEMENTS");
scanf("%d",&s);
for(i=l; i>=j; i++){
a[i+l]=a[i];
}
a[j]=s;
printf("\n\t—————————     \n);
printf("\n\t      NOW THE MODIFIED LIST IS:      \n");
printf("\n\t—————————     \n");
for(i=0;i<n;i++){
printf("%d\t",a[i]);
}
getch();
}
```

OUTPUT:

Enter number of elements in the given list:

7

Enter the elements in the given list:

10

20

30

40

50

60

70

```
-------------
Givens list is
-------------
10        20      30      40      50      60      70
Enter the number of element to be deleted
5
Now the list is:
10        20      30      40      60      70
Enter the value of deleted elements:
80
----------------
Now the modified list is:
----------------
10        20      30      40      80      60      70
---------------------------
```

57. **/*Program to find out the frequency occurrence of each character in the string except alphabet*/**

```
#include <stdio.h>
#include <conio.h>
#include <ctype.h>
void main(){
char a[10];
int i,j,ctr;
clrscr();
printf("enter any string::\n");
gets(a);
for(i=0;a[i]!='\0';i++){
if(isalpha(a[i])){
for(j=i-1;j>=0;j--){
if(a[i]==a[j])
```

```
break;
}
if(j<0){
ctr=l;
for(j=i+l;a[j]!='\0'; j++){
if(a[i]==a[j])
ctr++;
}
printf("the frequency occurence of %c is %d",a[i],ctr);
}
}
getch();
}
```

OUTPUT:

```
Enter any string: +++++– – –
The frequency counter of + is 5
The frequency counter of - is 6
```

58. **/*Program to find the frequency of special characters*/**

```
#include <stdio.h>
#include <conio.h>
#include <string.h>
void main(){
char a [20];
int i, n=0,l=0,j=0,k=0,t=0;
clrscr();
printf("ENTER ANY STRING YOU WANT ?\n");
fflush(stdin);
gets(a);
for(i=0; a[i]!='\0'; i++){
if(a[i]== '+')
```

```
n++;
if(a[i]== '-')
l++;
if(a[i]=='*')
m++;
if(a[i]== '/')
j++;
if(a[i]==' ')
k++;
}
printf("FREQUENCY OF '+':%d ",n);
printf("FREQUENCY OF '-':%d ",l);
printf("FREQUENCY OF '*':%d ",m);
printf("FREQUENCY OF '/':%d ",j);
printf("FREQUENCY OF ' ':%d",k);
getch();
}
```

OUTPUTs:

```
Enter any string u want:
+++++*****//////——
FREQUENCY OF '+':5:
FREQUENCY OF '-':4
FREQUENCY OF '*':5
FREQUENCY OF '/':6
FREQUENCY OF ' ':0
```

59. **/*Program to print 5 statements- one by one and at last to append each statement with the previous and print all of them in one line*/**

```
#include <stdio.h>
#include <conio.h>
void main(){
```

```
void   s1(),s2(),s3(),s4();
clrscr();
s1();
printf("\n");
s2();
printf("\n");
s3();
printf("\n");
s1();
printf("\n");
s4();
printf("\n");
s1();
s2();
s3();
sl();
s4();
getch();
}
void s1(){
printf("IIIIIII");
}
void s2(){
printf("NNNNNNN");
}
void s3(){
printf("DDDDDDD");
}
void s4(){
printf("AAAAAAA");
}
```

60. **/*Program to enter two string, sort them, and when any character is entered, it has to count the occurrence of only that character*/**

```
#include <stdio.h>
#1nclude <conio.h>
#include <string.h>
void main(){
char a[20][20],temp[20],ch;
int n,i,j,c=0;
clrscr();
printf("\n enter the number of students");
scanf("%d",&n);
fflush(stdin);
for(i=0;i<n; i++){
printf("\n enter the student names \n");
scanf("%c",&a);
for(i=0;i<n;i++)
gets(a[i]);
for(j=i+l;j<n;j++){
if(strcmp(a[i],a[j])>0){
strcpy(temp,a[i]);
strcpy(a[i],a[j]);
strcpy(a[j],temp);
}
}
}
printf(" the sorted list is\n");
for(i=0;i<n;i++)
printf("%s\t",a[i]);
printf("\n enter the string");
```

```
gets(a);
fflush(stdin);
printf("enter the character\n");
scanf("%c",&ch);
for(i=0;a[i]!='\0';i++){
if(a[i]==ch)
c++;
}
printf("frequency of given character is %d",c);
getch();
}
```

OUTPUT:

Enter the number of students: 2

Enter the student names: Revathi, Divya

The Sorted list is Divya, Revathi

Enter the String Revathi

Enter the character R

The frequency of given character is 1.

61. /*Program for sorting the given number of students in alphabetical order*/

```
#include <stdio.h>
#include <conio.h>
#include <string.h>
void main(){
char names[20][10],temp[10];
int i, j, n;
clrscr();
printf("enter the number of students");
scanf("%d",&n);
for(i=0; i<n; i++){
fflush(stdin);
```

```
gets(names[i]);
}
for(i=0;i<n;i++)
for(j=0;j<n;j++)
if(strcmp(names[i], names[j]<0){
strcpy (temp, names[i]);
strcpy(names[i], names[j]);
strcpy(names[j], temp);
}
printf("after sorting the names are");
for(i=0;i<n;i++)
printf("\n%s", names[i]);
getch();
}
```

OUTPUT:

```
Enter the number of students:
3
Ragini
Aruna
Manikumari
After sorting the names are:
Aruna
Manikumari
Ragini
```

62. /*Program to find out frequency counter of each alphabet in the string*/

```
#include <stdio.h>
#include <conio.h>
#include <ctype.h>
void main(){
char a [10];
```

```
int *p;
int * frequency(char *);
int i;
clrscr();
printf("enter any string");
gets(a);
p=frequency(a);
for(i=0;i<25;i++){
if(p[i]!=0)
printf("the frequency of %c is %d",i+65,p[i]);
}
getch();
}
int*frequency(char *a){
static int b[26];
int i;
for(i=0;a[i]!='\0';i++){
if(isalpha(a[i]))
b[toupper(a[i])-'A']++;
}
return (b);
}
```

INPUT:

malayalam

OUTPUT:

m-2

a-4

l-2

y-1

63. **/*Program to enter a string and print it of the required shape*/**

```
#include <stdio.h>
#include <conio.h>
void main(){
int i,j;
char a[7];
clrscr();
printf("enter your choice\n");
scanf("%s",&a);
printf("required output");
for(i=7; i>0;i--){
for(j=0;j<i;j++){
printf("%c",a[j]);
}
printf("\n");
}
getch();
}
```

OUTPUT:

```
Enter your choice:
JNTUCEH
Required output:
JNTUCEH
JNTUCE
JNTUC
JNTU
JNT
JN
J
```

64. /*Program to sort a list of strings and append any two stringss*/

```
#include <stdio.h>
#include <conio.h>
#include <stdlib.h>
#include <string.h>
int sort(char string[20][20], int size){
int i=0,j=0,compval=0;
char tempstr[20];
if(size<=0)
return 0;
for (i=0;i<size-l; i++){
for (j=i+l; j<size; j++){
compval = strcmp (string[i], string[j]);
if(compval>0){
strcpy(tempstr, string[i]);
strcpy(string[i],string[j]);
strcpy(string[i],tempstr);
}
}
}
return 1;
}
Void main(){
int n,i,j;
char string[20][20];
clrscr();
printf("ENTER NUMBER OF STRINGS\n");
scanf("%d",&n);
printf("ENTER THE STRINGS\n");
for(i=0;i<n;i++)
```

```
scanf("%s",string[i]);
sort(string,n);
printf("THE STRINGS IN THE SORTED ORDER ARE............. \n");
for(i=0;i<n;i++)
printf("%s\n",string[i]);
printf("APPENDING THE DESIRED TWO STRINGS..................\n");
printf("ENTER THE STRINGS OF YOUR CHOICE\n");
scanf("%d%d",&i,&j);
strcat(string[i], string[j]);
printf("%s\n",string[i]);
getch();
```

OUTPUT:

```
Enter number of strings:
5
Enter the strings:
ram
lakshman
krishna
arjun
hanuman
The srings in the sorterd order are:...................
arjun
hanuman
krishna
lakshman
ram
Appending the desired two strings.............
Renter the strings of your choice:
4 2
ramkrishna
```

65. **/*Program to find the occurrences of "a", "e", "i", "o", "u" in the entered strings*/**

```
#include <stdio.h>
#include <conio.h>
void main(){
int f=0,i,j=0,k=0,1=0,m=0,n=0,o,g=0,h=0;p=0,q=0;
char a[10],b[10],c[10],d[10],e[10];
clrscr();
printf("enter the first name");
gets(a);
for(i=0;i<10;i++){
if (a[i]=='a' || a[i]=='e' || a[i]=='i' || a[i]=='o' || a[i]=='u')
j++;
}
printf("the number of vowels in first name are %d\n\n",j);
printf("enter the second name");
gets(b);
for (i=0; i<10;i++){
if( b[i]=='a' || b[i]=='e' || b[i]=='i' || b[i]=='o' || b[i]=='u')
k++;
}
printf("the number of vowels in second name are %d\n\n",k);
printf("enter the third name");
gets(c);
for(i=0;i<10;i++){
if( c[i]=='a' || c[i]=='e' || c[i]=='i' || c[i]=='o' || c[i]=='u')
l++;
}
printf("the number of vowels in third name are %d\n\n",l);
printf("enter the fourth name");
```

```
gets(d);
for(i=0;i<10;i++){
if( d[i]=='a' || d[i]=='e' || d[i]=='i' || d[i]=='o' || d[i]=='u')
m++;
}
printf("the number of vowels in fourth name are %d\n\n",m);
printf("enter the fifth name");
gets(e);
for(i=0; i<10; i++){
if ( e[i]=='a' || e[i]=='e' || e[i]=='i' || e[i] =='o' ||e[i]=='u')
n++;
}
printf("the number of vowels in fifth name are %d\n\n",n);
o = j+k+l+m+n;
printf("the total number of vowels are %d\n\n",o);
for(i=0;i<10;i++){
if(a[i]=='a' || b[i]=='a' || c[i]=='a' || d[i]=='a' || e[i]=='a')
f++;
}
printf("the number of a's are %d\n\n",f);
for(i=0;i<10;i++){
if(a[i]=='e' || b[i]=='e' || c[i]=='e' || d[i]=='e' || e[i]=='e')
g++;
}
printf("the number of e's are %d\n\n",g);
for(i=0;i<10;i++){
if(a[i]=='i' || b[i]=='i' || c[i]=='i' || d[i]=='i' || e[i]=='i')
h++;
}
printf("the number of i's are %d\n\n",h);
for(i=0;i<10;i++){
```

```
if(a[i]==’o’|| b[i]==’o’|| c[i]==’o’|| d[i]==’o’|| e[i]==’o’)
p++;
}
printf(“the number of o’s are %d\n\n”,p);
for(i=0;i<10;i++){
if{a[i]==’u’|| b[i]==’u’|| c[i]==’u’|| d[i]==’u’|| e[i]==’u’)
q++;
}
printf(“the number of u’s are %d\n\n”,q);
getch();
}
```

OUTPUT :

Enter the first name — Akash

The number of vowels in first name is 2.

Enter the second, third, fourth and fifth name - Akhil, Gopi, Mahesh, Shekar.

The number of vowels in second, third, fourth and fifth name is 2, 2, 2 and 2 respectively

The number of a’s in the names: 5

The number of e’s in the names: 2

The number of i’s in the names: 2

The number of o’s in the names: 1

The number of u’s in the names: 0

The totals of vowels are: 10

Appendix –A

ASCII CHARACTER SET

Control Characters

Char	Oct	Dec	Hex	Control-Key	Control Action
NUL	0	0	0	^@	Null character
SOH	1	1	1	^A	Start of heading = console interrupt
STX	2	2	2	^B	Start of text, maintenance mode on HP console
ETX	3	3	3	^C	End of text
EOT	4	4	4	^D	End of transmission, not the same as ETB
ENQ	5	5	5	^E	Enquiry, goes with ACK; old HP flow control
ACK	6	6	6	^F	Acknowledge, clears ENQ logon hand
BEL	7	7	7	^G	Bell, rings the bell...
BS	10	8	8	^H	Backspace, works on HP terminals/computers
HT	11	9	9	^I	Horizontal tab, move to next tab stop
LF	12	10	a	^J	Line Feed
VT	13	11	b	^K	Vertical tab
FF	14	12	c	^L	Form Feed, page eject
CR	15	13	d	^M	Carriage Return
SO	16	14	e	^N	Shift Out, alternate character set
SI	17	15	f	^O	Shift In, resume default n character set
DLE	20	16	10	^P	Data link escape
DC1	21	17	11	^Q	XON, with XOFF to pause listings; ":okay to send".
DC2	22	18	12	^R	Device control 2, block-mode flow control
DC3	23	19	13	^S	XOFF, with XON is TERM=18 flow control
DC4	24	20	14	^T	Device control 4

NAK	25	21	15	^U	Negative acknowledge
SYN	26	22	16	^V	Synchronous idle
ETB	27	23	17	^W	End transmission block, not the same as EOT
CAN	30	24	18	^X	Cancel line, MPE echoes !!!
EM	31	25	19	^Y	End of medium, Control-Y interrupt
SUB	32	26	1a	^Z	Substitute
ESC	33	27	1b	^[	Escape, next character is not echoed
FS	34	28	1c	^\	File separator
GS	35	29	1d	^]	Group separator
RS	36	30	1e	^^	Record separator, block-mode terminator
US	37	31	1f	^_	Unit separator

Printing Characters

Char	Oct	Dec	Hex	Description
SP	40	32	20	Space
!	41	33	21	Exclamation mark
"	42	34	22	Quotation mark (" in HTML)
#	43	35	23	Cross hatch (number sign)
$	44	36	24	Dollar sign
%	45	37	25	Percent sign
&	46	38	26	Ampersand
'	47	39	27	Closing single quote (apostrophe)
(	50	40	28	Opening parentheses
)	51	41	29	Closing parentheses
*	52	42	2a	Asterisk (star, multiply)
+	53	43	2b	Plus
,	54	44	2c	Comma
-	55	45	2d	Hyphen, dash, minus
.	56	46	2e	Period
/	57	47	2f	Slant (forward slash, divide)
0	60	48	30	Zero
1	61	49	31	One
2	62	50	32	Two
3	63	51	33	Three
4	64	52	34	Four
5	65	53	35	Five
6	66	54	36	Six
7	67	55	37	Seven
8	70	56	38	Eight

9	71	57	39	Nine
:	72	58	3a	Colon
;	73	59	3b	Semicolon
<	74	60	3c	Less than sign (< in HTML)
=	75	61	3d	Equals sign
>	76	62	3e	Greater than sign (> in HTML)
?	77	63	3f	Question mark
@	100	64	40	At-sign
A	101	65	41	Uppercase A
B	102	66	42	Uppercase B
C	103	67	43	Uppercase C
D	104	68	44	Uppercase D
E	105	69	45	Uppercase E
F	106	70	46	Uppercase F
G	107	71	47	Uppercase G
H	110	72	48	Uppercase H
I	111	73	49	Uppercase I
J	112	74	4a	Uppercase J
K	113	75	4b	Uppercase K
L	114	76	4c	Uppercase L
M	115	77	4d	Uppercase M
N	116	78	4e	Uppercase N
O	117	79	4f	Uppercase O
P	120	80	50	Uppercase P
Q	121	81	51	Uppercase Q
R	122	82	52	Uppercase R
S	123	83	53	Uppercase S

T	124	84	54	Uppercase T
U	125	85	55	Uppercase U
V	126	86	56	Uppercase V
W	127	87	57	Uppercase W
X	130	88	58	Uppercase X
Y	131	89	59	Uppercase Y
Z	132	90	5a	Uppercase Z
[	133	91	5b	Opening square bracket
\	134	92	5c	Reverse slant (Backslash)
]	135	93	5d	Closing square bracket
^	136	94	5e	Caret (Circumflex)
_	137	95	5f	Underscore
'	140	96	60	Opening single quote
a	141	97	61	Lowercase a
b	142	98	62	Lowercase b
c	143	99	63	Lowercase c
d	144	100	64	Lowercase d
e	145	101	65	Lowercase e
f	146	102	66	Lowercase f
g	147	103	67	Lowercase g
h	150	104	68	Lowercase h
i	151	105	69	Lowercase i
j	152	106	6a	Lowercase j
k	153	107	6b	Lowercase k
l	154	108	6c	Lowercase l
m	155	109	6d	Lowercase m
n	156	110	6e	Lowercase n

o	157	111	6f	Lowercase o
p	160	112	70	Lowercase p
q	161	113	71	Lowercase q
r	162	114	72	Lowercase r
s	163	115	73	Lowercase s
t	164	116	74	Lowercase t
u	165	117	75	Lowercase u
v	166	118	76	Lowercase v
w	167	119	77	Lowercase w
x	170	120	78	Lowercase x
y	171	121	79	Lowercase y
z	172	122	7a	Lowercase z
{	173	123	7b	Opening curly brace
|	174	124	7c	Vertical line
}	175	125	7d	Closing curly brace
~	176	126	7e	Tilde (approximate)
DEL	177	127	47f	Delete (rubout), cross-hatch box

References

- Aho, Alfred V. and Jeffrey D. Ullman, 1983, Data Structures and Algorithms. Addison-Wesley, Reading, Massachusetts.
- Alfred Strohmeier, 2000, Algorithms and Data Structures, Swiss Federal Institute of Technology in Lausanne.
- Balagurusamy. E., 2009, C Programming and Data Structures, 4th Edition. McGraw-Hill.
- Brian W. Kernighan and Dennis M. Ritchie, 1988, The C Programming Language, Prentice-Hall.
- C Language Manual, Cosmic Software, Rev. 1.1, 2003.
- Champbell, M., 1993, Data Structures using C, Deakin University.
- Cormen, Thomas H., Charles E., 2001, Introduction to Algorithms, 2nd Edition. McGraw-Hill, New York
- Ellis Horowitz and Sartaj Sahani, 1991, Fundamentals of Computer Algorithms, Galgotia Publications Ltd.
- Granville Barnett and Luca Del Tongo, 2008, Data Structures and Algorithms: Annotated Reference with Examples, Dotnet Slackers Ltd.
- Greg McCarra, 2002, Algorithms and Data Structures, Napier University of Computing.
- Hanly J.R. and Koffman E.B., Problem Solving and Program Design in C, 5th Edition, Pearson.
- Kernighan B.W. and Ritchie D.M., 2002, C Programming Language, Pearson Education Asia, Delhi.
- Knuth, Donald E., 1998, The Art of Computer Programming, Volume 3, Sorting and Searching, Addison-Wesley, Reading, Massachusetts.
- Martin Richards, 2001, Data Structures and Algorithms, University of Cambridge.
- Muniswamy V.V., 2007, C & Data Structures, IK International Publications.
- Nitin Upadhyay, 2009, The Design and Analysis of Algorithms, Katson Publications.
- Pearson, Peter K., 1990, Fast Hashing of Variable-length Text Strings, Communications of the ACM, 33(6), pp. 677-680.
- Programming in C, 1999, CFS Documentation Cell, Centre for Electronics Design and Technology of India, New Delhi.

- Pugh, William, 1990, Skip Lists: A Probabilistic Alternative to Balanced Trees, Communications of the ACM, 33(6), pp.668-676.
- Srinivas Rao P.S.V., 2006, C Programming and Data Structures, SCITECH Publications.
- Rajaraman., R., 2007, Computer Programming in C, PHI.
- Rob Miles, 2007, Introduction to C Programming, The University of Hull.
- Samuel P. Harbison III, Guy L. Steele Jr., 2002, C – A Reference Manual – (5th edition); Prentice-Hall.
- Sanjay Dasgupta, Christos Papadimitriou, Umesh Vazirani, 2006, Algorithms.
- Stephen Gough and Brevan Miles, 1996, Programming in C, Oxford University Computing Services.
- Stephens, Rod, 1998, Ready-to-run Visual Basic Algorithms. John Wiley & Sons, New York.
- Ted Jenson, September 2003, A Tutorial on Pointers and Arrays in C, Version 1.2.
- Wirth N., 2004, Algorithms and Data Structures.

Index

A

B